BATMAN
KNIGHTFALL

PART TWO: WHO RULES THE NIGHT

Doug Moench   Chuck Dixon   Alan Grant
writers

Jim Aparo   Graham Nolan
Bret Blevins   Klaus Janson   Mike Manley
pencillers

Scott Hanna   Mike Manley   Klaus Janson
Bret Blevins   Steve George   Terry Austin
Rick Burchett   Dick Giordano
inkers

John Costanza   Ken Bruzenak
Todd Klein   Richard Starkings   Bob Pinaha
letterers

Adrienne Roy   Klaus Janson
colorists

Kelley Jones   Glenn Fabry   Brian Stelfreeze
covers

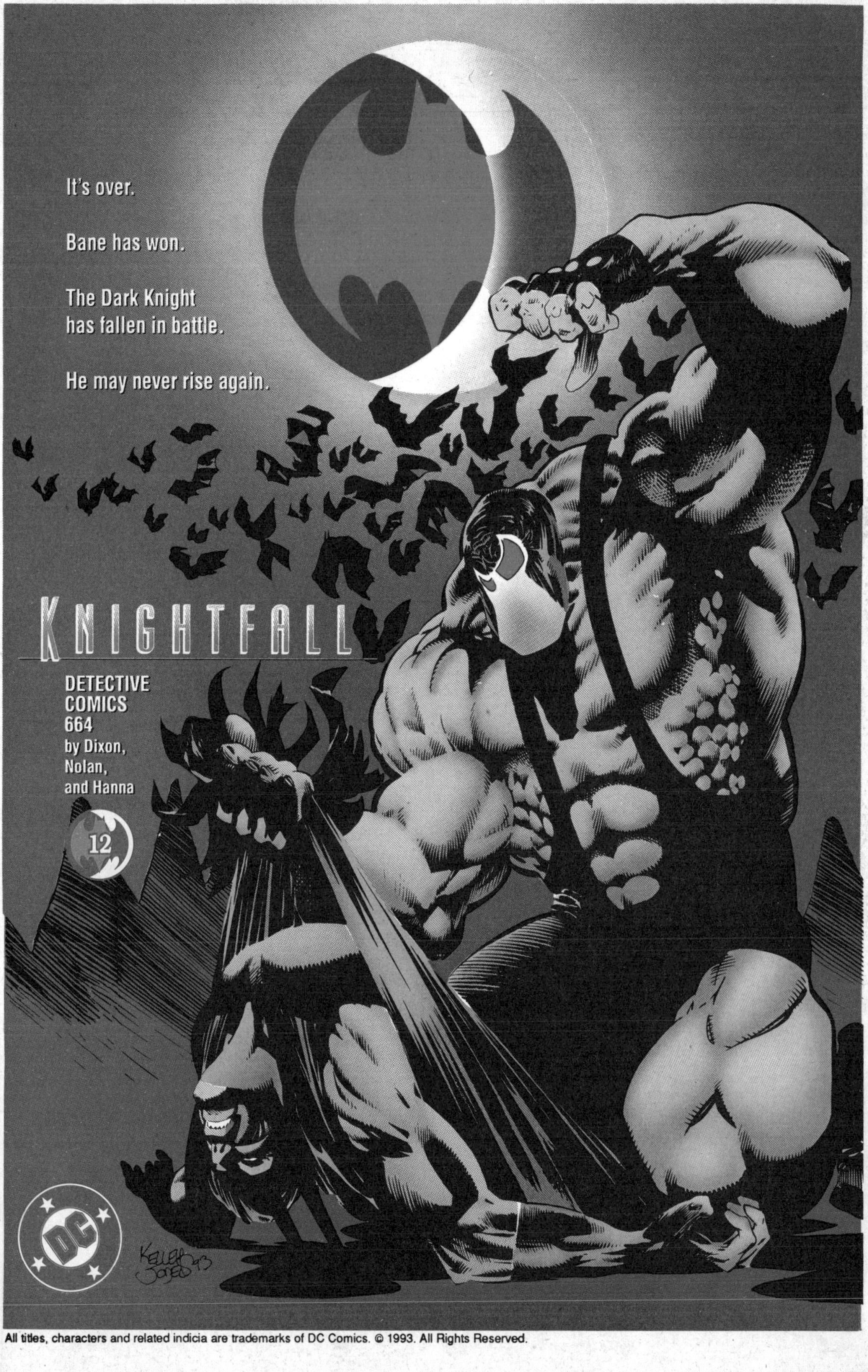
It's over.
Bane has won.
The Dark Knight
has fallen in battle.
He may never rise again.
KNIGHTFALL
DETECTIVE
COMICS
664
by Dixon,
Nolan,
and Hanna
12
DC
KELLEY JONES '93

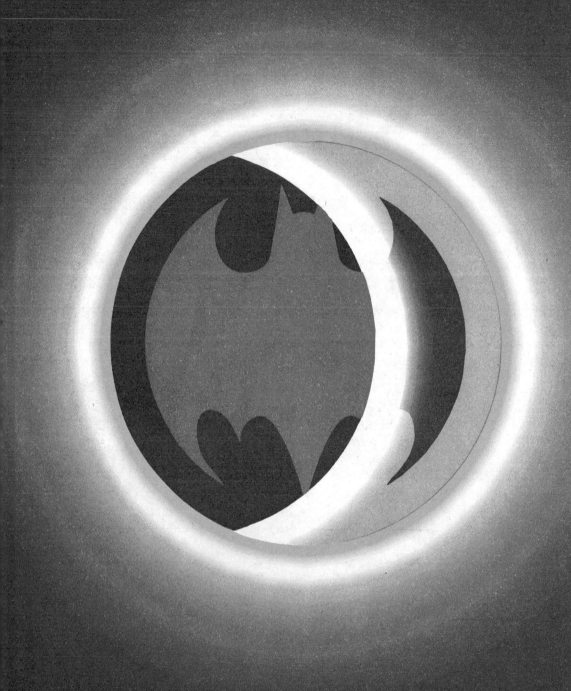

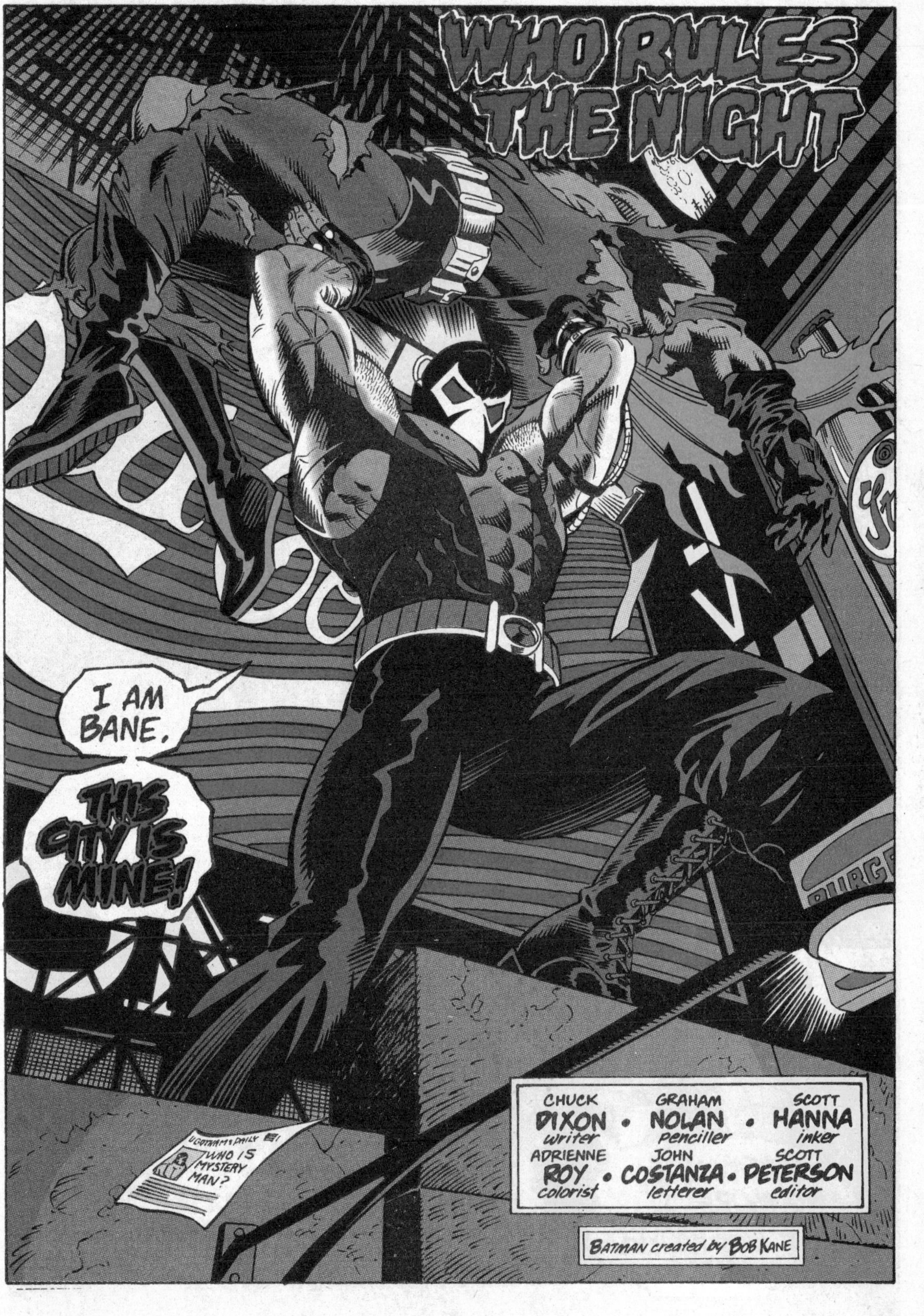
WHO RULES THE NIGHT
I AM BANE.
THIS CITY IS MINE!
GOTHAM DAILY
WHO IS MYSTERY MAN?
CHUCK DIXON writer • GRAHAM NOLAN penciller • SCOTT HANNA inker
ADRIENNE ROY colorist • JOHN COSTANZA letterer • SCOTT PETERSON editor
BATMAN created by BOB KANE

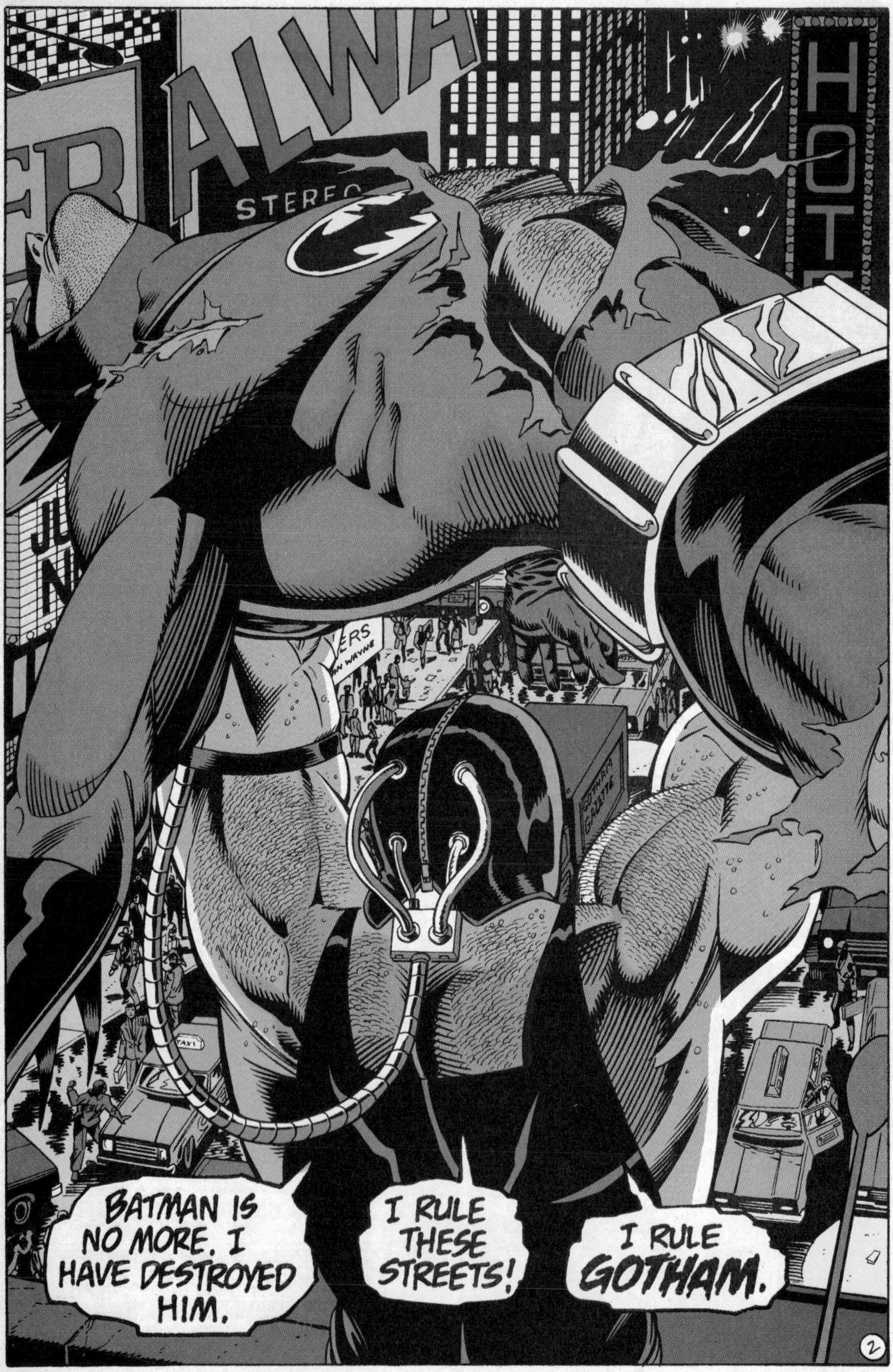
BATMAN IS NO MORE. I HAVE DESTROYED HIM.
I RULE THESE STREETS!
I RULE **GOTHAM.**
2

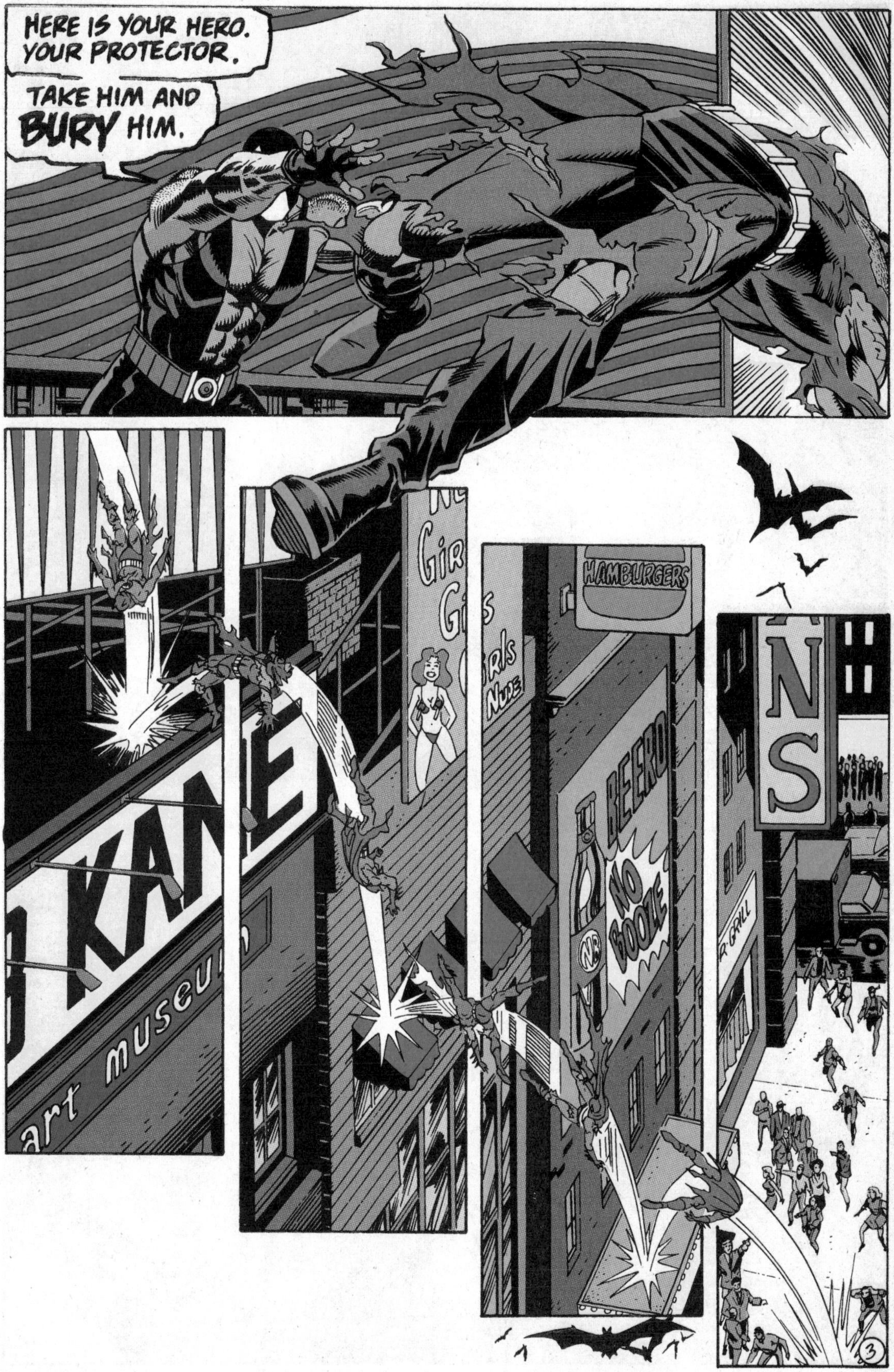
HERE IS YOUR HERO. YOUR PROTECTOR.
TAKE HIM AND BURY HIM.
HAMBURGERS
NO BOOZE
KANE

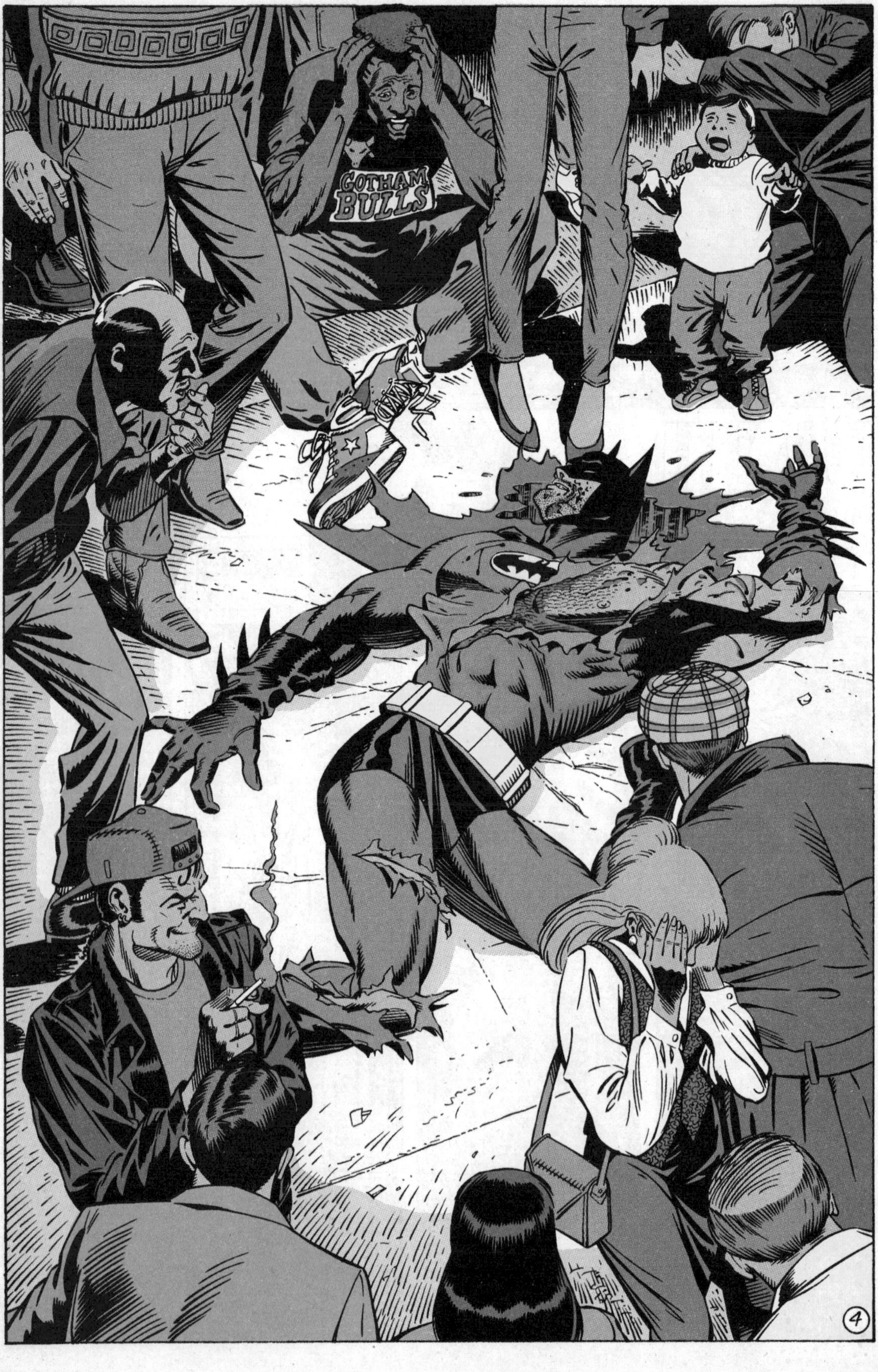
GOTHAM BULLS
4

WHERE'D THAT CREEP GET TO, MONTOYA? HE JUST TOSSED THE BATMAN AND RABBITED.

FORGET HIM, MARZ. WE DON'T WANT TO START A FIREFIGHT IN THE MIDDLE OF THIS CROWD.

"THAT GUY LOOKED LIKE HE WOULD ENJOY OFFING A FEW CITIZENS."

"CALL FOR AN AMBULANCE AND SOME BACK-UP. MAYBE THEY CAN HUNT FOR HIM."

...ROBINSON SQUARE, WE NEED AN EMERGENCY MEDICAL UNIT AND ANY AVAILABLE CARS. YEAH, I SAID THE BATMAN.

EVERYBODY GET BACK. WE CAN'T HELP THE MAN WITH YOU CROWDED IN HERE LIKE THIS.

EVERYBODY BACK, OKAY?

WE HAVE EMT UNITS ON THE WAY. CAN YOU HEAR ME?

UNNH..

HANG ON, THEY'RE ON THEIR WAY...

...A BIG GUY. BIG BIG. HAS ON A BLACK MASK AND LOOKS LIKE HE WEIGHS THREE HUNDRED PLUS. MOST OF IT IN HIS CHEST AND ARMS.

AMBULANCE IS HERE. GOTTA GO. TEN FOUR.

CLEAR THE ROAD, PEOPLE!

MERCY GENERAL EMT

PARK

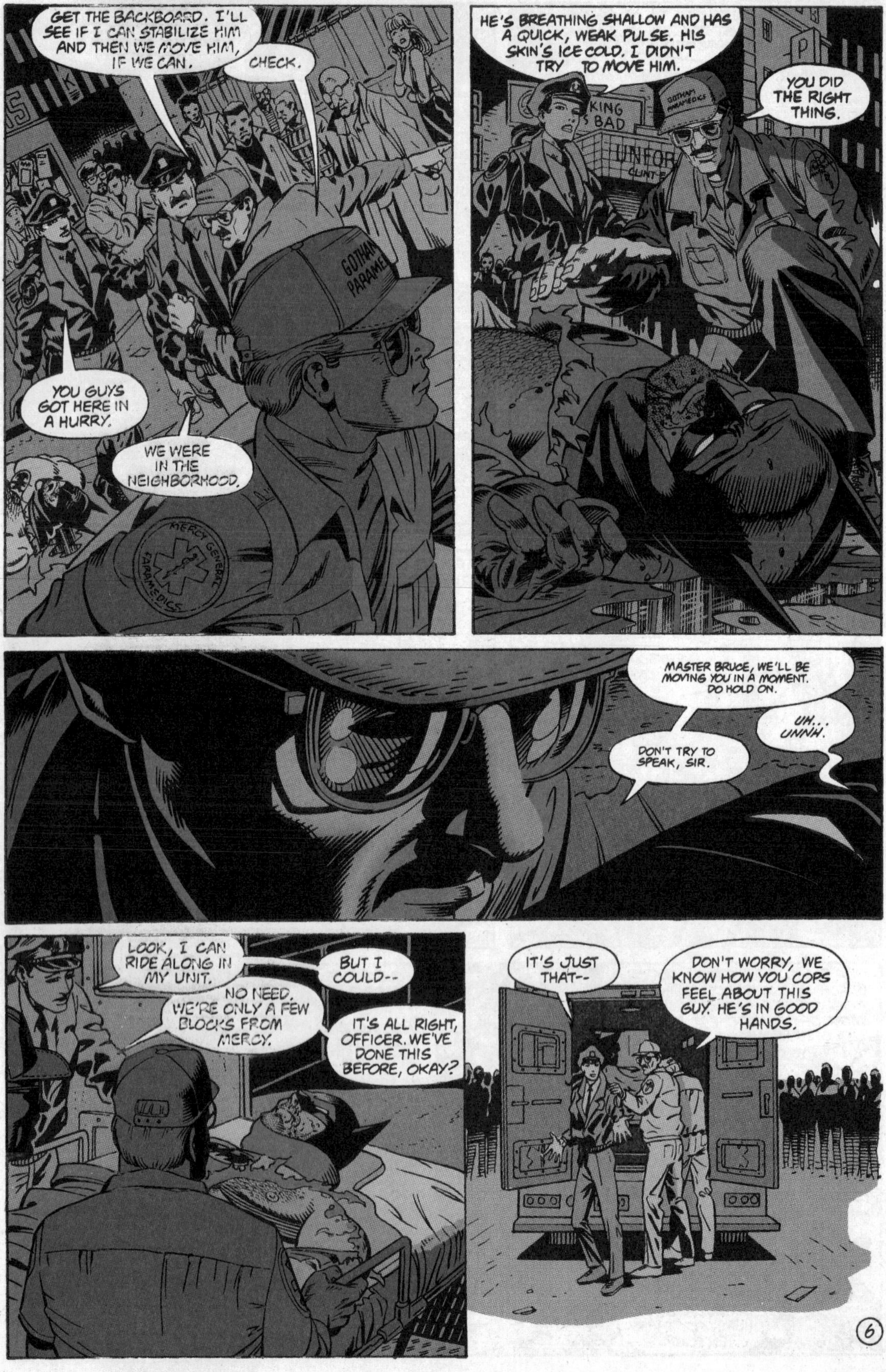
GET THE BACKBOARD. I'LL SEE IF I CAN STABILIZE HIM AND THEN WE MOVE HIM, IF WE CAN.
CHECK.
YOU GUYS GOT HERE IN A HURRY.
WE WERE IN THE NEIGHBORHOOD.
HE'S BREATHING SHALLOW AND HAS A QUICK, WEAK PULSE. HIS SKIN'S ICE COLD. I DIDN'T TRY TO MOVE HIM.
YOU DID THE RIGHT THING.
MASTER BRUCE, WE'LL BE MOVING YOU IN A MOMENT. DO HOLD ON.
UH... UNNH.
DON'T TRY TO SPEAK, SIR.
LOOK, I CAN RIDE ALONG IN MY UNIT.
NO NEED. WE'RE ONLY A FEW BLOCKS FROM MERCY.
BUT I COULD--
IT'S ALL RIGHT, OFFICER. WE'VE DONE THIS BEFORE, OKAY?
IT'S JUST THAT--
DON'T WORRY, WE KNOW HOW YOU COPS FEEL ABOUT THIS GUY. HE'S IN GOOD HANDS.
6

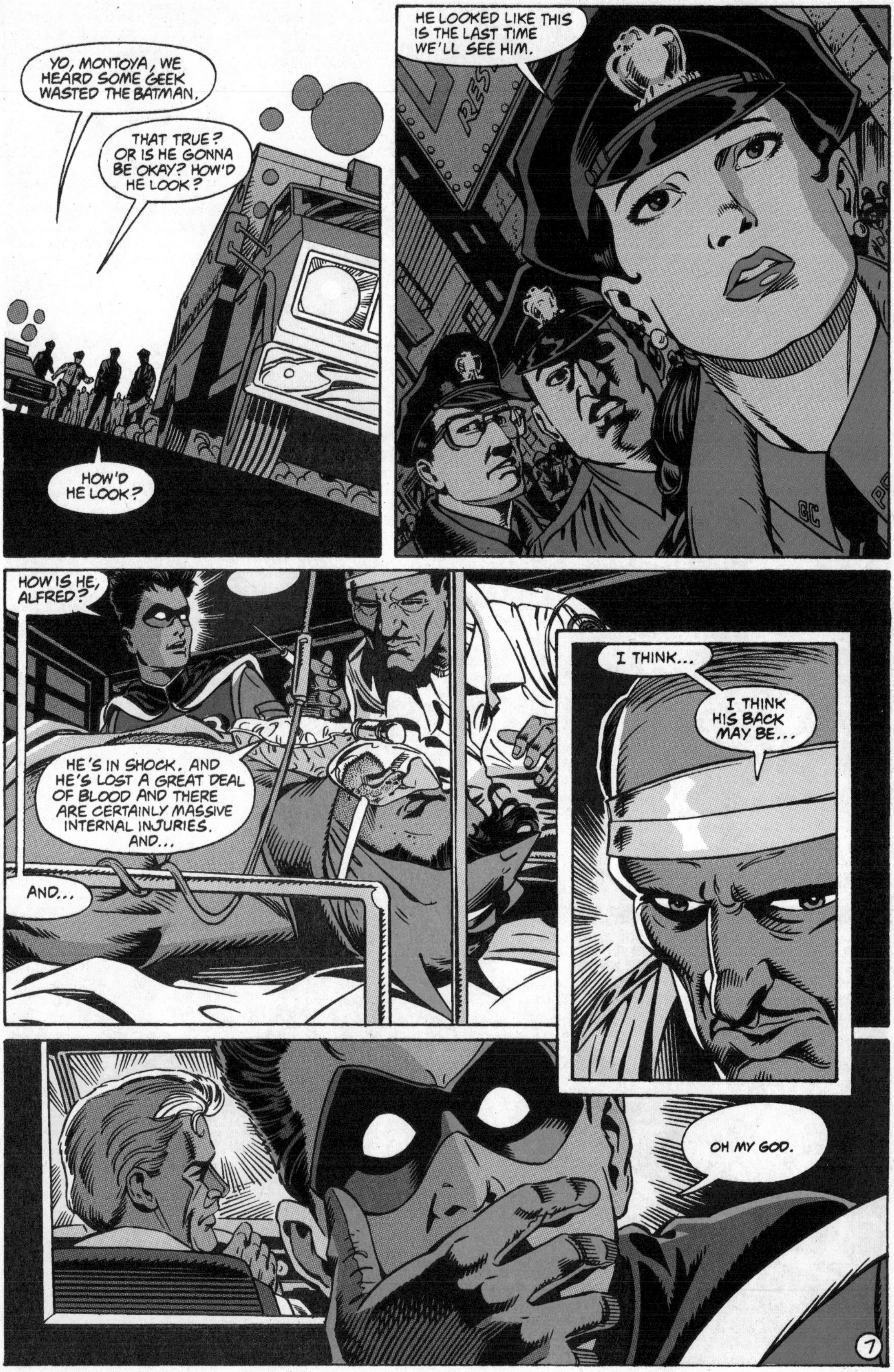
YO, MONTOYA, WE HEARD SOME GEEK WASTED THE BATMAN.
THAT TRUE? OR IS HE GONNA BE OKAY? HOW'D HE LOOK?
HOW'D HE LOOK?
HE LOOKED LIKE THIS IS THE LAST TIME WE'LL SEE HIM.
HOW IS HE, ALFRED?
HE'S IN SHOCK. AND HE'S LOST A GREAT DEAL OF BLOOD AND THERE ARE CERTAINLY MASSIVE INTERNAL INJURIES. AND...
AND...
I THINK...
I THINK HIS BACK MAY BE...
OH MY GOD.
7

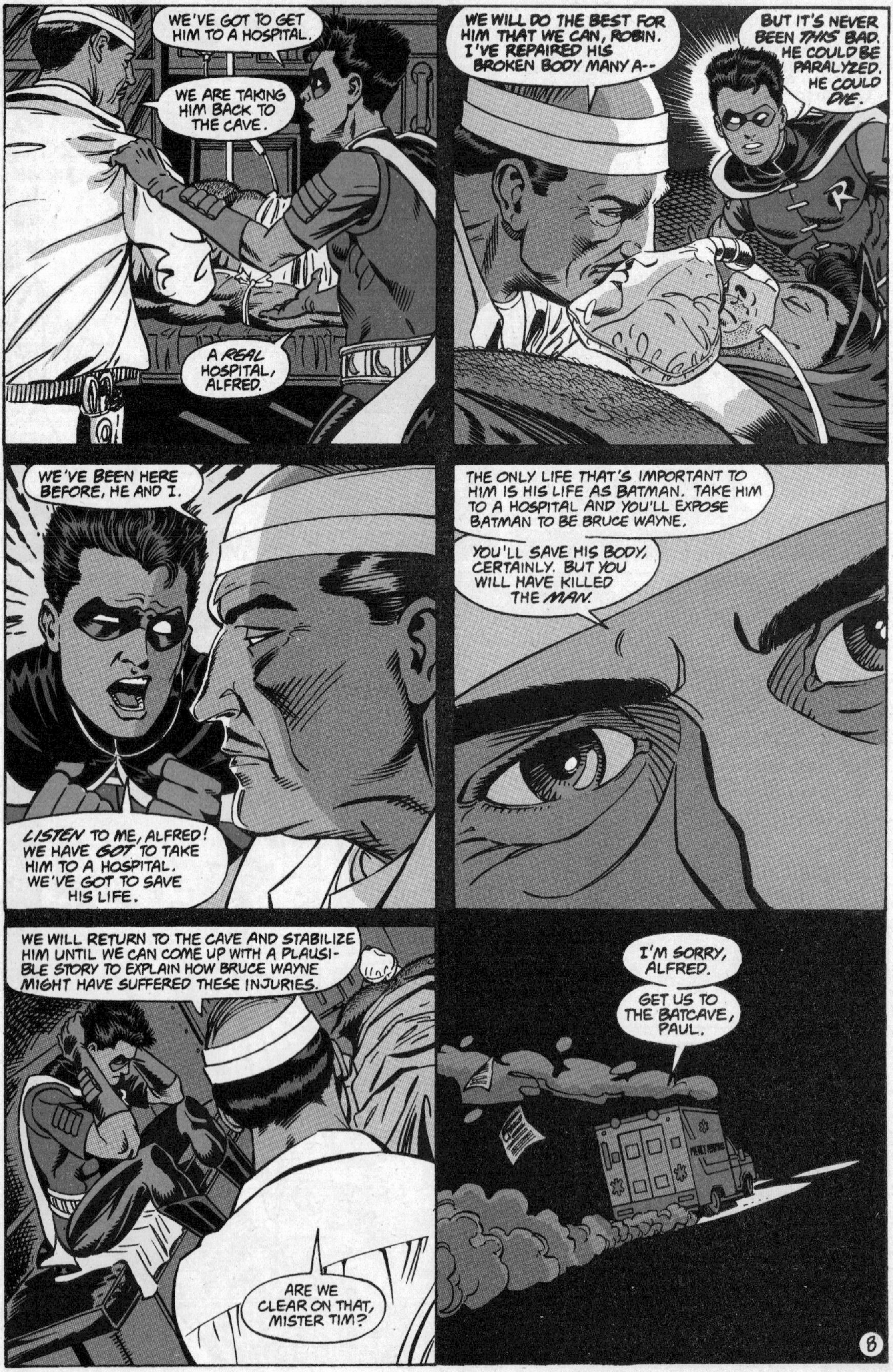

WE'VE GOT TO GET HIM TO A HOSPITAL.
WE ARE TAKING HIM BACK TO THE CAVE.
A *REAL* HOSPITAL, ALFRED.
WE WILL DO THE BEST FOR HIM THAT WE CAN, ROBIN. I'VE REPAIRED HIS BROKEN BODY MANY A--
BUT IT'S NEVER BEEN *THIS* BAD. HE COULD BE PARALYZED. HE COULD *DIE*.
WE'VE BEEN HERE BEFORE, HE AND I.
LISTEN TO ME, ALFRED! WE HAVE *GOT* TO TAKE HIM TO A HOSPITAL. WE'VE GOT TO SAVE HIS LIFE.
THE ONLY LIFE THAT'S IMPORTANT TO HIM IS HIS LIFE AS BATMAN. TAKE HIM TO A HOSPITAL AND YOU'LL EXPOSE BATMAN TO BE BRUCE WAYNE.
YOU'LL SAVE HIS BODY, CERTAINLY. BUT YOU WILL HAVE KILLED THE *MAN*.
WE WILL RETURN TO THE CAVE AND STABILIZE HIM UNTIL WE CAN COME UP WITH A PLAUSIBLE STORY TO EXPLAIN HOW BRUCE WAYNE MIGHT HAVE SUFFERED THESE INJURIES.
ARE WE CLEAR ON THAT, MISTER TIM?
I'M SORRY, ALFRED.
GET US TO THE BATCAVE, PAUL.
8

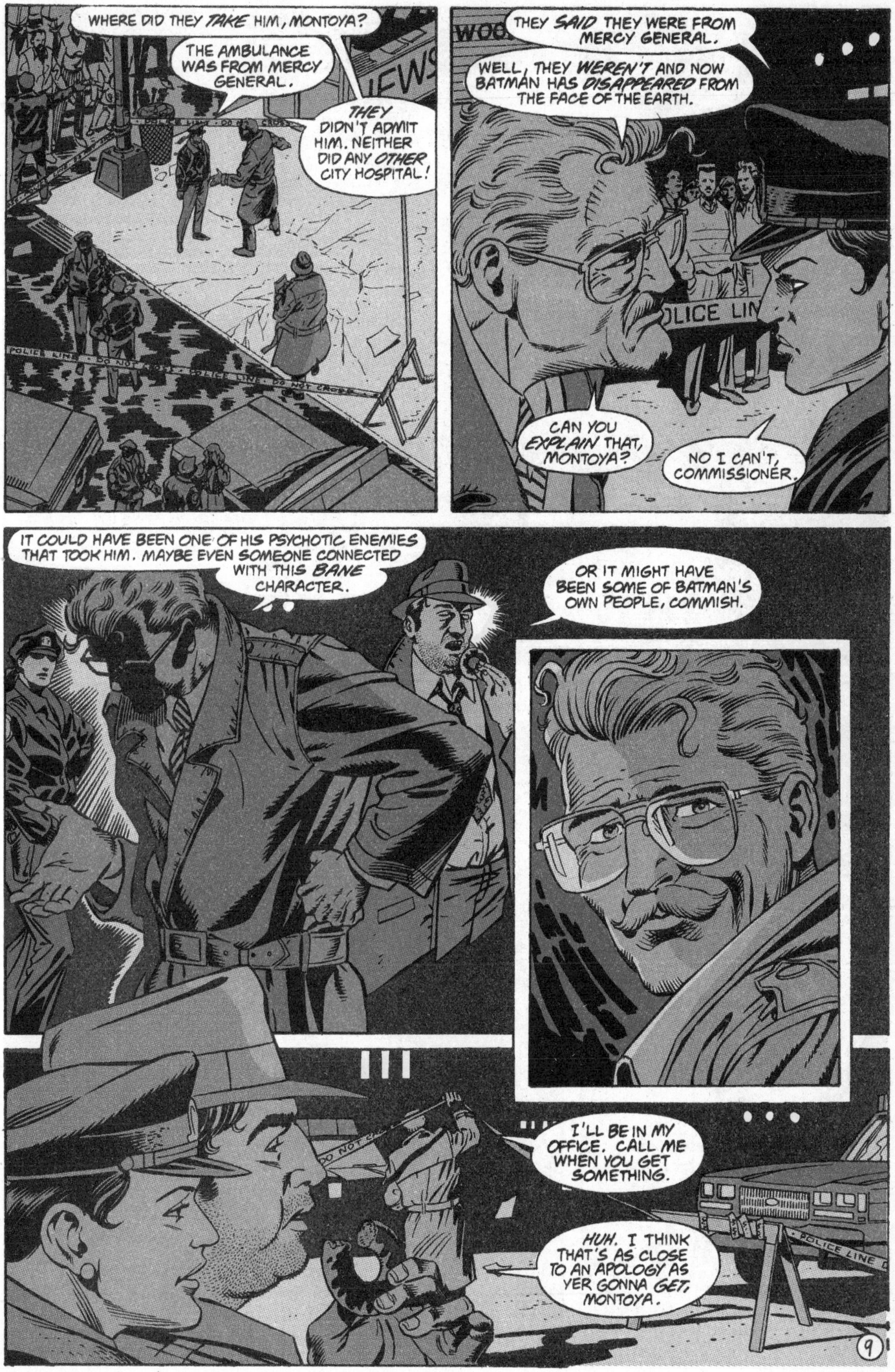
WHERE DID THEY TAKE HIM, MONTOYA?
THE AMBULANCE WAS FROM MERCY GENERAL.
THEY DIDN'T ADMIT HIM. NEITHER DID ANY OTHER CITY HOSPITAL!
THEY SAID THEY WERE FROM MERCY GENERAL.
WELL, THEY WEREN'T AND NOW BATMAN HAS DISAPPEARED FROM THE FACE OF THE EARTH.
CAN YOU EXPLAIN THAT, MONTOYA?
NO I CAN'T, COMMISSIONER.
IT COULD HAVE BEEN ONE OF HIS PSYCHOTIC ENEMIES THAT TOOK HIM. MAYBE EVEN SOMEONE CONNECTED WITH THIS BANE CHARACTER.
OR IT MIGHT HAVE BEEN SOME OF BATMAN'S OWN PEOPLE, COMMISH.
I'LL BE IN MY OFFICE. CALL ME WHEN YOU GET SOMETHING.
HUH. I THINK THAT'S AS CLOSE TO AN APOLOGY AS YER GONNA GET, MONTOYA.
9

...AND NOTHING IS KNOWN ABOUT THE WHEREABOUTS OF THE BATMAN OR THE MASKED STRANGER CALLING HIMSELF BANE.

OH, THIS IS RICH.

POLICE ARE STILL SCOURING THE ROBINSON SQUARE AREA AT THIS HOUR.

ISN'T IT *IRONIC*, SCARECROW? A LEGION OF BATTY'S BADDEST FOES TRY TO BRING HIM LOW AND SOME NEW *ROOKIE* COMES ALONG AND TRASHES HIM.

HILARIOUS.

WHY SO GLUM, SCARECHUM?

WE KIDNAP THE MAYOR, HOLD THE ENTIRE CITY AT BAY AND WHAT HAVE WE TO *SHOW* FOR IT?

NOTHING.

WELL, WE HAVE OUR BUDDING *FRIENDSHIP*, SCARY.

HUNH.

AND THIS MARVELOUS HIDEOUT, 'CROW.

A DUMP.

WATCH WHAT YOU SAY ABOUT LUCY. SHE HAS A LOOOOONG MEMORY.

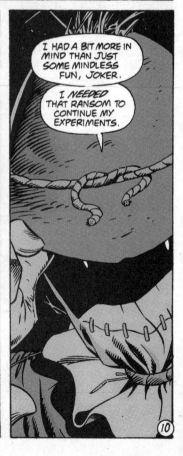

I HAD A BIT MORE IN MIND THAN JUST SOME MINDLESS FUN, JOKER.

I *NEEDED* THAT RANSOM TO CONTINUE MY EXPERIMENTS.

10

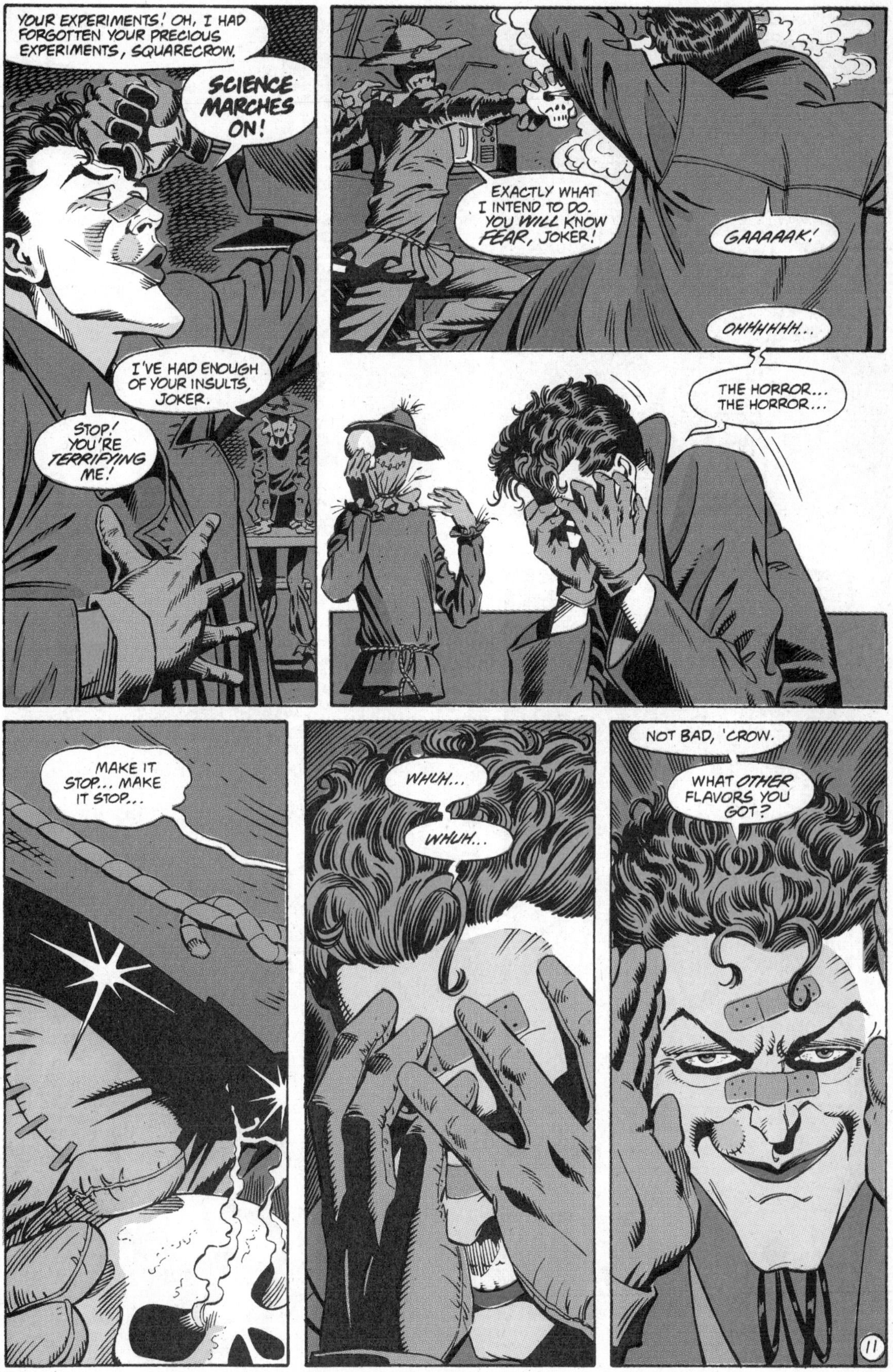
YOUR EXPERIMENTS! OH, I HAD FORGOTTEN YOUR PRECIOUS EXPERIMENTS, SQUARECROW.
SCIENCE MARCHES ON!
I'VE HAD ENOUGH OF YOUR INSULTS, JOKER.
STOP! YOU'RE TERRIFYING ME!
EXACTLY WHAT I INTEND TO DO. YOU WILL KNOW FEAR, JOKER!
GAAAAAK!
OHHHHHH...
THE HORROR... THE HORROR...
MAKE IT STOP... MAKE IT STOP...
WHUH...
WHUH...
NOT BAD, 'CROW.
WHAT OTHER FLAVORS YOU GOT?
11

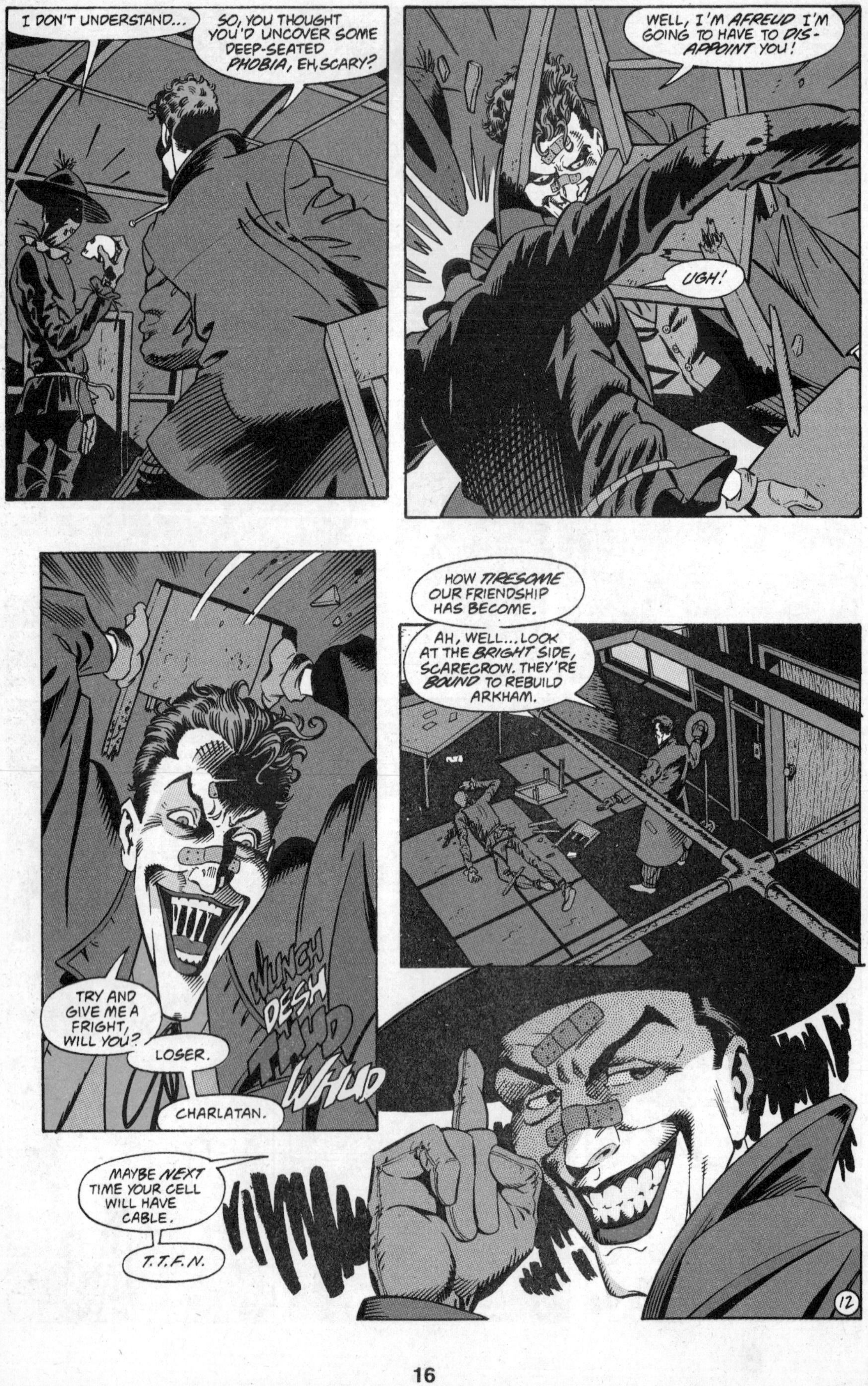
I DON'T UNDERSTAND...
SO, YOU THOUGHT YOU'D UNCOVER SOME DEEP-SEATED PHOBIA, EH, SCARY?
WELL, I'M AFREUD I'M GOING TO HAVE TO DIS-APPOINT YOU!
UGH!
TRY AND GIVE ME A FRIGHT, WILL YOU?
LOSER.
CHARLATAN.
WUNCH
DESH
THUD
WHUD
HOW TIRESOME OUR FRIENDSHIP HAS BECOME.
AH, WELL... LOOK AT THE BRIGHT SIDE, SCARECROW. THEY'RE BOUND TO REBUILD ARKHAM.
MAYBE NEXT TIME YOUR CELL WILL HAVE CABLE.
T.T.F.N.
12

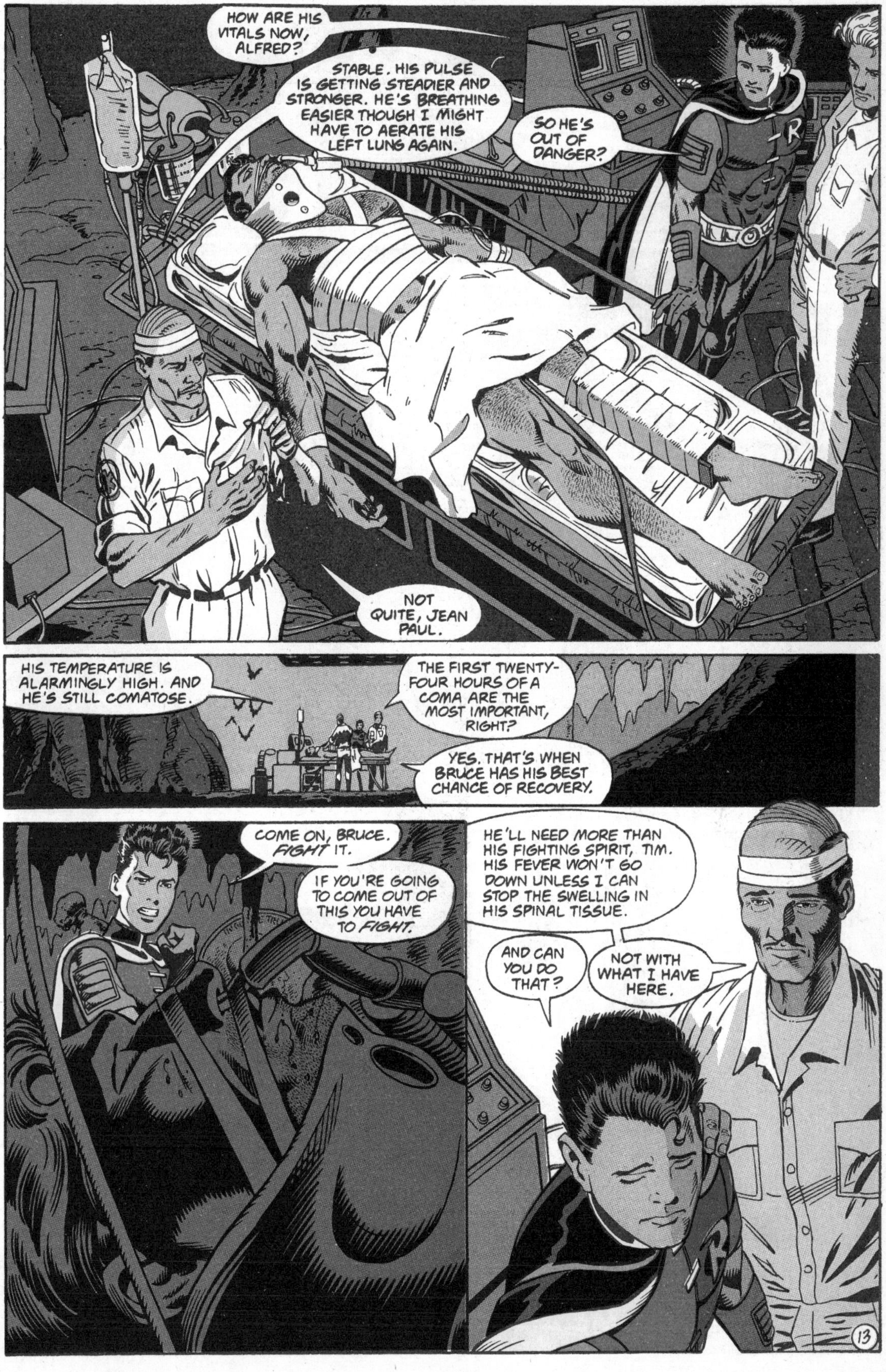
HOW ARE HIS VITALS NOW, ALFRED?
STABLE. HIS PULSE IS GETTING STEADIER AND STRONGER. HE'S BREATHING EASIER THOUGH I MIGHT HAVE TO AERATE HIS LEFT LUNG AGAIN.
SO HE'S OUT OF DANGER?
NOT QUITE, JEAN PAUL.
HIS TEMPERATURE IS ALARMINGLY HIGH. AND HE'S STILL COMATOSE.
THE FIRST TWENTY-FOUR HOURS OF A COMA ARE THE MOST IMPORTANT, RIGHT?
YES. THAT'S WHEN BRUCE HAS HIS BEST CHANCE OF RECOVERY.
COME ON, BRUCE. FIGHT IT.
IF YOU'RE GOING TO COME OUT OF THIS YOU HAVE TO FIGHT.
HE'LL NEED MORE THAN HIS FIGHTING SPIRIT, TIM. HIS FEVER WON'T GO DOWN UNLESS I CAN STOP THE SWELLING IN HIS SPINAL TISSUE.
AND CAN YOU DO THAT?
NOT WITH WHAT I HAVE HERE.
13

WE'LL NEED A DRUG CALLED DECADRON. IT'S SPECIFICALLY MADE FOR THE TREATMENT OF SPINAL TRAUMA.

IT'S THE ONLY WAY TO REDUCE THE SWELLING. BUT ONLY IF IT'S ADMINISTERED IN THE NEXT HOUR.

THEN WE'LL *GET* SOME. PAUL, WE'LL TAKE THE BATMOBILE.

I--

GO WITH HIM.

BUT THE BATMOBILE--

I DIDN'T TELL TIM EVERY-THING ABOUT BRUCE'S CONDITION...

WITHOUT THE DECADRON, EVEN IF MASTER BRUCE *DOES* AWAKEN, HE'LL BE PARALYZED FOR LIFE.

"GODSPEED, JEAN PAUL. GODSPEED."

IT'S A BREAK FOR US THAT BATMAN DIDN'T SECURE THE 'MOBILE WHEN HE PARKED IT.

ONLY *HE* KNOWS THE CODES.

YOU KNOW, IT WOULD BE BEST IF YOU PREPARED YOURSELF FOR THE WORST EVENTUALITY.

DON'T SAY IT, AZRAEL. I DON'T WANT TO *HEAR* IT.

THERE'LL ALWAYS BE A BATMAN.

ALWAYS.

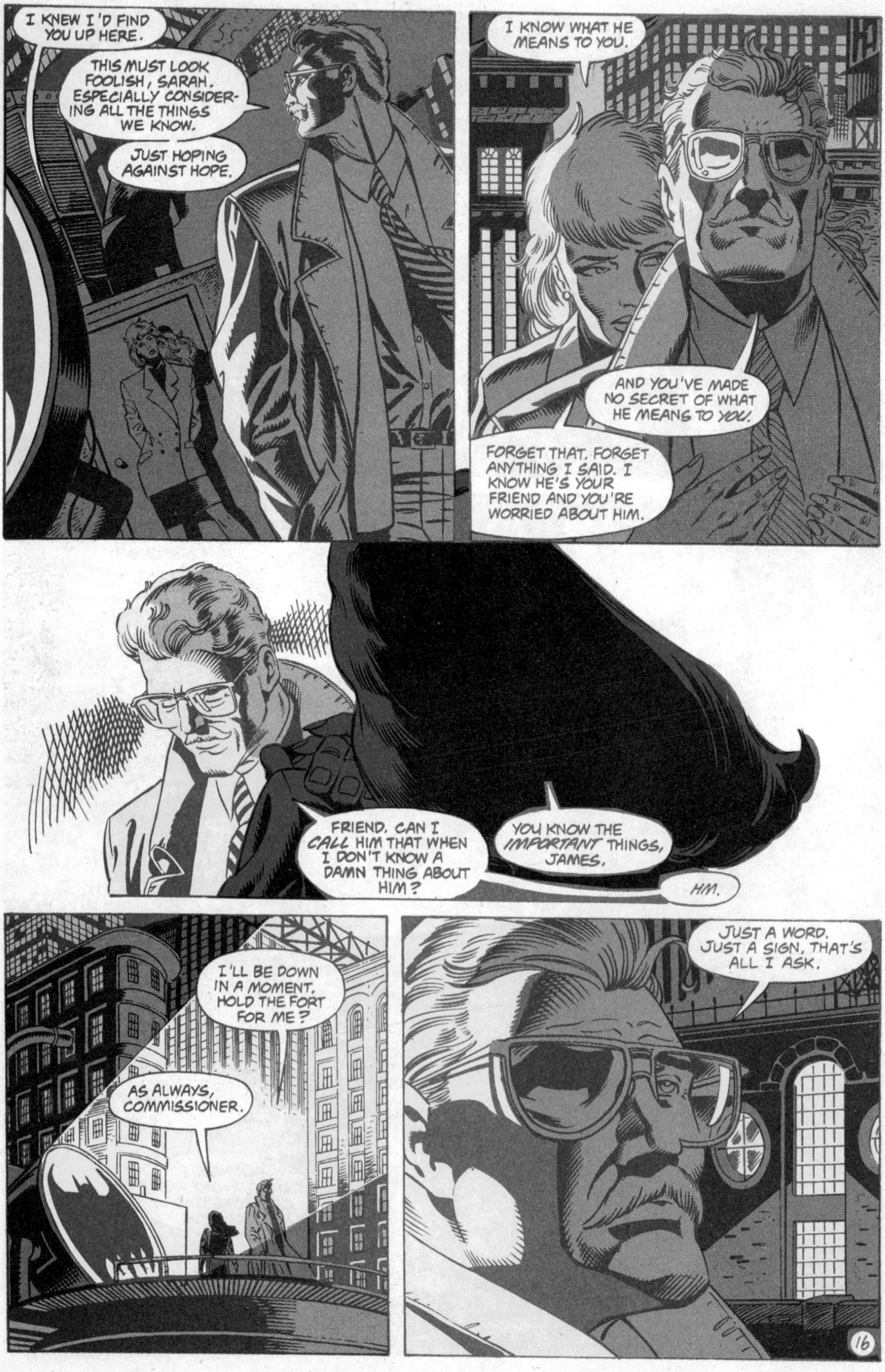
I KNEW I'D FIND YOU UP HERE.
THIS MUST LOOK FOOLISH, SARAH. ESPECIALLY CONSIDERING ALL THE THINGS WE KNOW.
JUST HOPING AGAINST HOPE.
I KNOW WHAT HE MEANS TO YOU.
AND YOU'VE MADE NO SECRET OF WHAT HE MEANS TO *YOU*.
FORGET THAT. FORGET ANYTHING I SAID. I KNOW HE'S YOUR FRIEND AND YOU'RE WORRIED ABOUT HIM.
FRIEND. CAN I *CALL* HIM THAT WHEN I DON'T KNOW A DAMN THING ABOUT HIM?
YOU KNOW THE *IMPORTANT* THINGS, JAMES.
HM.
I'LL BE DOWN IN A MOMENT. HOLD THE FORT FOR ME?
AS ALWAYS, COMMISSIONER.
JUST A WORD. JUST A SIGN, THAT'S ALL I ASK.
16

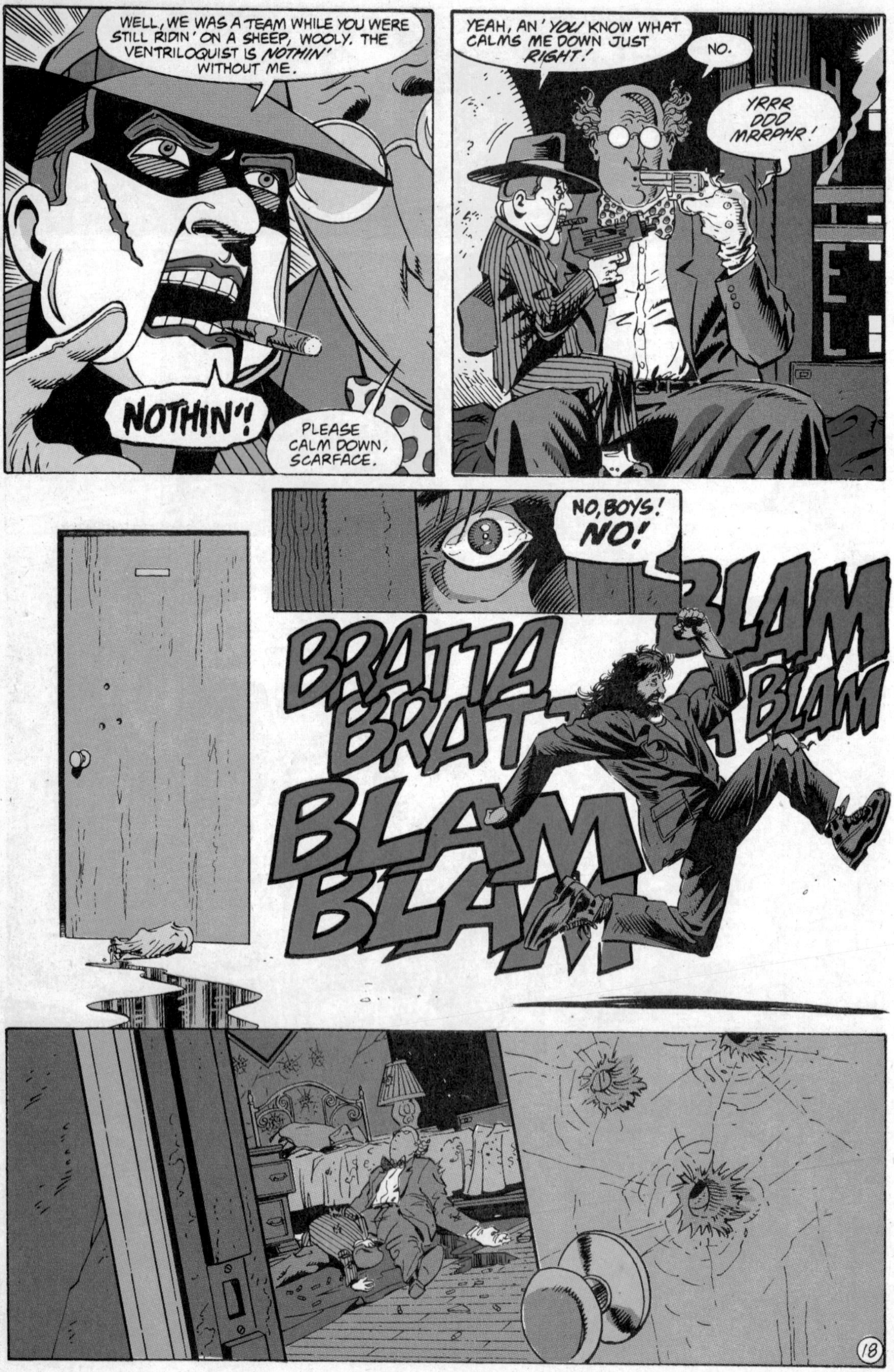

WELL, WE WAS A TEAM WHILE YOU WERE STILL RIDIN' ON A SHEEP, WOOLY. THE VENTRILOQUIST IS NOTHIN' WITHOUT ME.
NOTHIN'!
PLEASE CALM DOWN, SCARFACE.
YEAH, AN' YOU KNOW WHAT CALMS ME DOWN JUST RIGHT!
NO.
YRRR DDD MRRPHR!
NO, BOYS! NO!
BRATTA
BRATT
BLAM
BLAM
BLAM
BLAM
18

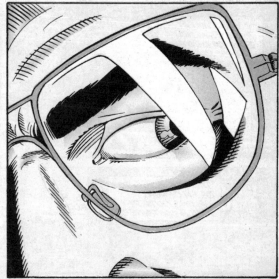

THANKS FOR LEAVING THE WINDOW OPEN.

YOU'RE ALONE.

I NEED YOUR HELP. *HE* NEEDS YOUR HELP.

ANYTHING.

A DRUG CALLED DECADRON. HE MIGHT DIE WITHOUT IT. WE NEED IT FAST.

WAIT HERE.

PATCH ME THROUGH TO BULLOCK'S UNIT.

BULLOCK, THIS IS THE COMMISSIONER, COME IN.

NO SIGN OF THIS BRAIN GUY, COMMISH. BUT HE CAN'T HIDE FOREVER.

IT'S *BANE*, HARV.

FORGET ABOUT THAT AND LISTEN UP...

19.

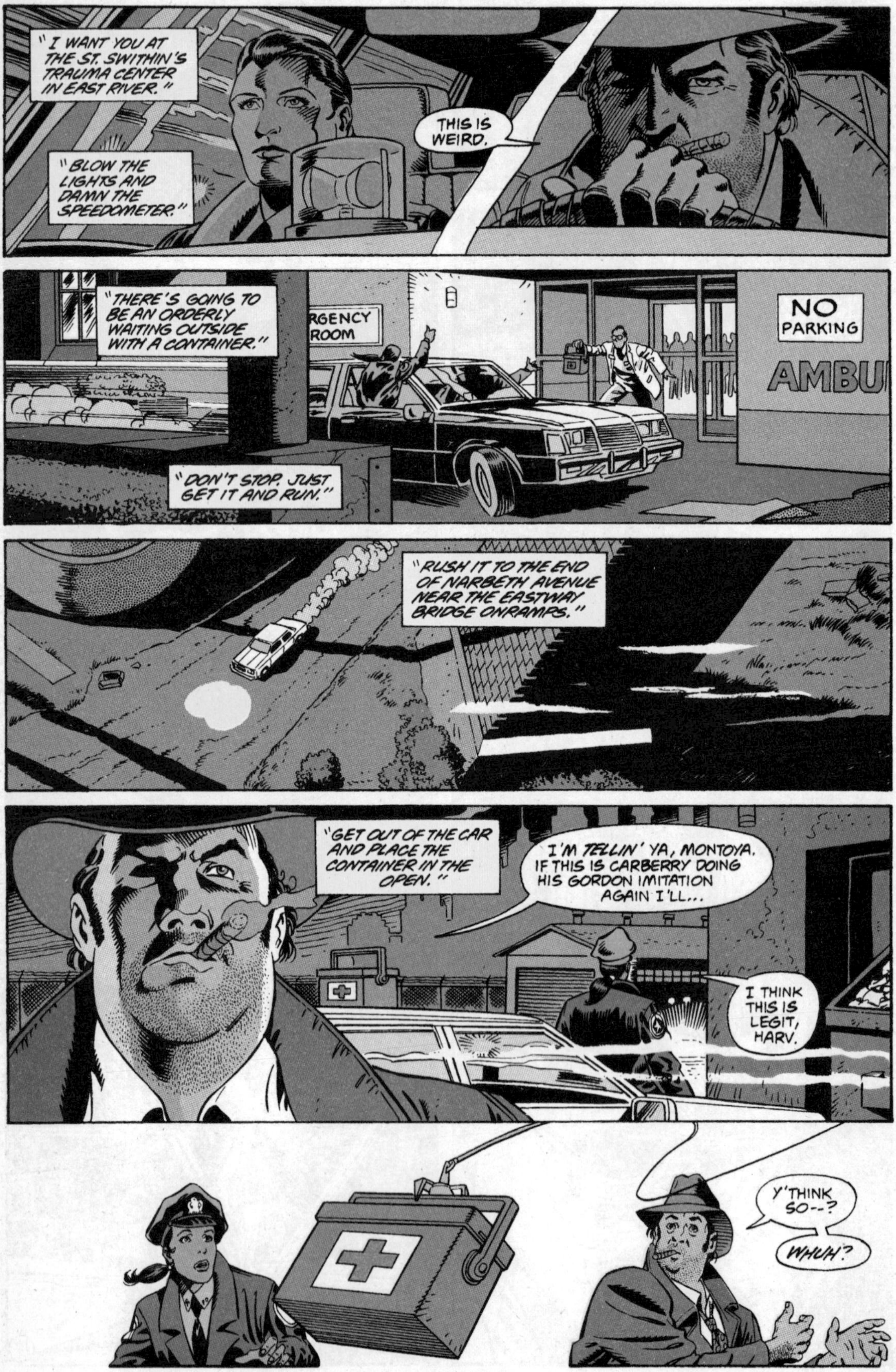
"I WANT YOU AT THE ST. SWITHIN'S TRAUMA CENTER IN EAST RIVER."
THIS IS WEIRD.
"BLOW THE LIGHTS AND DAMN THE SPEEDOMETER."
"THERE'S GOING TO BE AN ORDERLY WAITING OUTSIDE WITH A CONTAINER."
RGENCY ROOM
NO PARKING
AMBU
"DON'T STOP. JUST GET IT AND RUN."
"RUSH IT TO THE END OF NARBETH AVENUE NEAR THE EASTWAY BRIDGE ONRAMPS."
"GET OUT OF THE CAR AND PLACE THE CONTAINER IN THE OPEN."
I'M TELLIN' YA, MONTOYA. IF THIS IS CARBERRY DOING HIS GORDON IMITATION AGAIN I'LL...
I THINK THIS IS LEGIT, HARV.
Y'THINK SO--?
WHUH?

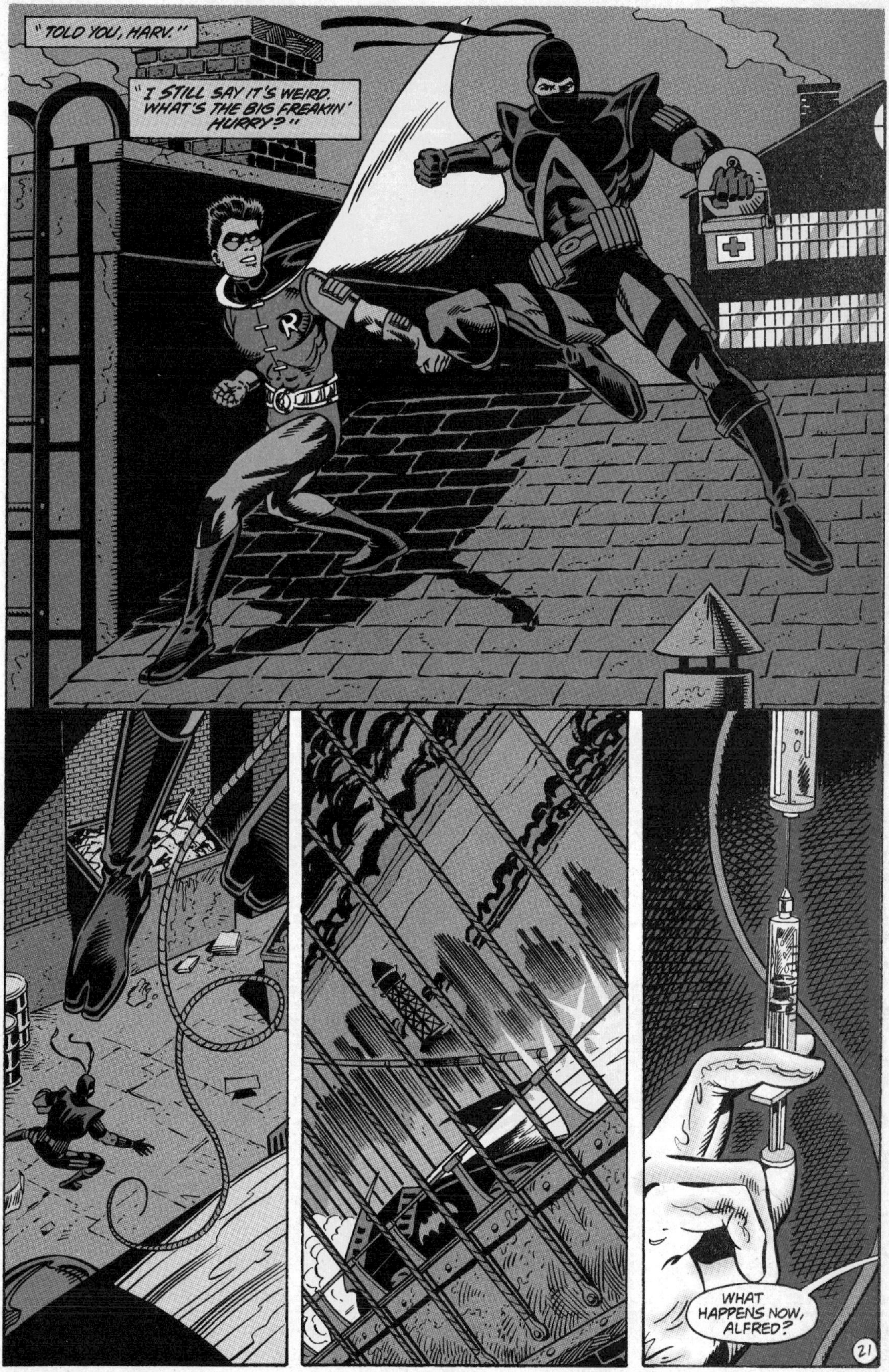
"TOLD YOU, HARV."
"I STILL SAY IT'S WEIRD. WHAT'S THE BIG FREAKIN' HURRY?"
WHAT HAPPENS NOW, ALFRED?
21

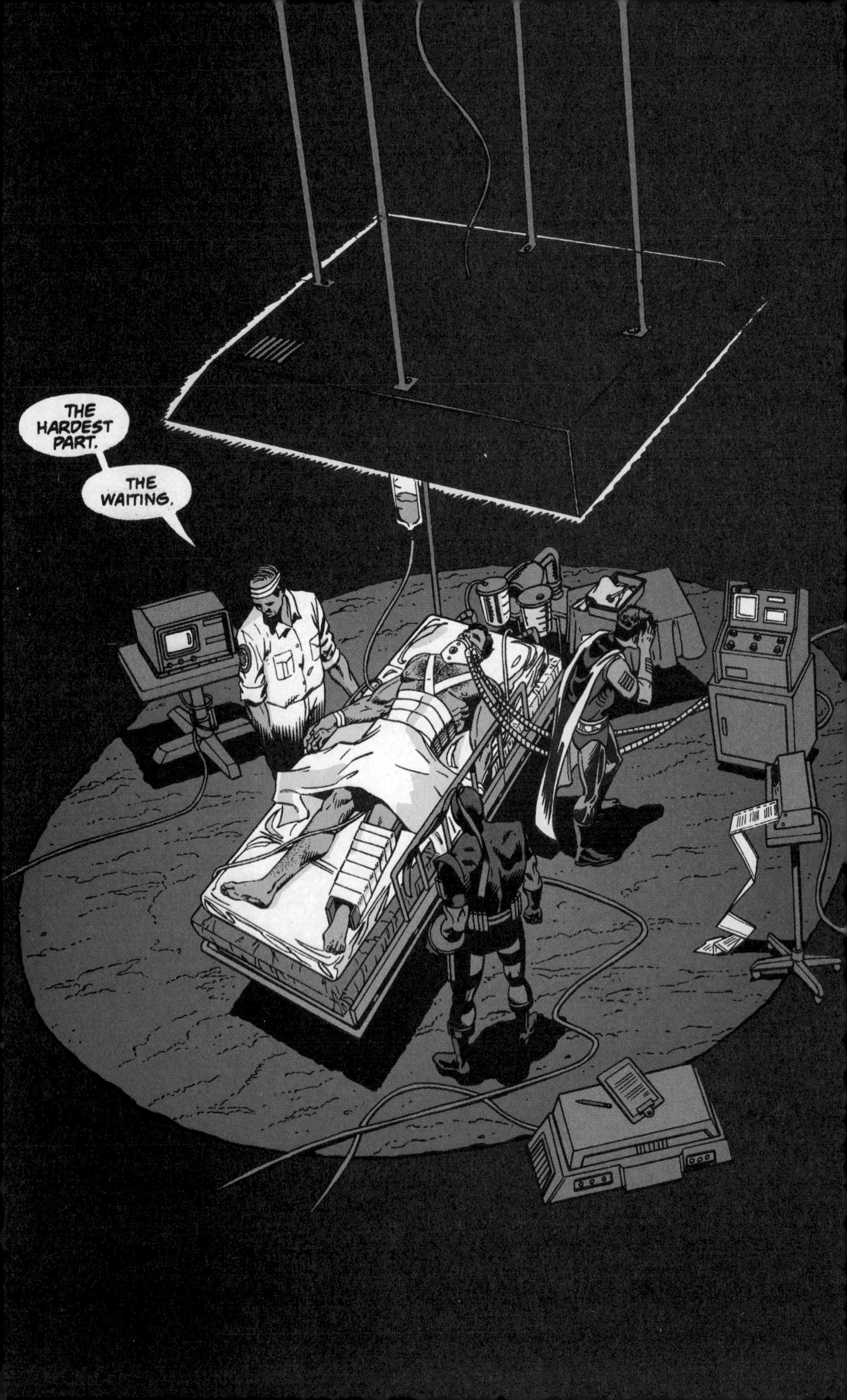
THE HARDEST PART.
THE WAITING.

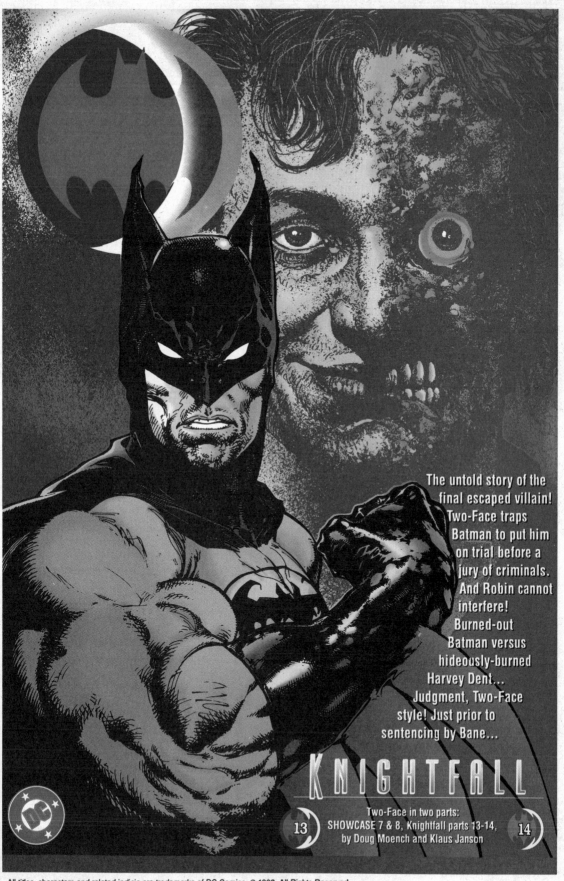

The untold story of the
final escaped villain!
Two-Face traps
Batman to put him
on trial before a
jury of criminals.
And Robin cannot
interfere!
Burned-out
Batman versus
hideously-burned
Harvey Dent...
Judgment, Two-Face
style! Just prior to
sentencing by Bane...

KNIGHTFALL

13   14

Two-Face in two parts:
SHOWCASE 7 & 8, Knightfall parts 13-14,
by Doug Moench and Klaus Janson

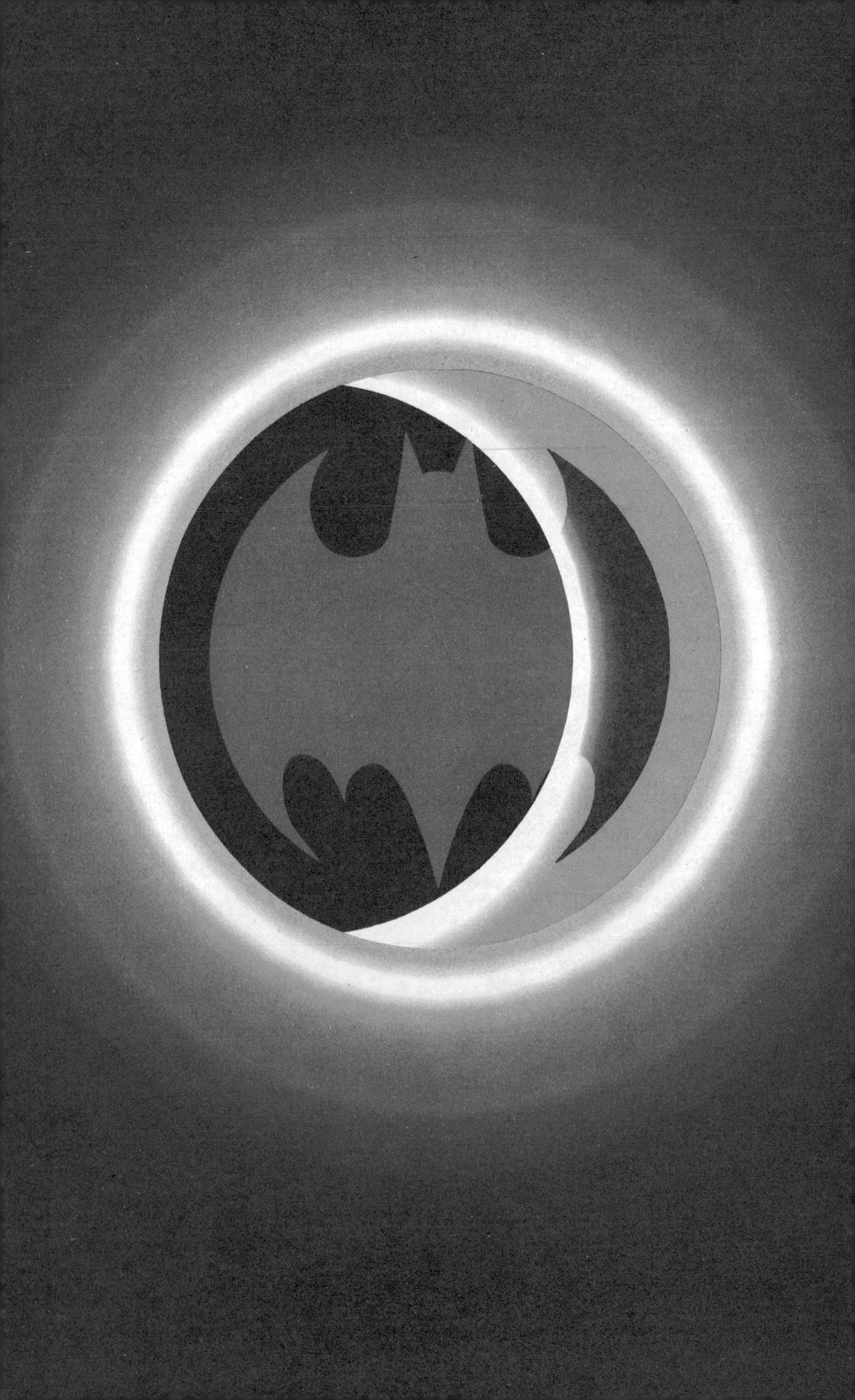

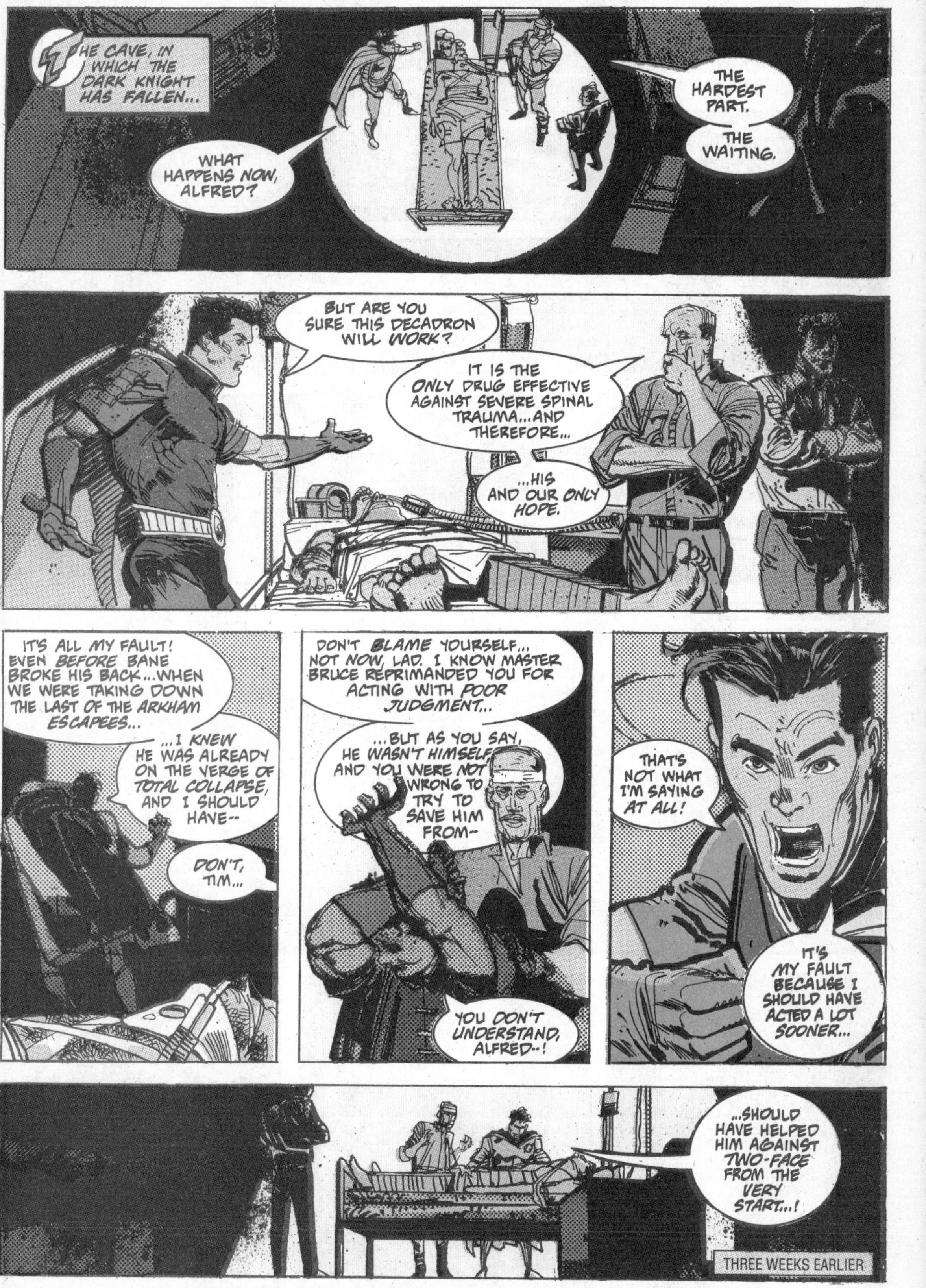
THE CAVE, IN WHICH THE DARK KNIGHT HAS FALLEN...
WHAT HAPPENS NOW, ALFRED?
THE HARDEST PART.
THE WAITING.
BUT ARE YOU SURE THIS DECADRON WILL WORK?
IT IS THE ONLY DRUG EFFECTIVE AGAINST SEVERE SPINAL TRAUMA...AND THEREFORE...
...HIS AND OUR ONLY HOPE.
IT'S ALL MY FAULT! EVEN BEFORE BANE BROKE HIS BACK...WHEN WE WERE TAKING DOWN THE LAST OF THE ARKHAM ESCAPEES...
...I KNEW HE WAS ALREADY ON THE VERGE OF TOTAL COLLAPSE, AND I SHOULD HAVE--
DON'T, TIM...
DON'T BLAME YOURSELF... NOT NOW, LAD. I KNOW MASTER BRUCE REPRIMANDED YOU FOR ACTING WITH POOR JUDGMENT...
...BUT AS YOU SAY, HE WASN'T HIMSELF, AND YOU WERE NOT WRONG TO TRY TO SAVE HIM FROM--
YOU DON'T UNDERSTAND, ALFRED--!
THAT'S NOT WHAT I'M SAYING AT ALL!
IT'S MY FAULT BECAUSE I SHOULD HAVE ACTED A LOT SOONER...
...SHOULD HAVE HELPED HIM AGAINST TWO-FACE FROM THE VERY START...!
THREE WEEKS EARLIER

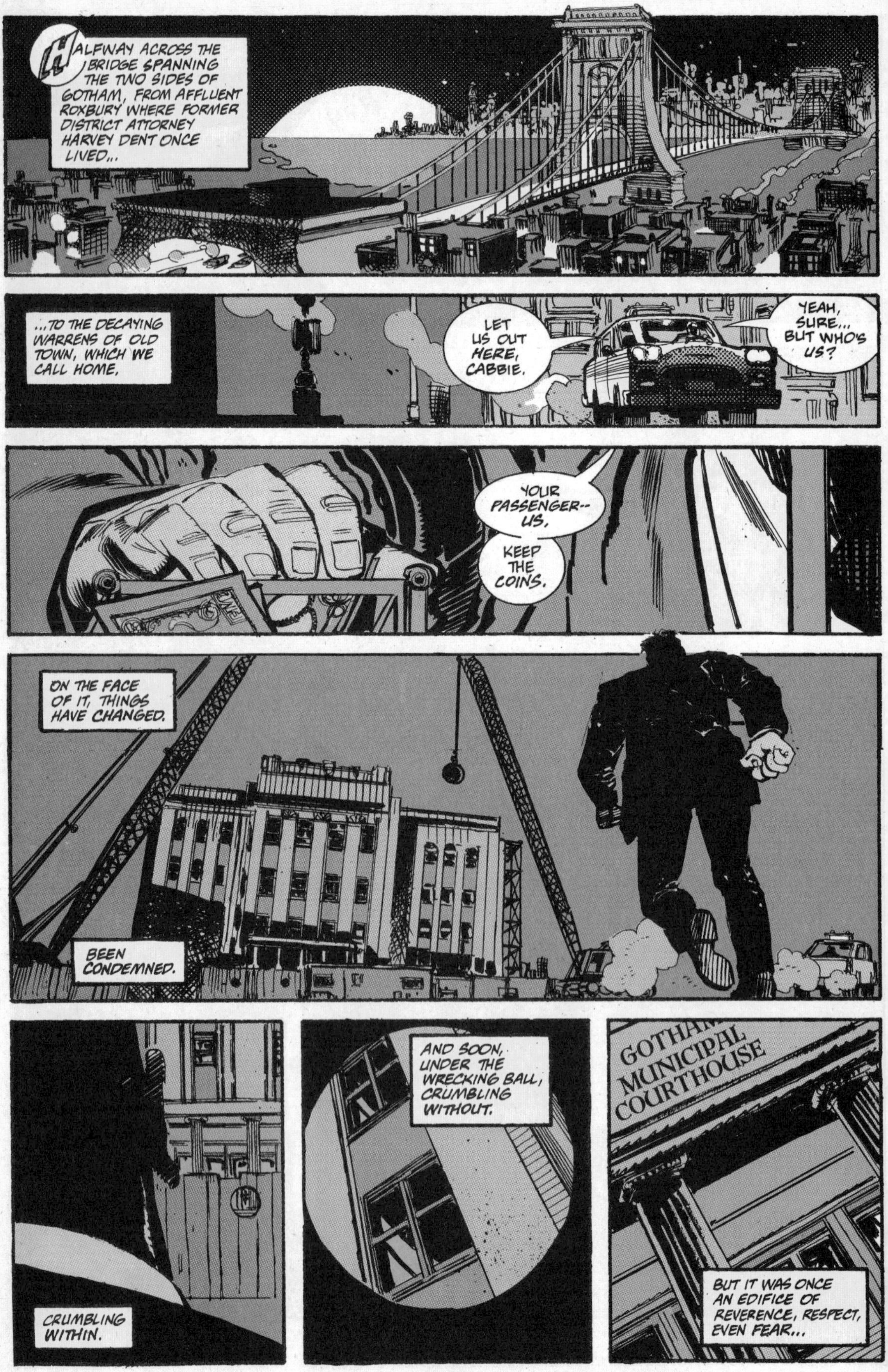
HALFWAY ACROSS THE BRIDGE SPANNING THE TWO SIDES OF GOTHAM, FROM AFFLUENT ROXBURY WHERE FORMER DISTRICT ATTORNEY HARVEY DENT ONCE LIVED...
...TO THE DECAYING WARRENS OF OLD TOWN, WHICH WE CALL HOME.
LET US OUT HERE, CABBIE.
YEAH, SURE... BUT WHO'S US?
YOUR PASSENGER-- US.
KEEP THE COINS.
ON THE FACE OF IT, THINGS HAVE CHANGED.
BEEN CONDEMNED.
CRUMBLING WITHIN.
AND SOON, UNDER THE WRECKING BALL, CRUMBLING WITHOUT.
GOTHAM MUNICIPAL COURTHOUSE
BUT IT WAS ONCE AN EDIFICE OF REVERENCE, RESPECT, EVEN FEAR...

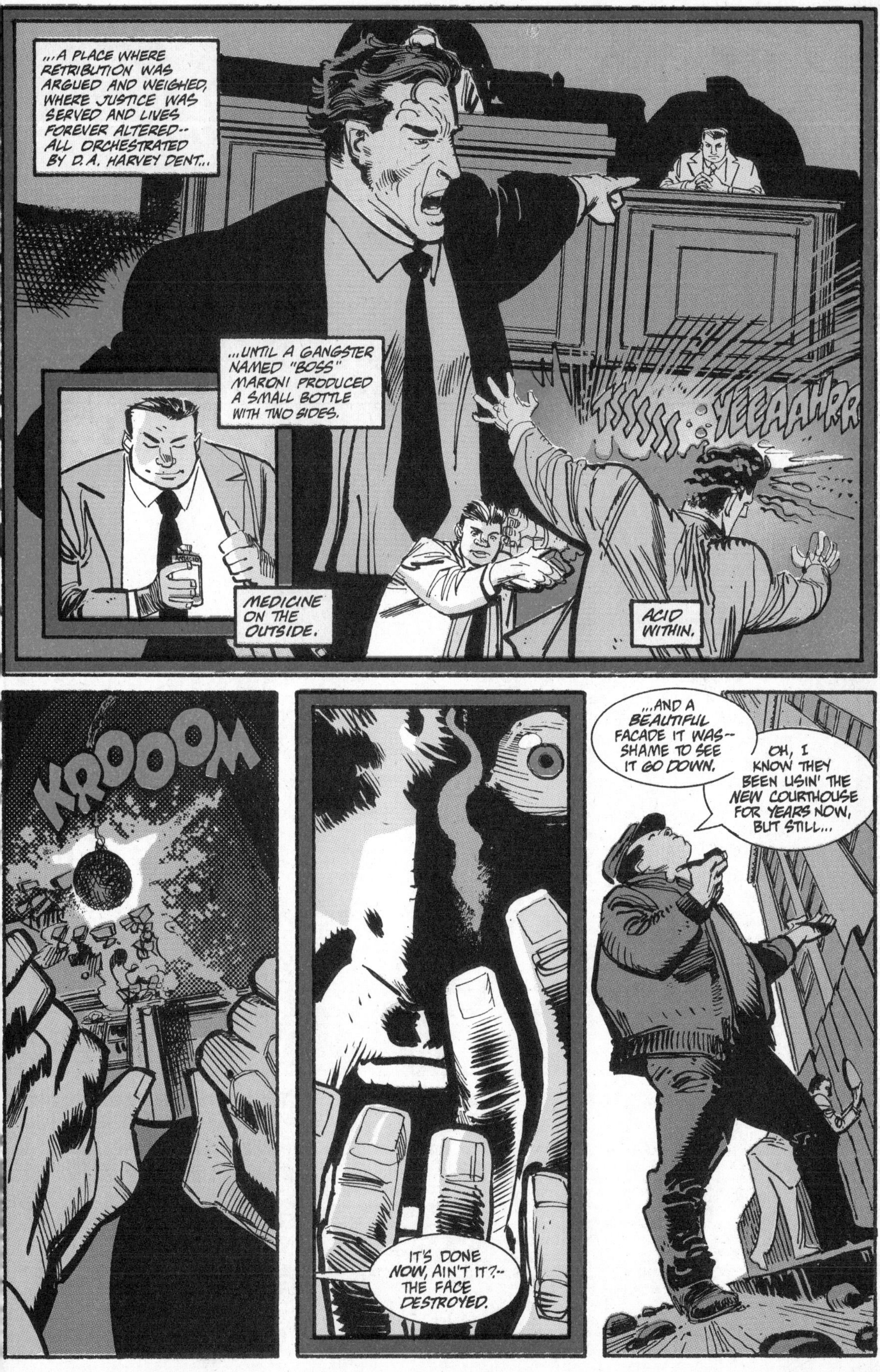
...A PLACE WHERE RETRIBUTION WAS ARGUED AND WEIGHED, WHERE JUSTICE WAS SERVED AND LIVES FOREVER ALTERED-- ALL ORCHESTRATED BY D.A. HARVEY DENT...
...UNTIL A GANGSTER NAMED "BOSS" MARONI PRODUCED A SMALL BOTTLE WITH TWO SIDES.
TSSSSS
YEEAAHRR
MEDICINE ON THE OUTSIDE.
ACID WITHIN.
KROOOM
IT'S DONE NOW, AIN'T IT?-- THE FACE DESTROYED.
...AND A BEAUTIFUL FACADE IT WAS-- SHAME TO SEE IT GO DOWN.
OH, I KNOW THEY BEEN USIN' THE NEW COURTHOUSE FOR YEARS NOW, BUT STILL...

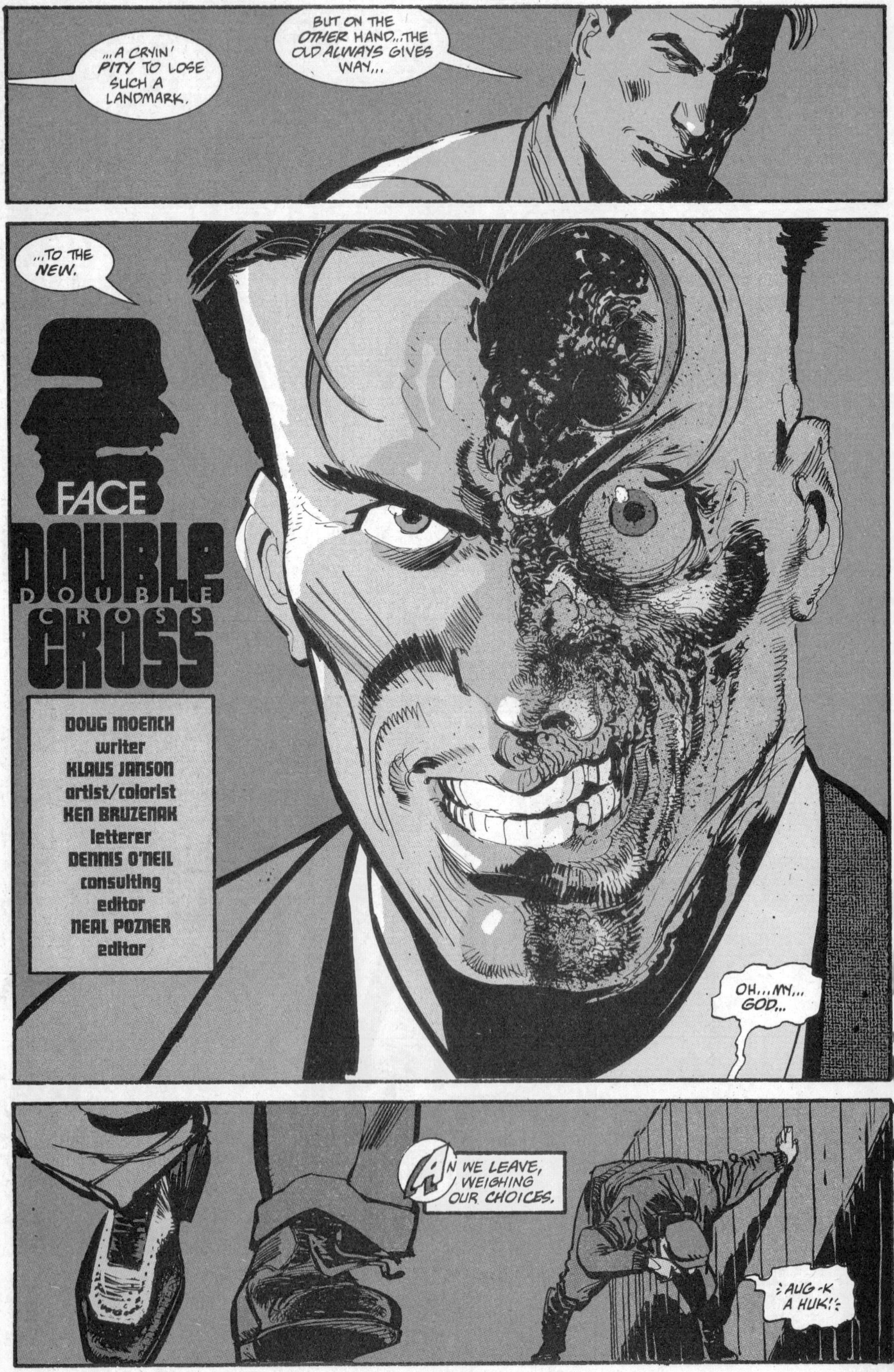
...A CRYIN' PITY TO LOSE SUCH A LANDMARK.
BUT ON THE OTHER HAND...THE OLD ALWAYS GIVES WAY...
...TO THE NEW.
2 FACE
DOUBLE
DOUBLE
CROSS
CROSS
DOUG MOENCH writer
KLAUS JANSON artist/colorist
KEN BRUZENAK letterer
DENNIS O'NEIL consulting editor
NEAL POZNER editor
OH... MY... GOD...
AN WE LEAVE, WEIGHING OUR CHOICES.
AUG-K A HUK!

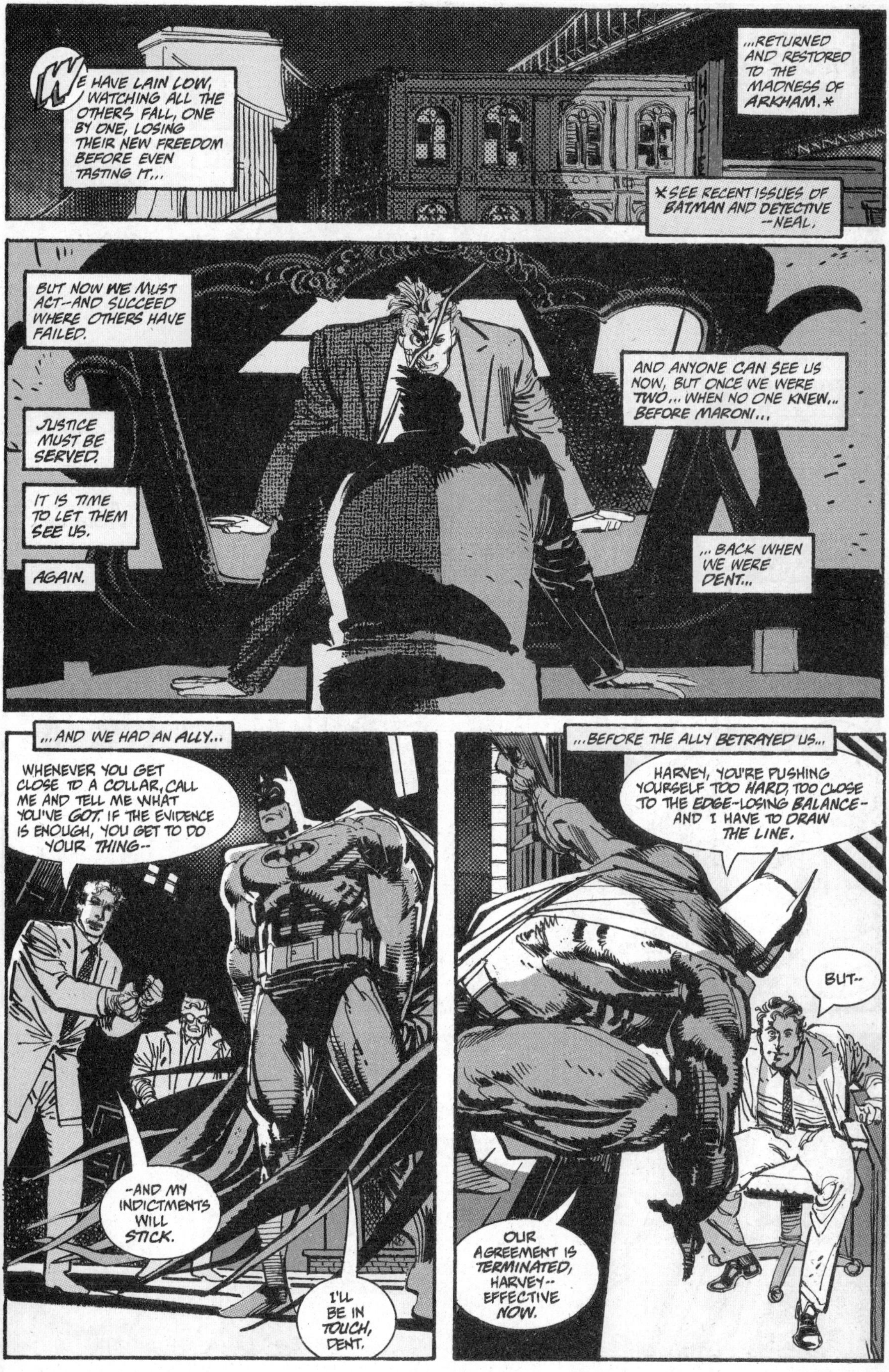
WE HAVE LAIN LOW, WATCHING ALL THE OTHERS FALL, ONE BY ONE, LOSING THEIR NEW FREEDOM BEFORE EVEN TASTING IT...
...RETURNED AND RESTORED TO THE MADNESS OF ARKHAM.*
*SEE RECENT ISSUES OF BATMAN AND DETECTIVE --NEAL.
BUT NOW WE MUST ACT--AND SUCCEED WHERE OTHERS HAVE FAILED.
JUSTICE MUST BE SERVED.
IT IS TIME TO LET THEM SEE US.
AGAIN.
AND ANYONE CAN SEE US NOW, BUT ONCE WE WERE TWO... WHEN NO ONE KNEW... BEFORE MARONI...
...BACK WHEN WE WERE DENT...
...AND WE HAD AN ALLY...
WHENEVER YOU GET CLOSE TO A COLLAR, CALL ME AND TELL ME WHAT YOU'VE GOT. IF THE EVIDENCE IS ENOUGH, YOU GET TO DO YOUR THING--
--AND MY INDICTMENTS WILL STICK.
I'LL BE IN TOUCH, DENT.
...BEFORE THE ALLY BETRAYED US...
HARVEY, YOU'RE PUSHING YOURSELF TOO HARD, TOO CLOSE TO THE EDGE--LOSING BALANCE--AND I HAVE TO DRAW THE LINE.
BUT--
OUR AGREEMENT IS TERMINATED, HARVEY--EFFECTIVE NOW.

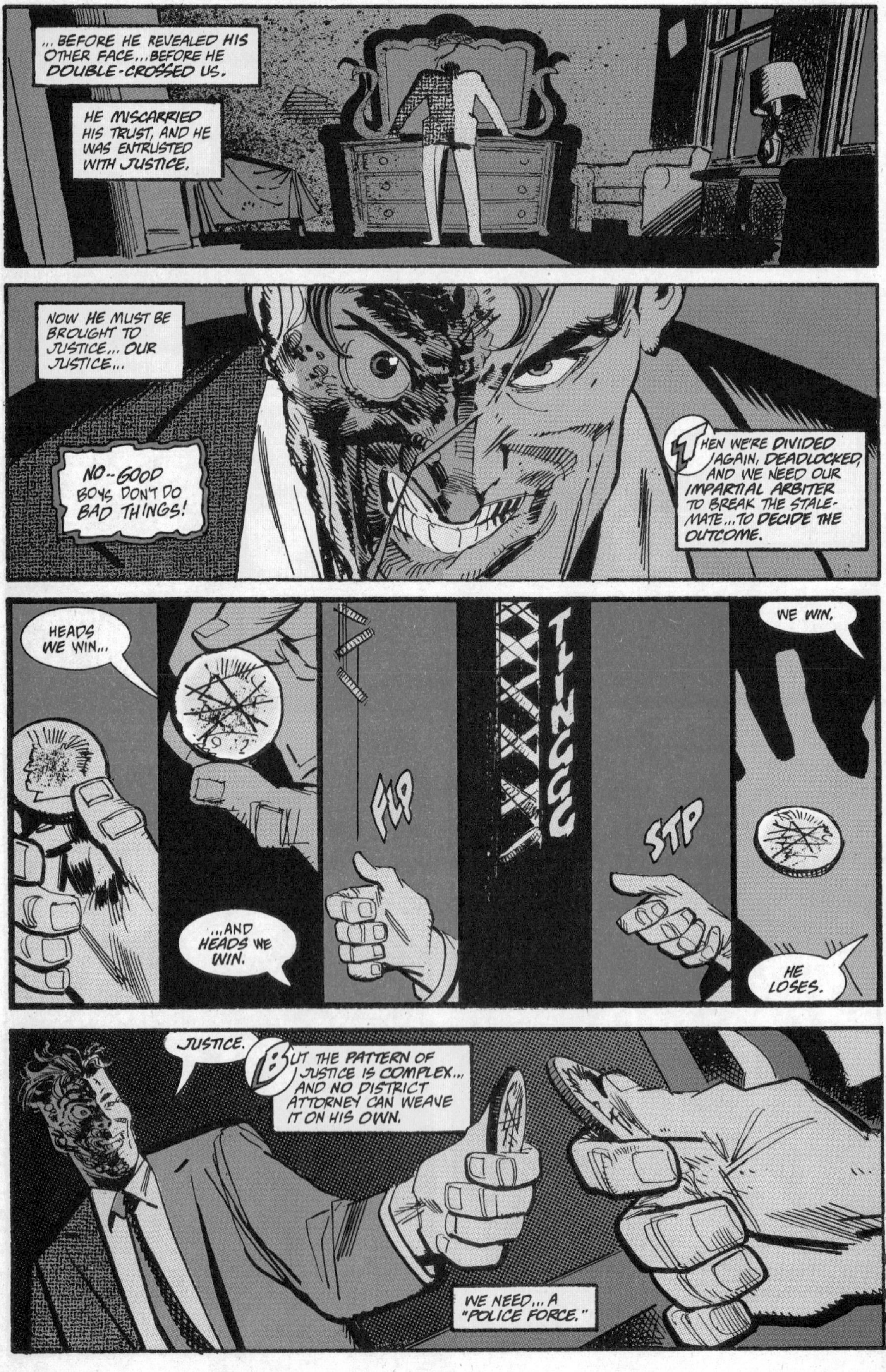
...BEFORE HE REVEALED HIS OTHER FACE...BEFORE HE DOUBLE-CROSSED US.
HE MISCARRIED HIS TRUST, AND HE WAS ENTRUSTED WITH JUSTICE.
NOW HE MUST BE BROUGHT TO JUSTICE... OUR JUSTICE...
NO--GOOD BOYS DON'T DO BAD THINGS!
THEN WE'RE DIVIDED AGAIN, DEADLOCKED, AND WE NEED OUR IMPARTIAL ARBITER TO BREAK THE STALE-MATE...TO DECIDE THE OUTCOME.
HEADS WE WIN...
...AND HEADS WE WIN.
FLP
TINGGG
STP
WE WIN.
HE LOSES.
JUSTICE.
BUT THE PATTERN OF JUSTICE IS COMPLEX... AND NO DISTRICT ATTORNEY CAN WEAVE IT ON HIS OWN.
WE NEED... A "POLICE FORCE."

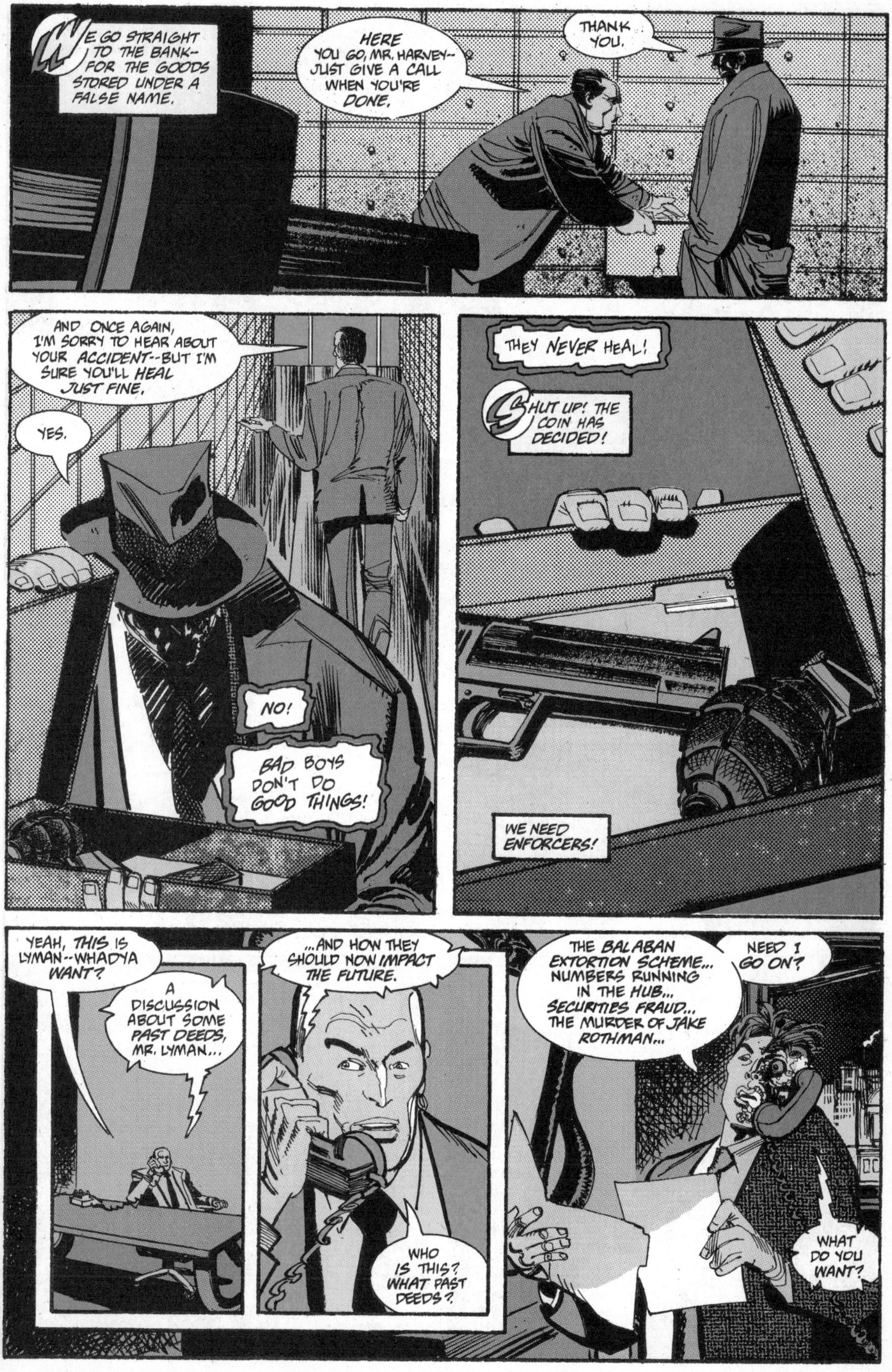
WE GO STRAIGHT TO THE BANK-- FOR THE GOODS STORED UNDER A FALSE NAME.
HERE YOU GO, MR. HARVEY-- JUST GIVE A CALL WHEN YOU'RE DONE.
THANK YOU.
AND ONCE AGAIN, I'M SORRY TO HEAR ABOUT YOUR ACCIDENT--BUT I'M SURE YOU'LL HEAL JUST FINE.
YES.
NO!
BAD BOYS DON'T DO GOOD THINGS!
THEY NEVER HEAL!
SHUT UP! THE COIN HAS DECIDED!
WE NEED ENFORCERS!
YEAH, THIS IS LYMAN--WHADYA WANT?
A DISCUSSION ABOUT SOME PAST DEEDS, MR. LYMAN...
...AND HOW THEY SHOULD NOW IMPACT THE FUTURE.
WHO IS THIS? WHAT PAST DEEDS?
THE BALABAN EXTORTION SCHEME... NUMBERS RUNNING IN THE HUB... SECURITIES FRAUD... THE MURDER OF JAKE ROTHMAN...
NEED I GO ON?
WHAT DO YOU WANT?

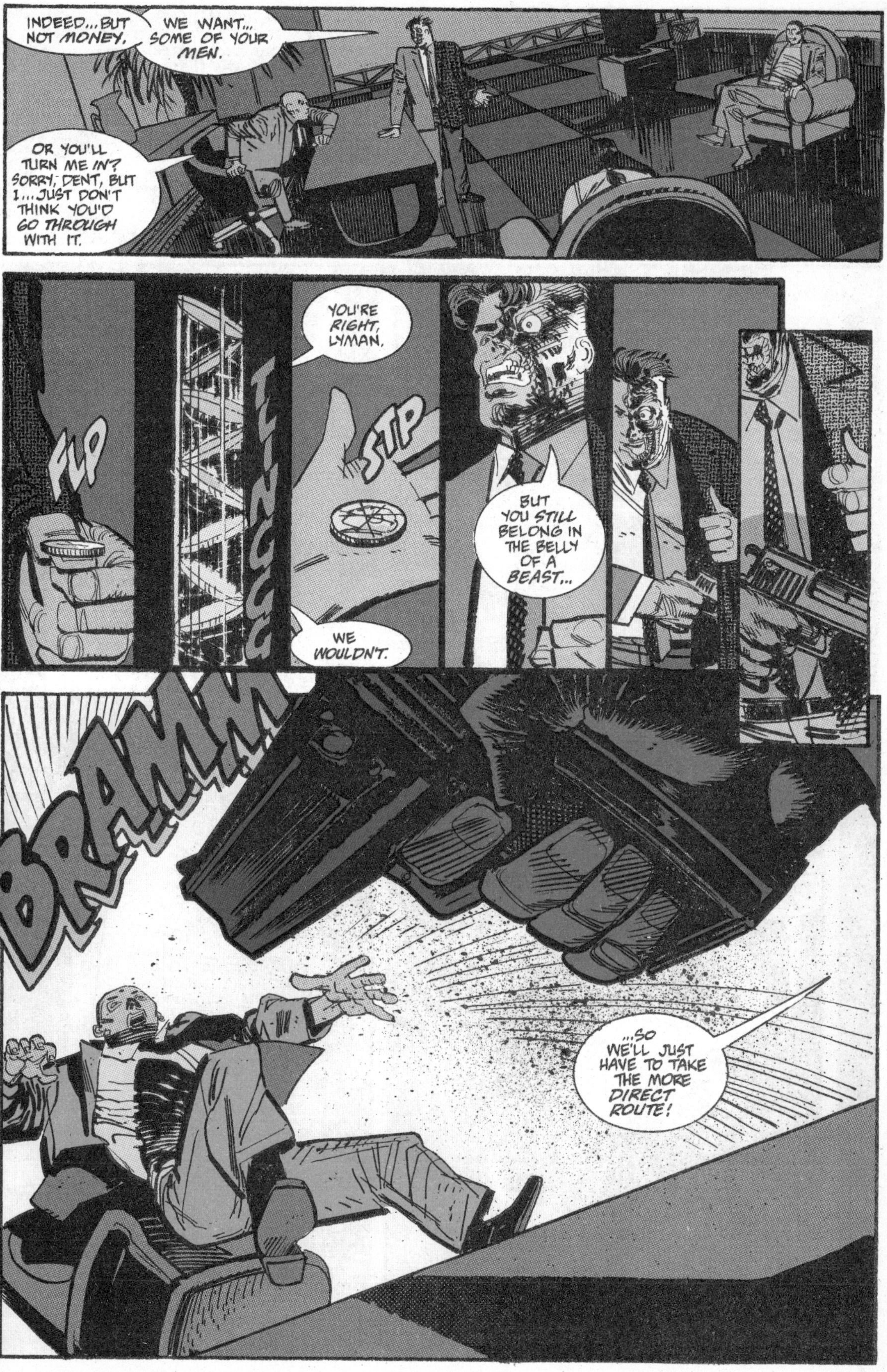
INDEED... BUT NOT MONEY.
WE WANT... SOME OF YOUR MEN.
OR YOU'LL TURN ME IN? SORRY, DENT, BUT I... JUST DON'T THINK YOU'D GO THROUGH WITH IT.
FLP
TLINGG
YOU'RE RIGHT, LYMAN.
STP
WE WOULDN'T.
BUT YOU STILL BELONG IN THE BELLY OF A BEAST...
BRAMM
...SO WE'LL JUST HAVE TO TAKE THE MORE DIRECT ROUTE!

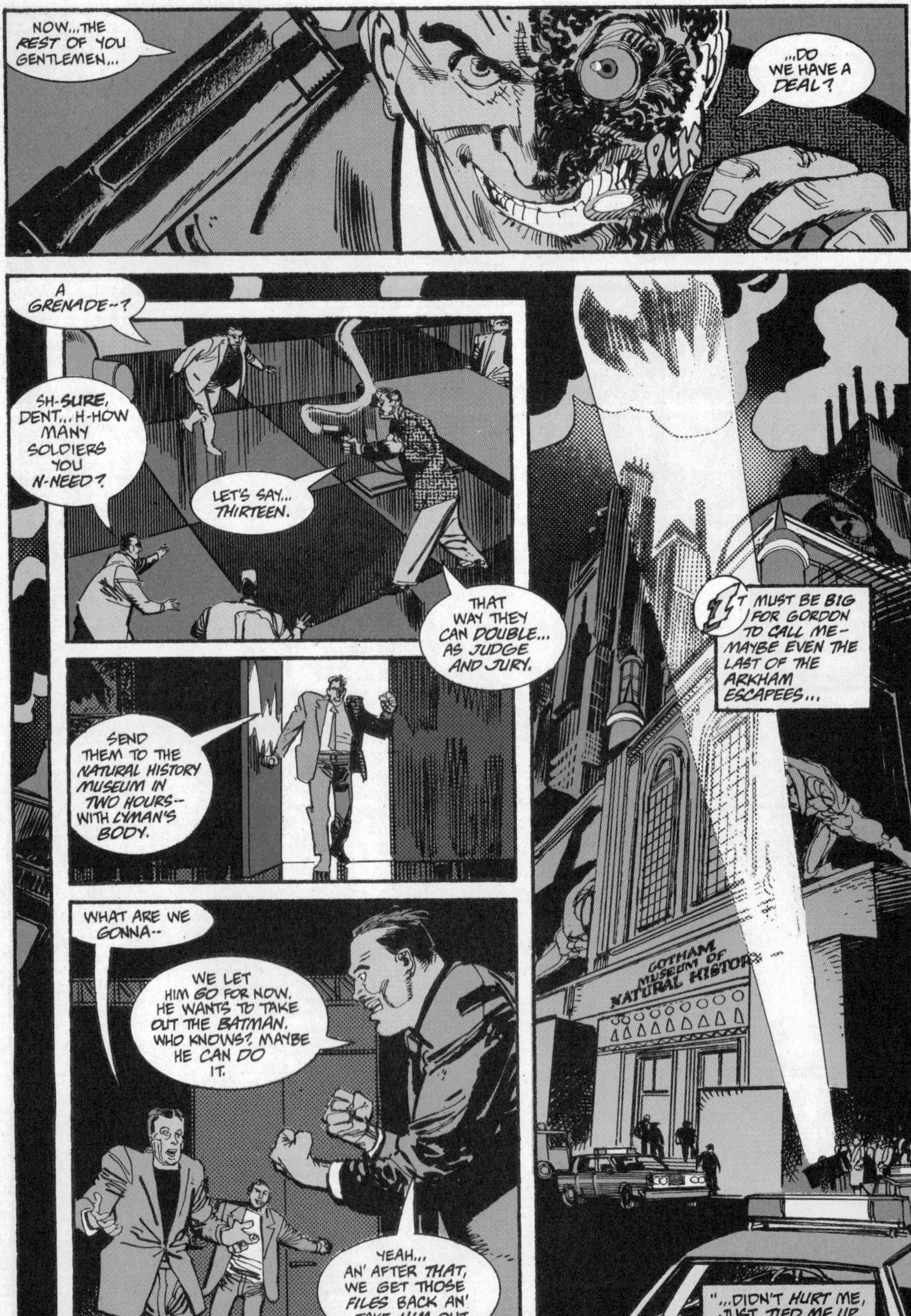
NOW... THE REST OF YOU GENTLEMEN...
...DO WE HAVE A DEAL?
A GRENADE--?
SH-SURE, DENT... H-HOW MANY SOLDIERS YOU N-NEED?
LET'S SAY... THIRTEEN.
THAT WAY THEY CAN DOUBLE... AS JUDGE AND JURY.
SEND THEM TO THE NATURAL HISTORY MUSEUM IN TWO HOURS-- WITH LYMAN'S BODY.
WHAT ARE WE GONNA--
WE LET HIM GO FOR NOW. HE WANTS TO TAKE OUT THE BATMAN. WHO KNOWS? MAYBE HE CAN DO IT.
YEAH... AN' AFTER THAT, WE GET THOSE FILES BACK AN' TAKE HIM OUT.
IT MUST BE BIG FOR GORDON TO CALL ME-- MAYBE EVEN THE LAST OF THE ARKHAM ESCAPEES...
GOTHAM MUSEUM OF NATURAL HISTOR
"...DIDN'T HURT ME, JUST TIED ME UP AND TAPED MY MOUTH..."

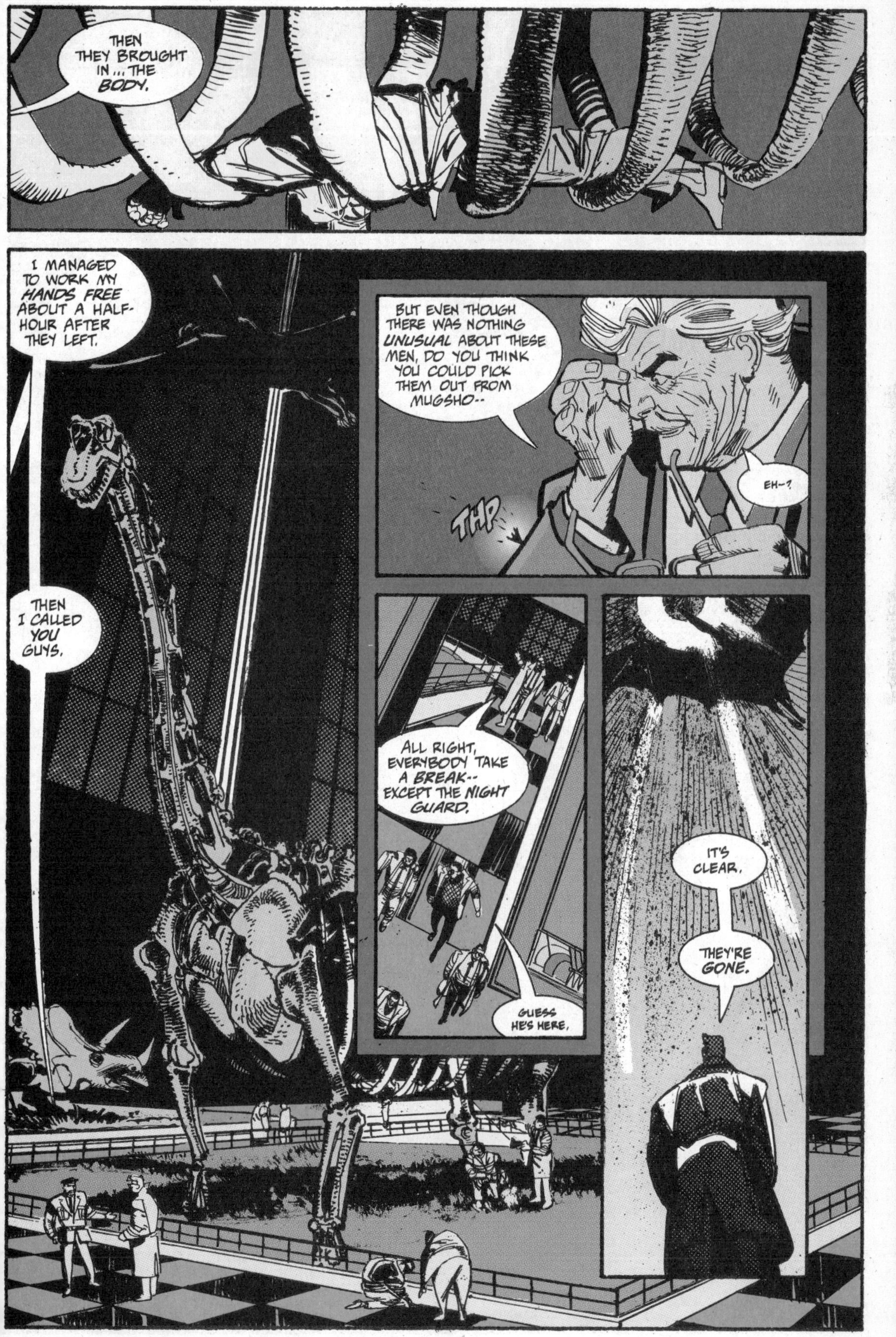
THEN THEY BROUGHT IN ... THE BODY.
I MANAGED TO WORK MY HANDS FREE ABOUT A HALF-HOUR AFTER THEY LEFT.
THEN I CALLED YOU GUYS.
BUT EVEN THOUGH THERE WAS NOTHING UNUSUAL ABOUT THESE MEN, DO YOU THINK YOU COULD PICK THEM OUT FROM MUGSHO--
THP
EH--?
ALL RIGHT, EVERYBODY TAKE A BREAK-- EXCEPT THE NIGHT GUARD.
GUESS HE'S HERE.
IT'S CLEAR.
THEY'RE GONE.

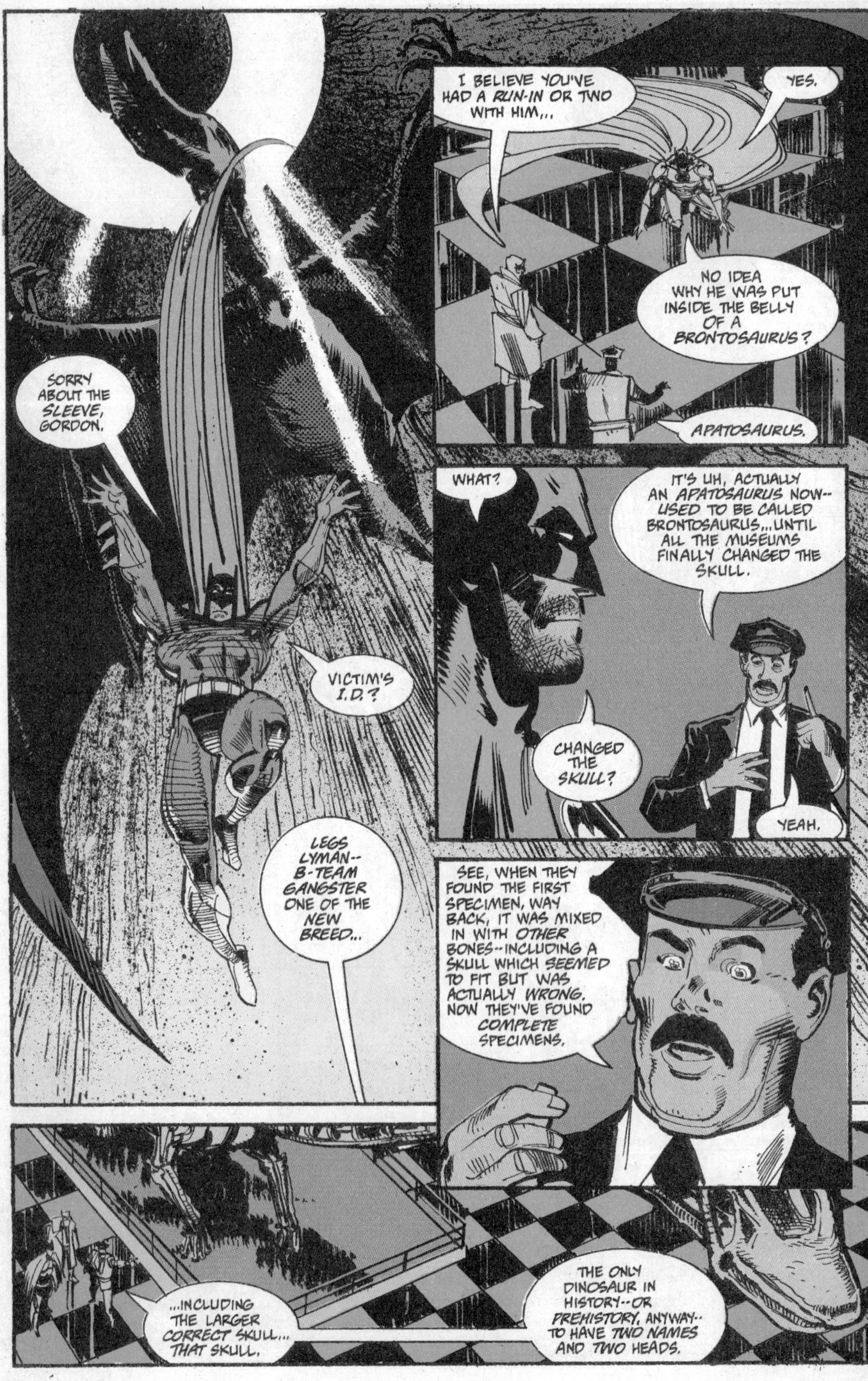
I BELIEVE YOU'VE HAD A RUN-IN OR TWO WITH HIM...
YES.
NO IDEA WHY HE WAS PUT INSIDE THE BELLY OF A BRONTOSAURUS?
APATOSAURUS.
SORRY ABOUT THE SLEEVE, GORDON.
WHAT?
IT'S UH, ACTUALLY AN APATOSAURUS NOW-- USED TO BE CALLED BRONTOSAURUS... UNTIL ALL THE MUSEUMS FINALLY CHANGED THE SKULL.
CHANGED THE SKULL?
YEAH.
VICTIM'S I.D.?
LEGS LYMAN-- B-TEAM GANGSTER ONE OF THE NEW BREED...
SEE, WHEN THEY FOUND THE FIRST SPECIMEN, WAY BACK, IT WAS MIXED IN WITH OTHER BONES--INCLUDING A SKULL WHICH SEEMED TO FIT BUT WAS ACTUALLY WRONG. NOW THEY'VE FOUND COMPLETE SPECIMENS.
...INCLUDING THE LARGER CORRECT SKULL... THAT SKULL.
THE ONLY DINOSAUR IN HISTORY--OR PREHISTORY, ANYWAY-- TO HAVE TWO NAMES AND TWO HEADS.

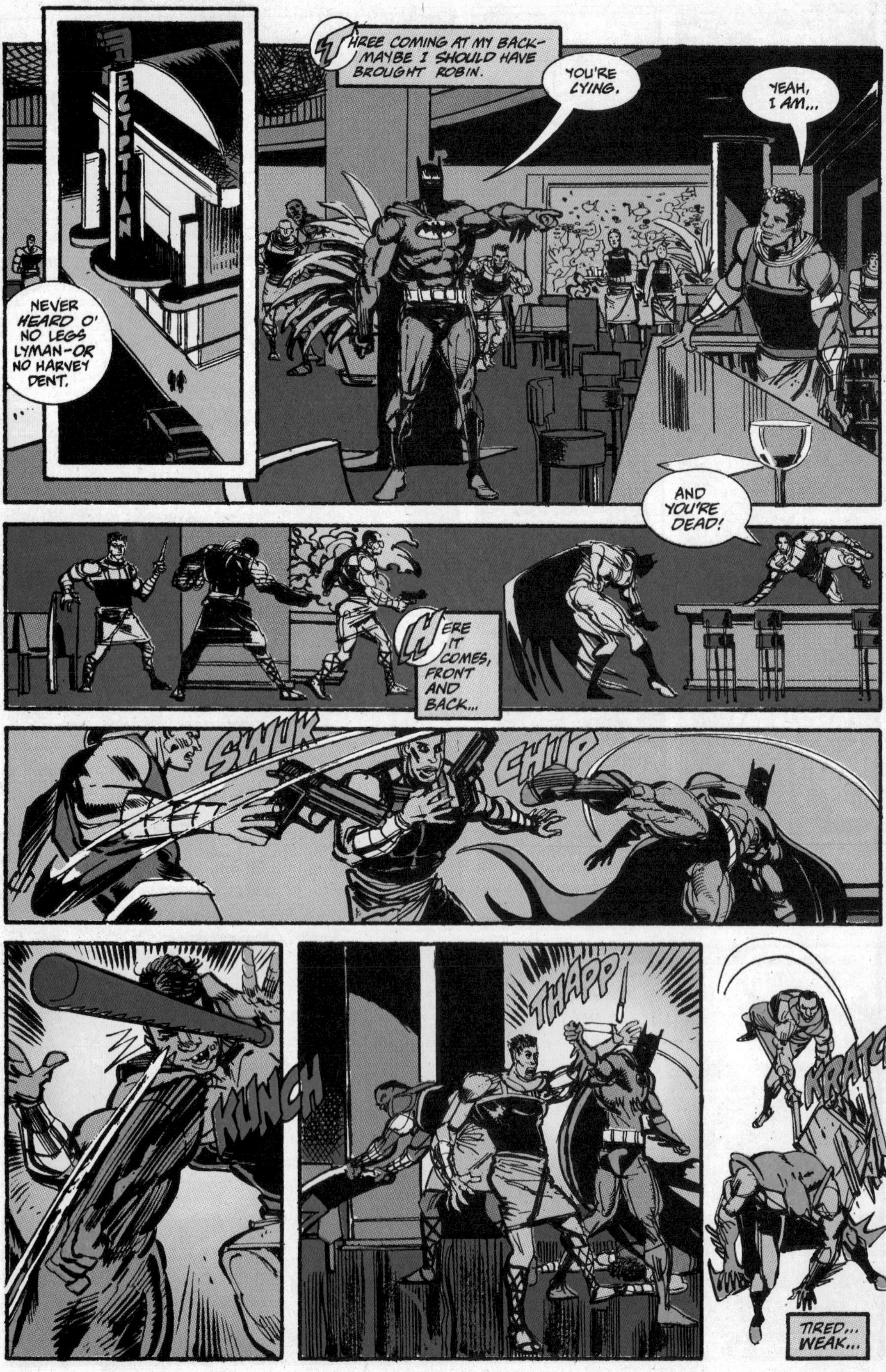
THREE COMING AT MY BACK- MAYBE I SHOULD HAVE BROUGHT ROBIN.
NEVER HEARD O' NO LEGS LYMAN-OR NO HARVEY DENT.
...
YOU'RE LYING.
YEAH, I AM...
AND YOU'RE DEAD!
HERE IT COMES, FRONT AND BACK...
SWUK
CHUP
KUNCH
THAPP
KRATCH
TIRED... WEAK...

By NOW, ALL FOUR SHOULD BE DOWN TO STAY...

SWOKK

...THE FIGHT FINISHED IN SECONDS...

BUT INSTEAD--

KWUMP

UHN--!

--THEY JUST KEEP COMING...

CHUFT

...BIG AND CLUMSY...

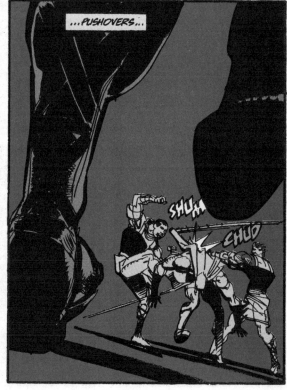

...PUSHOVERS...

SHU

CHUD

43

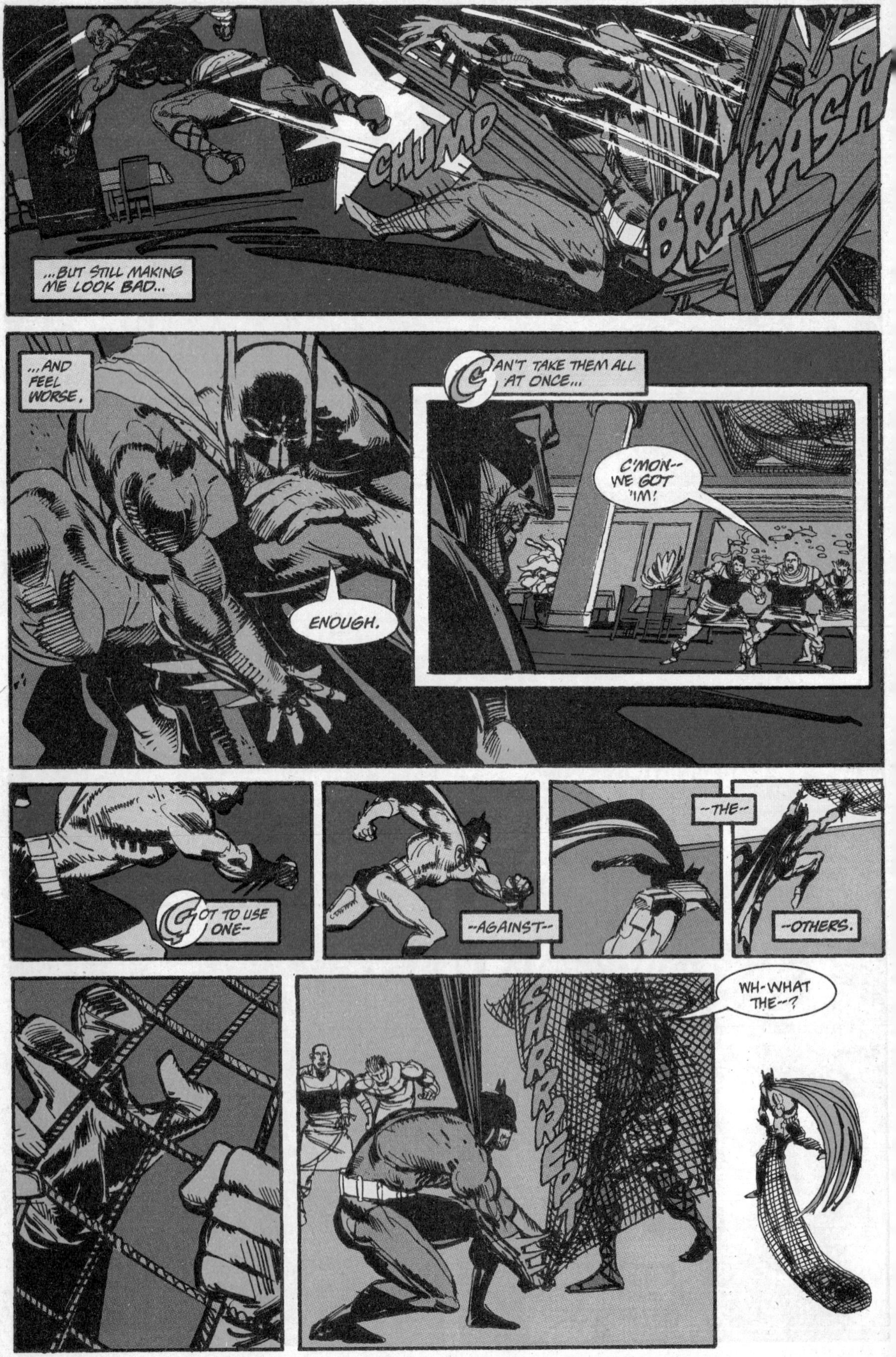
CHUMP
BRAKASH
...BUT STILL MAKING ME LOOK BAD...
...AND FEEL WORSE.
CAN'T TAKE THEM ALL AT ONCE...
C'MON-- WE GOT 'IM!
ENOUGH.
GOT TO USE ONE-
--AGAINST--
--THE--
--OTHERS.
WH-WHAT THE--?

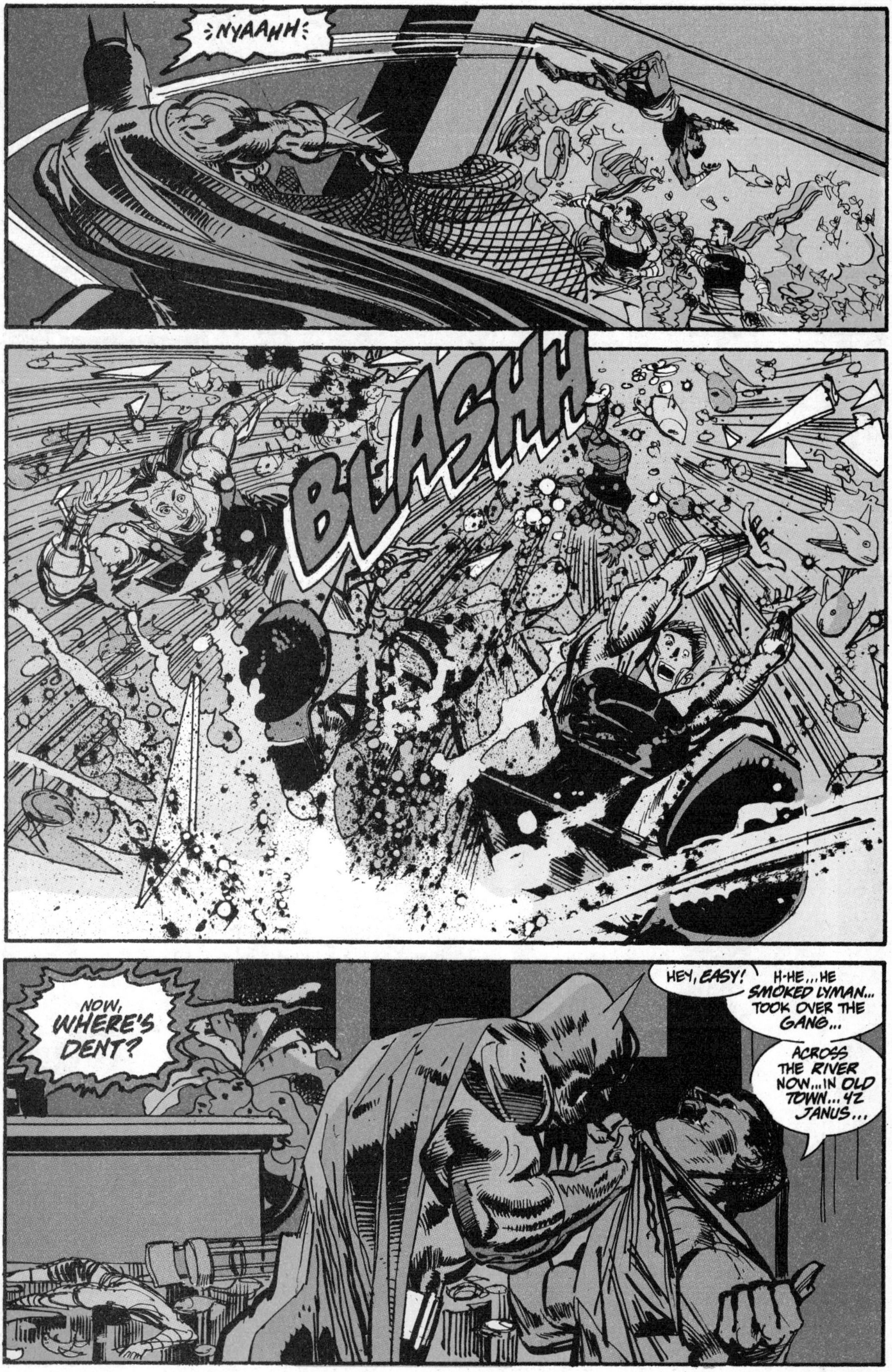
NYAAHH
BLASHH
NOW, WHERE'S DENT?
HEY, EASY! H-HE... HE SMOKED LYMAN... TOOK OVER THE GANG...
ACROSS THE RIVER NOW... IN OLD TOWN... 42 JANUS...

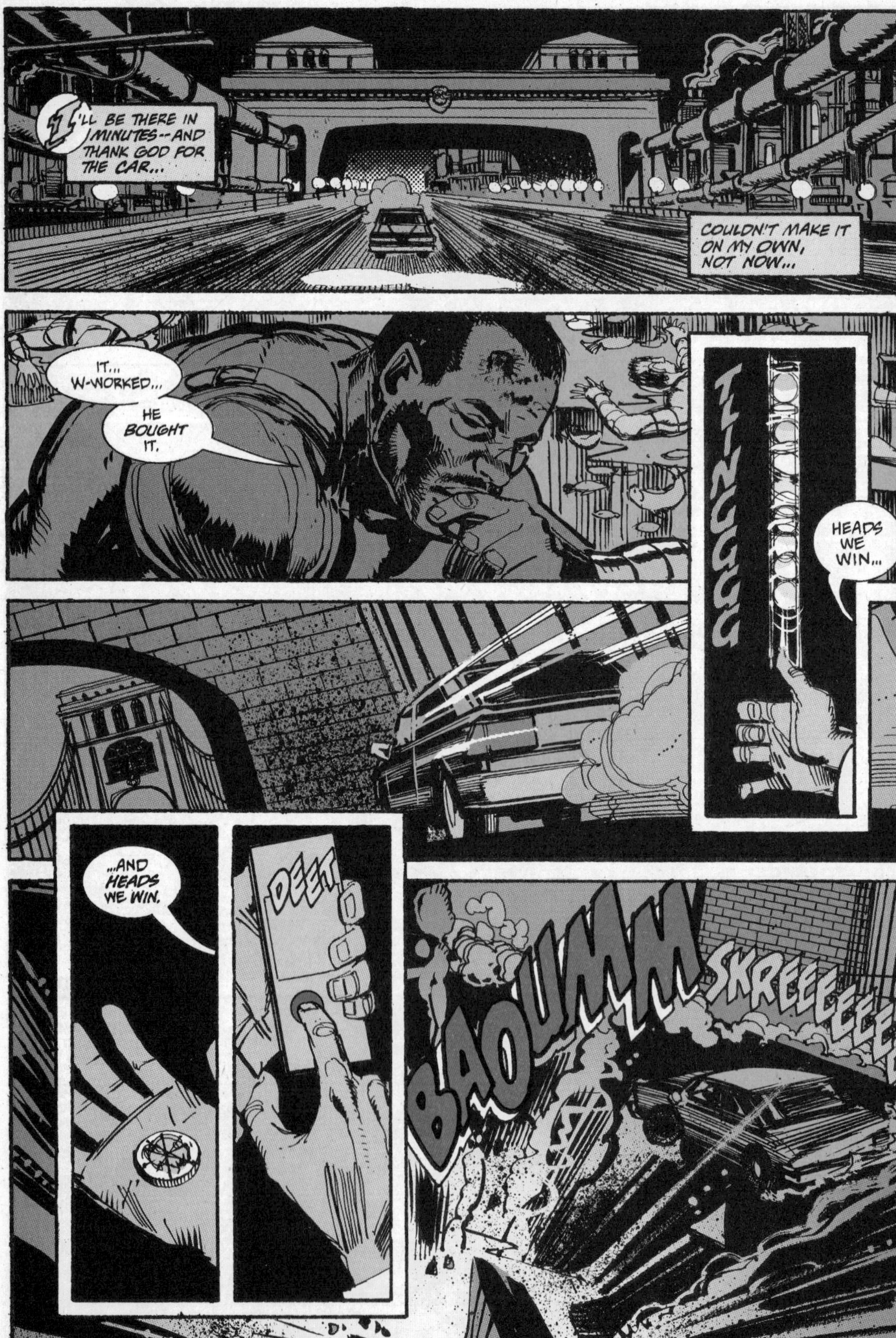
I'LL BE THERE IN MINUTES--AND THANK GOD FOR THE CAR...
COULDN'T MAKE IT ON MY OWN, NOT NOW...
IT... W-WORKED...
HE BOUGHT IT.
TINGGGG
HEADS WE WIN...
...AND HEADS WE WIN.
DEET
BAOUMM
SKREEEEEEE

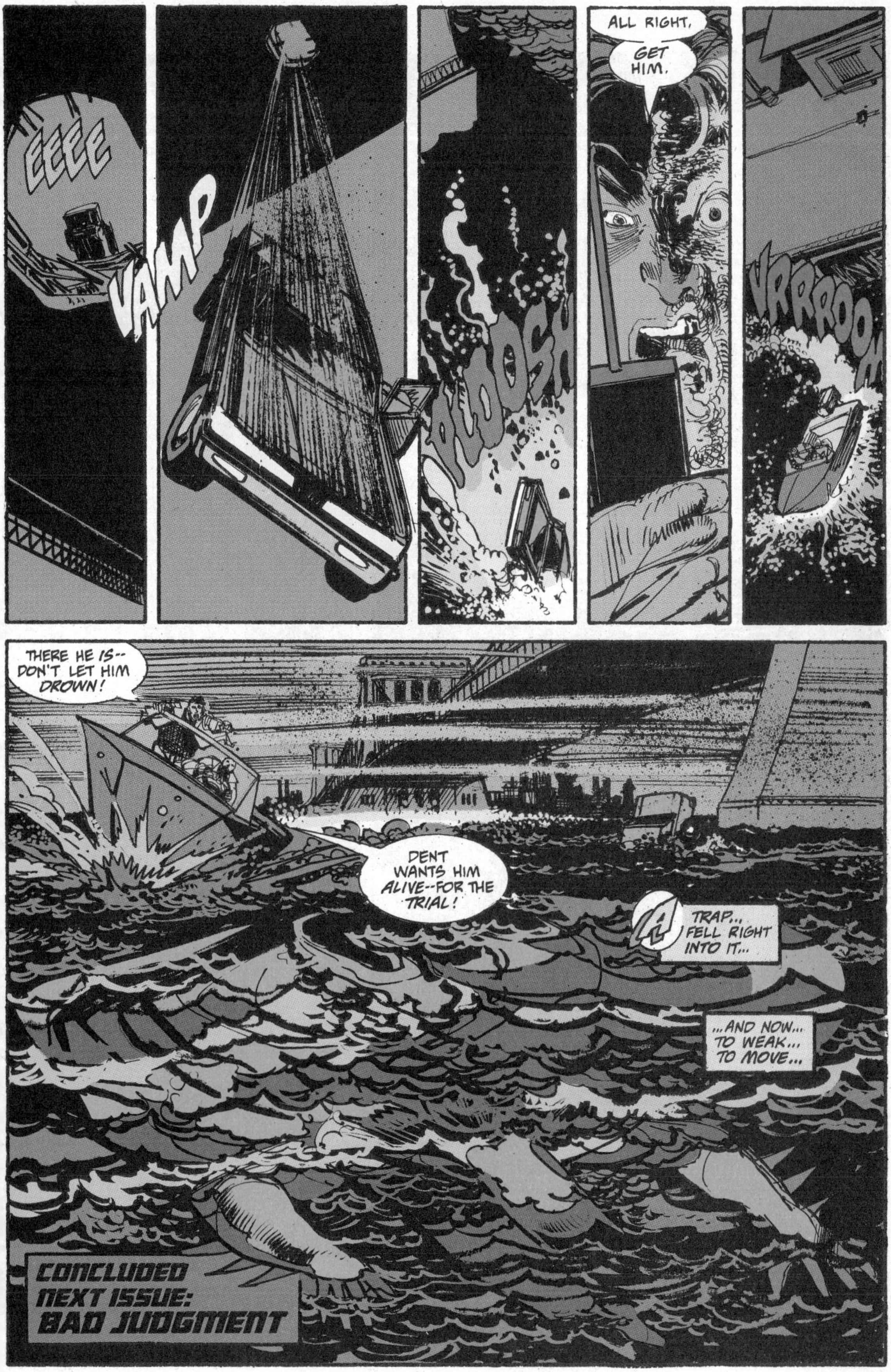
EEEE
VAMP
SHOOSH
ALL RIGHT,
GET HIM.
VRRROOM
THERE HE IS-- DON'T LET HIM DROWN!
DENT WANTS HIM ALIVE--FOR THE TRIAL!
TRAP... FELL RIGHT INTO IT...
...AND NOW... TO WEAK... TO MOVE...
CONCLUDED NEXT ISSUE: BAD JUDGMENT

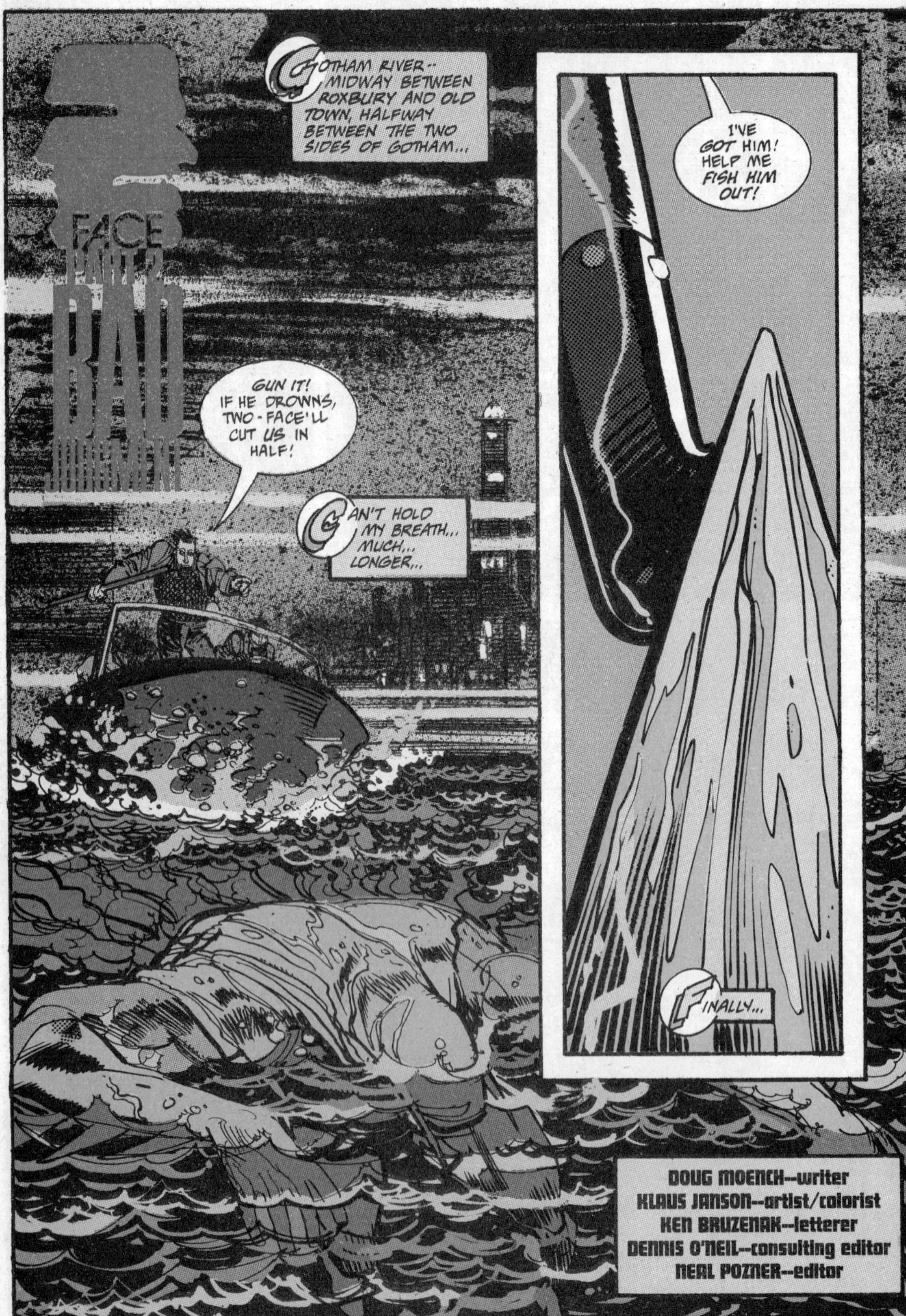
FACE
BAD
GOTHAM RIVER-- MIDWAY BETWEEN ROXBURY AND OLD TOWN, HALFWAY BETWEEN THE TWO SIDES OF GOTHAM...
GUN IT! IF HE DROWNS, TWO-FACE'LL CUT US IN HALF!
CAN'T HOLD MY BREATH... MUCH... LONGER...
I'VE GOT HIM! HELP ME FISH HIM OUT!
FINALLY...
DOUG MOENCH--writer
KLAUS JANSON--artist/colorist
KEN BRUZENAK--letterer
DENNIS O'NEIL--consulting editor
NEAL POZNER--editor

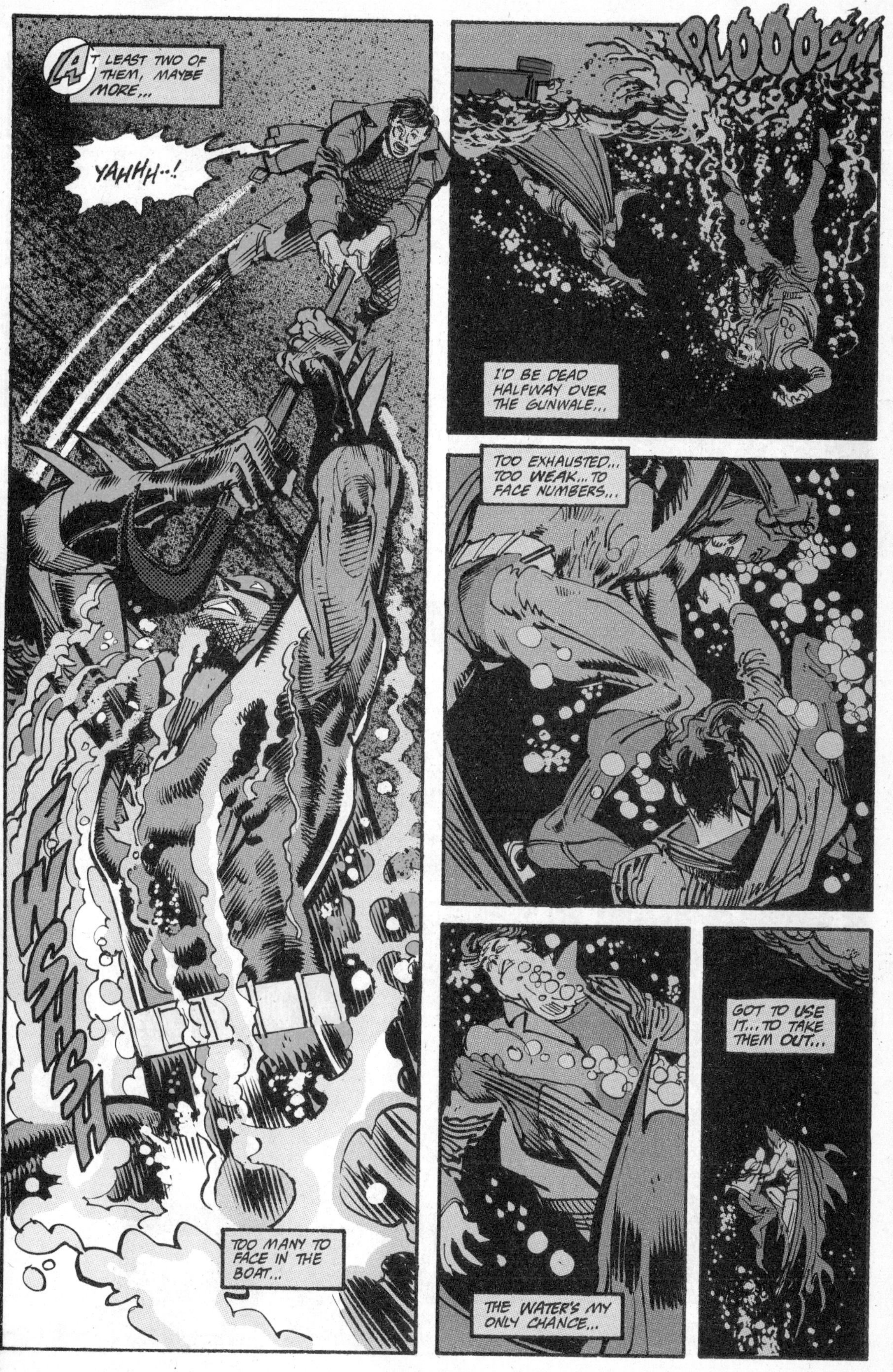

AT LEAST TWO OF THEM, MAYBE MORE...
YAHHH--!
TOO MANY TO FACE IN THE BOAT...
PLOOOSH
I'D BE DEAD HALFWAY OVER THE GUNWALE...
TOO EXHAUSTED... TOO WEAK... TO FACE NUMBERS...
THE WATER'S MY ONLY CHANCE...
GOT TO USE IT... TO TAKE THEM OUT...

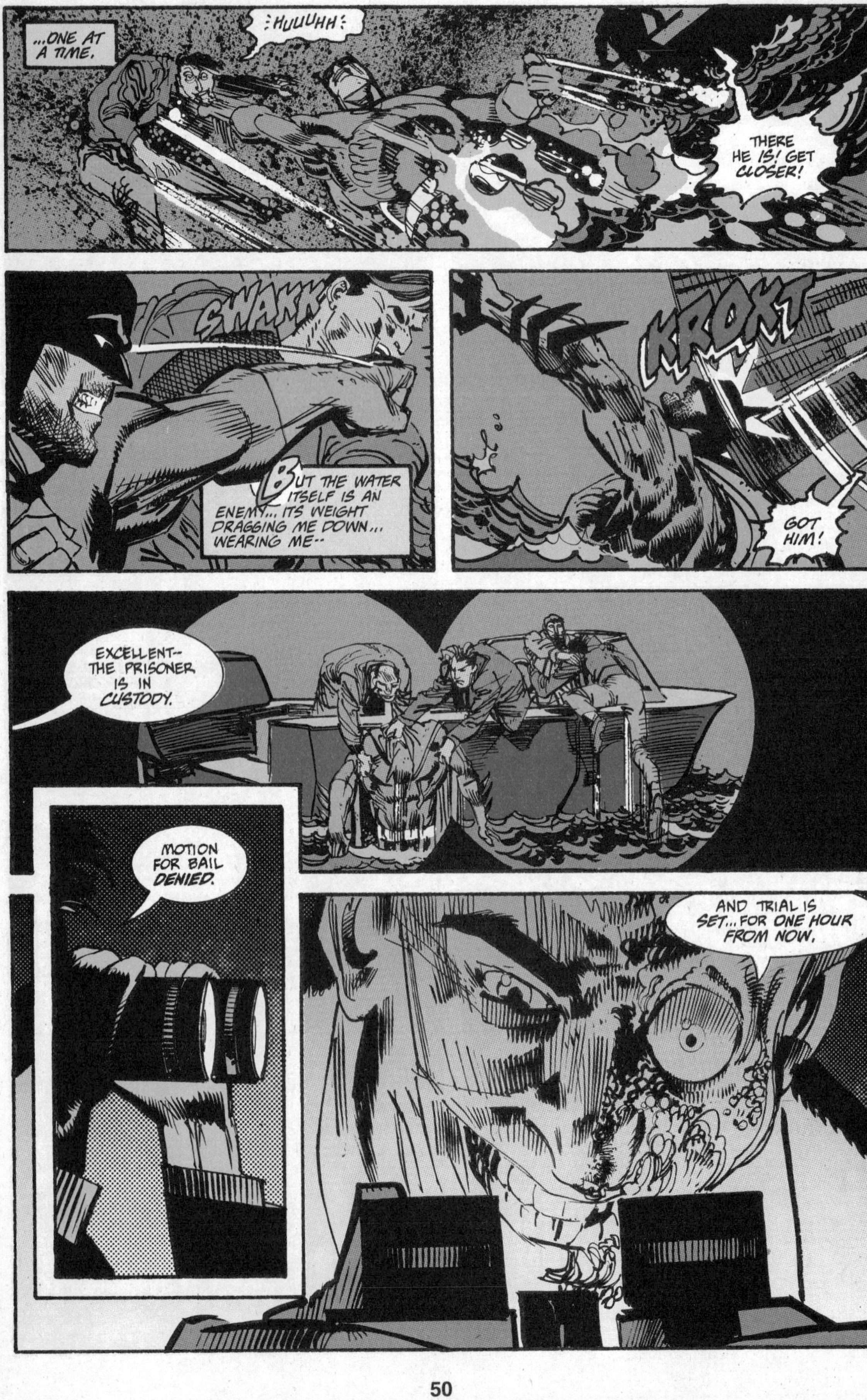
...ONE AT A TIME.
HUUUHH
THERE HE IS! GET CLOSER!
SNAKK
BUT THE WATER ITSELF IS AN ENEMY... ITS WEIGHT DRAGGING ME DOWN... WEARING ME--
KROKT
GOT HIM!
EXCELLENT-- THE PRISONER IS IN CUSTODY.
MOTION FOR BAIL DENIED.
AND TRIAL IS SET... FOR ONE HOUR FROM NOW.

IF YOU'RE ADAMANT ABOUT TRYING TO ASSIST THE MASTER, TIM, I SUGGEST WE FORTIFY OURSELVES BEFORE--

I'LL EAT YOUR SANDWICHES, ALFIE...

...BUT OUR ONLY ASSISTANCE MAY BE PARKING THE BATMOBILE WHEN HE GETS BACK.

NO LUCK IN THE COMPUTER FILES?

NADA-- ZIP...

ONLY THING I'VE LEARNED IS THAT CHILD ABUSE SCARRED HARVEY DENT'S SOUL LONG BEFORE BOSS MARONI'S ACID HIT HIS FACE.

...LONG ENOUGH TO BECOME A DYNAMITE DISTRICT ATTORNEY.

BUT EVEN SO, IT SEEMS HE WAS ABLE TO KEEP HIS BAD SIDE DOWN FOR QUITE A WHILE...

YES, THE MASTER HAS OFTEN COMMENTED ON WHAT A TRAGEDY HIS CASE IS-- AND THAT HARVEY DENT WAS ONCE A GENUINELY GOOD MAN.

WELL, HE'S TWO MEN NOW...

...HIS BAD-CRAZY DARK SIDE HELD IN CHECK ONLY BY THE TOSS OF A COIN.

AND SINCE I CAN'T FIND A CLUE AS TO WHERE HE MIGHT BE HOLED UP, OR WHERE BATMAN MIGHT HAVE GONE LOOKING FOR HIM...

...ALL WE CAN DO IS WAIT-- AND WONDER WHICH SIDE OF THE COIN WILL TURN UP.

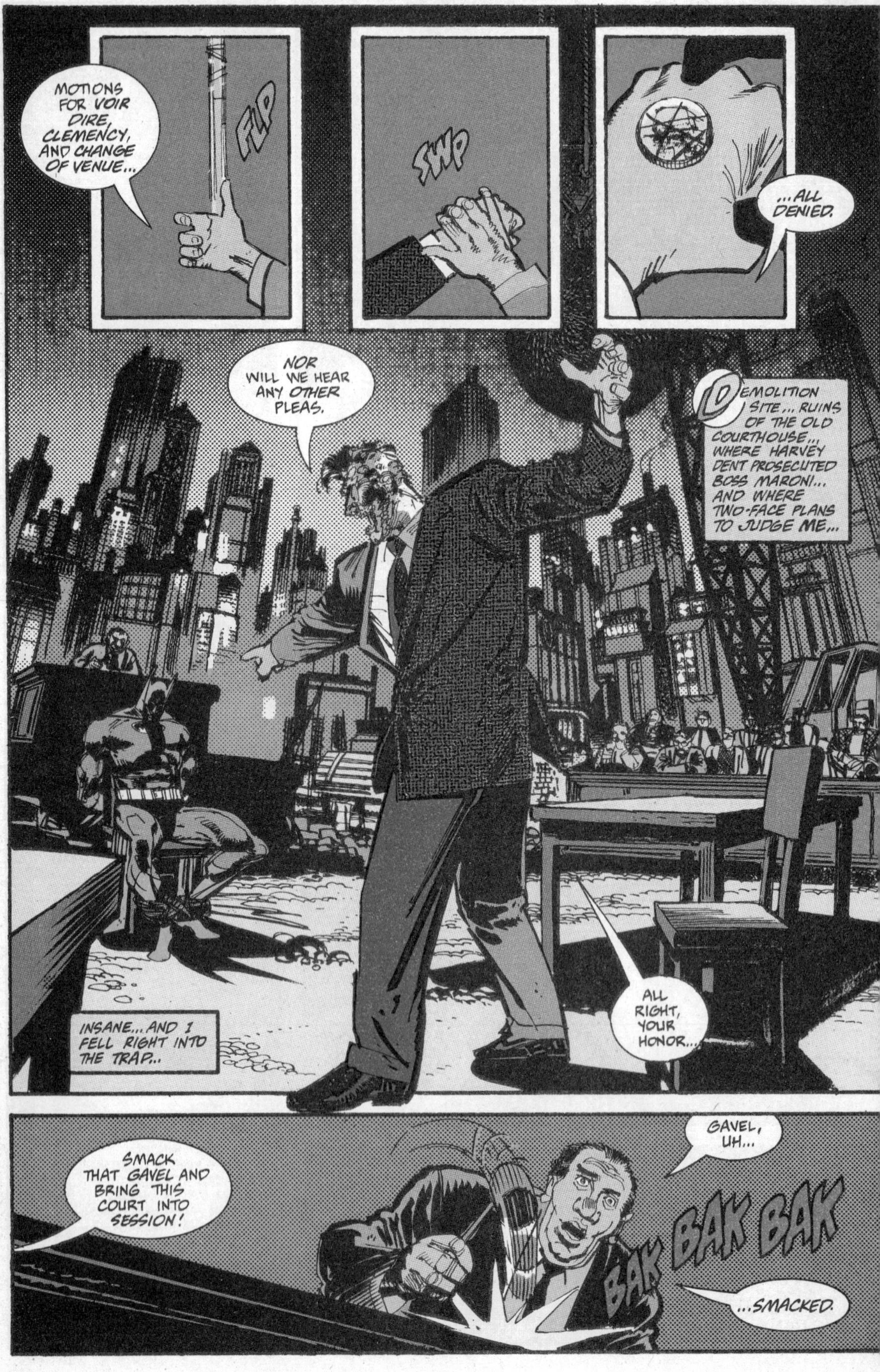
MOTIONS FOR VOIR DIRE, CLEMENCY, AND CHANGE OF VENUE...
FLP
SWP
...ALL DENIED.
NOR WILL WE HEAR ANY OTHER PLEAS.
DEMOLITION SITE... RUINS OF THE OLD COURTHOUSE... WHERE HARVEY DENT PROSECUTED BOSS MARONI... AND WHERE TWO-FACE PLANS TO JUDGE ME...
INSANE... AND I FELL RIGHT INTO THE TRAP...
ALL RIGHT, YOUR HONOR...
SMACK THAT GAVEL AND BRING THIS COURT INTO SESSION!
GAVEL, UH...
BAK BAK BAK
...SMACKED.

GENTLEMEN OF THE JURY, I AM THE *PROSECUTOR*-- AND *THAT* MAN IS THE *CRIMINAL!*

NOTICE THE *MASK?*

IF HE DIDN'T HAVE SOMETHING TO HIDE, WHY WOULD HE WEAR IT?

THE "*JUDGE*" ...AND "*JURY*"...

HIS CRIMES ARE MANY AND INSIDIOUS! THEY DEMAND JUSTICE--AND RETRIBUTION!

STILL GROGGY... EXHAUSTED...

LYMAN'S FORMER THUGS... TWO-FACE'S NEW GANG...

JUST FOR STARTERS, HE IS CHARGED WITH *TWO-FACED DUPLICITY, DOUBLE-DEALING, TWO COUNTS OF BETRAYAL,* AND *DOUBLE-CROSS!*

ONCE CONVICTED, HIS PUNISHMENT WILL BE SEVERE--AND PERSONALLY ENFORCED BY *ME!*

I INSIST ON THE *DEATH* PENALTY, GENTLEMEN--

--AND THAT PUNISHMENT WILL BE PRECEDED BY NOTHING LESS THAN THE *REMOVAL* OF HIS MASK--THE STRIPPING AWAY OF THE *SECOND FACE* BEHIND WHICH HE HIDES!

WITHOUT THE MASK, HIS SINS WILL NO LONGER BE *COVERED UP!* THEY WILL BE *NAKED* FOR ALL TO SEE!

WITHOUT *THE MASK,* HE WILL BE *DESTROYED*-- WITH A BULLET RIGHT THROUGH HIS *OTHER FACE*-- HIS *REAL FACE!*

WITHOUT THE *MASK,* HE WILL BE EXPOSED FOR WHAT HE TRULY IS!

WAS WRONG TO EXCLUDE ROBIN...BAD JUDGMENT...LOSING MY EDGE MORE EVERY DAY...ACTUALLY NEED HELP NOW...

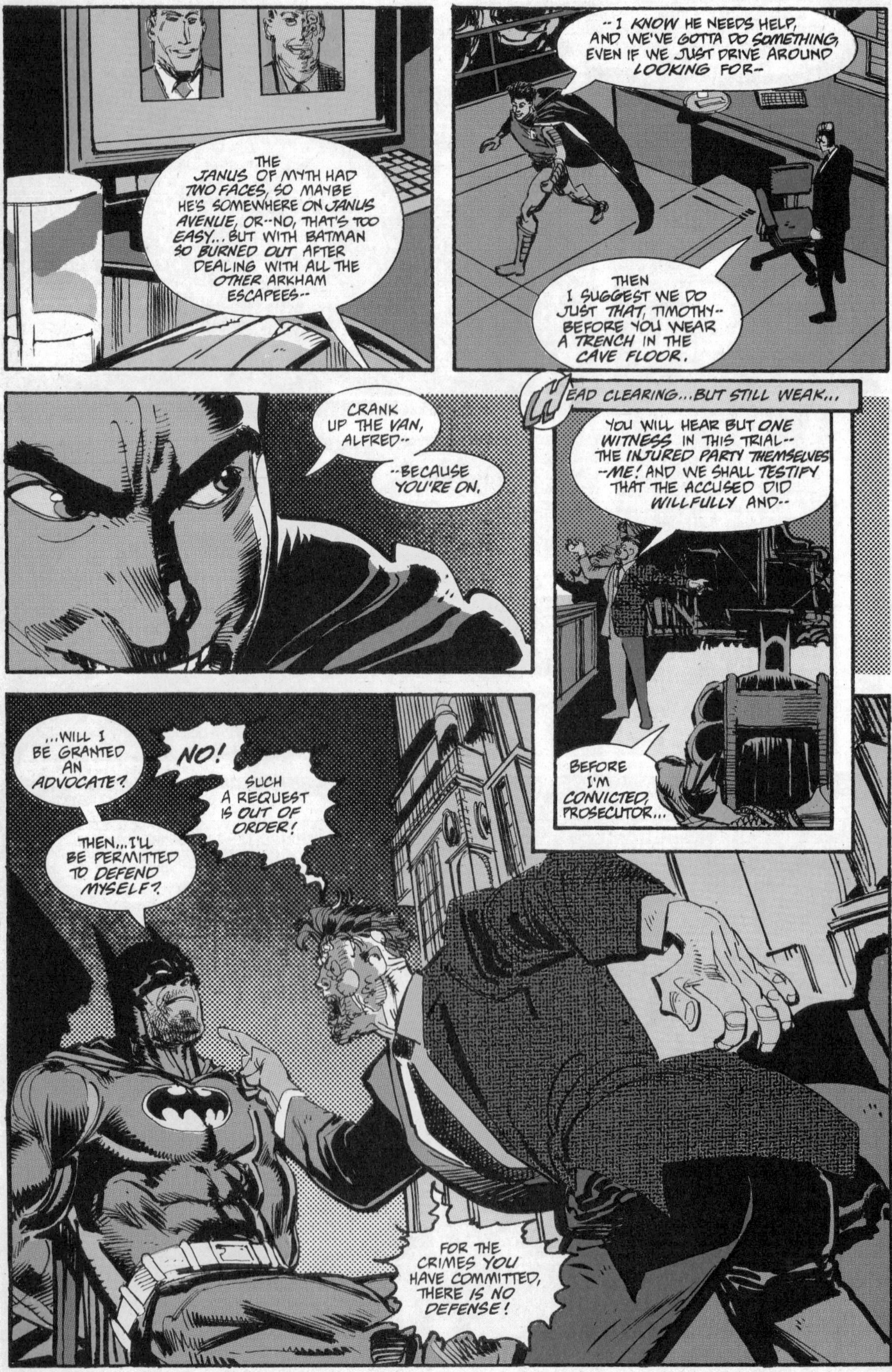
THE JANUS OF MYTH HAD TWO FACES, SO MAYBE HE'S SOMEWHERE ON JANUS AVENUE, OR--NO, THAT'S TOO EASY... BUT WITH BATMAN SO BURNED OUT AFTER DEALING WITH ALL THE OTHER ARKHAM ESCAPEES--
--I KNOW HE NEEDS HELP, AND WE'VE GOTTA DO SOMETHING, EVEN IF WE JUST DRIVE AROUND LOOKING FOR--
THEN I SUGGEST WE DO JUST THAT, TIMOTHY-- BEFORE YOU WEAR A TRENCH IN THE CAVE FLOOR.
CRANK UP THE VAN, ALFRED--
--BECAUSE YOU'RE ON.
CH
HEAD CLEARING... BUT STILL WEAK...
YOU WILL HEAR BUT ONE WITNESS IN THIS TRIAL-- THE INJURED PARTY THEMSELVES --ME! AND WE SHALL TESTIFY THAT THE ACCUSED DID WILLFULLY AND--
BEFORE I'M CONVICTED, PROSECUTOR...
...WILL I BE GRANTED AN ADVOCATE?
NO!
SUCH A REQUEST IS OUT OF ORDER!
THEN... I'LL BE PERMITTED TO DEFEND MYSELF?
FOR THE CRIMES YOU HAVE COMMITTED, THERE IS NO DEFENSE!

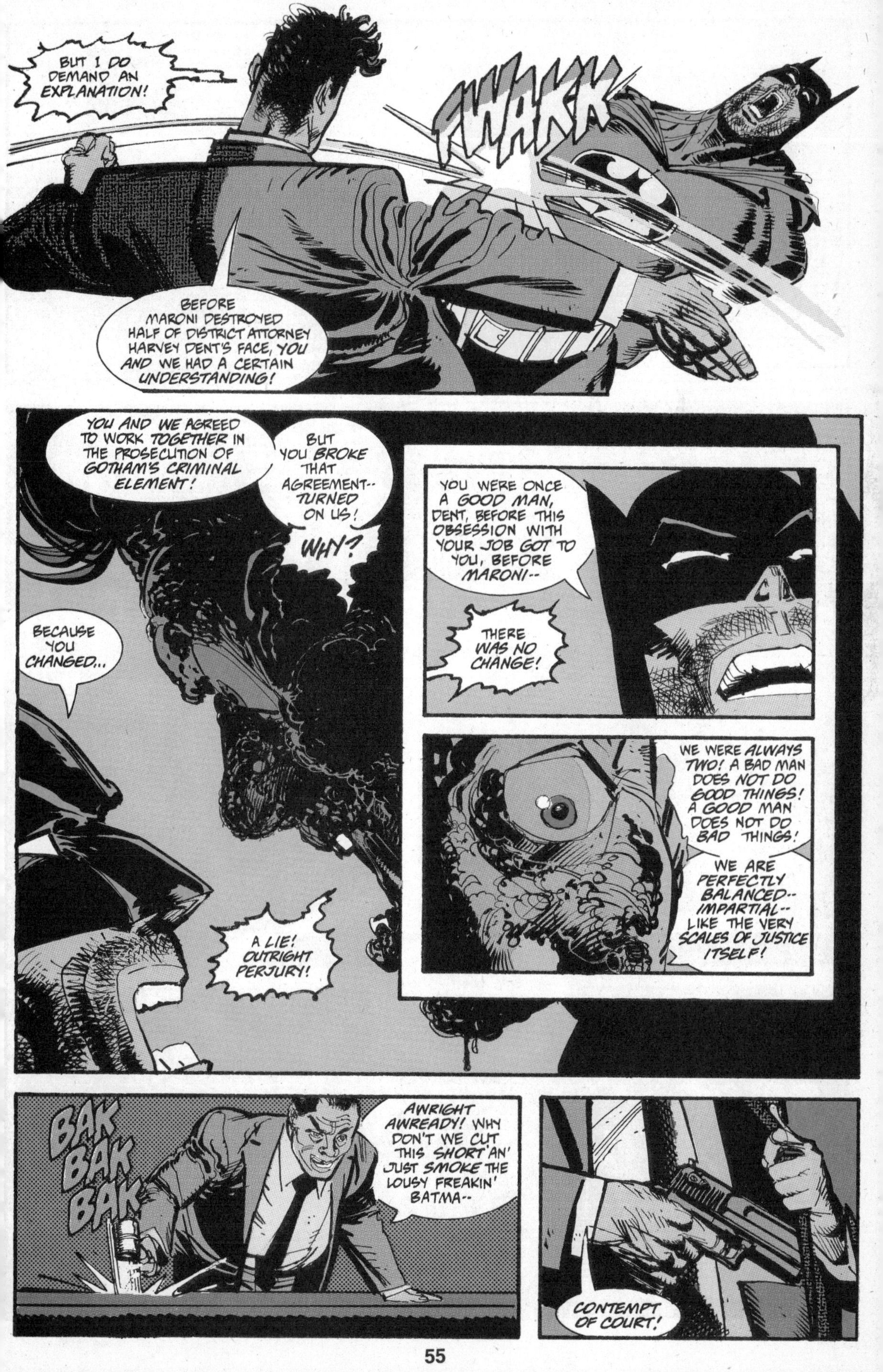
BUT I DO DEMAND AN EXPLANATION!
THWAKK
BEFORE MARONI DESTROYED HALF OF DISTRICT ATTORNEY HARVEY DENT'S FACE, YOU AND WE HAD A CERTAIN UNDERSTANDING!
YOU AND WE AGREED TO WORK TOGETHER IN THE PROSECUTION OF GOTHAM'S CRIMINAL ELEMENT!
BUT YOU BROKE THAT AGREEMENT-- TURNED ON US!
WHY?
YOU WERE ONCE A GOOD MAN, DENT, BEFORE THIS OBSESSION WITH YOUR JOB GOT TO YOU, BEFORE MARONI--
THERE WAS NO CHANGE!
BECAUSE YOU CHANGED...
WE WERE ALWAYS TWO! A BAD MAN DOES NOT DO GOOD THINGS! A GOOD MAN DOES NOT DO BAD THINGS!
WE ARE PERFECTLY BALANCED-- IMPARTIAL-- LIKE THE VERY SCALES OF JUSTICE ITSELF!
A LIE! OUTRIGHT PERJURY!
BAK BAK BAK
AWRIGHT AWREADY! WHY DON'T WE CUT THIS SHORT 'AN' JUST SMOKE THE LOUSY FREAKIN' BATMA--
CONTEMPT OF COURT!

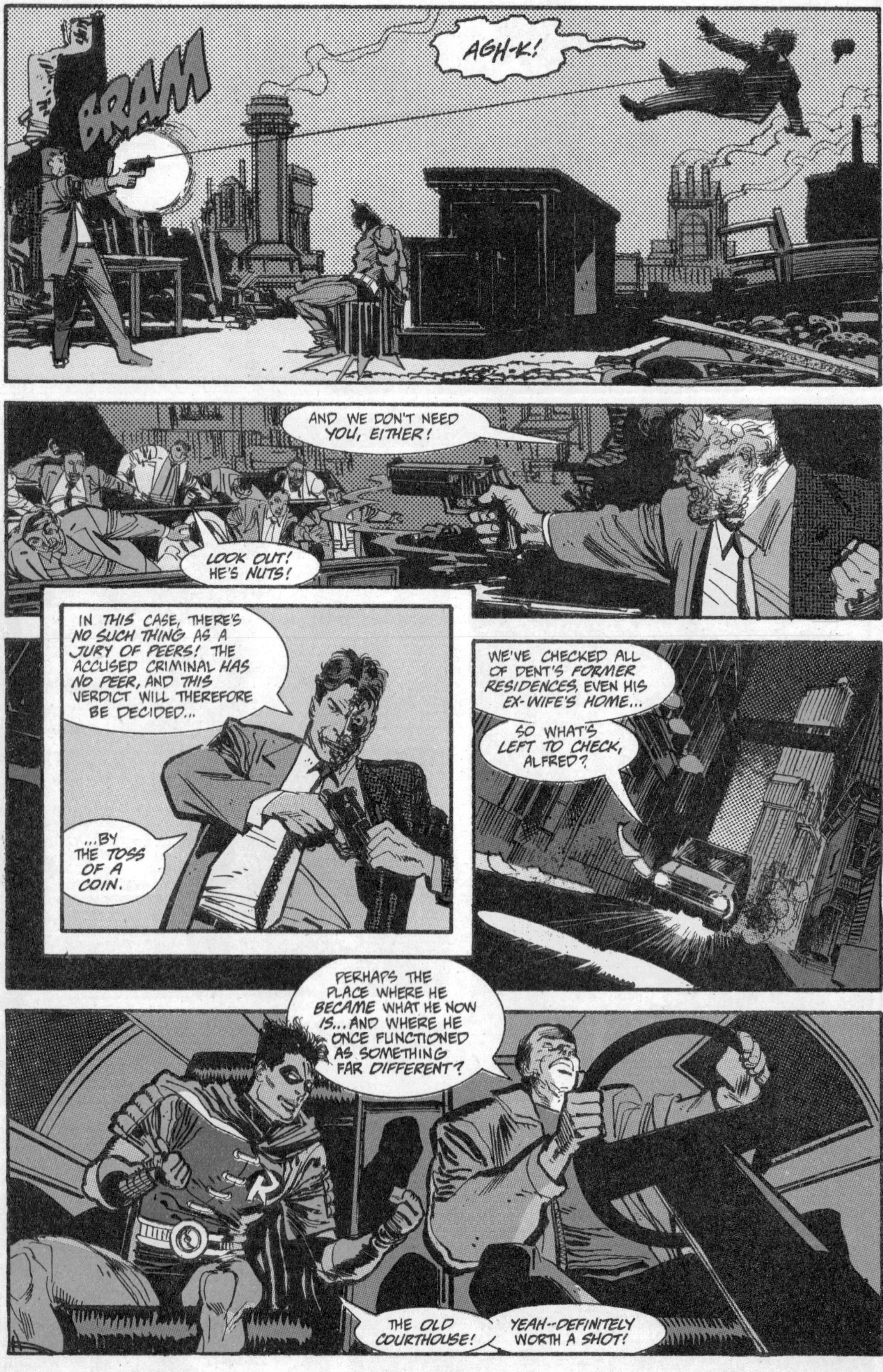
BRAM
AGH-K!
AND WE DON'T NEED YOU, EITHER!
LOOK OUT! HE'S NUTS!
IN THIS CASE, THERE'S NO SUCH THING AS A JURY OF PEERS! THE ACCUSED CRIMINAL HAS NO PEER, AND THIS VERDICT WILL THEREFORE BE DECIDED...
...BY THE TOSS OF A COIN.
WE'VE CHECKED ALL OF DENT'S FORMER RESIDENCES, EVEN HIS EX-WIFE'S HOME...
SO WHAT'S LEFT TO CHECK, ALFRED?
PERHAPS THE PLACE WHERE HE BECAME WHAT HE NOW IS... AND WHERE HE ONCE FUNCTIONED AS SOMETHING FAR DIFFERENT?
THE OLD COURTHOUSE!
YEAH--DEFINITELY WORTH A SHOT!

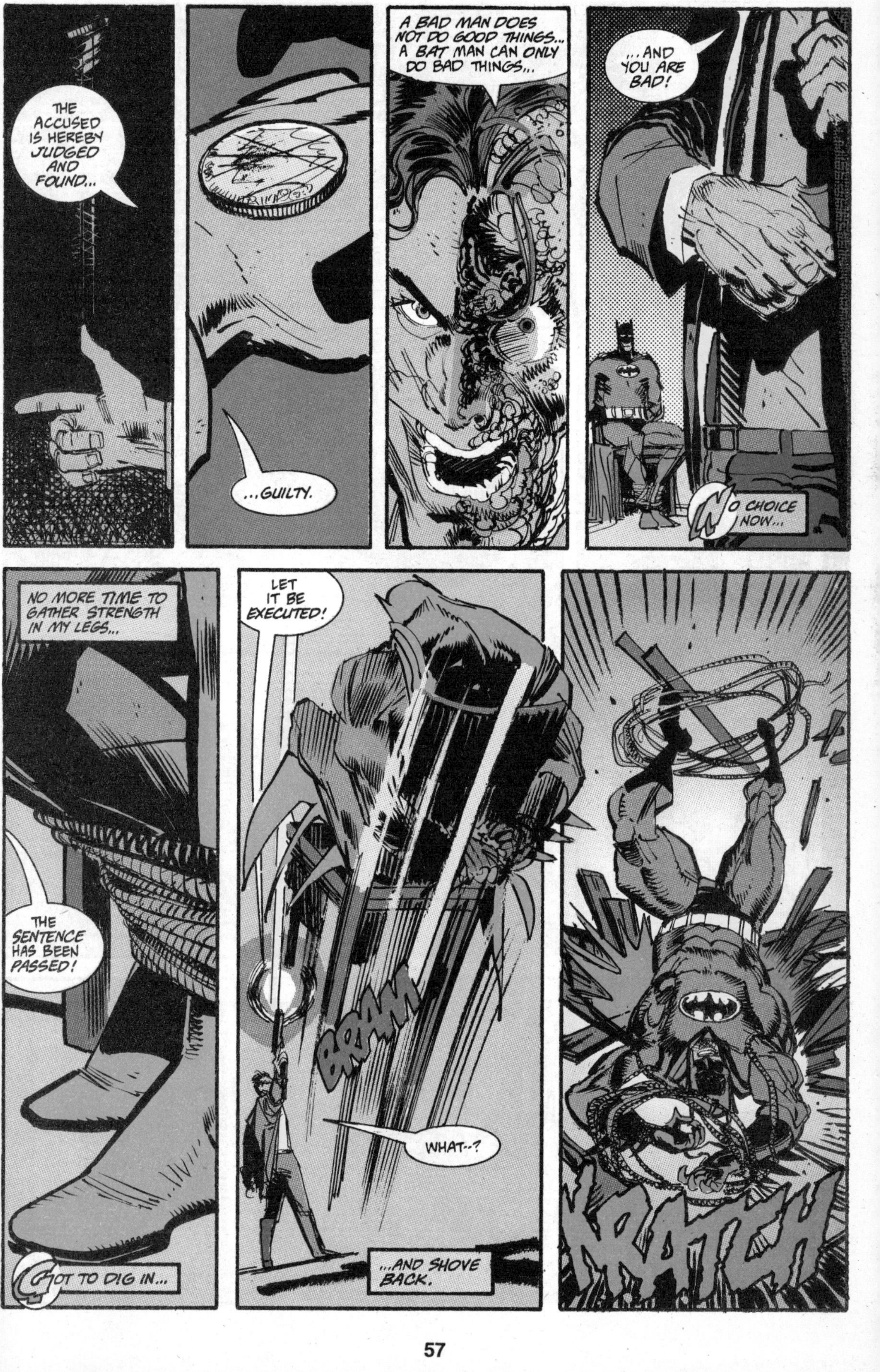
THE ACCUSED IS HEREBY JUDGED AND FOUND...
...GUILTY.
A BAD MAN DOES NOT DO GOOD THINGS... A BAT MAN CAN ONLY DO BAD THINGS...
...AND YOU ARE BAD!
NO CHOICE NOW...
NO MORE TIME TO GATHER STRENGTH IN MY LEGS...
THE SENTENCE HAS BEEN PASSED!
GOT TO DIG IN...
LET IT BE EXECUTED!
BRAM
WHAT--?
...AND SHOVE BACK.
KRATCH

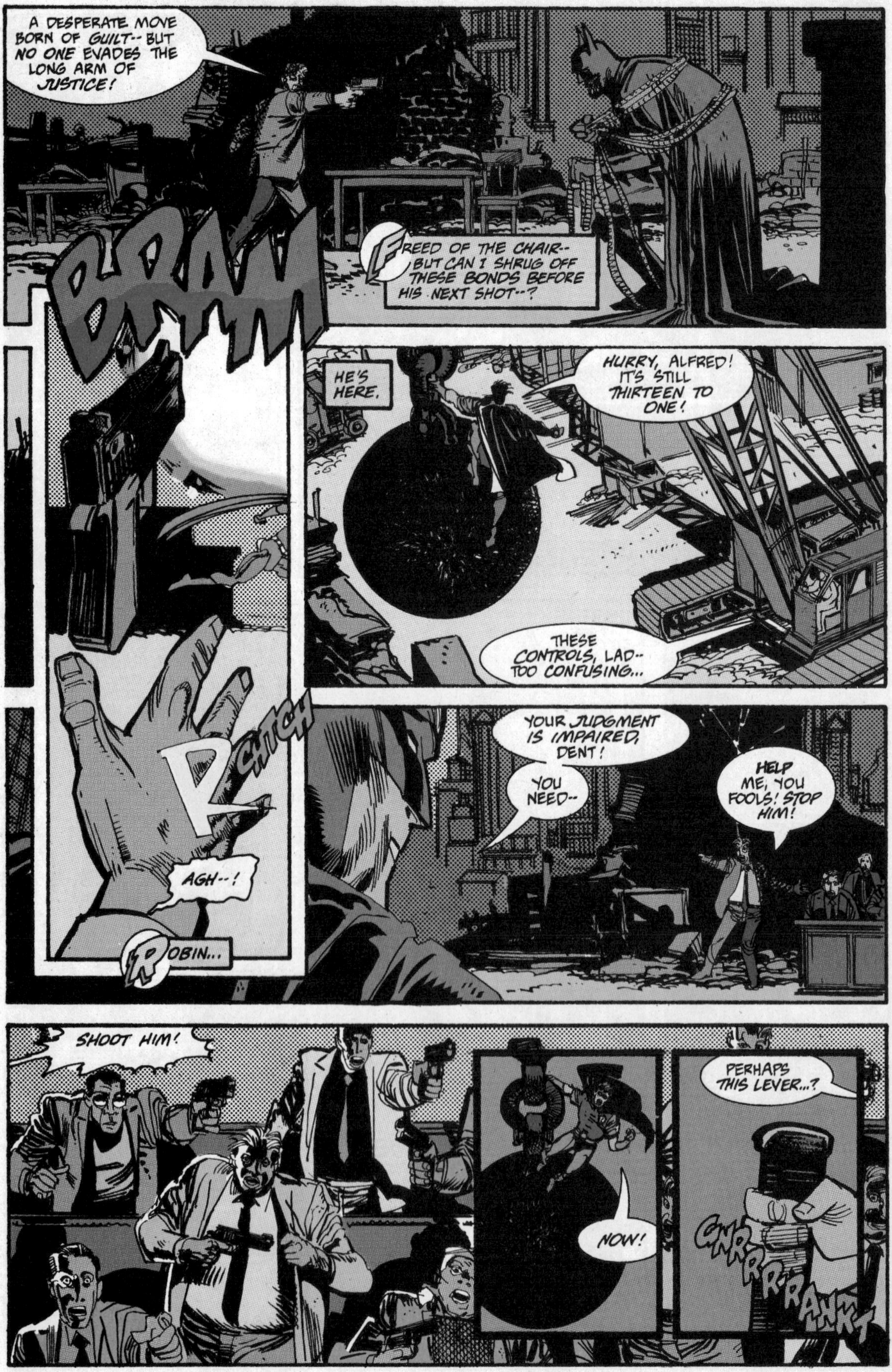

A DESPERATE MOVE BORN OF GUILT-- BUT NO ONE EVADES THE LONG ARM OF JUSTICE!
BRAM
FREED OF THE CHAIR-- BUT CAN I SHRUG OFF THESE BONDS BEFORE HIS NEXT SHOT--?
HE'S HERE.
HURRY, ALFRED! IT'S STILL THIRTEEN TO ONE!
THESE CONTROLS, LAD-- TOO CONFUSING...
RCHTCH
AGH--!
ROBIN...
YOUR JUDGMENT IS IMPAIRED, DENT!
YOU NEED--
HELP ME, YOU FOOLS! STOP HIM!
SHOOT HIM!
NOW!
PERHAPS THIS LEVER...?
CNRRR-RANK

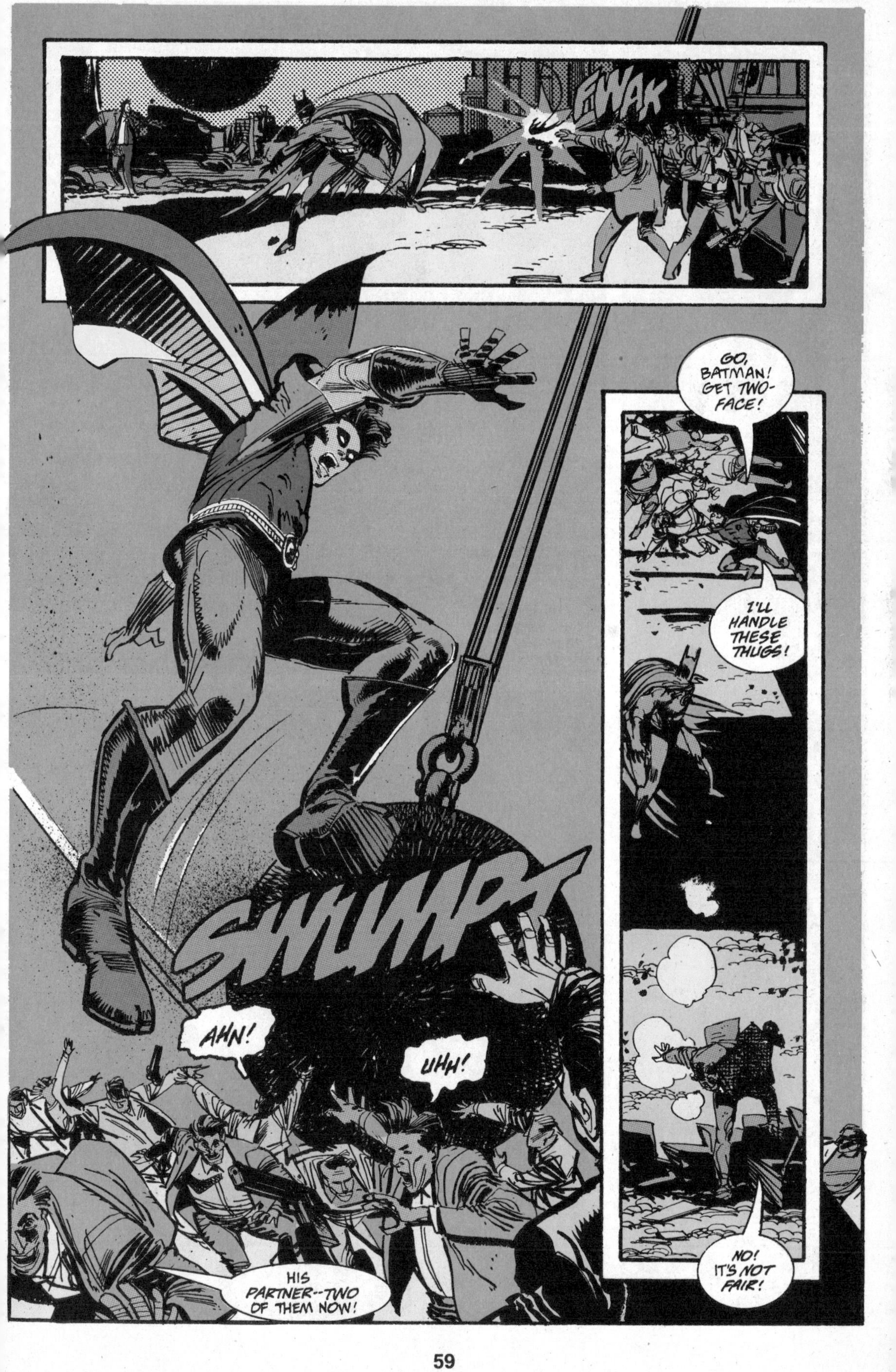
FWAK
GO, BATMAN! GET TWO-FACE!
I'LL HANDLE THESE THUGS!
SHWUMP
AHN!
UHH!
HIS PARTNER--TWO OF THEM NOW!
NO! IT'S NOT FAIR!

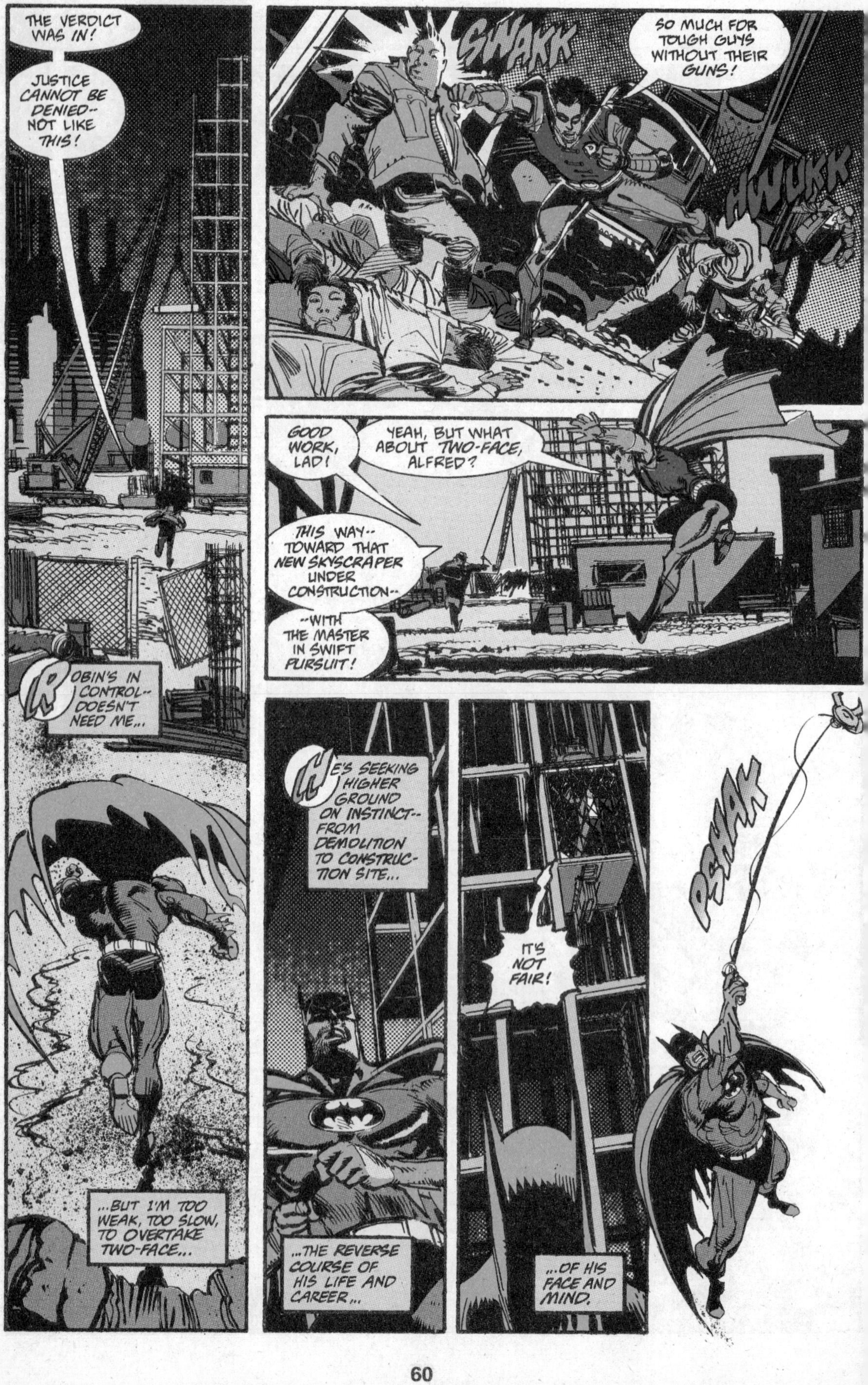
THE VERDICT WAS IN!
JUSTICE CANNOT BE DENIED-- NOT LIKE THIS!
SWAKK
SO MUCH FOR TOUGH GUYS WITHOUT THEIR GUNS!
HWUKK
GOOD WORK, LAD!
YEAH, BUT WHAT ABOUT TWO-FACE, ALFRED?
THIS WAY-- TOWARD THAT NEW SKYSCRAPER UNDER CONSTRUCTION--
--WITH THE MASTER IN SWIFT PURSUIT!
ROBIN'S IN CONTROL-- DOESN'T NEED ME...
...BUT I'M TOO WEAK, TOO SLOW, TO OVERTAKE TWO-FACE...
HE'S SEEKING HIGHER GROUND ON INSTINCT-- FROM DEMOLITION TO CONSTRUCTION SITE...
...THE REVERSE COURSE OF HIS LIFE AND CAREER...
IT'S NOT FAIR!
...OF HIS FACE AND MIND.
PSHAK

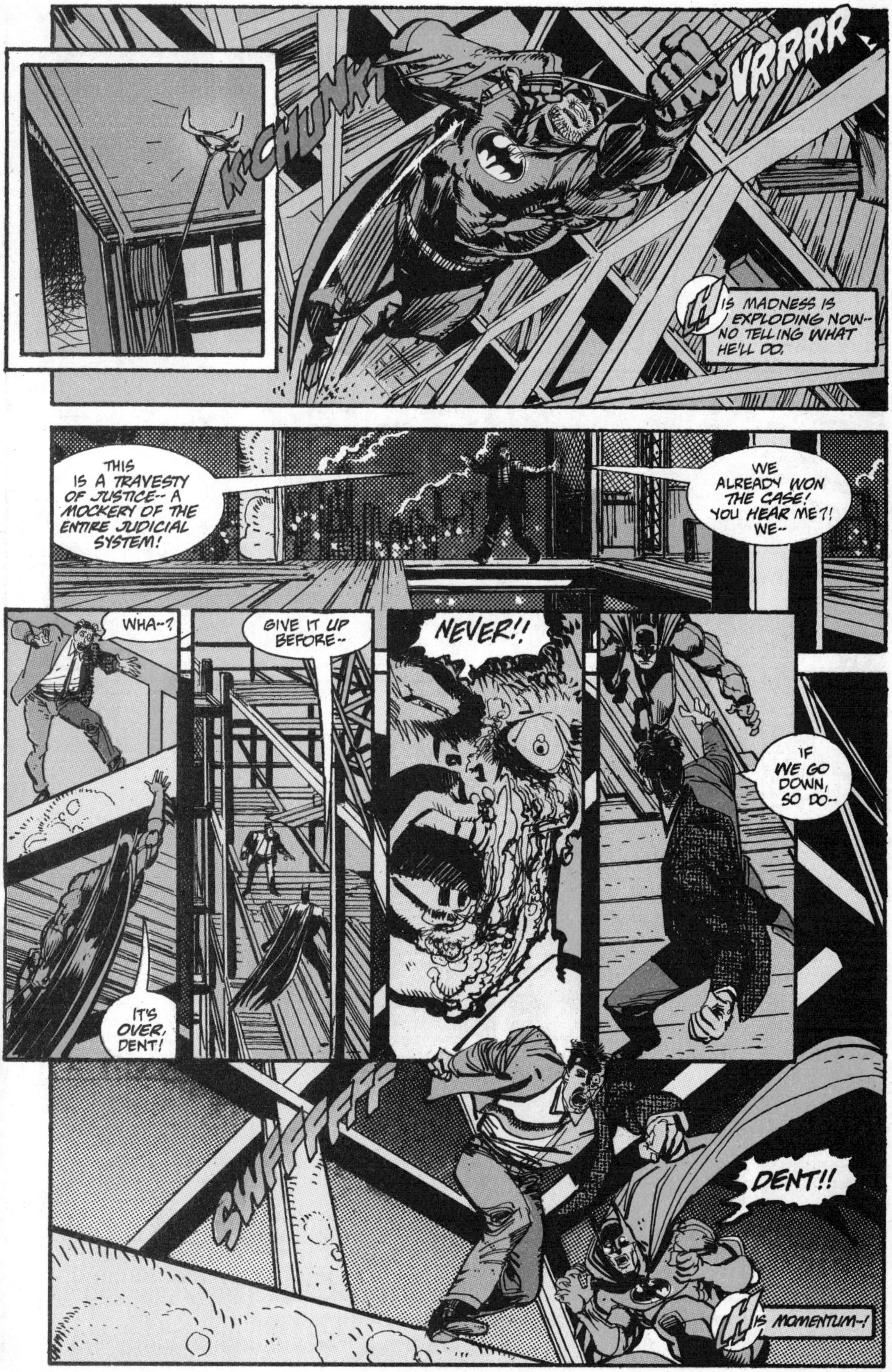
K-CHUNK!
VRRRR
HIS MADNESS IS EXPLODING NOW-- NO TELLING WHAT HE'LL DO.
THIS IS A TRAVESTY OF JUSTICE-- A MOCKERY OF THE ENTIRE JUDICIAL SYSTEM!
WE ALREADY WON THE CASE! YOU HEAR ME?! WE--
WHA--?
IT'S OVER, DENT!
GIVE IT UP BEFORE--
NEVER!!
IF WE GO DOWN, SO DO--
SWFFFF
DENT!!
HIS MOMENTUM--!

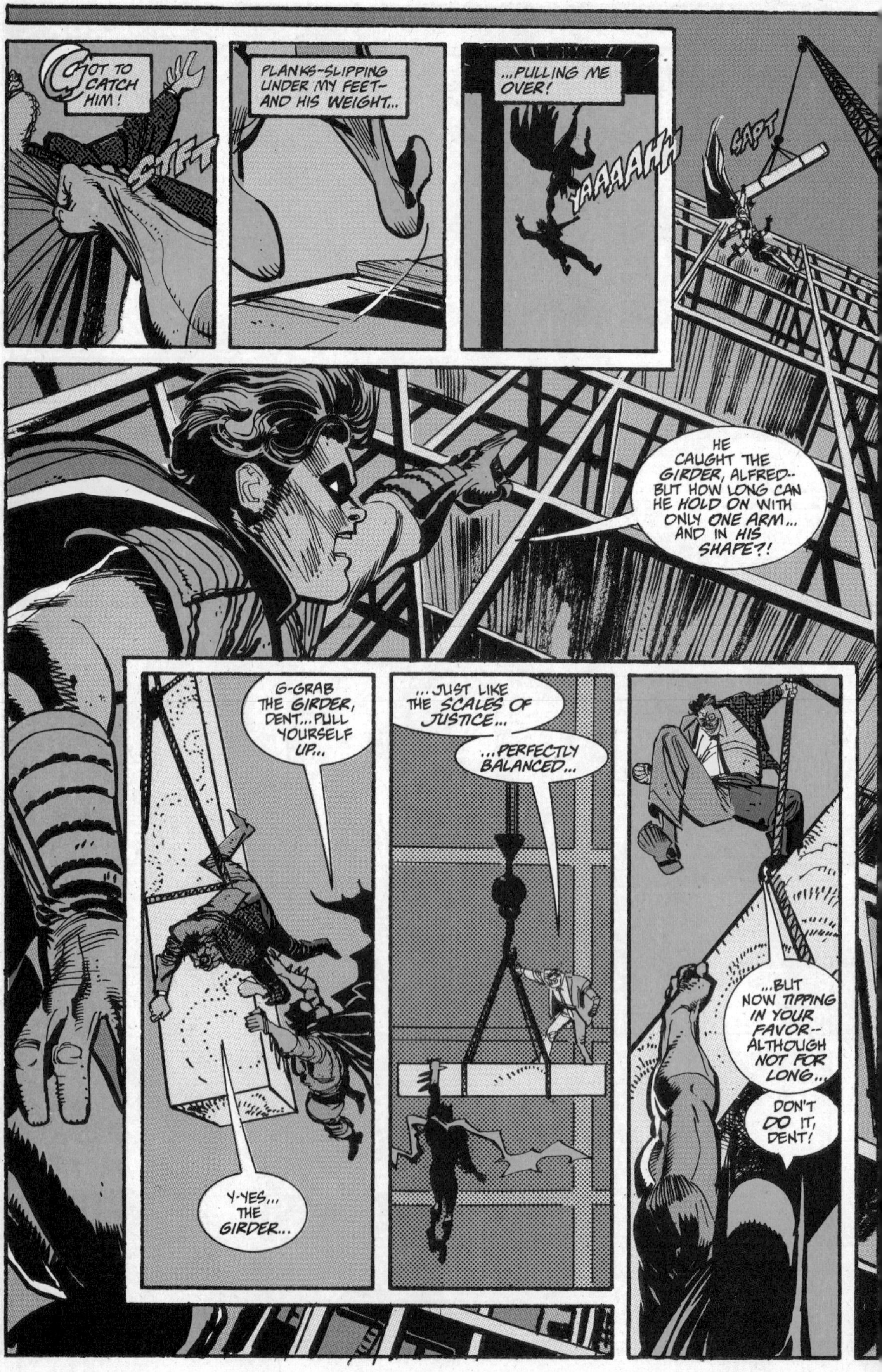
GOT TO CATCH HIM!
SSTFT
PLANKS-SLIPPING UNDER MY FEET-AND HIS WEIGHT...
...PULLING ME OVER!
YAAAAHH
HE CAUGHT THE GIRDER, ALFRED-- BUT HOW LONG CAN HE HOLD ON WITH ONLY ONE ARM... AND IN HIS SHAPE?!
G-GRAB THE GIRDER, DENT... PULL YOURSELF UP...
Y-YES... THE GIRDER...
...JUST LIKE THE SCALES OF JUSTICE...
...PERFECTLY BALANCED...
...BUT NOW TIPPING IN YOUR FAVOR-- ALTHOUGH NOT FOR LONG...
DON'T DO IT, DENT!

63

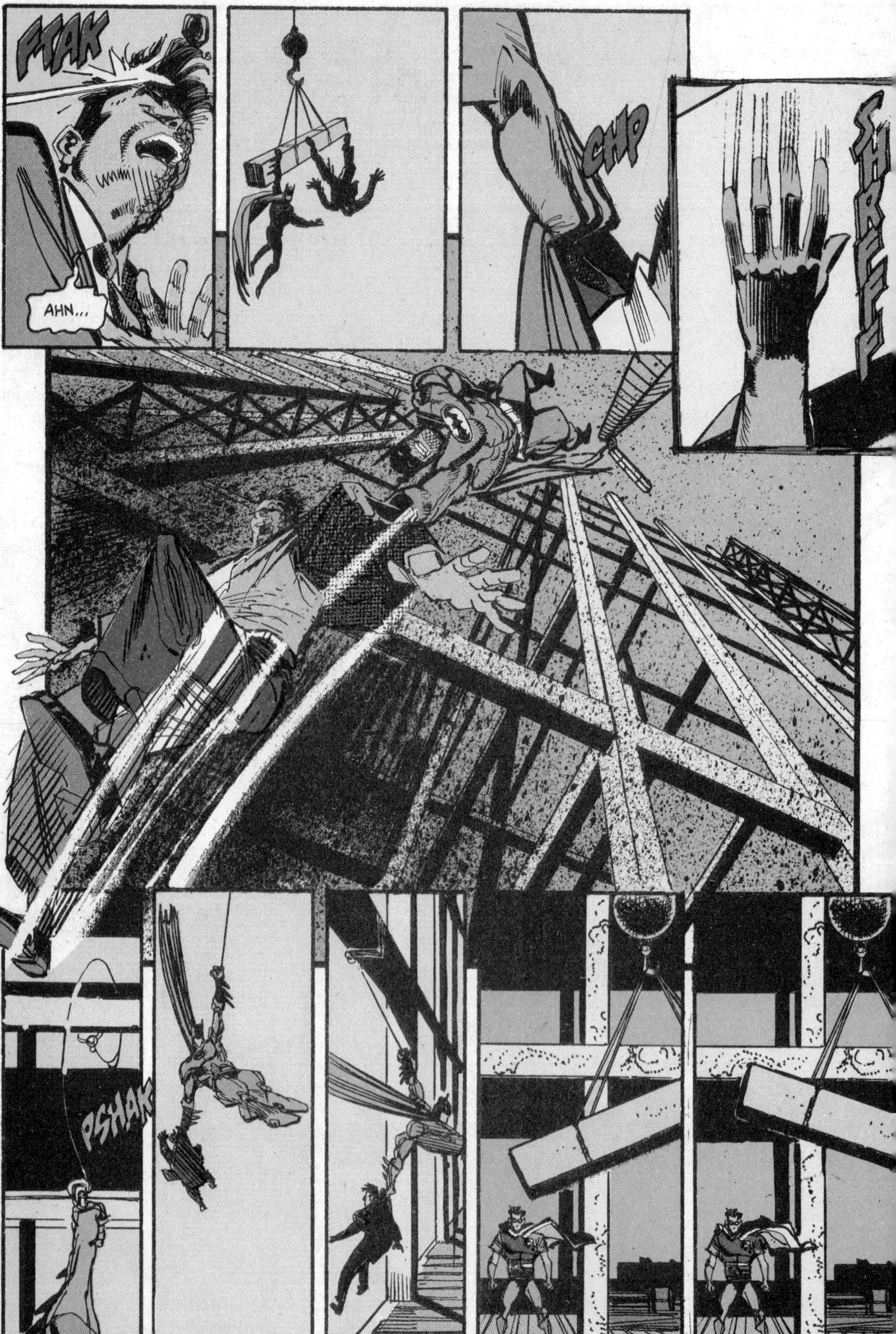
FTAK
AHN...
CHP
SHREFF
PSHAK

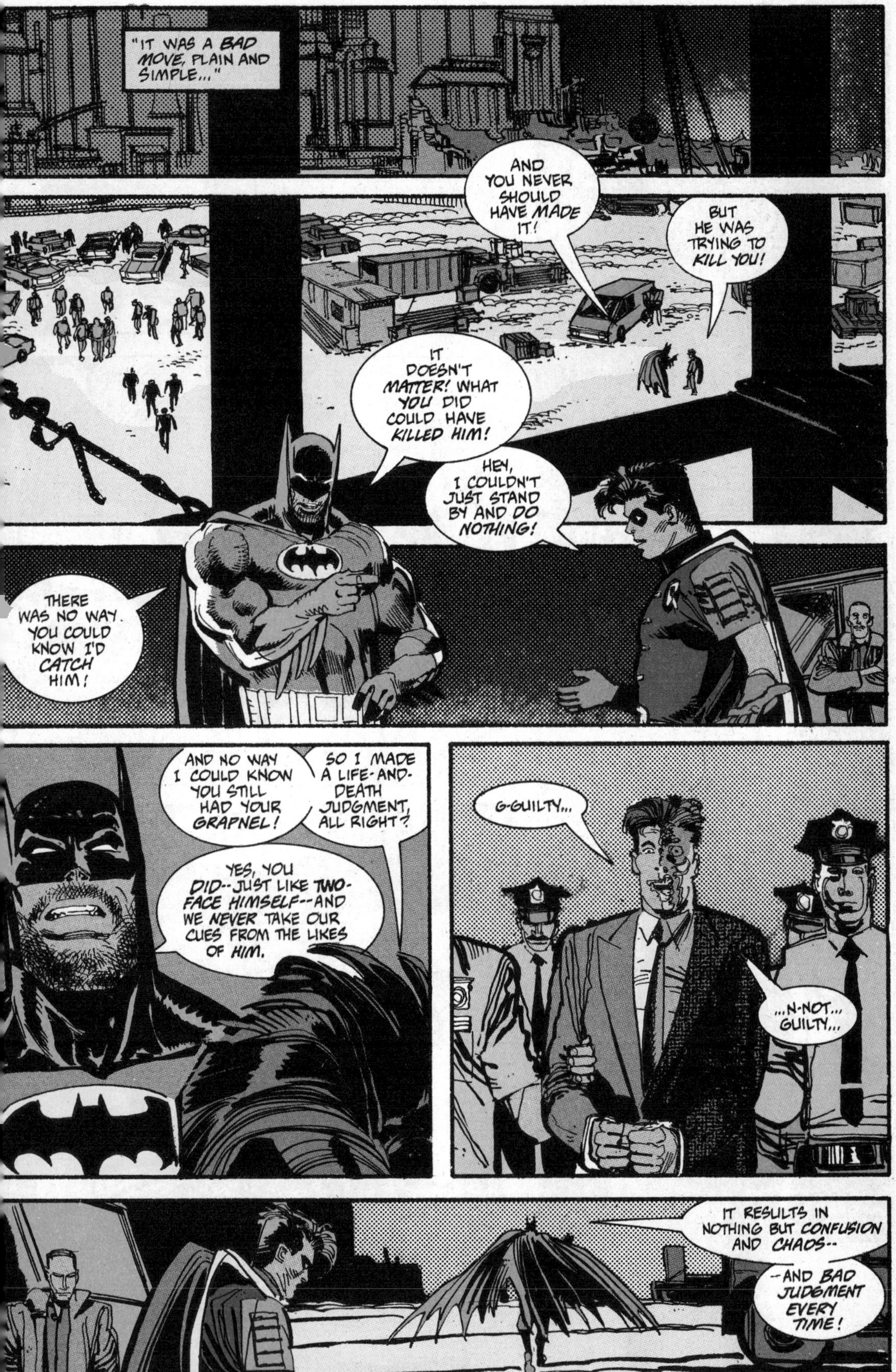
"IT WAS A BAD MOVE, PLAIN AND SIMPLE..."
AND YOU NEVER SHOULD HAVE MADE IT!
BUT HE WAS TRYING TO KILL YOU!
IT DOESN'T MATTER! WHAT YOU DID COULD HAVE KILLED HIM!
HEY, I COULDN'T JUST STAND BY AND DO NOTHING!
THERE WAS NO WAY YOU COULD KNOW I'D CATCH HIM!
AND NO WAY I COULD KNOW YOU STILL HAD YOUR GRAPNEL!
SO I MADE A LIFE-AND-DEATH JUDGMENT, ALL RIGHT?
YES, YOU DID--JUST LIKE TWO-FACE HIMSELF--AND WE NEVER TAKE OUR CUES FROM THE LIKES OF HIM.
G-GUILTY...
...N-NOT... GUILTY...
IT RESULTS IN NOTHING BUT CONFUSION AND CHAOS--
--AND BAD JUDGMENT EVERY TIME!

THE CAVE, WHERE THE DARK KNIGHT LIES FALLEN AND SILENT, THREE WEEKS LATER...

AND NOW... WHAT IF HE... IF HE DOESN'T WAKE UP?

ONE OF OUR LAST MEMORIES COULD BE... HIM BLAMING ME... BLAMING ME FOR ALL THE WRONG REASONS...

ALL MY FAULT... SHOULD HAVE ACTED SOONER...

...NO MATTER WHAT HE SAID...

PLEASE, SIR... YOU'RE STRONGER THAN THIS...

I... I KNOW YOU ARE.

A-ALFRED?

THE DECADRON-- IT WORKED!

YOU'RE BACK, SIR-- THANK GOD, YOU'RE BACK!

I'M HERE, BRUCE-- I'VE BEEN HERE!

R-ROBIN...

ABOUT T-TWO-FACE... YOU... YOU DID RIGHT...

...AND IT... IT WASN'T BAD JUDGMENT... NOT AT ALL.

End

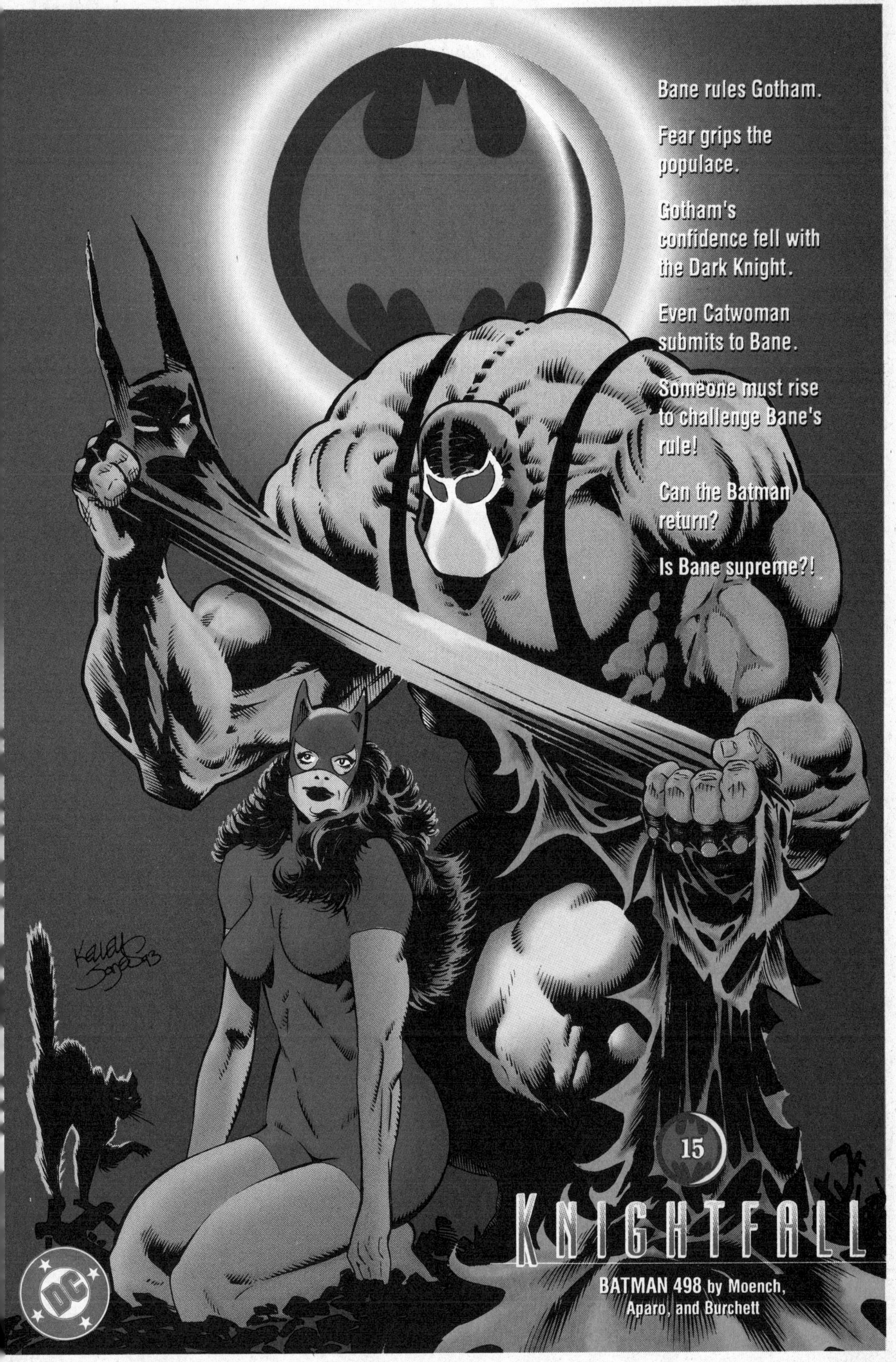

Bane rules Gotham.
Fear grips the populace.
Gotham's confidence fell with the Dark Knight.
Even Catwoman submits to Bane.
Someone must rise to challenge Bane's rule!
Can the Batman return?
Is Bane supreme?!
15
KNIGHTFALL
BATMAN 498 by Moench, Aparo, and Burchett

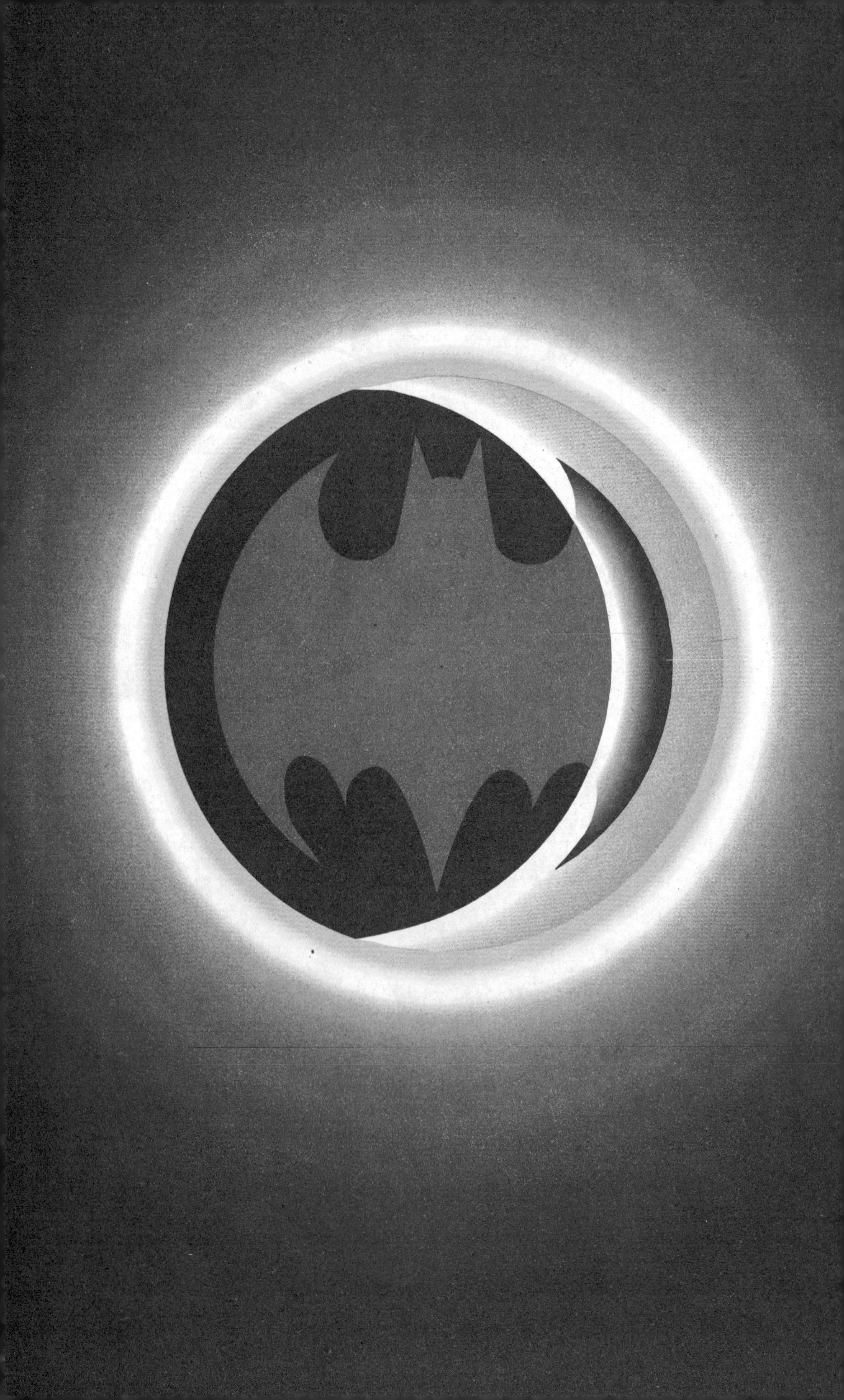

KNIGHTS IN DARKNESS

DOUG MOENCH
WRITER

JIM APARO
PENCILLER

RICK BURCHETT
INKER

ADRIENNE ROY
COLORIST

RICHARD STARKINGS
LETTERER

JORDAN B. GORFINKEL
ASSISTANT EDITOR

DENNIS O'NEIL
EDITOR

BATMAN CREATED BY BOB KANE

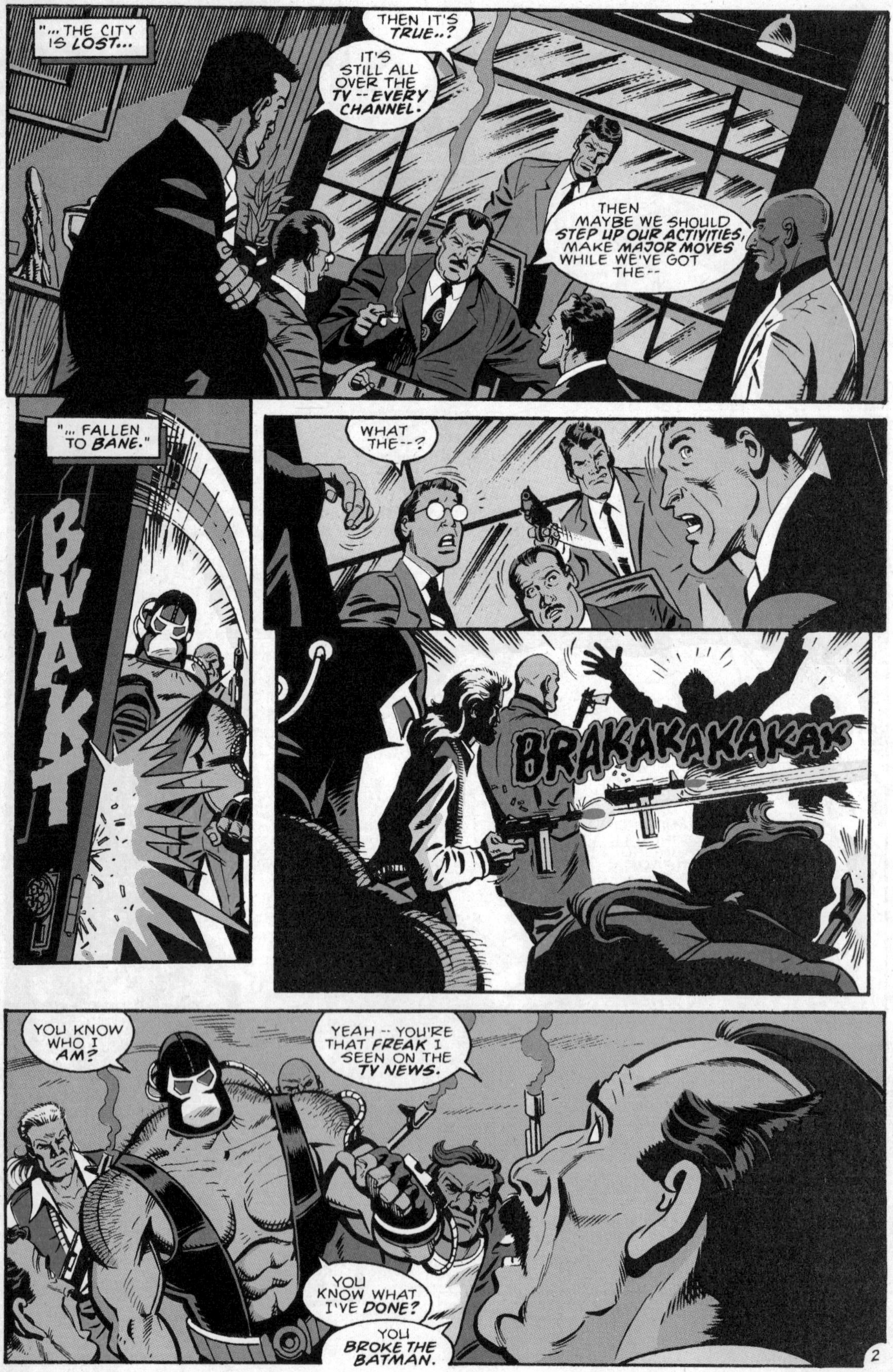
"... THE CITY IS LOST...
THEN IT'S TRUE..?
IT'S STILL ALL OVER THE TV -- EVERY CHANNEL.
THEN MAYBE WE SHOULD STEP UP OUR ACTIVITIES, MAKE MAJOR MOVES WHILE WE'VE GOT THE--
"... FALLEN TO BANE."
BWAKT
WHAT THE--?
BRAKAKAKAKAKAK
YOU KNOW WHO I AM?
YEAH -- YOU'RE THAT FREAK I SEEN ON THE TV NEWS.
YOU KNOW WHAT I'VE DONE?
YOU BROKE THE BATMAN.
2

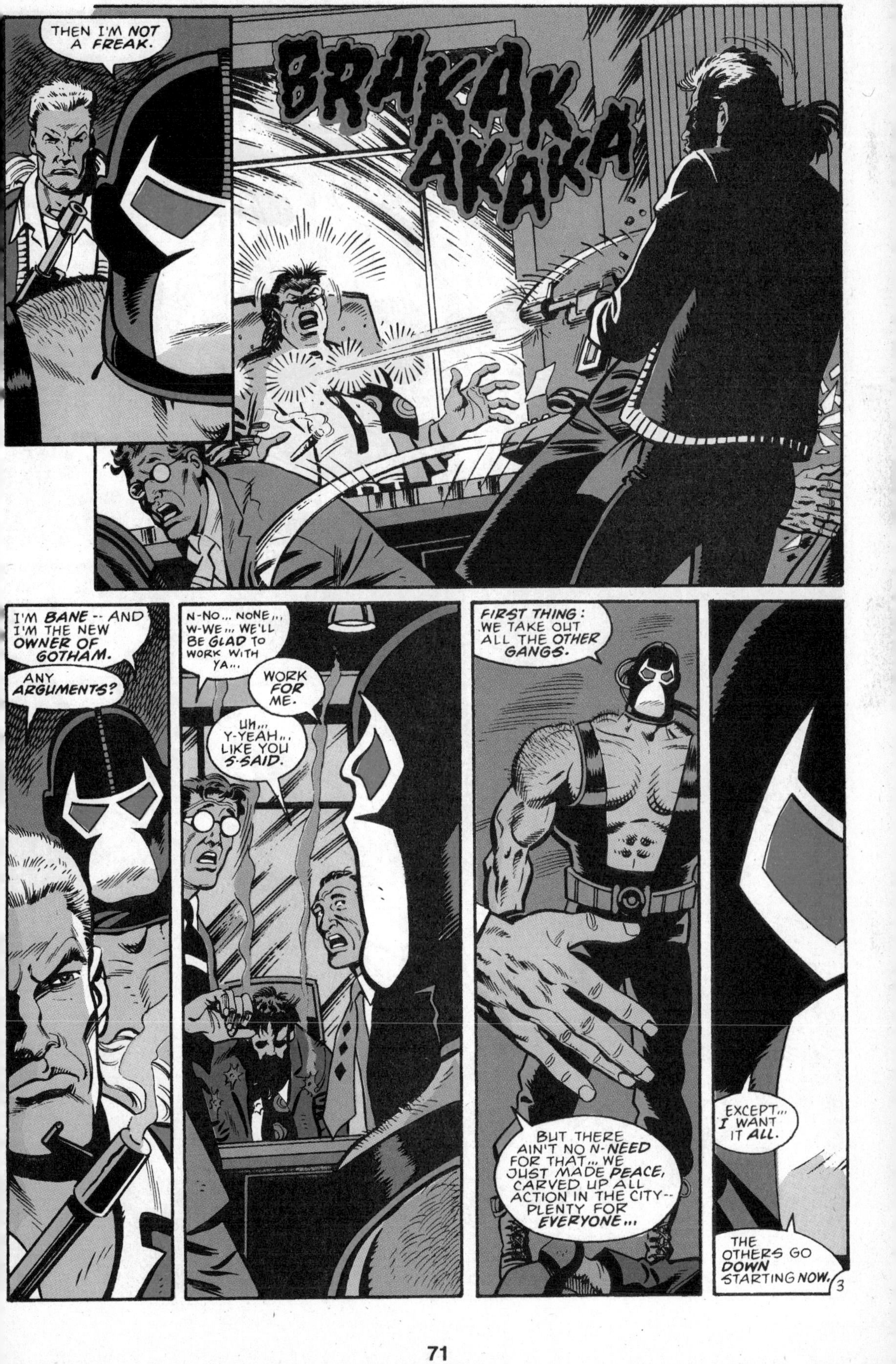

THEN I'M NOT A FREAK.
BRAKAKAKAKAKAKA
I'M BANE -- AND I'M THE NEW OWNER OF GOTHAM.
ANY ARGUMENTS?
N-NO... NONE... W-WE... WE'LL BE GLAD TO WORK WITH YA...
WORK FOR ME.
UH... Y-YEAH... LIKE YOU S-SAID.
FIRST THING: WE TAKE OUT ALL THE OTHER GANGS.
BUT THERE AIN'T NO N-NEED FOR THAT... WE JUST MADE PEACE, CARVED UP ALL ACTION IN THE CITY-- PLENTY FOR EVERYONE...
EXCEPT... I WANT IT ALL.
THE OTHERS GO DOWN STARTING NOW.
3

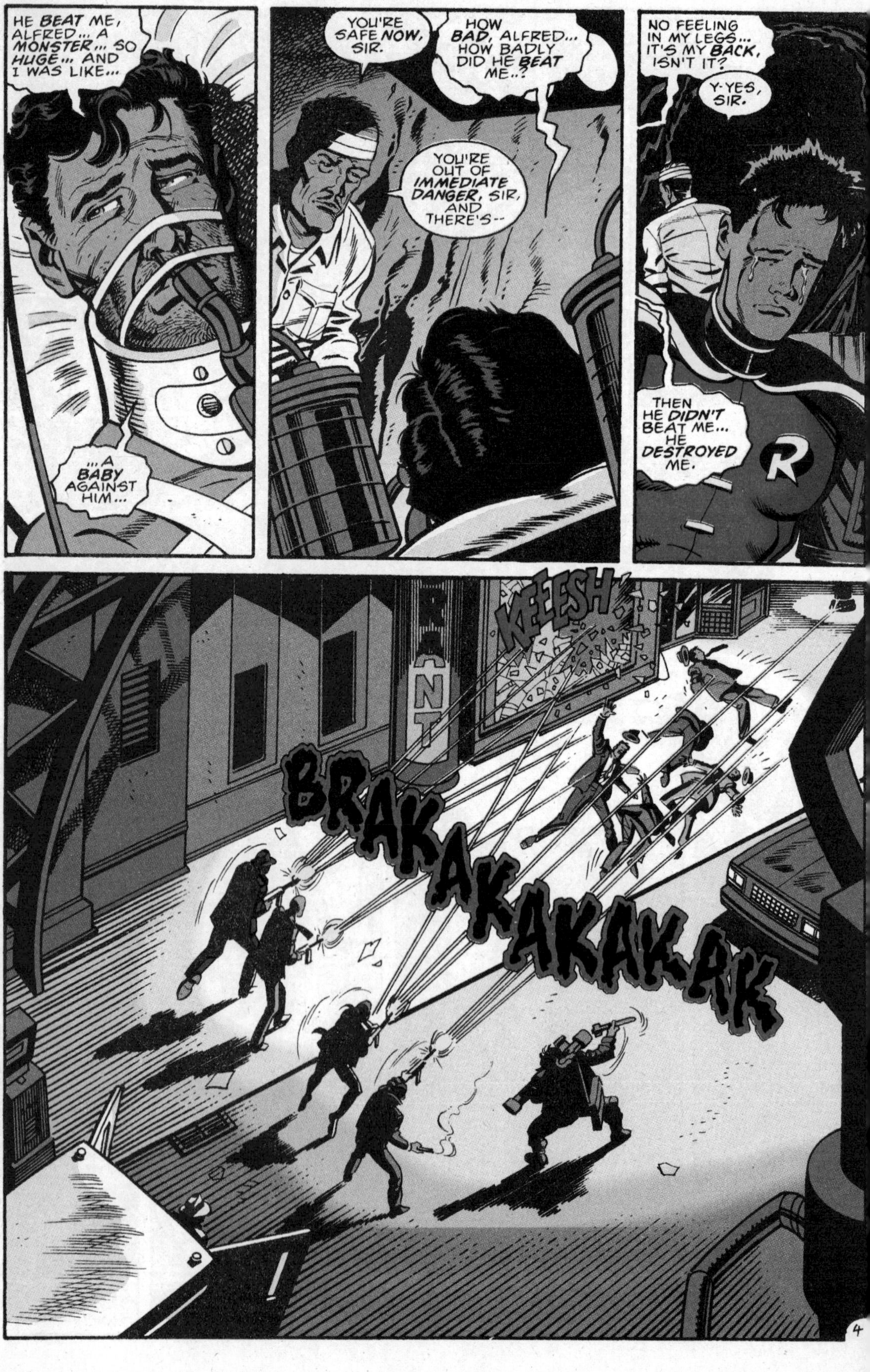
HE BEAT ME, ALFRED... A MONSTER... SO HUGE... AND I WAS LIKE...
...A BABY AGAINST HIM...
YOU'RE SAFE NOW, SIR.
HOW BAD, ALFRED... HOW BADLY DID HE BEAT ME..?
YOU'RE OUT OF IMMEDIATE DANGER, SIR, AND THERE'S--
NO FEELING IN MY LEGS... IT'S MY BACK, ISN'T IT?
Y-YES, SIR.
THEN HE DIDN'T BEAT ME... HE DESTROYED ME.
KEEESH
BRAKAKAKAKAKAK
4

COME ON, TROGG — DUMP YOUR *ROCKET* AND LET'S *MOVE*!!

VBOOSH

KA ROOOM

WE GOT US A *BUSY* NIGHT.

DESTROYED ME...

I CAN'T *STAND* IT, ALFRED -- WHY IS HE ACTING SO... *SO WEAK?*

IT'S HIS FIRST *REAL* FAILURE, TIMOTHY...

EVEN WHEN HE... LOST JASON... IT WAS *OUT OF HIS CONTROL...*

THIS IS THE *FIRST TIME* HE HAS FACED ANOTHER MAN SQUARELY AND *LOST.*

YEAH, BUT --

BEAR IN MIND, LAD, THE ENORMOUS *STRESS* HE'S BEEN UNDER -- FOR *MONTHS* NOW...

5

73

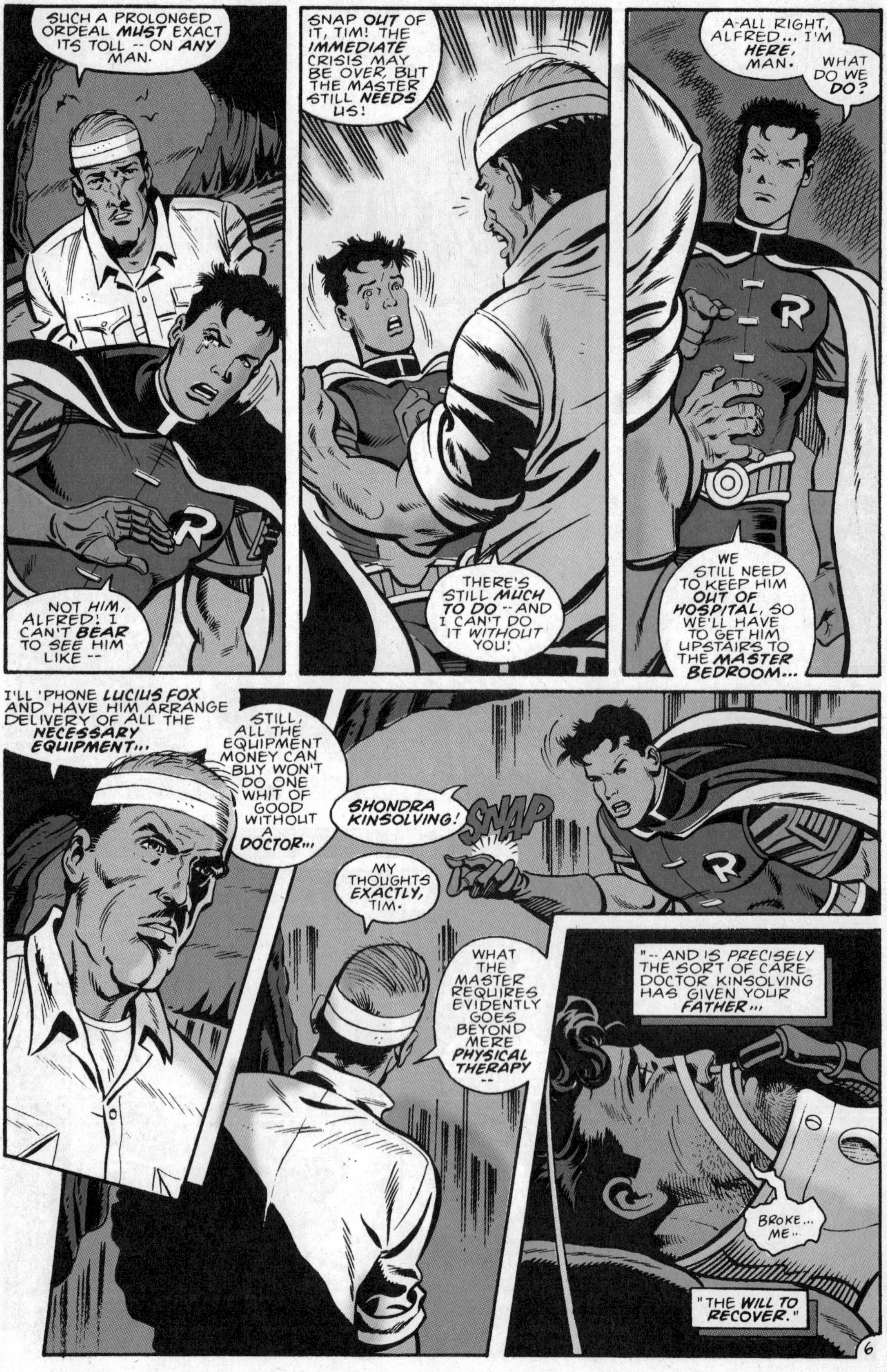

SUCH A PROLONGED ORDEAL MUST EXACT ITS TOLL -- ON ANY MAN.
NOT HIM, ALFRED! I CAN'T BEAR TO SEE HIM LIKE --
SNAP OUT OF IT, TIM! THE IMMEDIATE CRISIS MAY BE OVER, BUT THE MASTER STILL NEEDS US!
THERE'S STILL MUCH TO DO -- AND I CAN'T DO IT WITHOUT YOU!
A-ALL RIGHT, ALFRED... I'M HERE, MAN.
WHAT DO WE DO?
WE STILL NEED TO KEEP HIM OUT OF HOSPITAL, SO WE'LL HAVE TO GET HIM UPSTAIRS TO THE MASTER BEDROOM...
I'LL 'PHONE LUCIUS FOX AND HAVE HIM ARRANGE DELIVERY OF ALL THE NECESSARY EQUIPMENT...
STILL, ALL THE EQUIPMENT MONEY CAN BUY WON'T DO ONE WHIT OF GOOD WITHOUT A DOCTOR...
SHONDRA KINSOLVING!
SNAP
MY THOUGHTS EXACTLY, TIM.
WHAT THE MASTER REQUIRES EVIDENTLY GOES BEYOND MERE PHYSICAL THERAPY --
"-- AND IS PRECISELY THE SORT OF CARE DOCTOR KINSOLVING HAS GIVEN YOUR FATHER...
BROKE... ME...
"THE WILL TO RECOVER."
6

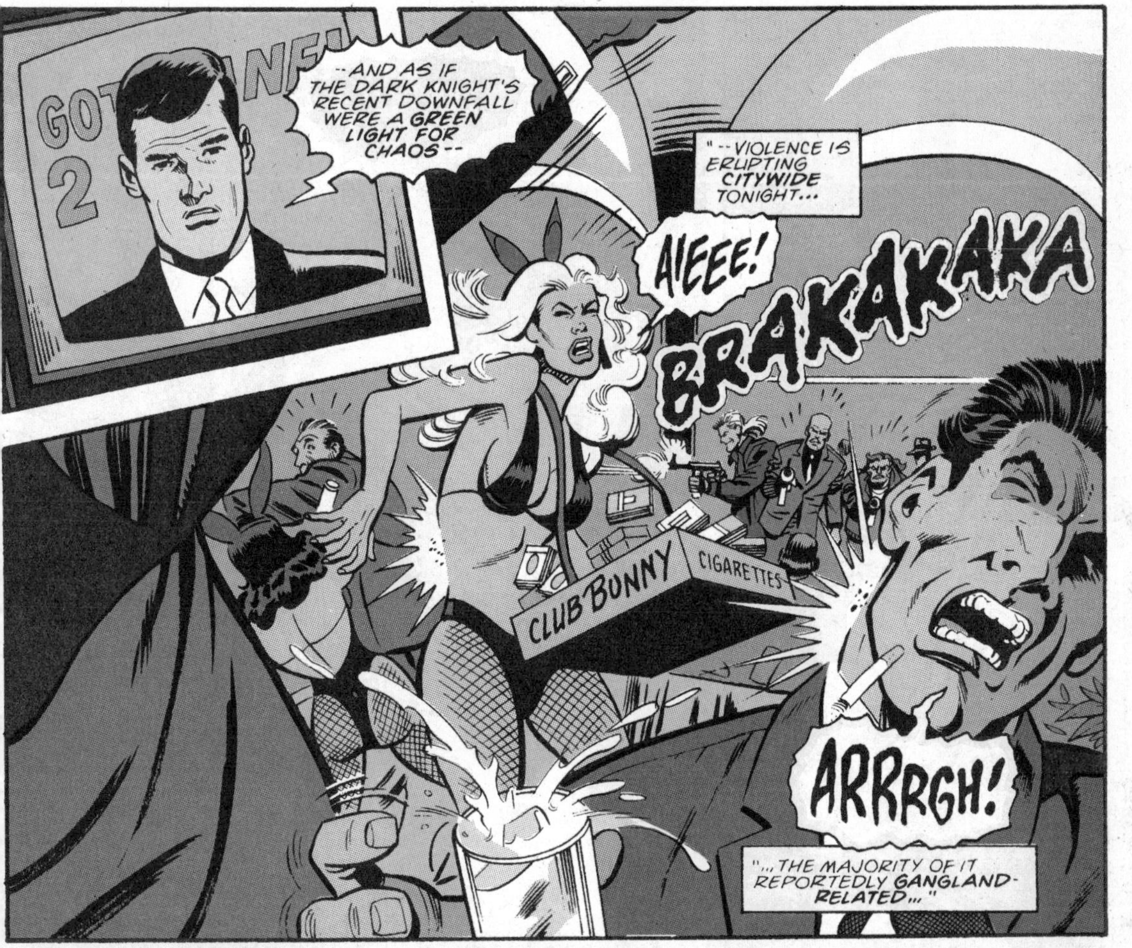
GOT
2
--AND AS IF THE DARK KNIGHT'S RECENT DOWNFALL WERE A GREEN LIGHT FOR CHAOS--
"--VIOLENCE IS ERUPTING CITYWIDE TONIGHT...
AIEEE!
BRAKAKAKA
CLUB BUNNY CIGARETTES
ARRRGH!
"...THE MAJORITY OF IT REPORTEDLY GANGLAND-RELATED..."

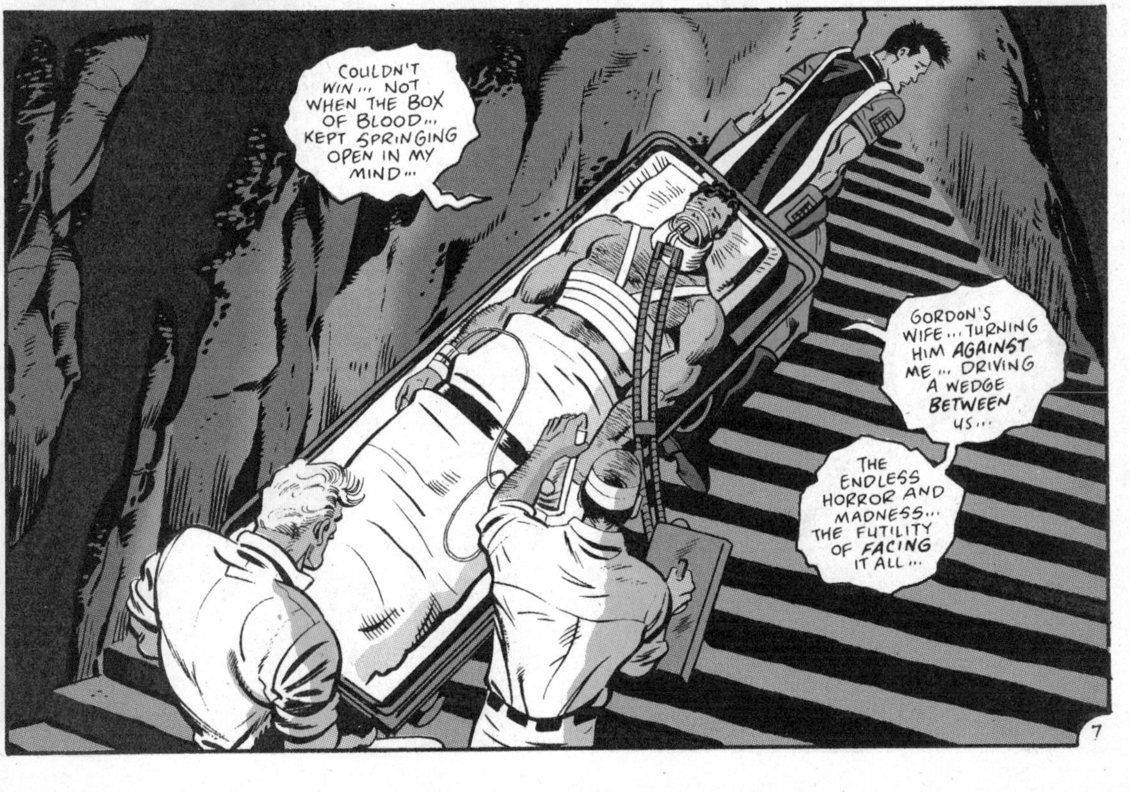
COULDN'T WIN... NOT WHEN THE BOX OF BLOOD... KEPT SPRINGING OPEN IN MY MIND...
GORDON'S WIFE... TURNING HIM AGAINST ME... DRIVING A WEDGE BETWEEN US...
THE ENDLESS HORROR AND MADNESS... THE FUTILITY OF FACING IT ALL...
7

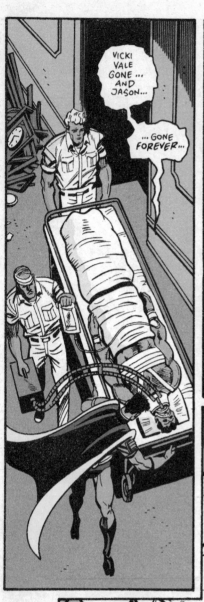

VICKI VALE GONE... AND JASON...

...GONE FOREVER...

THE FEAR THAT MY NEXT MISTAKE... COULD MEAN THE DEATH OF--

YOU'RE HOME NOW, SIR-- YOU'RE SAFE.

IS THERE ANYTHING YOU--

NO... JUST TURN OUT THE LIGHTS AND LEAVE ME...

...IN THE DARK.

JEAN PAUL, YOU GO 'PHONE SAL FIORINI AND GET TO WORK ON THE SECURITY SYSTEM.

AT ONCE, ALFRED.

TIM, BEFORE WE GO FETCH DOCTOR KINSOLVING, WE'LL NEED A COVER STORY... SOME SORT OF ACCIDENT LOGICALLY INVOLVING BRUCE WAY--

A CAR WRECK-- HE TOTALED THE PORSCHE.

GOOD LAD-- THERE ARE SLEDGE-HAMMERS IN THE SHED.

8

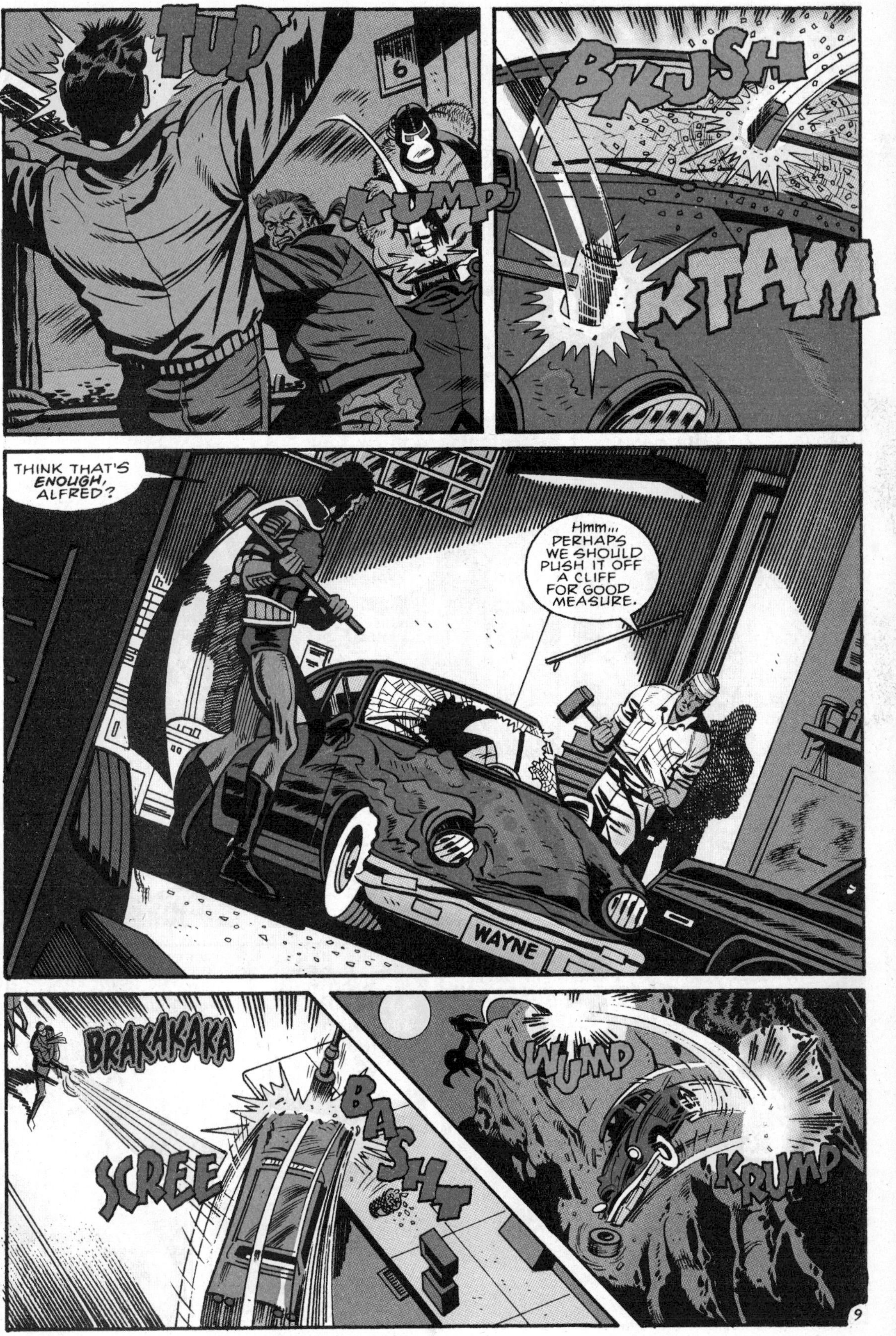
TUD
KUMP
BKJSH
KTAM
THINK THAT'S *ENOUGH*, ALFRED?
Hmm... PERHAPS WE SHOULD PUSH IT OFF A CLIFF FOR GOOD MEASURE.
WAYNE
BRAKAKAKA
SCREE
BASHT
WUMP
KRUMP
9

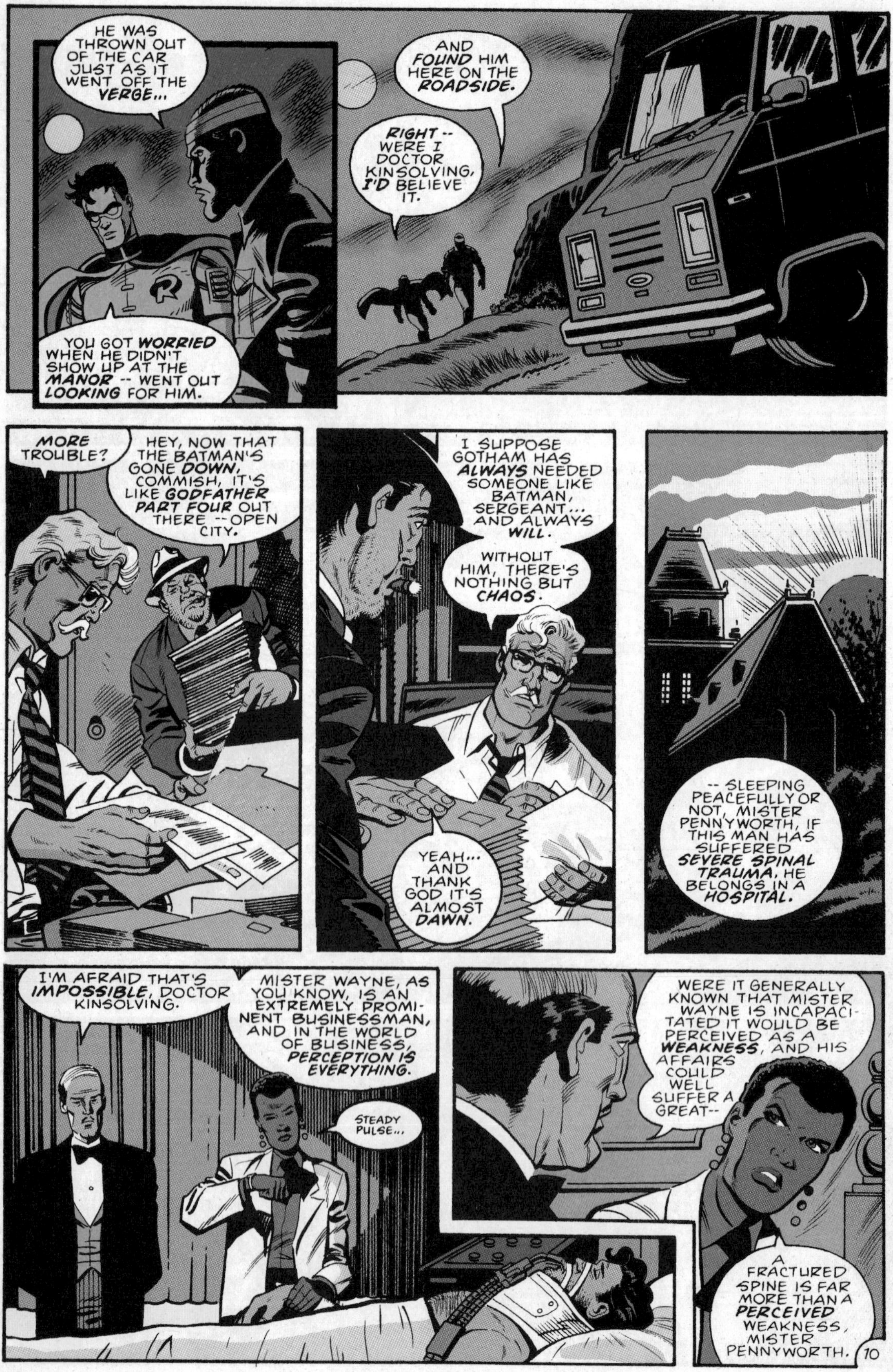
HE WAS THROWN OUT OF THE CAR JUST AS IT WENT OFF THE VERGE...
YOU GOT WORRIED WHEN HE DIDN'T SHOW UP AT THE MANOR -- WENT OUT LOOKING FOR HIM.
AND FOUND HIM HERE ON THE ROADSIDE.
RIGHT -- WERE I DOCTOR KINSOLVING, I'D BELIEVE IT.
MORE TROUBLE?
HEY, NOW THAT THE BATMAN'S GONE DOWN, COMMISH, IT'S LIKE GODFATHER PART FOUR OUT THERE -- OPEN CITY.
I SUPPOSE GOTHAM HAS ALWAYS NEEDED SOMEONE LIKE BATMAN, SERGEANT... AND ALWAYS WILL.
WITHOUT HIM, THERE'S NOTHING BUT CHAOS.
YEAH... AND THANK GOD IT'S ALMOST DAWN.
-- SLEEPING PEACEFULLY OR NOT, MISTER PENNYWORTH, IF THIS MAN HAS SUFFERED SEVERE SPINAL TRAUMA, HE BELONGS IN A HOSPITAL.
I'M AFRAID THAT'S IMPOSSIBLE, DOCTOR KINSOLVING.
MISTER WAYNE, AS YOU KNOW, IS AN EXTREMELY PROMINENT BUSINESSMAN, AND IN THE WORLD OF BUSINESS, PERCEPTION IS EVERYTHING.
STEADY PULSE...
WERE IT GENERALLY KNOWN THAT MISTER WAYNE IS INCAPACITATED IT WOULD BE PERCEIVED AS A WEAKNESS, AND HIS AFFAIRS COULD WELL SUFFER A GREAT--
A FRACTURED SPINE IS FAR MORE THAN A PERCEIVED WEAKNESS, MISTER PENNYWORTH.
10

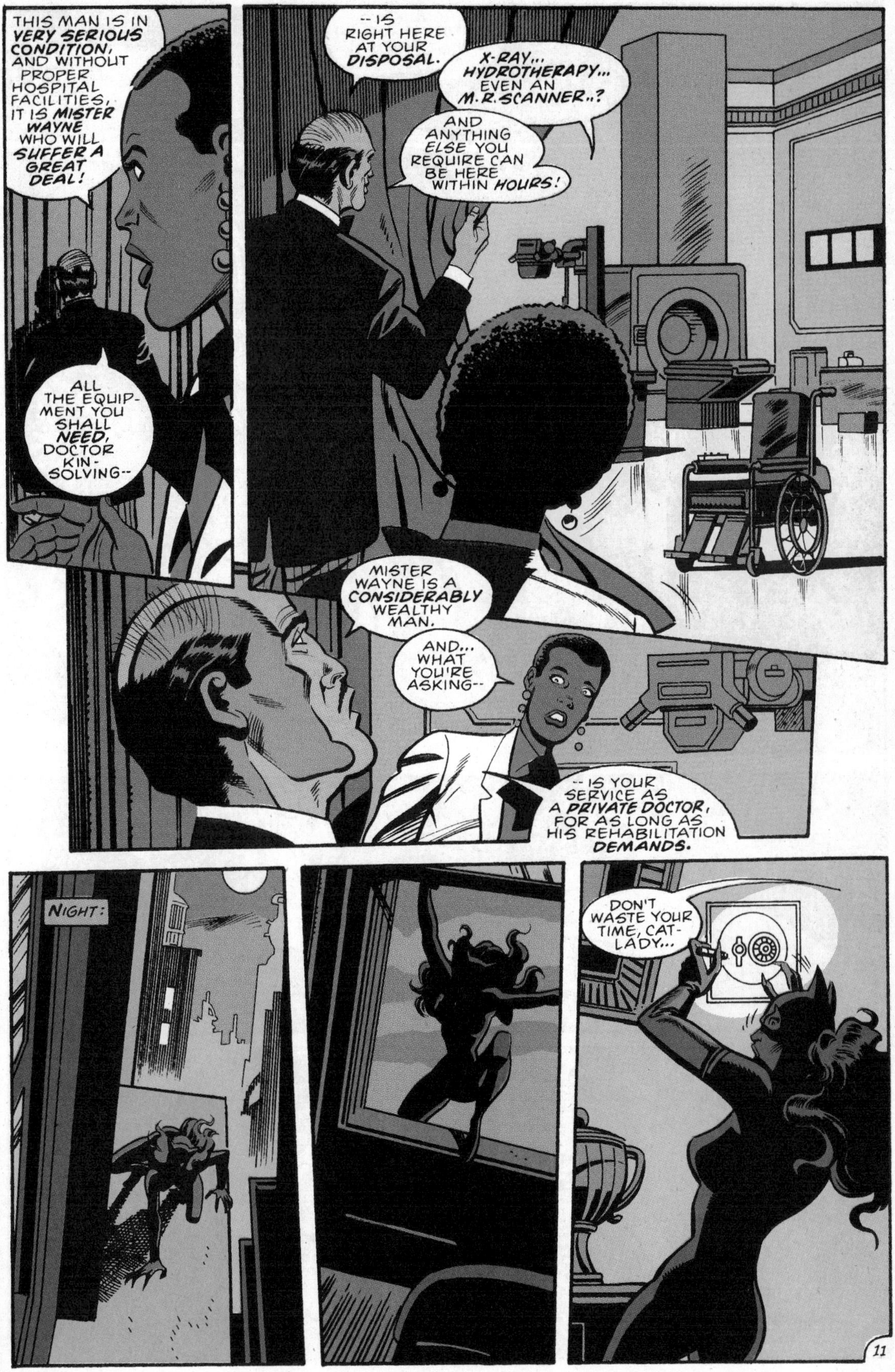
THIS MAN IS IN VERY SERIOUS CONDITION, AND WITHOUT PROPER HOSPITAL FACILITIES, IT IS MISTER WAYNE WHO WILL SUFFER A GREAT DEAL!
ALL THE EQUIPMENT YOU SHALL NEED, DOCTOR KINSOLVING--
--IS RIGHT HERE AT YOUR DISPOSAL.
X-RAY... HYDROTHERAPY... EVEN AN M.R. SCANNER..?
AND ANYTHING ELSE YOU REQUIRE CAN BE HERE WITHIN HOURS!
MISTER WAYNE IS A CONSIDERABLY WEALTHY MAN.
AND... WHAT YOU'RE ASKING--
--IS YOUR SERVICE AS A PRIVATE DOCTOR, FOR AS LONG AS HIS REHABILITATION DEMANDS.
NIGHT:
DON'T WASTE YOUR TIME, CAT-LADY...
11

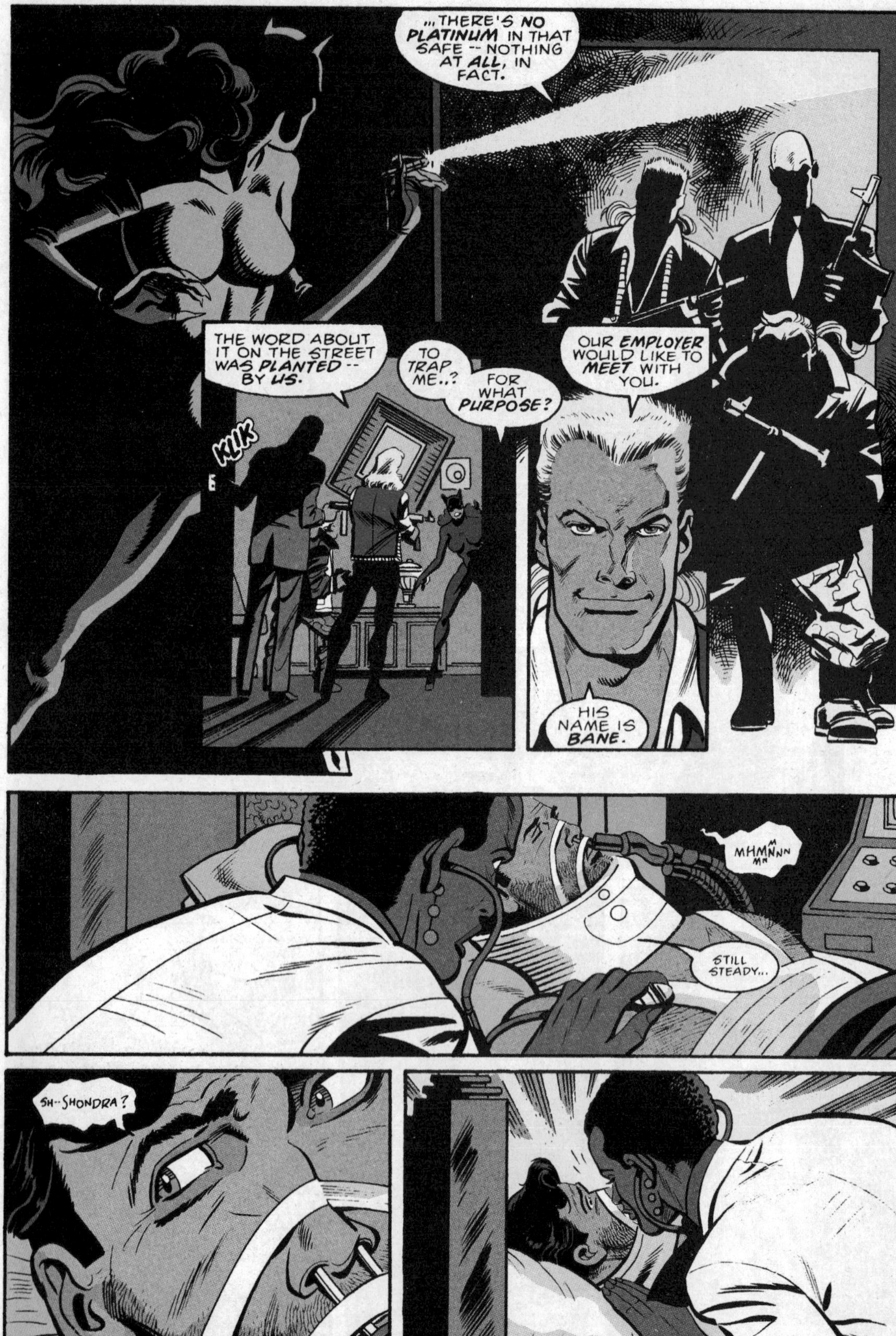
...THERE'S NO PLATINUM IN THAT SAFE -- NOTHING AT ALL, IN FACT.
THE WORD ABOUT IT ON THE STREET WAS PLANTED -- BY US.
TO TRAP ME..?
FOR WHAT PURPOSE?
OUR EMPLOYER WOULD LIKE TO MEET WITH YOU.
KLIK
HIS NAME IS BANE.
MHMMMNNN
STILL STEADY...
SH--SHONDRA?
12

STILL NO WORD ON WHERE HE *IS*, COMMISH?

NO.

GOIN' UP TO THE *ROOF?*

IT CAN'T *HURT*, SERGEANT, TO *TRY*.

ABOUT WHAT HAPPENED WHEN YOU *WOKE UP*, BRUCE, I ... *WELL*, I CAN'T REALLY *EXPLAIN* IT...

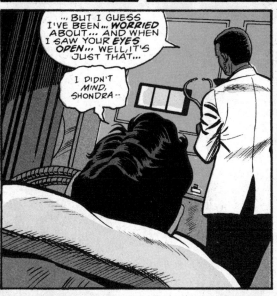

...BUT I GUESS I'VE BEEN... *WORRIED* ABOUT... AND WHEN I SAW YOUR *EYES OPEN*... WELL, IT'S JUST THAT...

I DIDN'T *MIND*, SHONDRA--

YOU *DIDN'T?*

OTHER THAN... *WEAKNESS* AND *PAIN*... IT WAS THE FIRST TIME, IN FAR TOO LONG, THAT I'VE FELT *ANYTHING*.

YES, AND ALFRED AND TIMOTHY TOLD ME YOU'RE EXPERIENCING SOME *DEPRESSION*...

I'VE SUFFERED A ... *LOSS* ... *BEYOND* THE INJURY...

I HOPE YOU'RE NOT TALKING ABOUT A MERE *CAR.*

CAR?!?

Ahem...

THE *PORSCHE*, SIR.

YOU WERE IN *SHOCK* WHEN I FOUND YOU BY THE *ROADSIDE*, REMEMBER -- WITH LITTLE OR NO *MEMORY* OF YOUR ACCIDENT.

13

IT MAY TAKE A WHILE, DOCTOR, FOR MISTER WAYNE TO --

IF ANYONE CAN HEAL HIM, MISTER PENNYWORTH, *I WILL.*

MIGHTY CONFIDENT...

EXACTLY, BRUCE, AND THAT'S WHAT YOU MUST BE -- *BOTH OF US* -- TOGETHER.

FROM WHAT I *KNOW* OF YOU, YOU'RE NOT THE TYPE WHO *QUITS*... EVEN IF YOU ARE CAPABLE OF *LYING.*

LYING..?

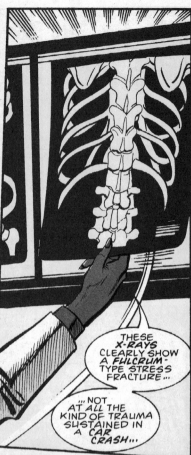

THESE *X-RAYS* CLEARLY SHOW A *FULCRUM-*TYPE STRESS FRACTURE...

...NOT AT ALL THE KIND OF TRAUMA SUSTAINED IN A *CAR CRASH*...

...WHICH, IN ANY CASE, WOULD HAVE *SHATTERED* YOUR *LEGS* BEFORE AFFECTING YOUR *BACK.*

I...

HE WAS *THROWN* FROM THE CAR -- BEFORE IT WENT OVER THE *VERGE* -- LANDED ON A *LARGE ROCK.*

THAT'S ALL RIGHT -- I *LIKE* IT.

You... *DO?!*

YOU'RE A *MYSTERY* TO ME, BRUCE -- AND THE FACT THAT YOU'RE *CLINGING* TO YOUR MYSTERY PROVES YOU *HAVEN'T GIVEN UP!*

BESIDES, THE *DIAGNOSTICIAN* IN ME ENJOYS PEELING *MYSTERIES OPEN*... ONE LAYER AT A *TIME.*

14

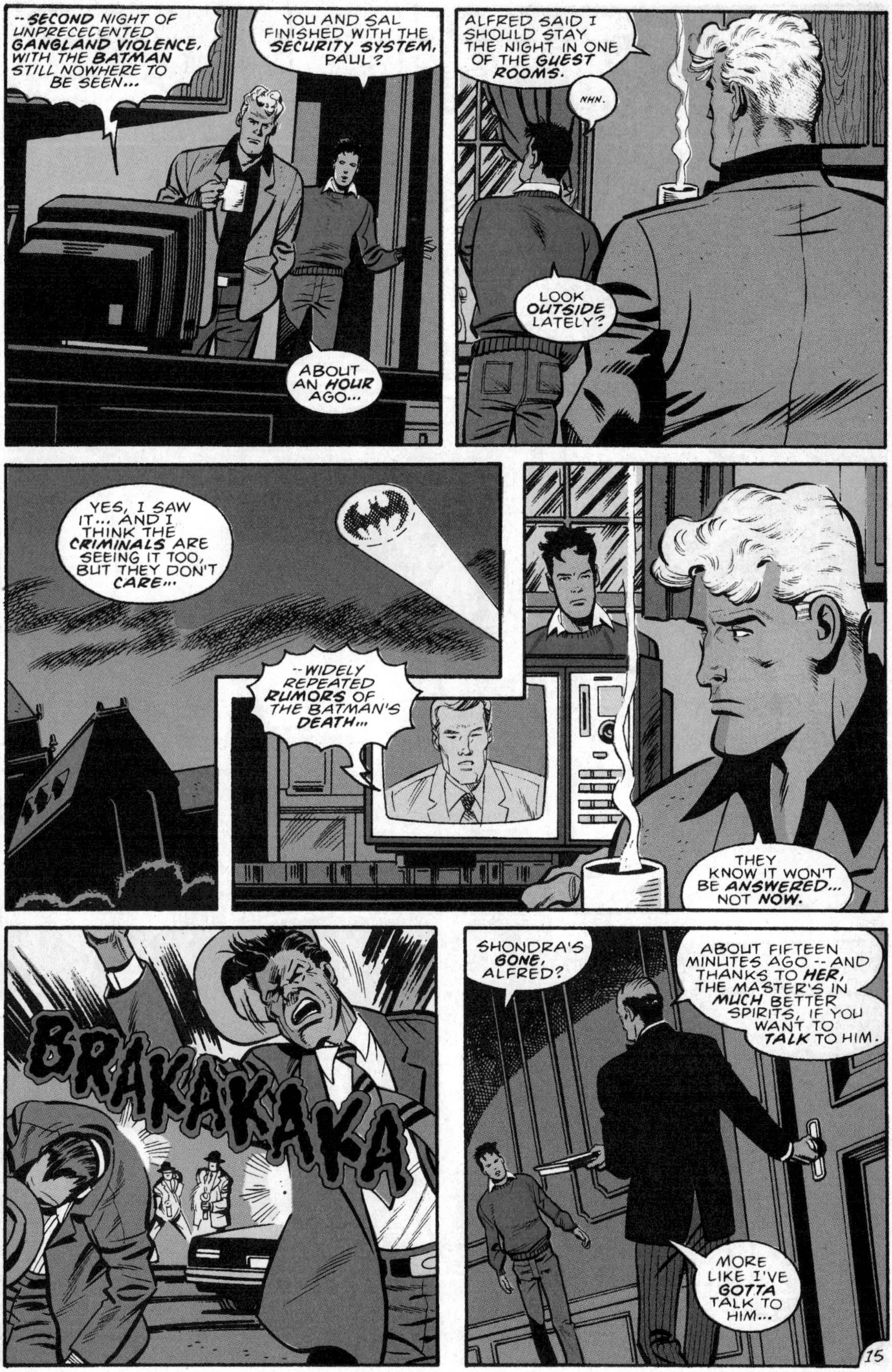
--SECOND NIGHT OF UNPRECEDENTED GANGLAND VIOLENCE, WITH THE BATMAN STILL NOWHERE TO BE SEEN...
YOU AND SAL FINISHED WITH THE SECURITY SYSTEM, PAUL?
ABOUT AN HOUR AGO...
ALFRED SAID I SHOULD STAY THE NIGHT IN ONE OF THE GUEST ROOMS.
NHN.
LOOK OUTSIDE LATELY?
YES, I SAW IT... AND I THINK THE CRIMINALS ARE SEEING IT TOO, BUT THEY DON'T CARE...
--WIDELY REPEATED RUMORS OF THE BATMAN'S DEATH...
THEY KNOW IT WON'T BE ANSWERED... NOT NOW.
BRAKAKAKAKA
SHONDRA'S GONE, ALFRED?
ABOUT FIFTEEN MINUTES AGO -- AND THANKS TO HER, THE MASTER'S IN MUCH BETTER SPIRITS, IF YOU WANT TO TALK TO HIM.
MORE LIKE I'VE GOTTA TALK TO HIM...
15

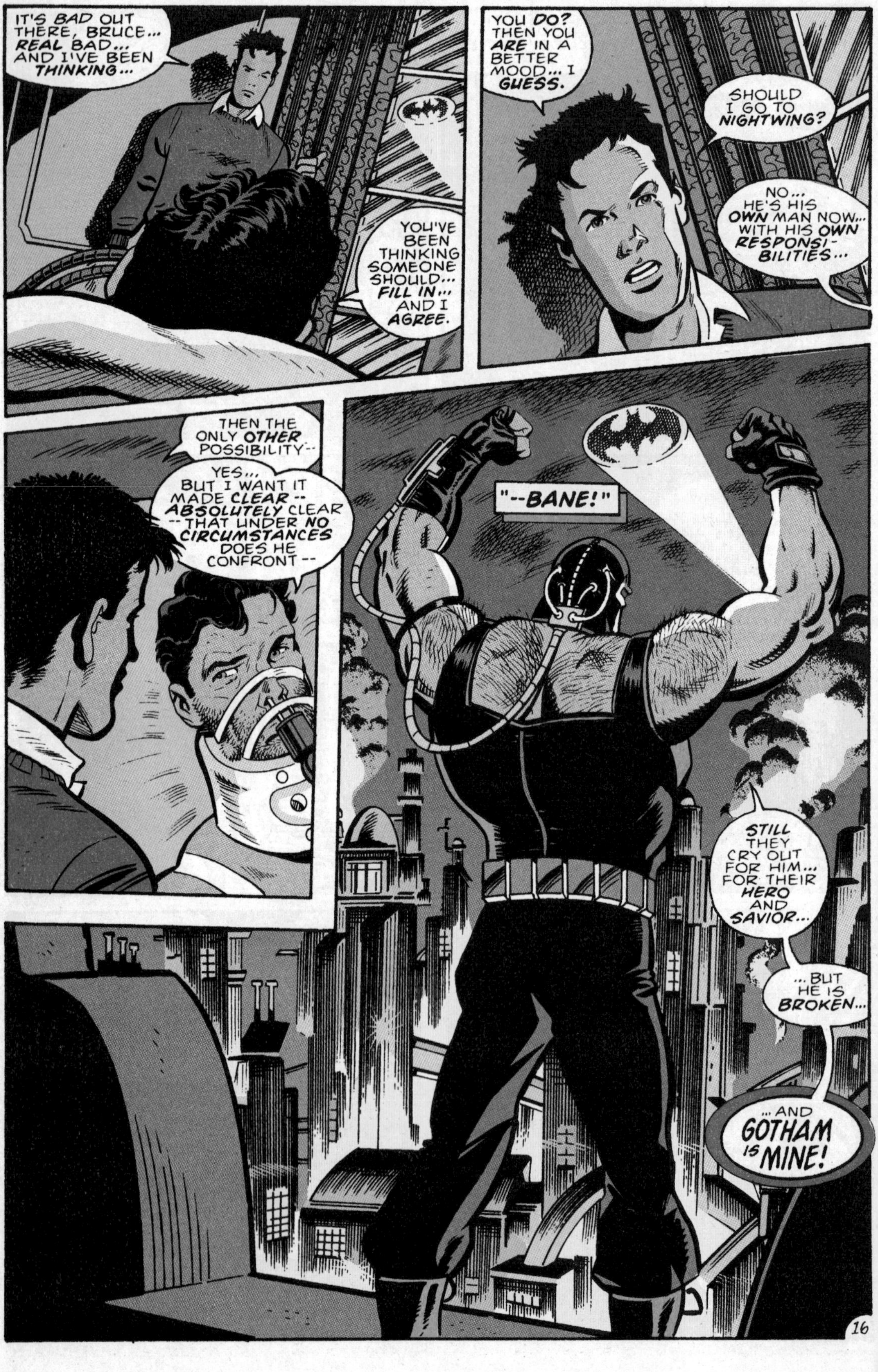
IT'S BAD OUT THERE, BRUCE... REAL BAD... AND I'VE BEEN THINKING...
YOU'VE BEEN THINKING SOMEONE SHOULD... FILL IN... AND I AGREE.
YOU DO? THEN YOU ARE IN A BETTER MOOD... I GUESS.
SHOULD I GO TO NIGHTWING?
NO... HE'S HIS OWN MAN NOW... WITH HIS OWN RESPONSI-BILITIES...
THEN THE ONLY OTHER POSSIBILITY--
YES... BUT I WANT IT MADE CLEAR -- ABSOLUTELY CLEAR -- THAT UNDER NO CIRCUMSTANCES DOES HE CONFRONT --
"--BANE!"
STILL THEY CRY OUT FOR HIM... FOR THEIR HERO AND SAVIOR...
...BUT HE IS BROKEN...
...AND GOTHAM IS MINE!
16

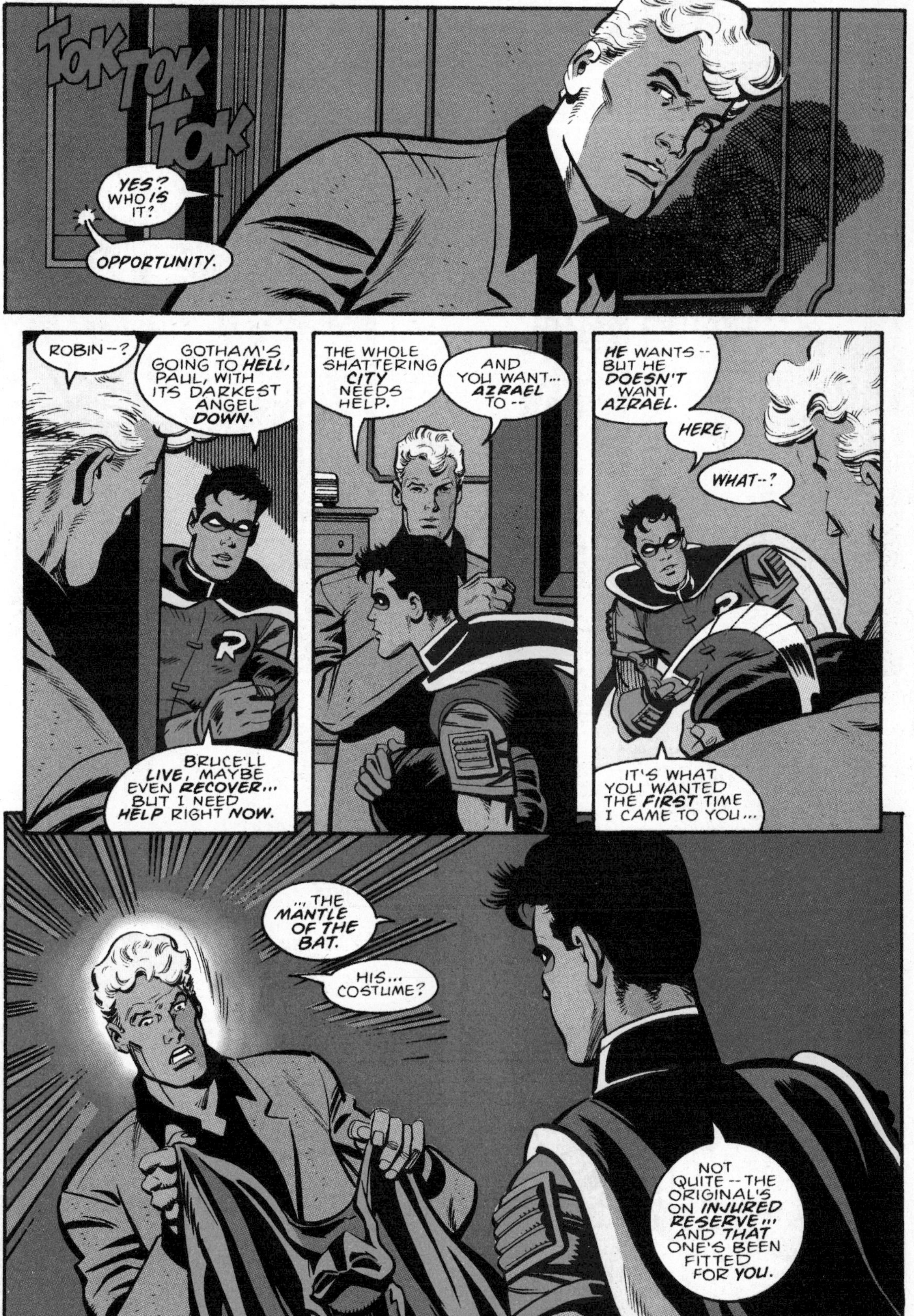
TOK TOK TOK
YES? WHO IS IT?
OPPORTUNITY.
ROBIN--?
GOTHAM'S GOING TO HELL, PAUL, WITH ITS DARKEST ANGEL DOWN.
BRUCE'LL LIVE, MAYBE EVEN RECOVER... BUT I NEED HELP RIGHT NOW.
THE WHOLE SHATTERING CITY NEEDS HELP.
AND YOU WANT... AZRAEL TO --
HE WANTS -- BUT HE DOESN'T WANT AZRAEL.
HERE.
WHAT--?
IT'S WHAT YOU WANTED THE FIRST TIME I CAME TO YOU...
... THE MANTLE OF THE BAT.
HIS... COSTUME?
NOT QUITE -- THE ORIGINAL'S ON INJURED RESERVE... AND THAT ONE'S BEEN FITTED FOR YOU.
17

86

OUR BUSINESS IS WITH THE *CATWOMAN*, TROGG, NOT --

YOU'VE GOT *YOUR* FLUNKIES, BANE -- I'VE GOT *MINE*.

SAY *"HELLO"* TO THE MAN, LEOPOLD.

GOT A *LIGHT*, MAN..?

OR DO I HAVE TO *CHAIN*?

MY OFFER IS TO *YOU* -- NOT YOUR *"FLUNKY."*

SO I'LL *CHAIN* IT.

AND JUST *WHAT IS* YOUR OFFER, BANE?

BASICALLY, YOU CONTINUE DOING WHAT YOU DO SO WELL -- *STEALING*.

MY ONLY DEMAND IS THAT YOU NOW FENCE ALL GOODS THROUGH *MY* ORGANIZATION.

RATE HE'S *GOING* LAST FEW NIGHTS, WON'T *BE* ANY *OTHER* ORGANIZATIONS.

YOU SAID *"BASICALLY."*

FROM TIME TO TIME, I MAY REQUIRE YOUR SPECIALIZED SKILLS FOR CERTAIN *OTHER* JOBS... *SURVEILLANCE*, PERHAPS, THE THEFT OF *INFORMATION* ...

FOR THESE... *ACTIVITIES*, YOU WILL BE PAID FAR MORE THAN THE VALUE OF *ANYTHING* YOU COULD FENCE.

19

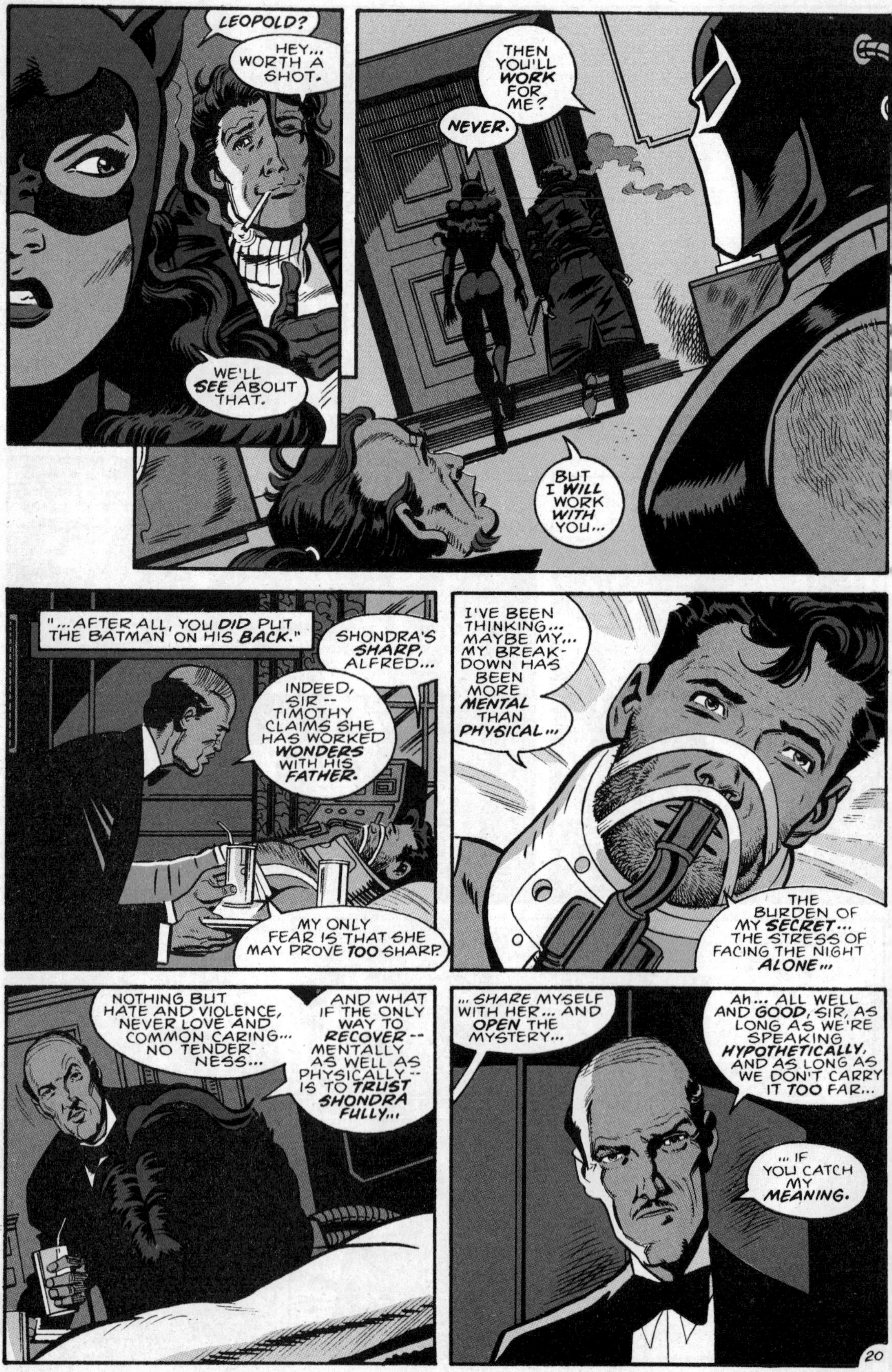
LEOPOLD?
HEY... WORTH A SHOT.
WE'LL SEE ABOUT THAT.
THEN YOU'LL WORK FOR ME?
NEVER.
BUT I WILL WORK WITH YOU...
"...AFTER ALL, YOU DID PUT THE BATMAN ON HIS BACK."
SHONDRA'S SHARP, ALFRED...
INDEED, SIR -- TIMOTHY CLAIMS SHE HAS WORKED WONDERS WITH HIS FATHER.
MY ONLY FEAR IS THAT SHE MAY PROVE TOO SHARP.
I'VE BEEN THINKING... MAYBE MY... MY BREAK-DOWN HAS BEEN MORE MENTAL THAN PHYSICAL...
THE BURDEN OF MY SECRET... THE STRESS OF FACING THE NIGHT ALONE...
NOTHING BUT HATE AND VIOLENCE, NEVER LOVE AND COMMON CARING... NO TENDER-NESS...
AND WHAT IF THE ONLY WAY TO RECOVER -- MENTALLY AS WELL AS PHYSICALLY -- IS TO TRUST SHONDRA FULLY...
...SHARE MYSELF WITH HER... AND OPEN THE MYSTERY...
Ah... ALL WELL AND GOOD, SIR, AS LONG AS WE'RE SPEAKING HYPOTHETICALLY, AND AS LONG AS WE DON'T CARRY IT TOO FAR...
...IF YOU CATCH MY MEANING.
20

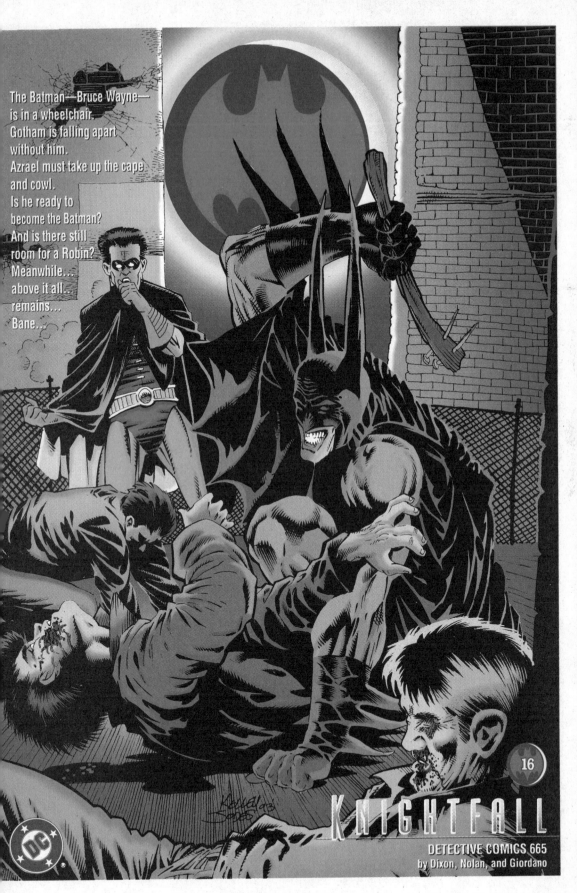

The Batman—Bruce Wayne—is in a wheelchair. Gotham is falling apart without him. Azrael must take up the cape and cowl. Is he ready to become the Batman? And is there still room for a Robin? Meanwhile... above it all... remains... Bane...

16

KNIGHTFALL

DETECTIVE COMICS 665
by Dixon, Nolan, and Giordano

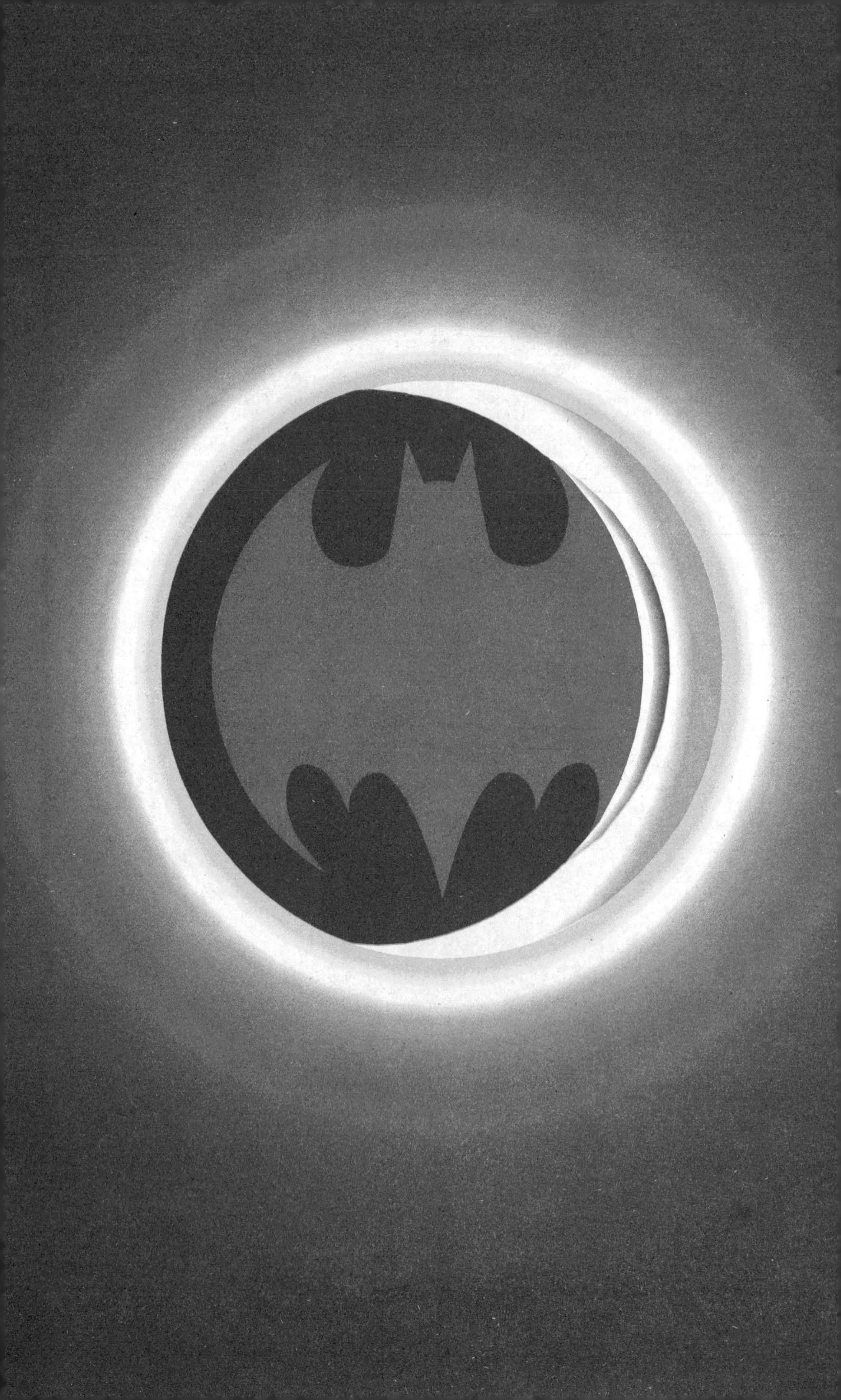

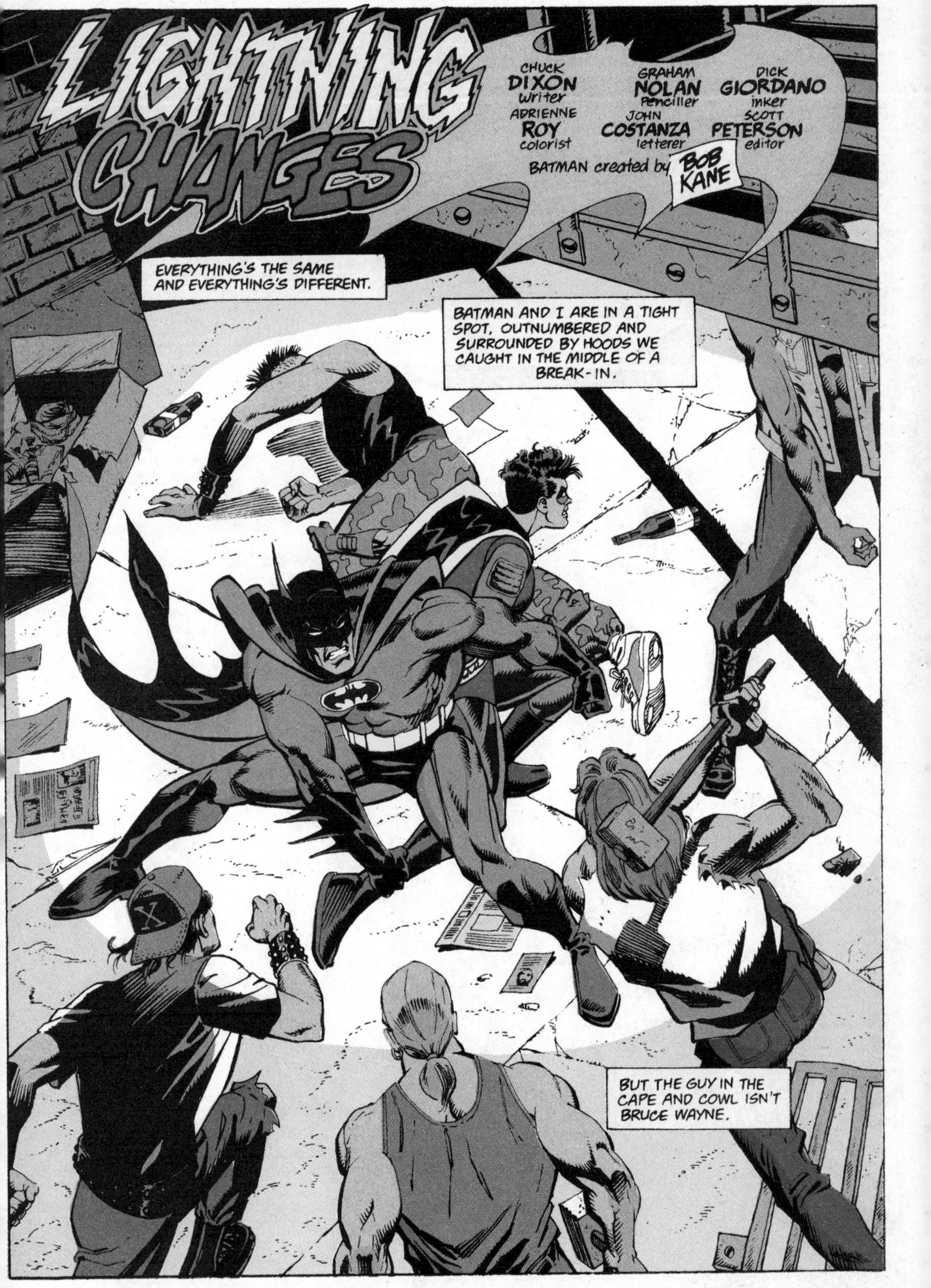
LIGHTNING CHANGES
CHUCK DIXON writer
GRAHAM NOLAN penciller
DICK GIORDANO inker
ADRIENNE ROY colorist
JOHN COSTANZA letterer
SCOTT PETERSON editor
BATMAN created by BOB KANE
EVERYTHING'S THE SAME AND EVERYTHING'S DIFFERENT.
BATMAN AND I ARE IN A TIGHT SPOT, OUTNUMBERED AND SURROUNDED BY HOODS WE CAUGHT IN THE MIDDLE OF A BREAK-IN.
BUT THE GUY IN THE CAPE AND COWL ISN'T BRUCE WAYNE.

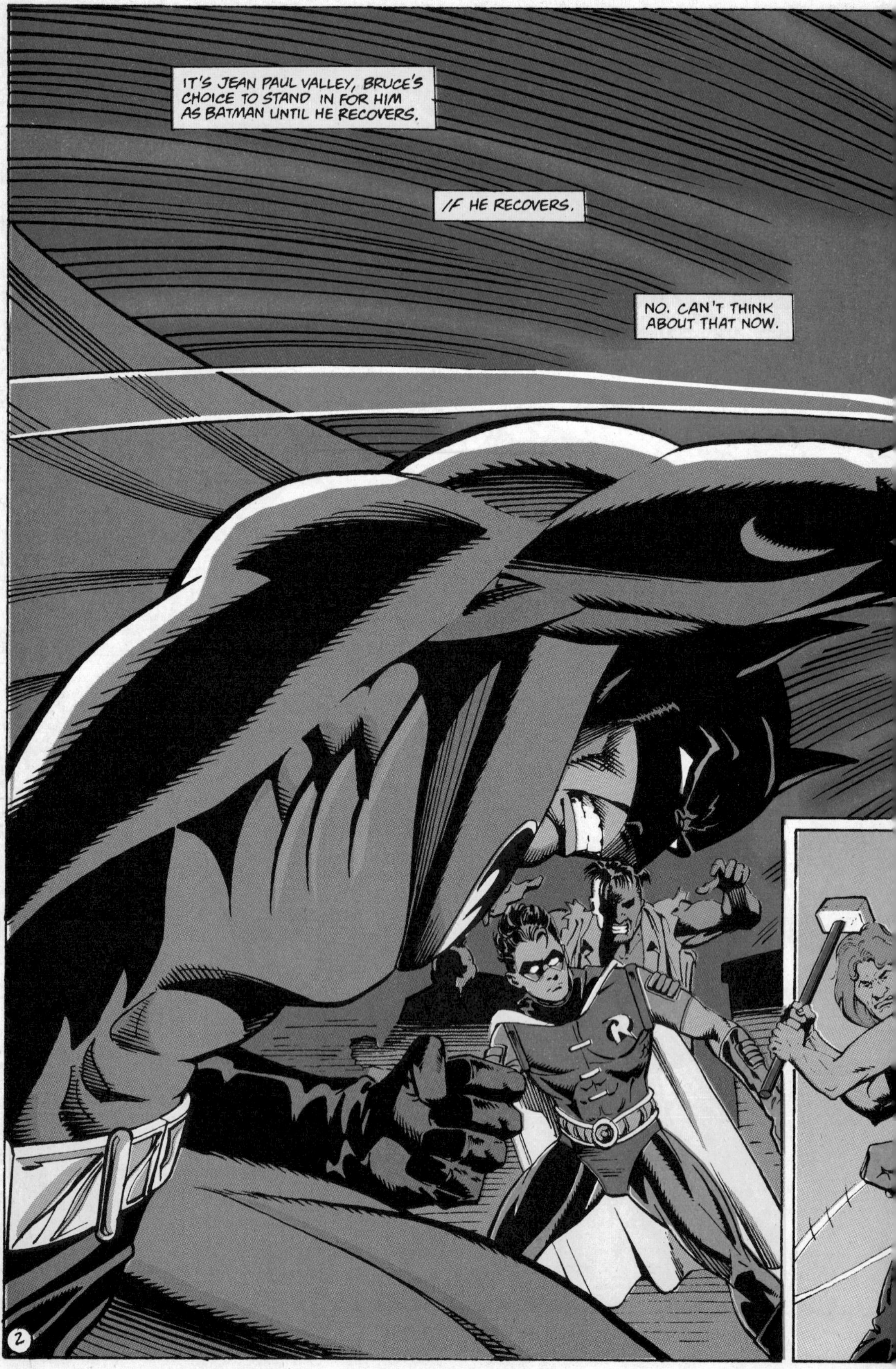
IT'S JEAN PAUL VALLEY, BRUCE'S CHOICE TO STAND IN FOR HIM AS BATMAN UNTIL HE RECOVERS.
IF HE RECOVERS.
NO. CAN'T THINK ABOUT THAT NOW.

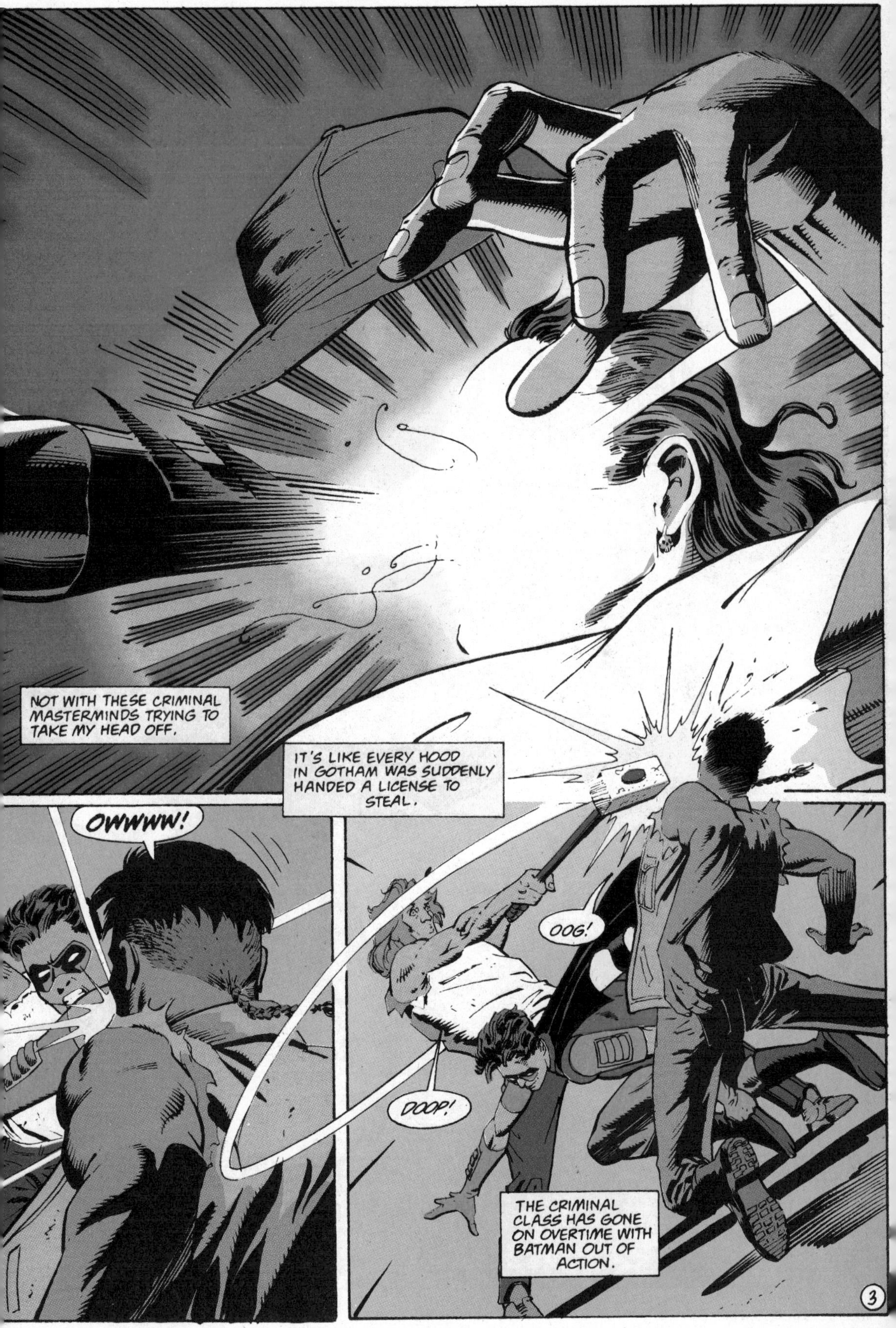
NOT WITH THESE CRIMINAL MASTERMINDS TRYING TO TAKE MY HEAD OFF.
IT'S LIKE EVERY HOOD IN GOTHAM WAS SUDDENLY HANDED A LICENSE TO STEAL.
OWWWW!
OOG!
DOOP!
THE CRIMINAL CLASS HAS GONE ON OVERTIME WITH BATMAN OUT OF ACTION.
3

OUR PRESENCE ON THE STREET SHOULD CHANGE THAT.

EVEN IF IT ISN'T THE REAL BATMAN.

AND PAUL'S DOING A GOOD JOB FILLING IN.

MAYBE A LITTLE *TOO* GOOD.

HE'S *INTO* IT, ALL RIGHT. HE'S QUICK AND TOUGH AND SCARY.

UNNH!

BUT SOMEHOW HE'S SCARY IN ALL THE *WRONG* WAYS.

SCUM!

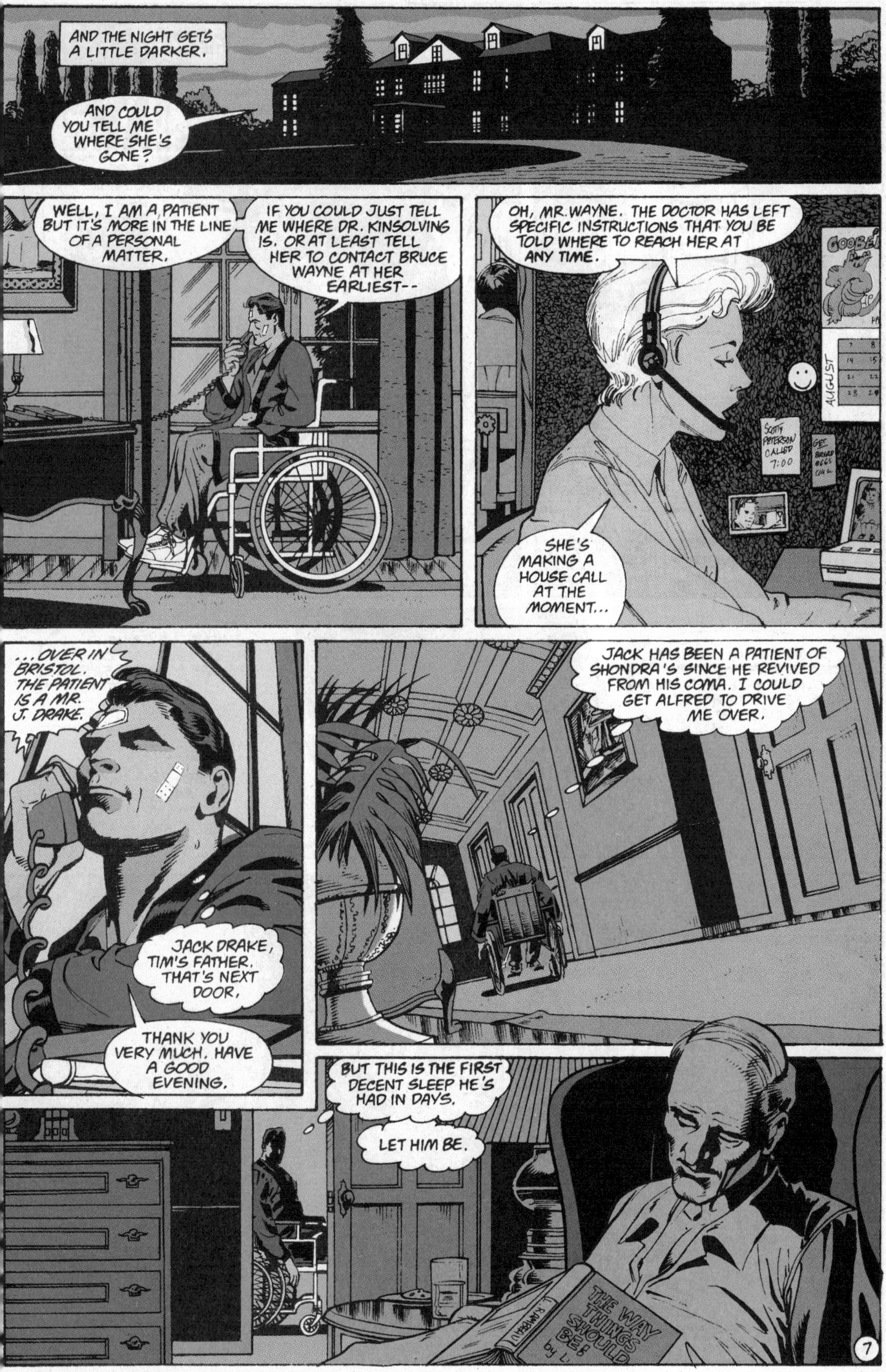
AND THE NIGHT GETS A LITTLE DARKER.
AND COULD YOU TELL ME WHERE SHE'S GONE?
WELL, I AM A PATIENT BUT IT'S MORE IN THE LINE OF A PERSONAL MATTER.
IF YOU COULD JUST TELL ME WHERE DR. KINSOLVING IS. OR AT LEAST TELL HER TO CONTACT BRUCE WAYNE AT HER EARLIEST--
OH, MR. WAYNE. THE DOCTOR HAS LEFT SPECIFIC INSTRUCTIONS THAT YOU BE TOLD WHERE TO REACH HER AT ANY TIME.
SHE'S MAKING A HOUSE CALL AT THE MOMENT...
AUGUST
...OVER IN BRISTOL. THE PATIENT IS A MR. J. DRAKE.
JACK DRAKE, TIM'S FATHER. THAT'S NEXT DOOR.
THANK YOU VERY MUCH. HAVE A GOOD EVENING.
JACK HAS BEEN A PATIENT OF SHONDRA'S SINCE HE REVIVED FROM HIS COMA. I COULD GET ALFRED TO DRIVE ME OVER.
BUT THIS IS THE FIRST DECENT SLEEP HE'S HAD IN DAYS.
LET HIM BE.
THE WAY THINGS SHOULD BE
7

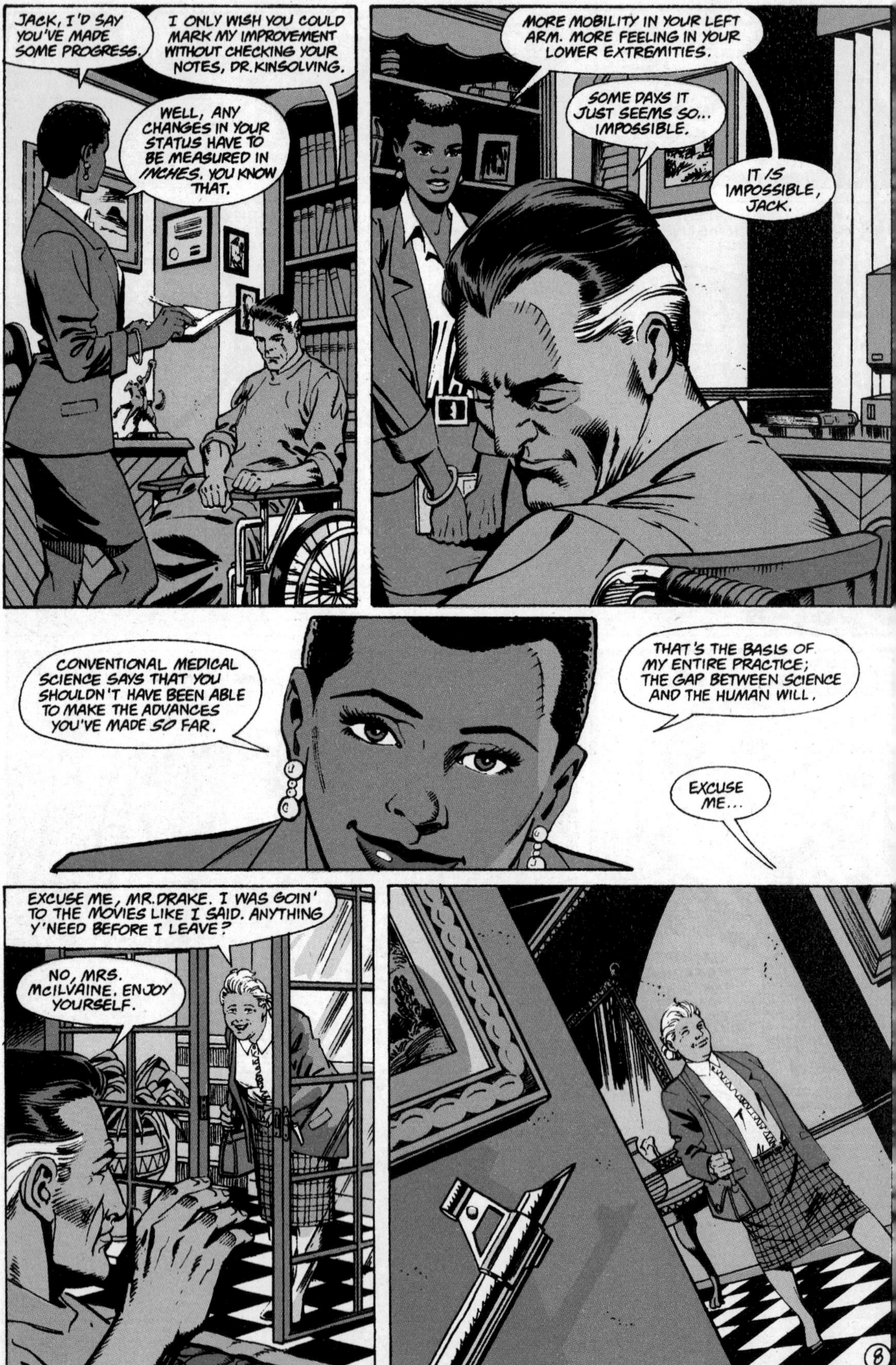
JACK, I'D SAY YOU'VE MADE SOME PROGRESS.
I ONLY WISH YOU COULD MARK MY IMPROVEMENT WITHOUT CHECKING YOUR NOTES, DR. KINSOLVING.
WELL, ANY CHANGES IN YOUR STATUS HAVE TO BE MEASURED IN INCHES, YOU KNOW THAT.
MORE MOBILITY IN YOUR LEFT ARM. MORE FEELING IN YOUR LOWER EXTREMITIES.
SOME DAYS IT JUST SEEMS SO... IMPOSSIBLE.
IT IS IMPOSSIBLE, JACK.
CONVENTIONAL MEDICAL SCIENCE SAYS THAT YOU SHOULDN'T HAVE BEEN ABLE TO MAKE THE ADVANCES YOU'VE MADE SO FAR.
THAT'S THE BASIS OF MY ENTIRE PRACTICE; THE GAP BETWEEN SCIENCE AND THE HUMAN WILL.
EXCUSE ME...
EXCUSE ME, MR. DRAKE. I WAS GOIN' TO THE MOVIES LIKE I SAID. ANYTHING Y'NEED BEFORE I LEAVE?
NO, MRS. MCILVAINE. ENJOY YOURSELF.
8

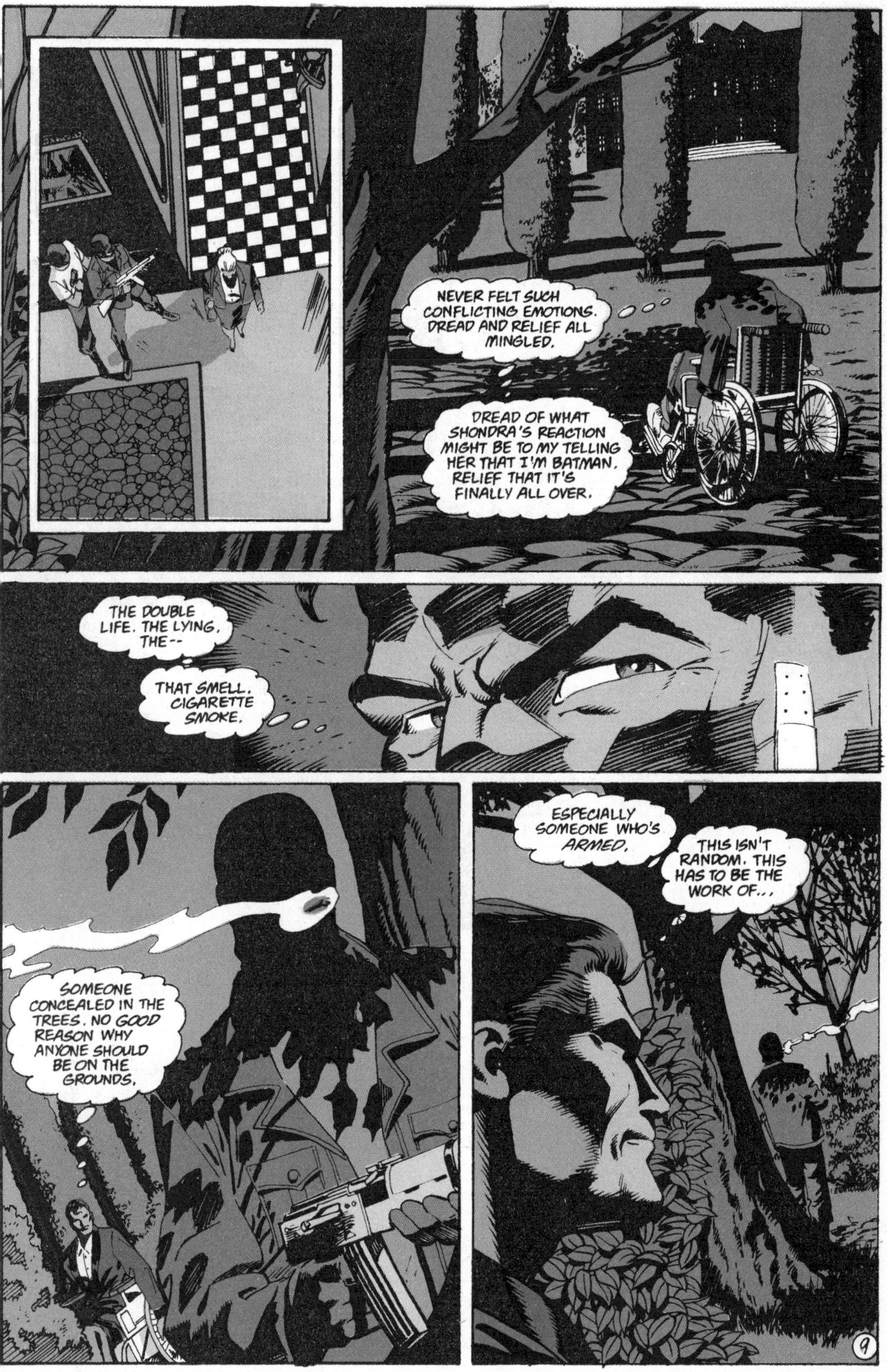
NEVER FELT SUCH CONFLICTING EMOTIONS. DREAD AND RELIEF ALL MINGLED.
DREAD OF WHAT SHONDRA'S REACTION MIGHT BE TO MY TELLING HER THAT I'M BATMAN. RELIEF THAT IT'S FINALLY ALL OVER.
THE DOUBLE LIFE. THE LYING. THE--
THAT SMELL. CIGARETTE SMOKE.
SOMEONE CONCEALED IN THE TREES. NO GOOD REASON WHY ANYONE SHOULD BE ON THE GROUNDS.
ESPECIALLY SOMEONE WHO'S ARMED.
THIS ISN'T RANDOM. THIS HAS TO BE THE WORK OF...
9

"...BANE."

DRUGS. SMUGGLING. GAMBLING. EXTORTION. CAR THEFT. BANK BURGLARY.

FROM THE HIGHEST ROLLER TO THE LOWEST STREET PUNK. OUT OF EVERY DOLLAR TAKEN IN WE GET FIFTY CENTS.

THE UNIONS, BANE. WE STILL DON'T HAVE A GRIP ON *THEM.*

FROM CREST POINT TO SOMERSET. IT IS *ALL* MINE. MY INFLUENCE AND POWER ARE FELT IN EVERY CORNER OF GOTHAM.

CONSTRUCTION, TRUCKING AND TRADE UNIONS ARE THE *MOST* LUCRATIVE RACKETS. THE MEN WHO CONTROL THEM HOLD ON TO THEM DEARLY.

WE HAVE ALREADY DRIVEN A WEDGE INTO THEIR ORGAN- IZATION.

IT WILL TAKE A LOT OF MUSCLE TO TAKE THEM AND MORE TO *HOLD* THEM.

THEY WILL DRIVE IT DEEPER, MY FRIENDS. YOU WILL SEE.

10

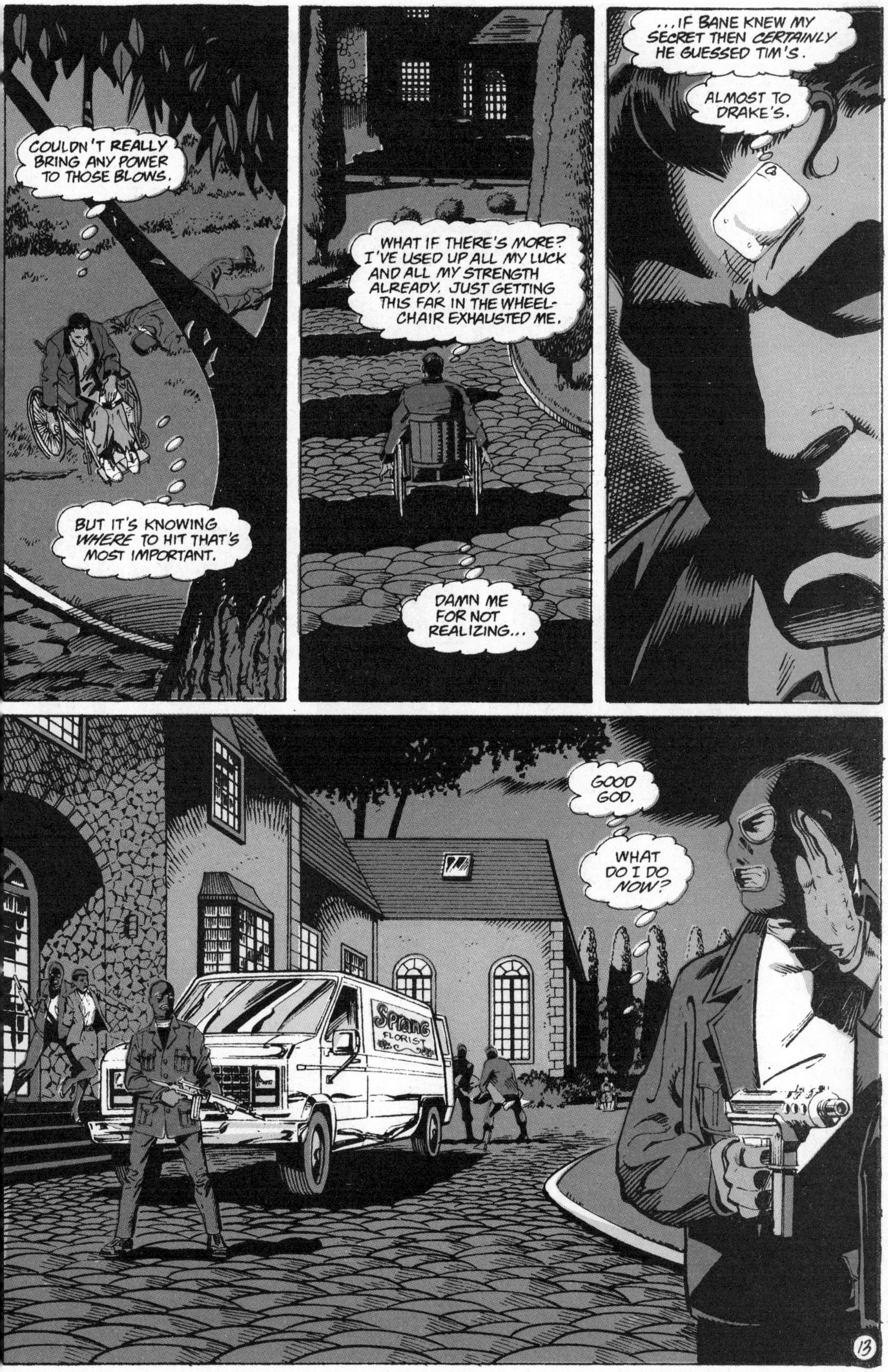
COULDN'T REALLY BRING ANY POWER TO THOSE BLOWS.
BUT IT'S KNOWING *WHERE* TO HIT THAT'S MOST IMPORTANT.
WHAT IF THERE'S MORE? I'VE USED UP ALL MY LUCK AND ALL MY STRENGTH ALREADY. JUST GETTING THIS FAR IN THE WHEEL-CHAIR EXHAUSTED ME.
DAMN ME FOR NOT REALIZING...
...IF BANE KNEW MY SECRET THEN *CERTAINLY* HE GUESSED TIM'S.
ALMOST TO DRAKE'S.
GOOD GOD.
WHAT DO I DO *NOW*?
Sprang FLORIST
13

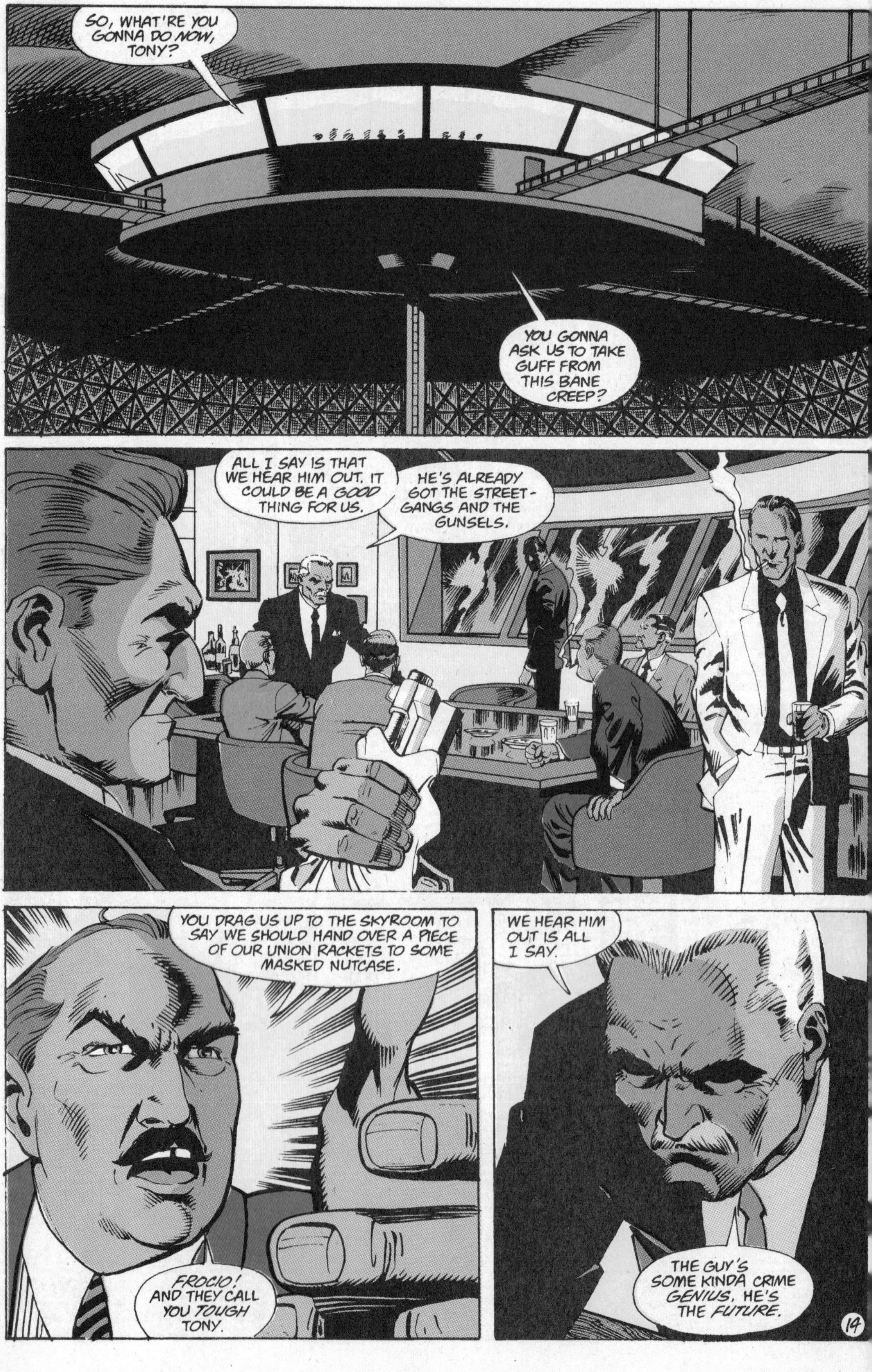
SO, WHAT'RE YOU GONNA DO NOW, TONY?
YOU GONNA ASK US TO TAKE GUFF FROM THIS BANE CREEP?
ALL I SAY IS THAT WE HEAR HIM OUT. IT COULD BE A GOOD THING FOR US.
HE'S ALREADY GOT THE STREET-GANGS AND THE GUNSELS.
YOU DRAG US UP TO THE SKYROOM TO SAY WE SHOULD HAND OVER A PIECE OF OUR UNION RACKETS TO SOME MASKED NUTCASE.
FROCIO! AND THEY CALL YOU TOUGH TONY.
WE HEAR HIM OUT IS ALL I SAY.
THE GUY'S SOME KINDA CRIME GENIUS, HE'S THE FUTURE.
14

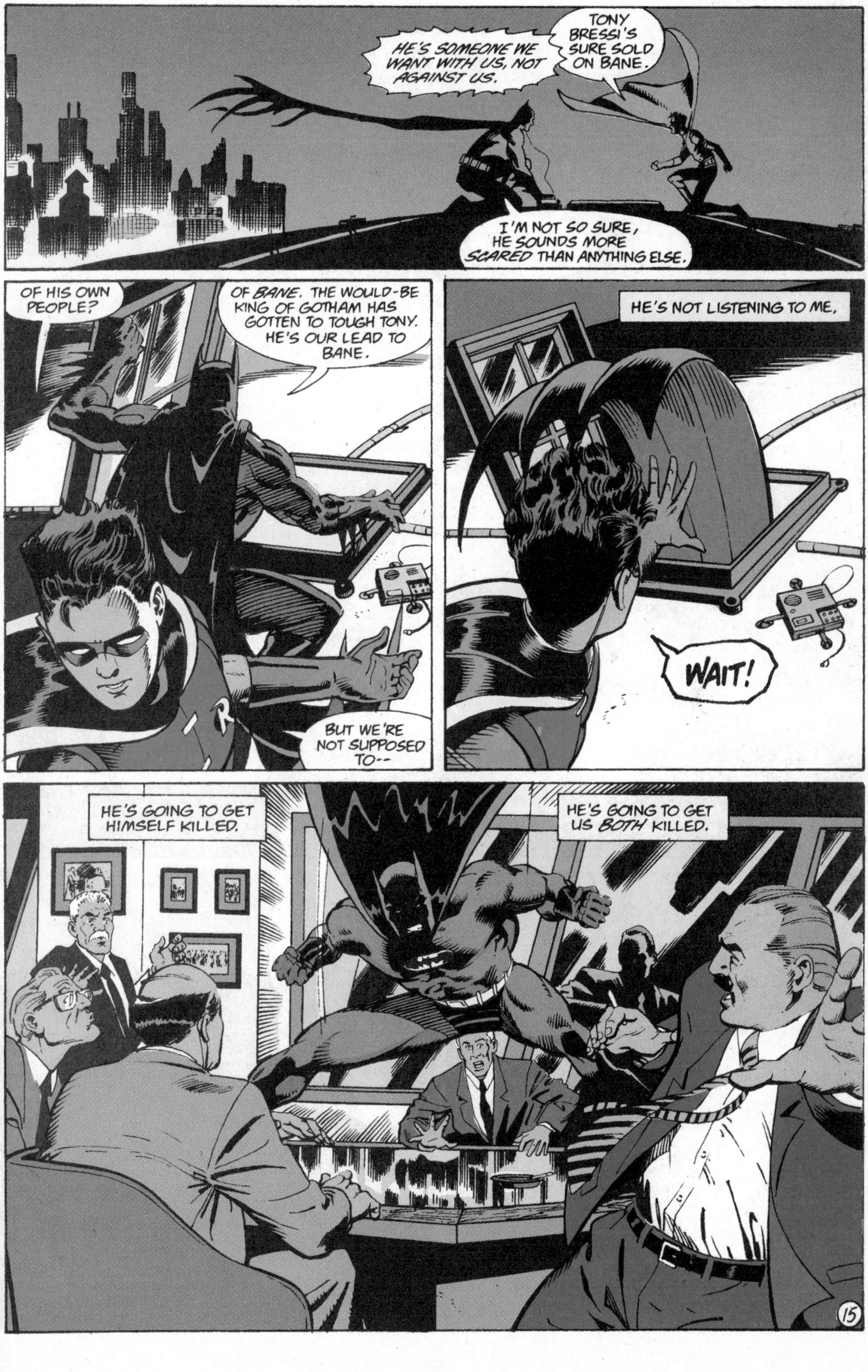
HE'S SOMEONE WE WANT WITH US, NOT AGAINST US.
TONY BRESSI'S SURE SOLD ON BANE.
I'M NOT SO SURE, HE SOUNDS MORE SCARED THAN ANYTHING ELSE.
OF HIS OWN PEOPLE?
OF BANE. THE WOULD-BE KING OF GOTHAM HAS GOTTEN TO TOUGH TONY. HE'S OUR LEAD TO BANE.
BUT WE'RE NOT SUPPOSED TO--
HE'S NOT LISTENING TO ME.
WAIT!
HE'S GOING TO GET HIMSELF KILLED.
HE'S GOING TO GET US BOTH KILLED.
15

THIS SITUATION IS GOING TO BE HARD TO CONTROL.

SHONDRA!

WE DO NOT *NEED* WITNESSES! GET *RID* OF HIM!

NO!

DON'T *HURT* HIM! YOU DON'T WANT HIM, YOU WANT *US!*

YOU CAN'T TAKE THEM! I WON'T *LET* YOU!

AND WHAT WILL YOU *DO* TO ME, EH?

OUT OF THE *WAY*, TAZ. I'LL *KILL* HIM!

YOU GOING TO ROLL OVER MY FOOT WITH YOUR CHAIR, EH?

HEY!

LET ME GET A CLEAR *SHOT* AT HIM!

UNH!

WE'RE SUPPOSED TO ACT AS A TEAM.

I FEEL MORE ALONE THAN WHEN I'M SOLO.

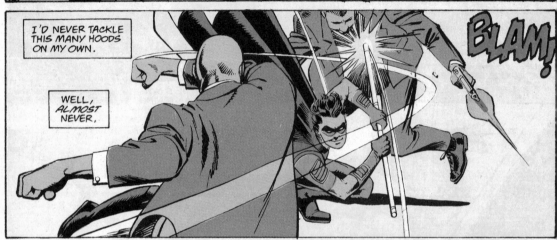

I'D NEVER TACKLE THIS MANY HOODS ON MY OWN.

WELL, ALMOST NEVER.

BLAM!

ROBIN! I'M GOING AFTER TOUGH TONY! CAN YOU HANDLE THINGS HERE?

WELL, ACTUALLY... NO.

HE'S OUR ONLY LEAD TO BANE. I CAN'T LET HIM SLIP AWAY.

SHOULD I GIVE PAUL ANOTHER CHANCE OR TELL BRUCE ABOUT TONIGHT?

18

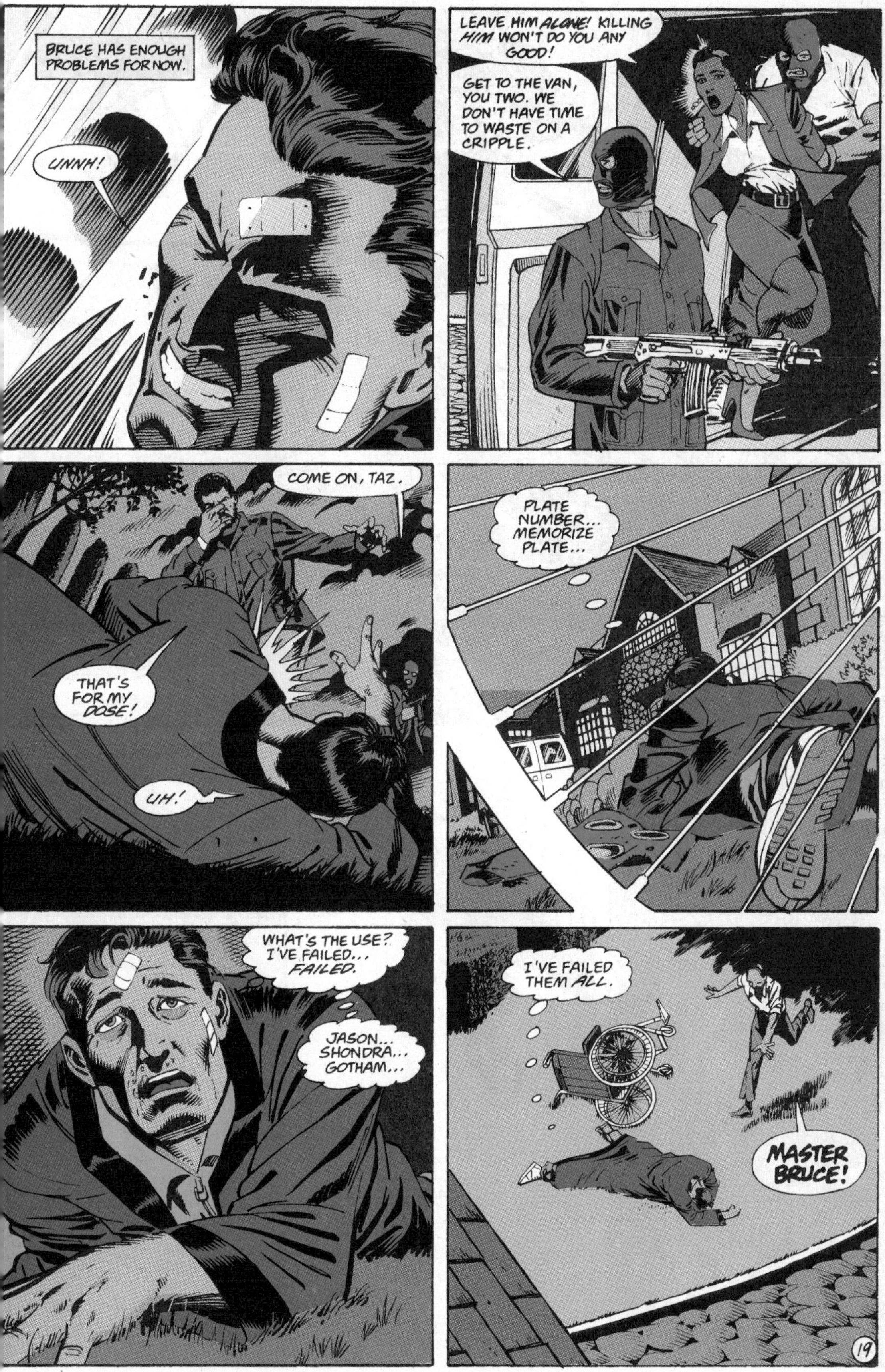

BRUCE HAS ENOUGH PROBLEMS FOR NOW.
UNNH!
LEAVE HIM ALONE! KILLING HIM WON'T DO YOU ANY GOOD!
GET TO THE VAN, YOU TWO. WE DON'T HAVE TIME TO WASTE ON A CRIPPLE.
COME ON, TAZ.
THAT'S FOR MY DOSE!
UH!
PLATE NUMBER... MEMORIZE PLATE...
WHAT'S THE USE? I'VE FAILED... FAILED.
JASON... SHONDRA... GOTHAM...
I'VE FAILED THEM ALL.
MASTER BRUCE!
19

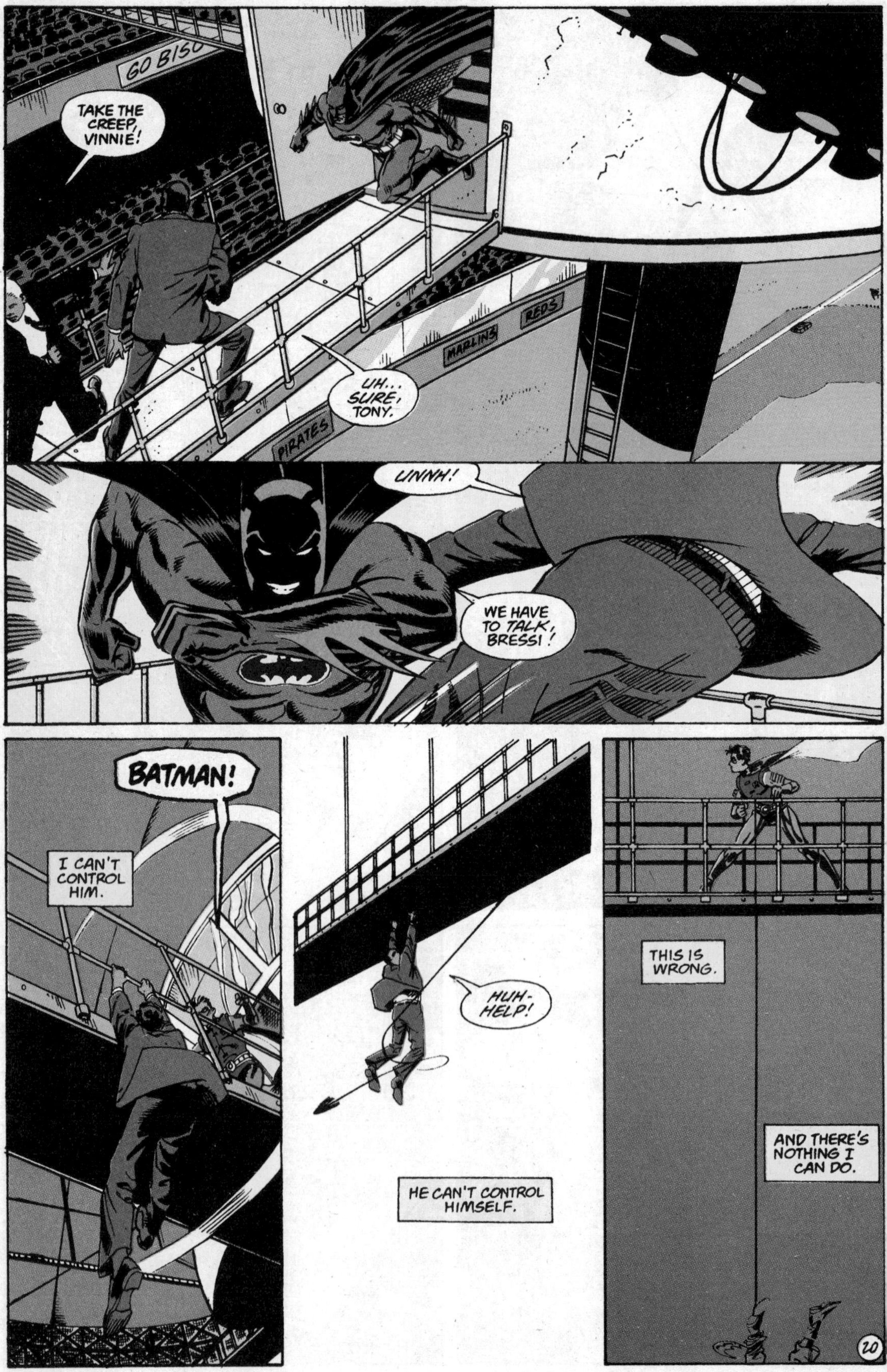

GO BISO
TAKE THE CREEP, VINNIE!
UH... SURE, TONY.
MARLINS
REDS
PIRATES
UNNH!
WE HAVE TO TALK, BRESSI!
BATMAN!
I CAN'T CONTROL HIM.
HUH-HELP!
HE CAN'T CONTROL HIMSELF.
THIS IS WRONG.
AND THERE'S NOTHING I CAN DO.
20

WHAT DID HE DO TO YOU? WHY ARE YOU SO SCARED OF HIM?

I--I DON'T KNOW WHO YOU'RE *TALKING* ABOUT!

BANE.

YOU'RE SO *TERRIFIED* OF HIM YOU'RE TRYING TO GET THE OTHERS TO KNUCKLE UNDER TO HIM. TO PAY TRIBUTE.

YOU WERE AN *IRON MAN*, BRESSI. YOU BEAT DOWN SOME OF THE STRONGEST CRIME BOSSES IN GOTHAM TO GET WHERE YOU ARE.

WHAT'S THE *HOLD* HE HAS ON YOU, BRESSI? TALK OR *DIE!*

YOU *CAN'T!* WE DON'T *WORK* THAT WAY!

THEN MAYBE WE SHOULD START RIGHT NOW.

I DIDN'T *ASK* YOU TO COME ALONG.

MY *KIDS!*

JEEZE... HE'S GOT MY KIDS...

HE SAID HE'D SEND ME THEIR *EYES*... IF I DIDN'T GET THE OTHERS TO TOE THE LINE...

NOW WE'RE GETTING SOMEWHERE.

21.

113

114

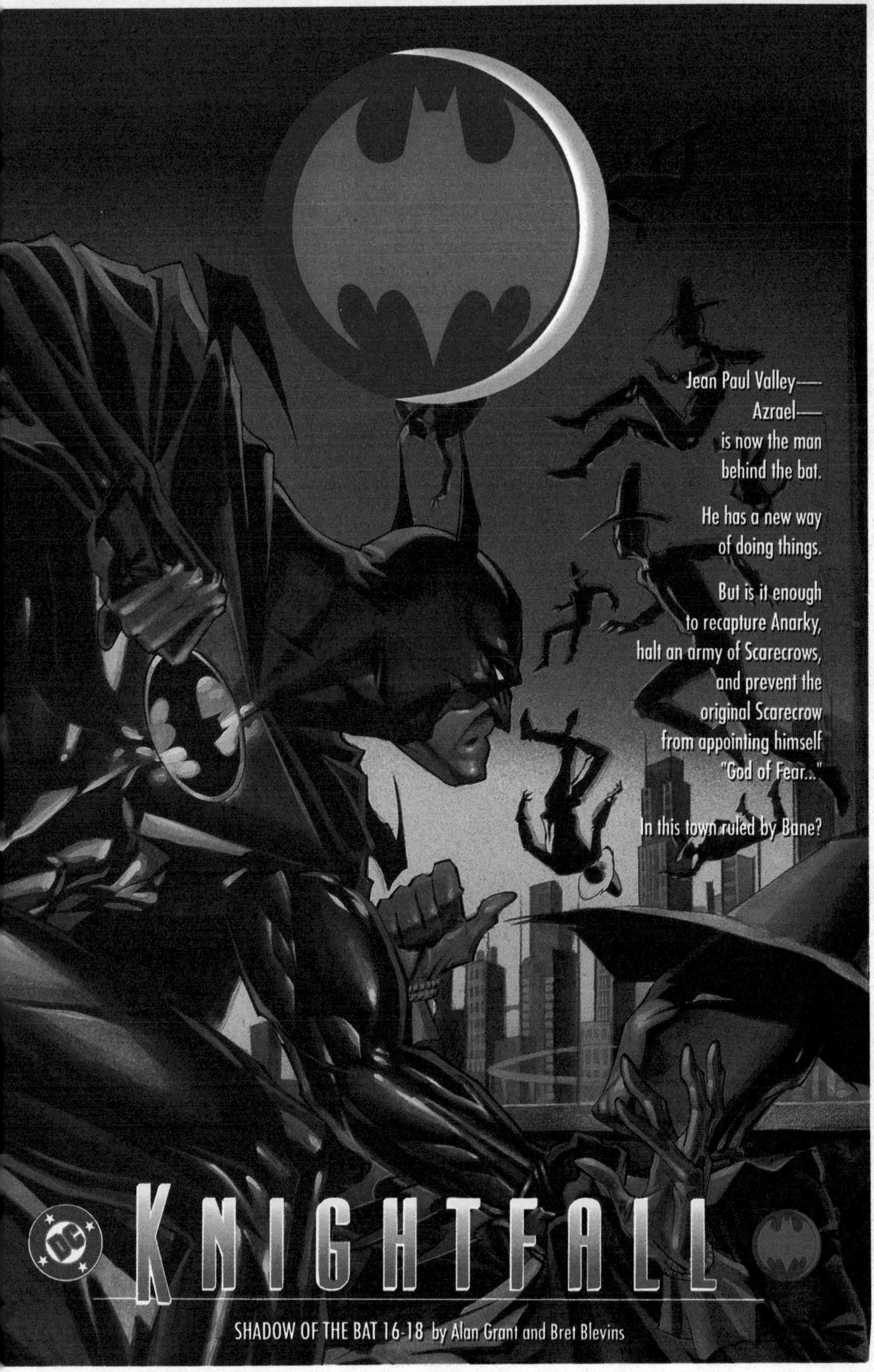
Jean Paul Valley—
Azrael—
is now the man
behind the bat.
He has a new way
of doing things.
But is it enough
to recapture Anarky,
halt an army of Scarecrows,
and prevent the
original Scarecrow
from appointing himself
"God of Fear..."
In this town ruled by Bane?
KNIGHTFALL
SHADOW OF THE BAT 16-18 by Alan Grant and Bret Blevins

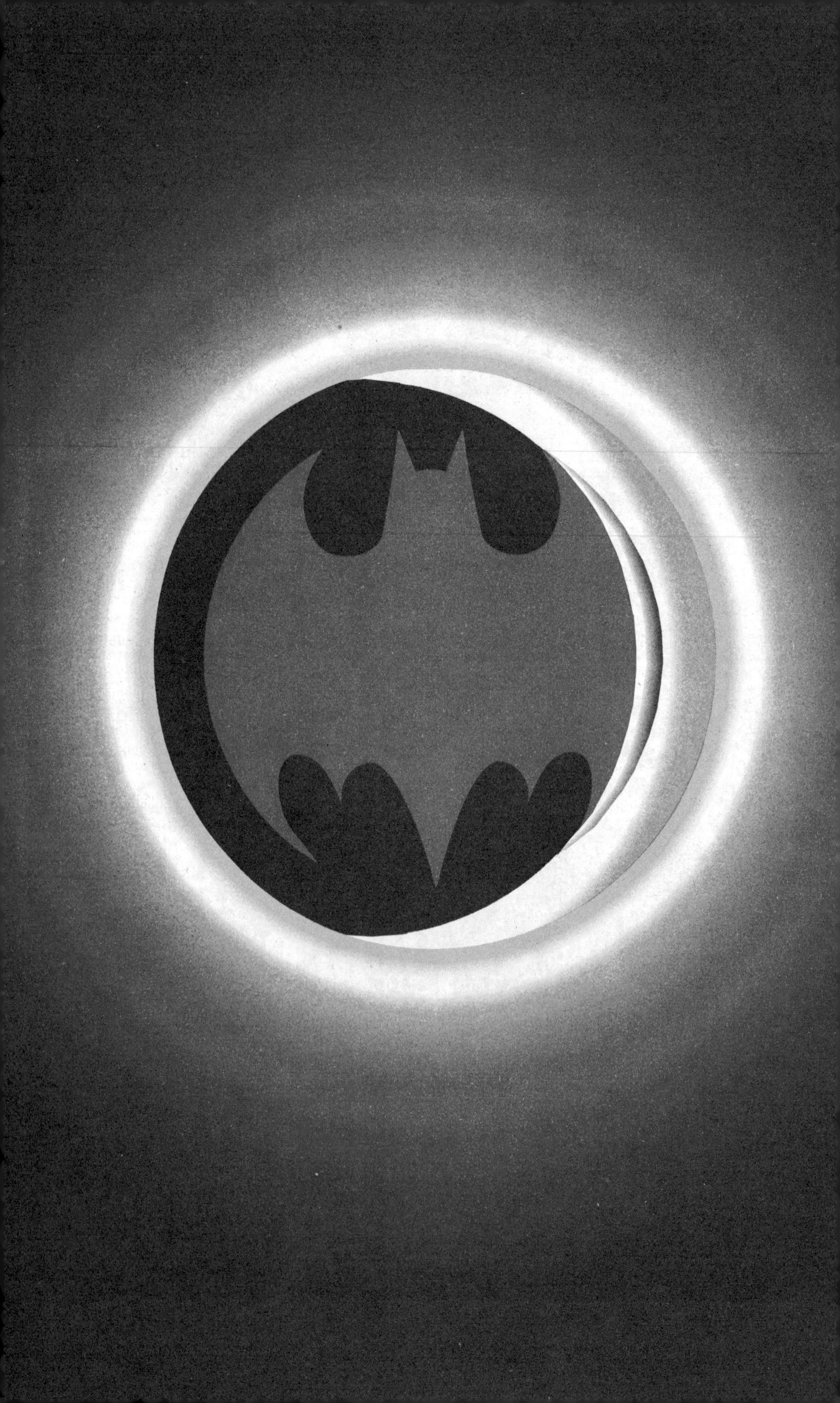

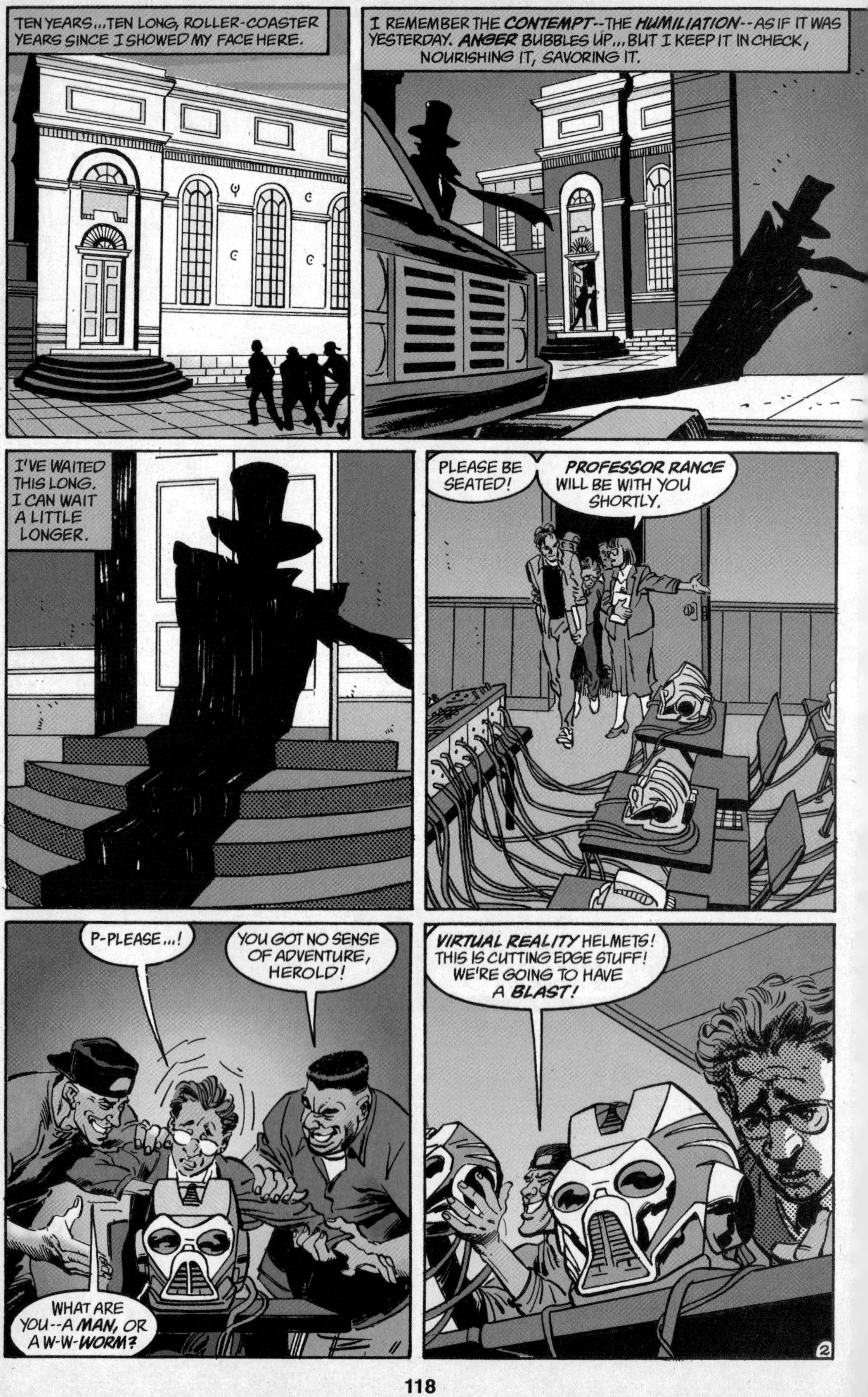
TEN YEARS...TEN LONG, ROLLER-COASTER YEARS SINCE I SHOWED MY FACE HERE.
I REMEMBER THE CONTEMPT--THE HUMILIATION--AS IF IT WAS YESTERDAY. ANGER BUBBLES UP... BUT I KEEP IT IN CHECK, NOURISHING IT, SAVORING IT.
I'VE WAITED THIS LONG. I CAN WAIT A LITTLE LONGER.
PLEASE BE SEATED!
PROFESSOR RANCE WILL BE WITH YOU SHORTLY.
P-PLEASE...!
YOU GOT NO SENSE OF ADVENTURE, HEROLD!
WHAT ARE YOU--A MAN, OR A W-W-WORM?
VIRTUAL REALITY HELMETS! THIS IS CUTTING EDGE STUFF! WE'RE GOING TO HAVE A BLAST!
2

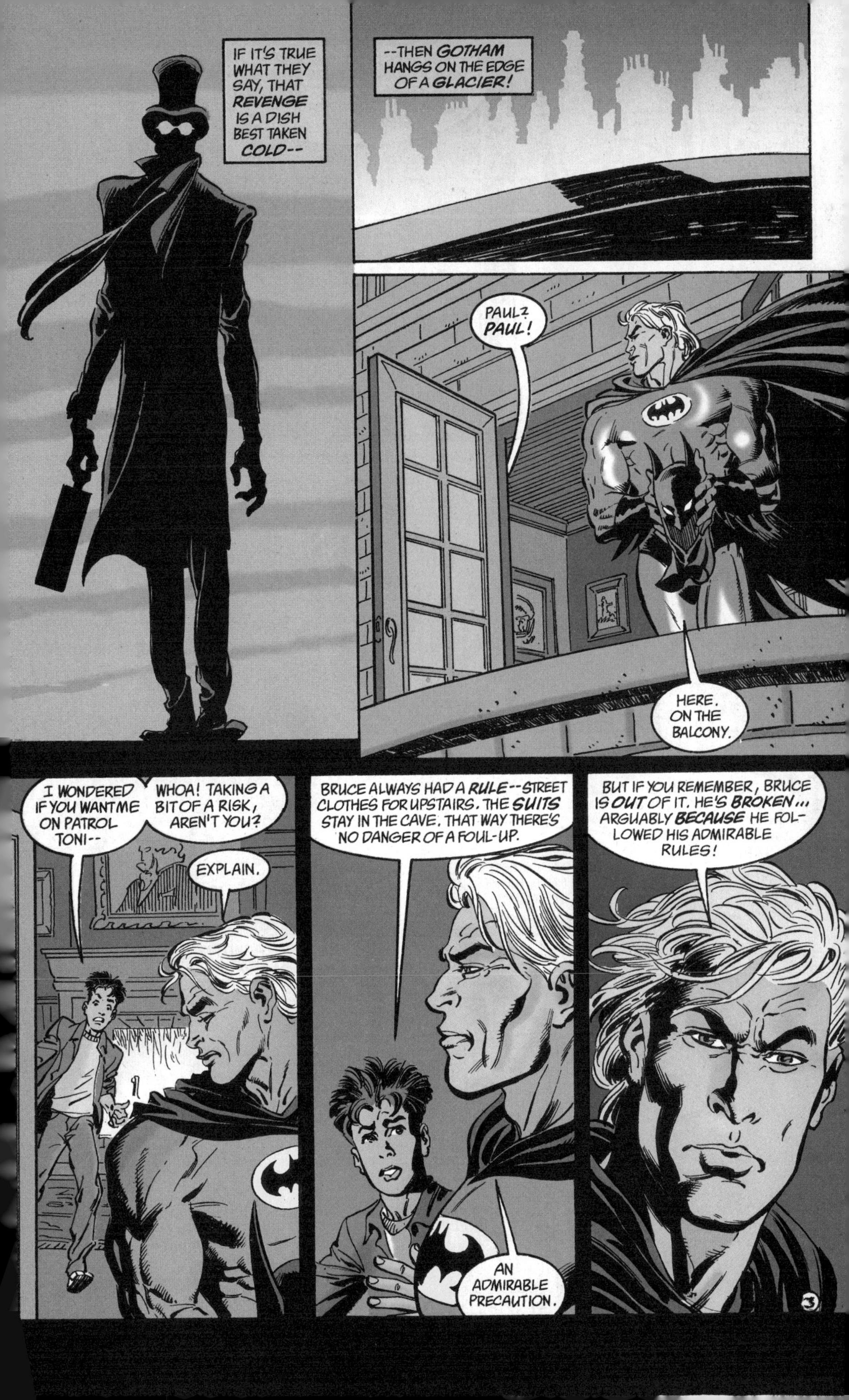

IF IT'S TRUE WHAT THEY SAY, THAT REVENGE IS A DISH BEST TAKEN COLD--
--THEN GOTHAM HANGS ON THE EDGE OF A GLACIER!
PAUL? PAUL!
HERE. ON THE BALCONY.
I WONDERED IF YOU WANT ME ON PATROL TONI--
WHOA! TAKING A BIT OF A RISK, AREN'T YOU?
EXPLAIN.
BRUCE ALWAYS HAD A RULE--STREET CLOTHES FOR UPSTAIRS. THE SUITS STAY IN THE CAVE. THAT WAY THERE'S NO DANGER OF A FOUL-UP.
AN ADMIRABLE PRECAUTION.
BUT IF YOU REMEMBER, BRUCE IS OUT OF IT. HE'S BROKEN... ARGUABLY BECAUSE HE FOLLOWED HIS ADMIRABLE RULES!
3

"BUT MOST OF ALL, AFRAID FOR *JEAN PAUL VALLEY*.

"YOU MAY BE WEARING THE *SUIT*, PAUL. YOU MAY EVEN HAVE BRUCE WAYNE'S *BLESSING*--

"BUT IF YOU WANT TO BE EVEN *HALF* THE MAN HE IS, YOU STILL HAVE A *WHOLE* LOT TO *LEARN!*"

THE CREEPS JUST NEVER GET IT!

THE ESSENCE OF ANARCHY IS *SURPRISE*-- SPONTANEOUS ACTION...

...EVEN WHEN IT *DOES* REQUIRE A LITTLE *PLANNING!*

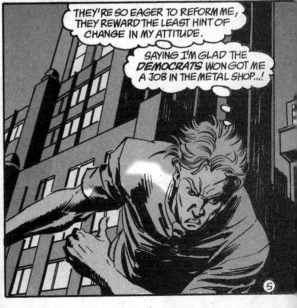

THEY'RE SO EAGER TO REFORM ME, THEY REWARD THE LEAST HINT OF CHANGE IN MY ATTITUDE.

SAYING I'M GLAD THE *DEMOCRATS* WON GOT ME A JOB IN THE METAL SHOP...!

5

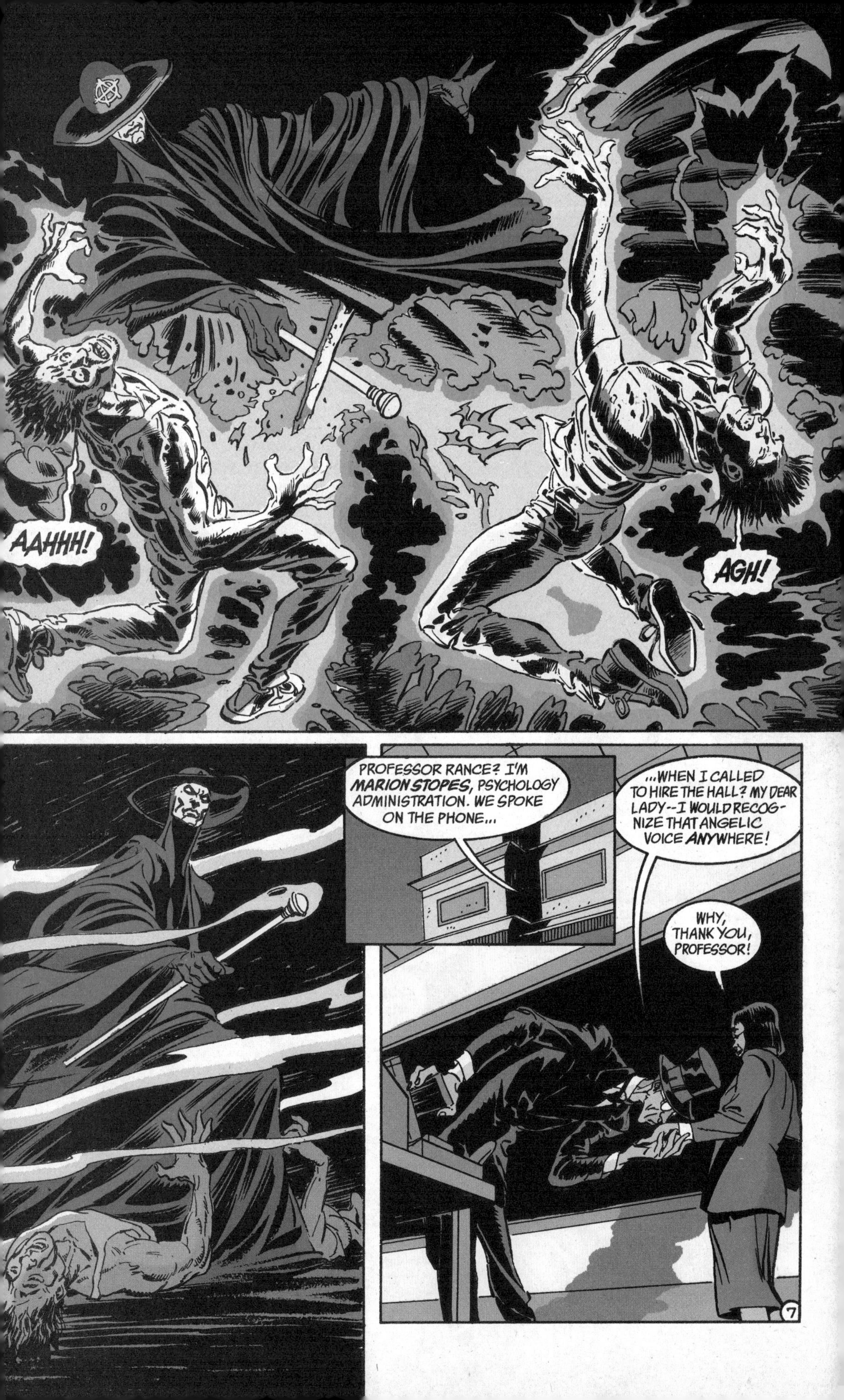
AAHHH!
AGH!
PROFESSOR RANCE? I'M MARION STOPES, PSYCHOLOGY ADMINISTRATION. WE SPOKE ON THE PHONE...
...WHEN I CALLED TO HIRE THE HALL? MY DEAR LADY--I WOULD RECOGNIZE THAT ANGELIC VOICE ANYWHERE!
WHY, THANK YOU, PROFESSOR!

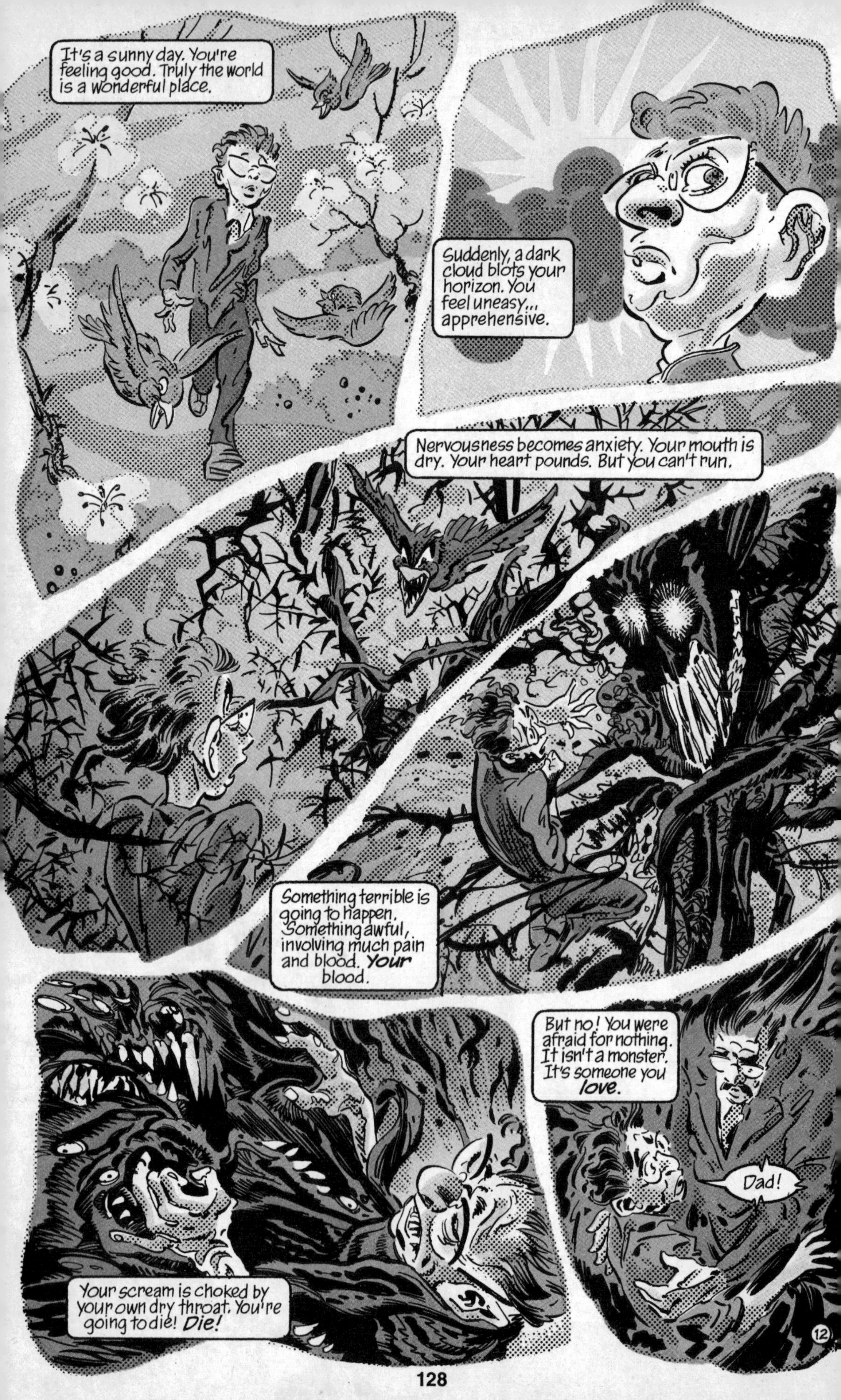
It's a sunny day. You're feeling good. Truly the world is a wonderful place.
Suddenly, a dark cloud blots your horizon. You feel uneasy... apprehensive.
Nervousness becomes anxiety. Your mouth is dry. Your heart pounds. But you can't run.
Something terrible is going to happen. Something awful, involving much pain and blood. *Your* blood.
Your scream is choked by your own dry throat. You're going to die! *Die!*
But no! You were afraid for nothing. It isn't a monster. It's someone you *love*.
Dad!
12

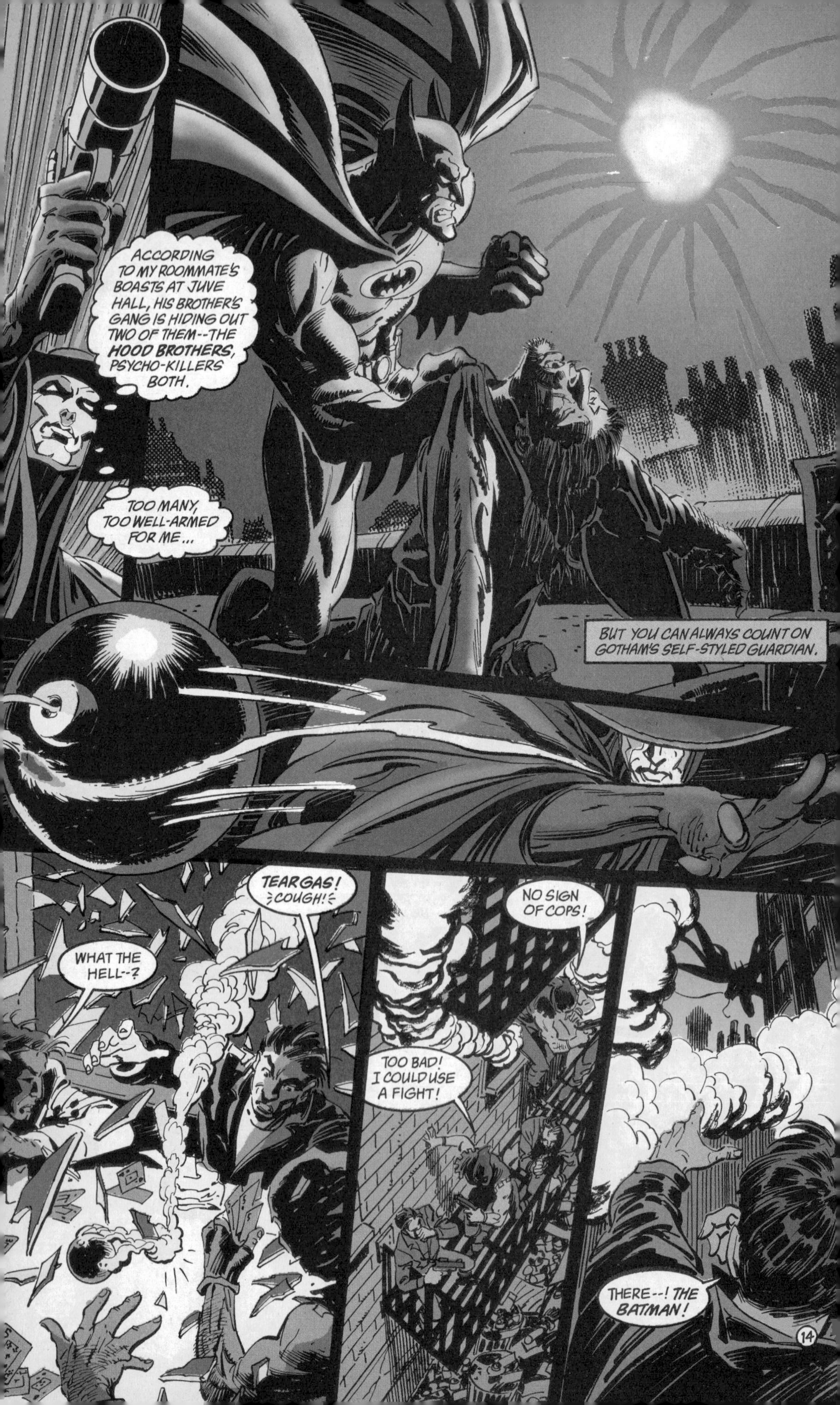
ACCORDING TO MY ROOMMATE'S BOASTS AT JUVE HALL, HIS BROTHER'S GANG IS HIDING OUT TWO OF THEM--THE **HOOD BROTHERS**, PSYCHO-KILLERS BOTH.
TOO MANY, TOO WELL-ARMED FOR ME...
BUT YOU CAN ALWAYS COUNT ON GOTHAM'S SELF-STYLED GUARDIAN.
WHAT THE HELL--?
TEARGAS! COUGH!
NO SIGN OF COPS!
TOO BAD! I COULD USE A FIGHT!
THERE--! THE **BATMAN**!
14

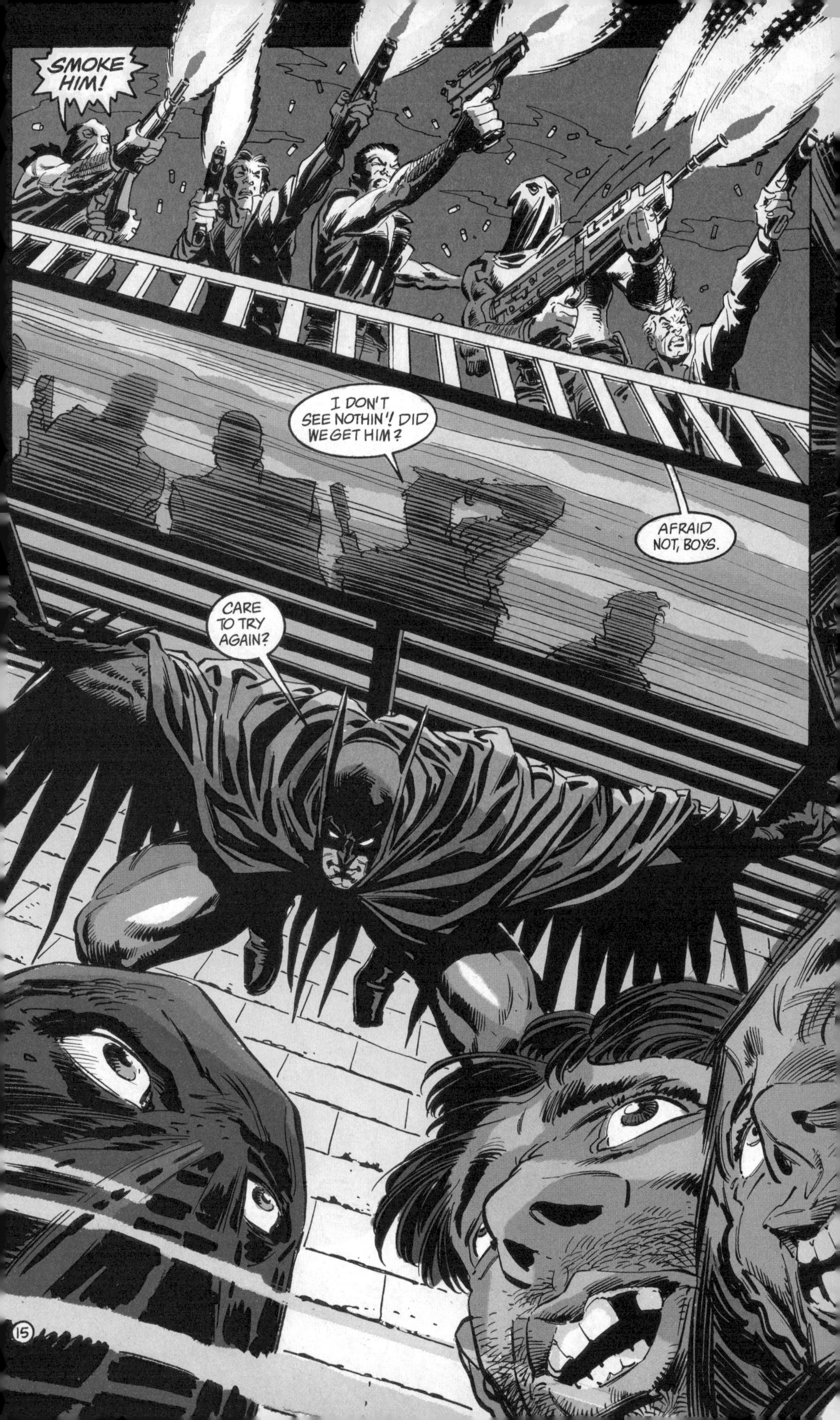
SMOKE HIM!
I DON'T SEE NOTHIN'! DID WE GET HIM?
AFRAID NOT, BOYS.
CARE TO TRY AGAIN?

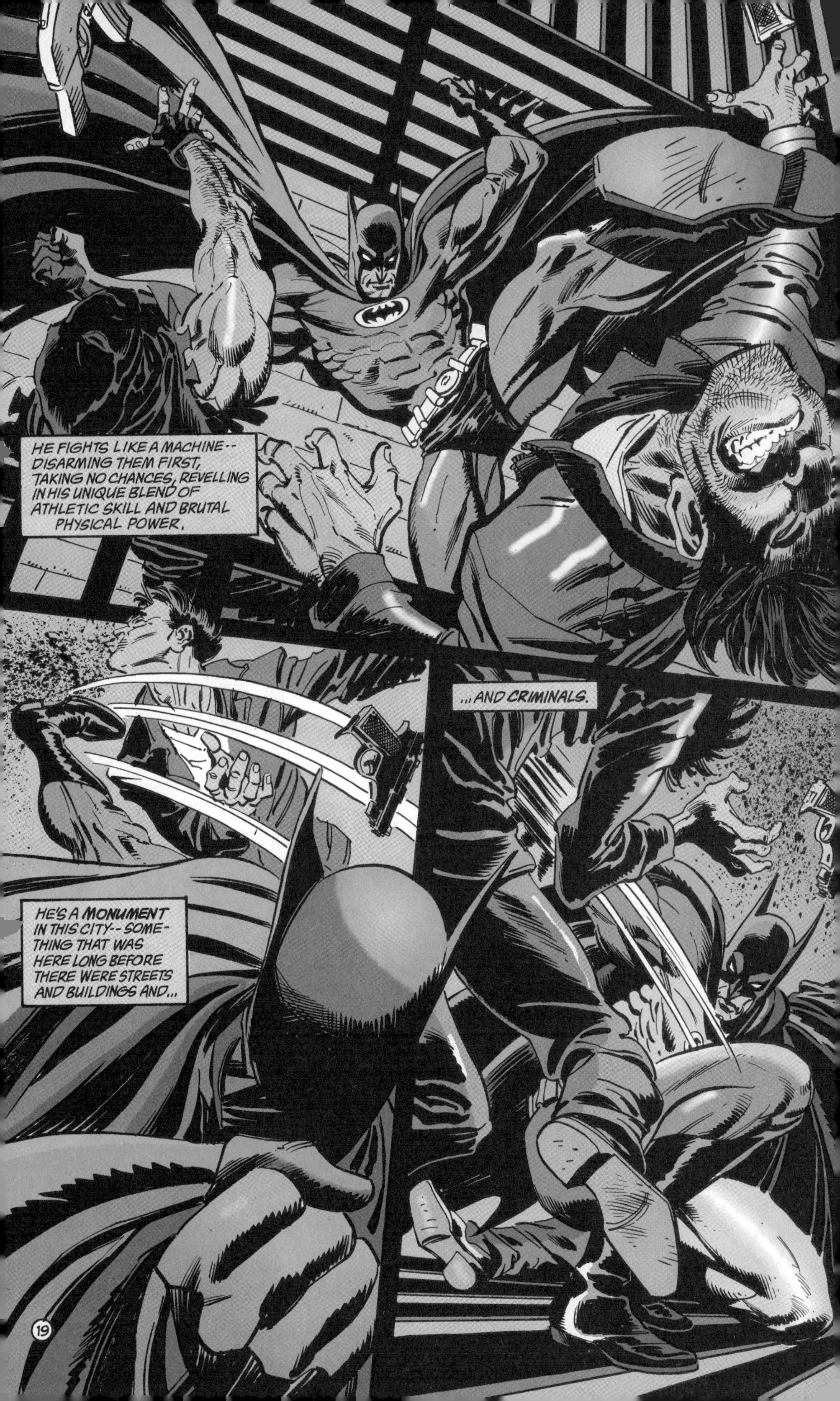
HE FIGHTS LIKE A MACHINE-- DISARMING THEM FIRST, TAKING NO CHANCES, REVELLING IN HIS UNIQUE BLEND OF ATHLETIC SKILL AND BRUTAL PHYSICAL POWER.
HE'S A MONUMENT IN THIS CITY-- SOMETHING THAT WAS HERE LONG BEFORE THERE WERE STREETS AND BUILDINGS AND...
...AND CRIMINALS.
19

NEXT   I, SCARECROW!

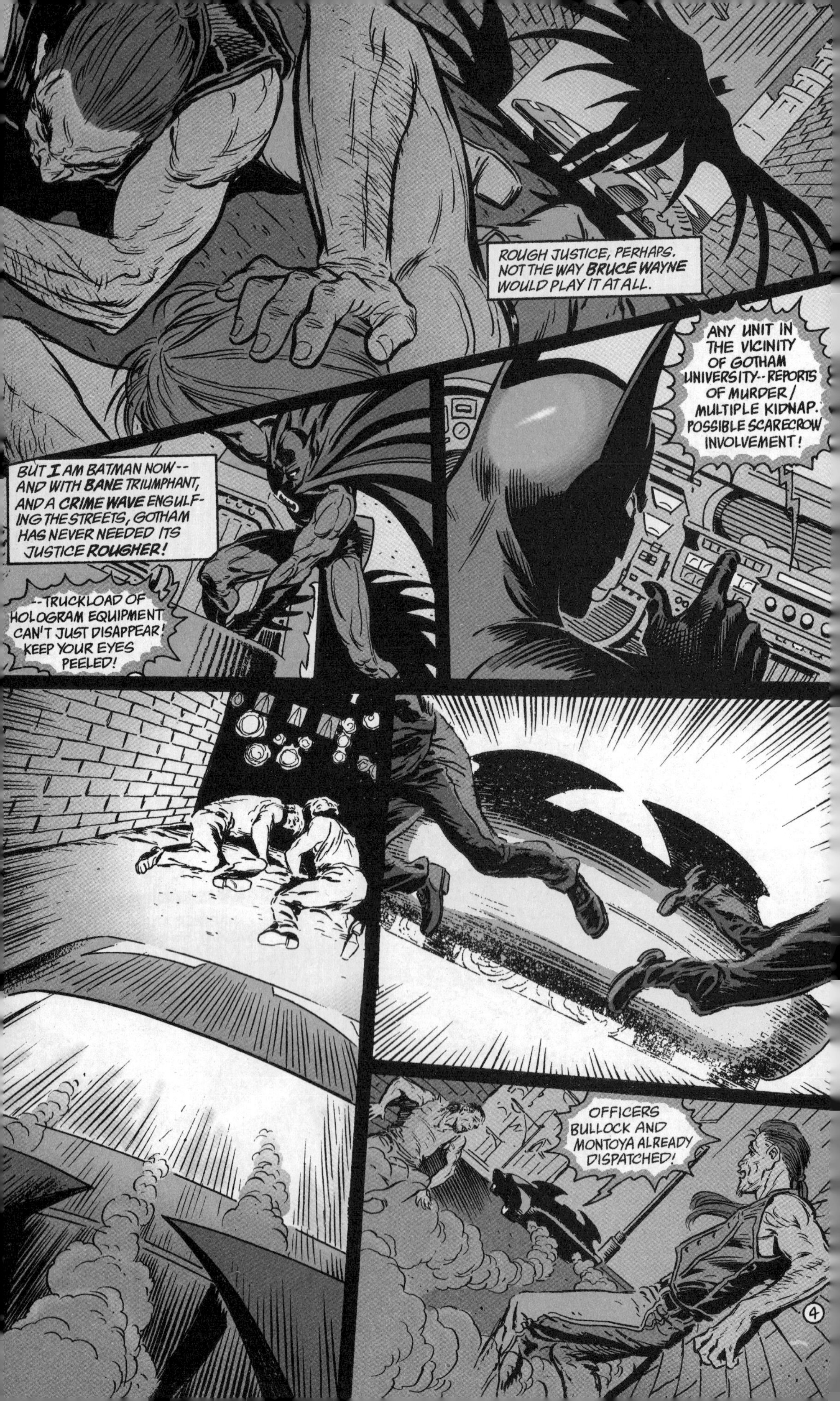

ROUGH JUSTICE, PERHAPS. NOT THE WAY BRUCE WAYNE WOULD PLAY IT AT ALL.
ANY UNIT IN THE VICINITY OF GOTHAM UNIVERSITY--REPORTS OF MURDER/ MULTIPLE KIDNAP. POSSIBLE SCARECROW INVOLVEMENT!
BUT I AM BATMAN NOW--AND WITH BANE TRIUMPHANT, AND A CRIME WAVE ENGULFING THE STREETS, GOTHAM HAS NEVER NEEDED ITS JUSTICE ROUGHER!
--TRUCKLOAD OF HOLOGRAM EQUIPMENT CAN'T JUST DISAPPEAR! KEEP YOUR EYES PEELED!
OFFICERS BULLOCK AND MONTOYA ALREADY DISPATCHED!

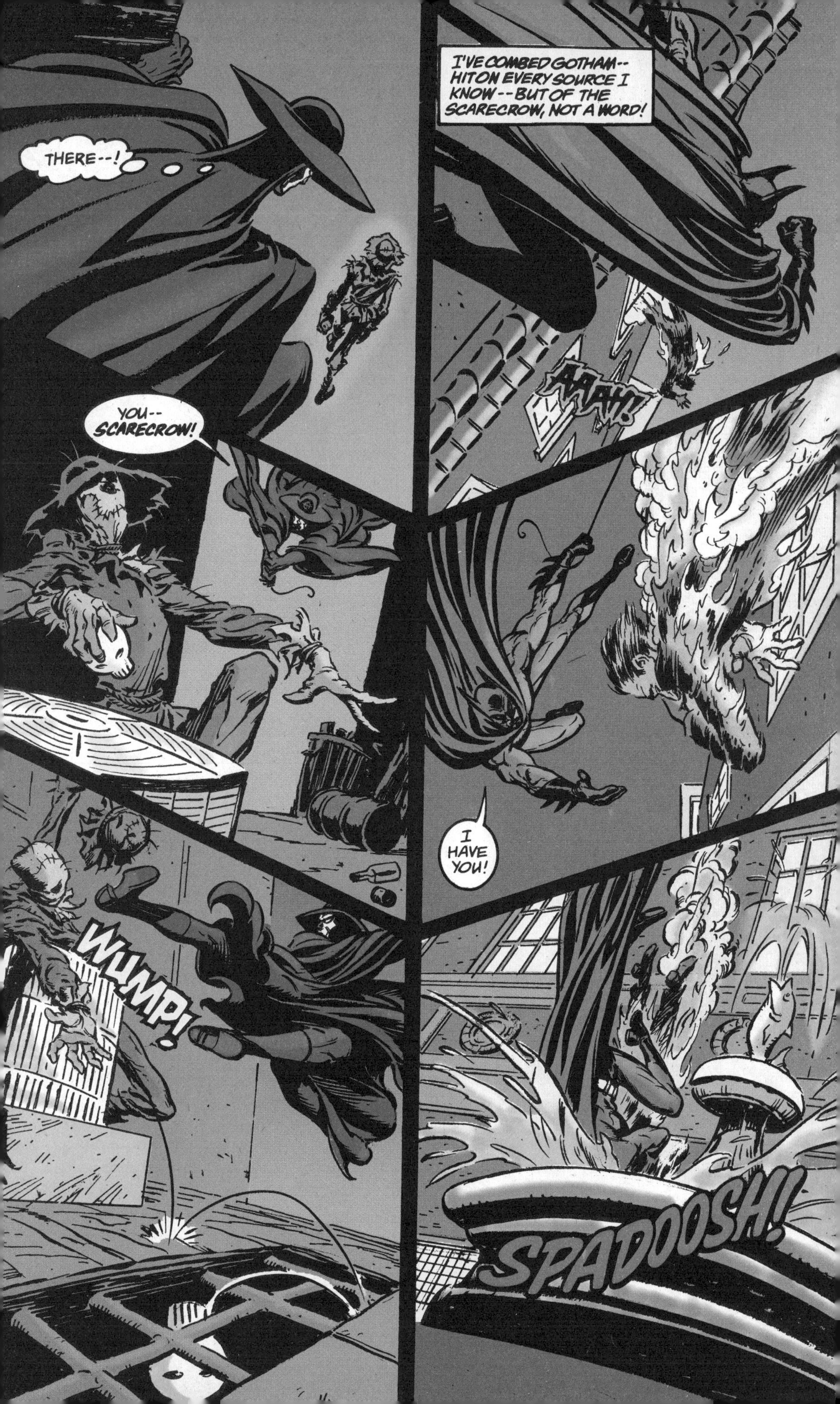
THERE--!
YOU--
SCARECROW!
WUMP!
I'VE COMBED GOTHAM--
HIT ON EVERY SOURCE I
KNOW--BUT OF THE
SCARECROW, NOT A WORD!
AAAH!
I
HAVE
YOU!
SPADOOSH!

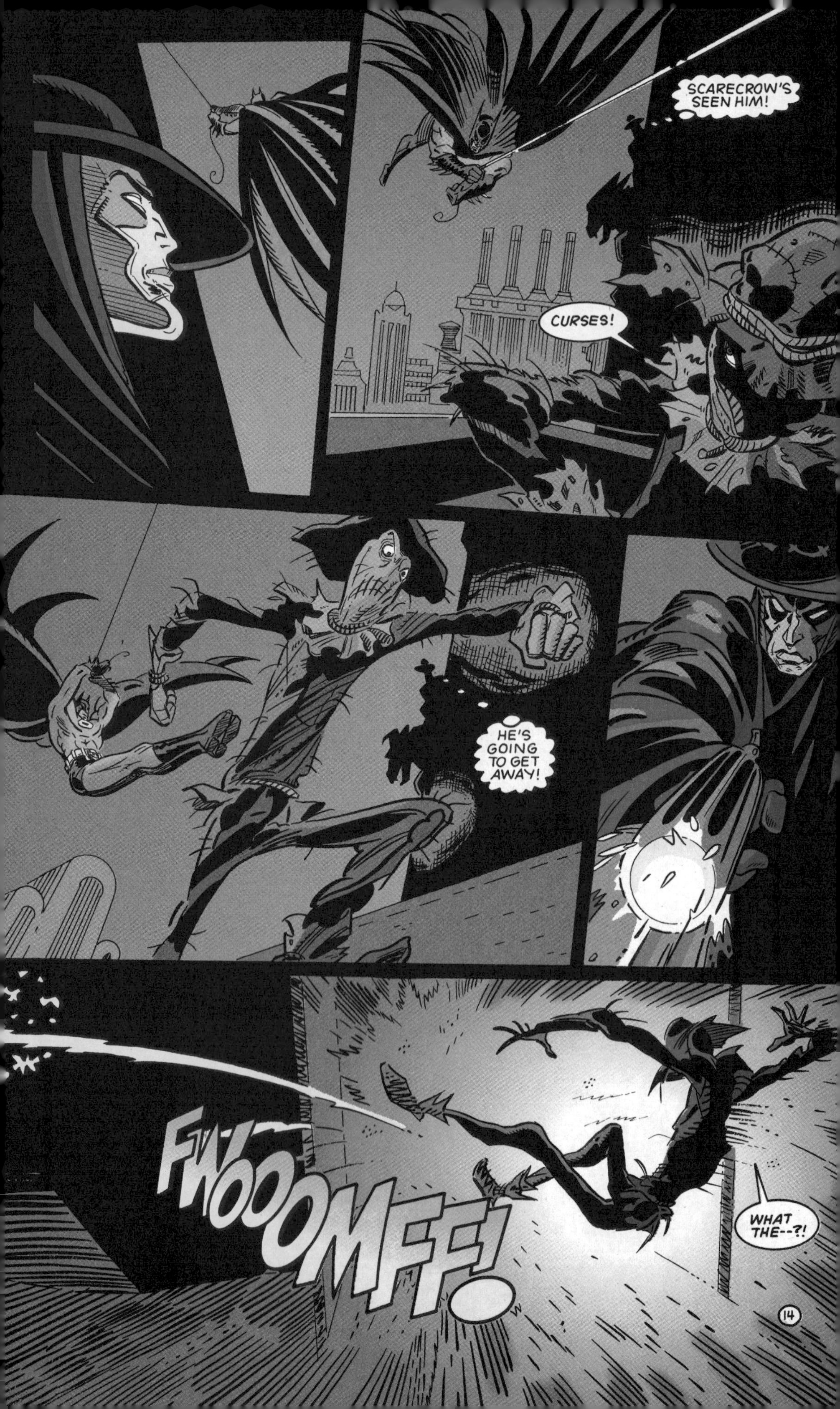
SCARECROW'S SEEN HIM!
CURSES!
HE'S GOING TO GET AWAY!
FWOOOMFF!
WHAT THE--?!
14

--I MEANT IT!

WAKK!

I'M NOT ONE OF YOUR CHEAP STREET PUNKS, BATMAN!

I STAND POISED ON THE EDGE OF GODHOOD--

I'VE ALWAYS PREFERRED TO RELY ON MY MIND'S NATURAL GENIUS-- BUT I'M NOT AVERSE TO A SPOT OF ROUGH AND TUMBLE!

THE CRANE STYLE--

--AND NO MERE MORTAL WILL STOP ME!

--APT, DON'T YOU THINK?

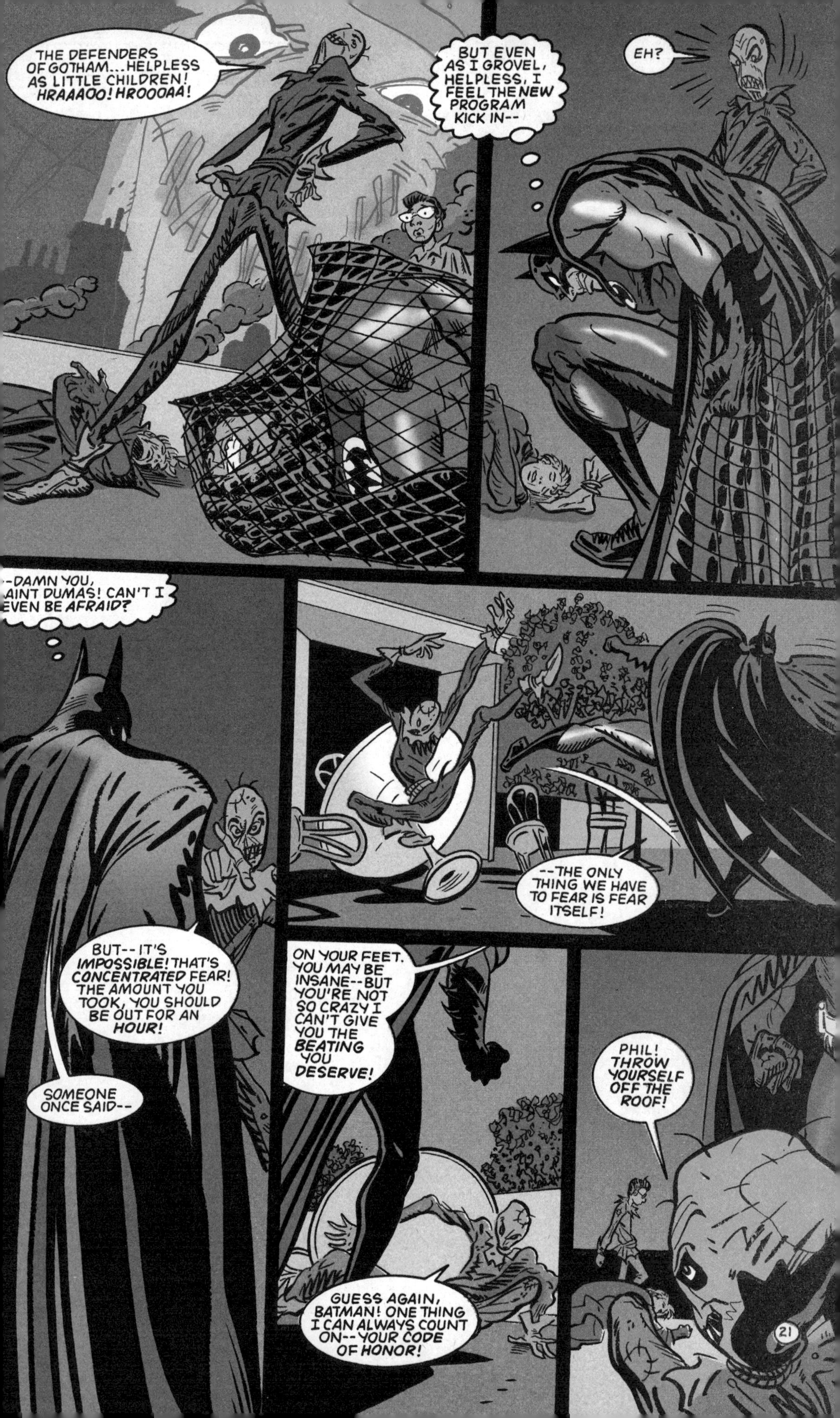
THE DEFENDERS OF GOTHAM... HELPLESS AS LITTLE CHILDREN! HRAAAOO! HROOOAA!
BUT EVEN AS I GROVEL, HELPLESS, I FEEL THE NEW PROGRAM KICK IN--
EH?
--DAMN YOU, AINT DUMAS! CAN'T I EVEN BE AFRAID?
BUT-- IT'S IMPOSSIBLE! THAT'S CONCENTRATED FEAR! THE AMOUNT YOU TOOK, YOU SHOULD BE OUT FOR AN HOUR!
SOMEONE ONCE SAID--
--THE ONLY THING WE HAVE TO FEAR IS FEAR ITSELF!
ON YOUR FEET. YOU MAY BE INSANE--BUT YOU'RE NOT SO CRAZY I CAN'T GIVE YOU THE BEATING YOU DESERVE!
GUESS AGAIN, BATMAN! ONE THING I CAN ALWAYS COUNT ON-- YOUR CODE OF HONOR!
PHIL! THROW YOURSELF OFF THE ROOF!
21

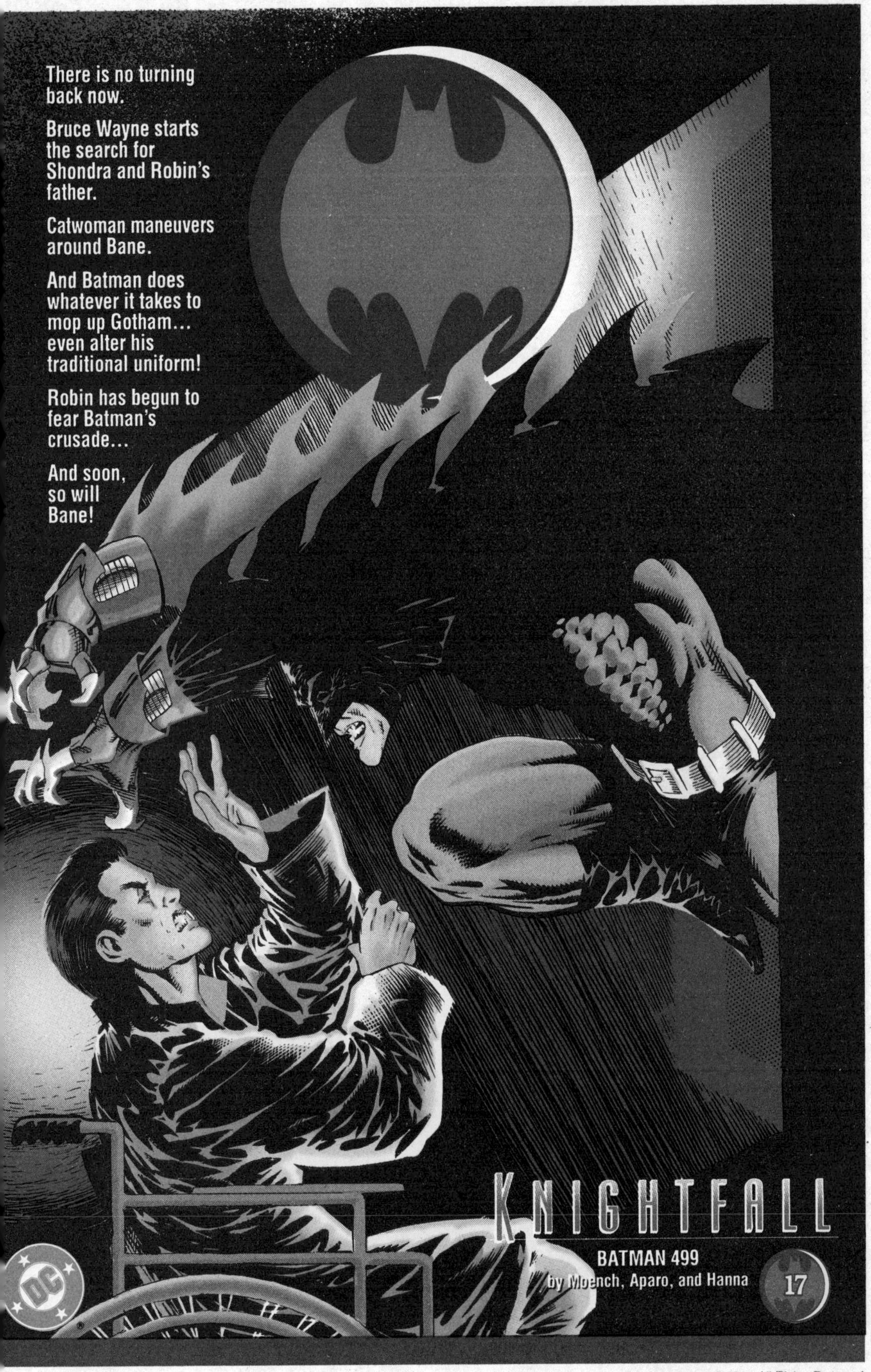
There is no turning back now.
Bruce Wayne starts the search for Shondra and Robin's father.
Catwoman maneuvers around Bane.
And Batman does whatever it takes to mop up Gotham... even alter his traditional uniform!
Robin has begun to fear Batman's crusade...
And soon, so will Bane!
KNIGHTFALL
BATMAN 499
by Moench, Aparo, and Hanna
17
DC

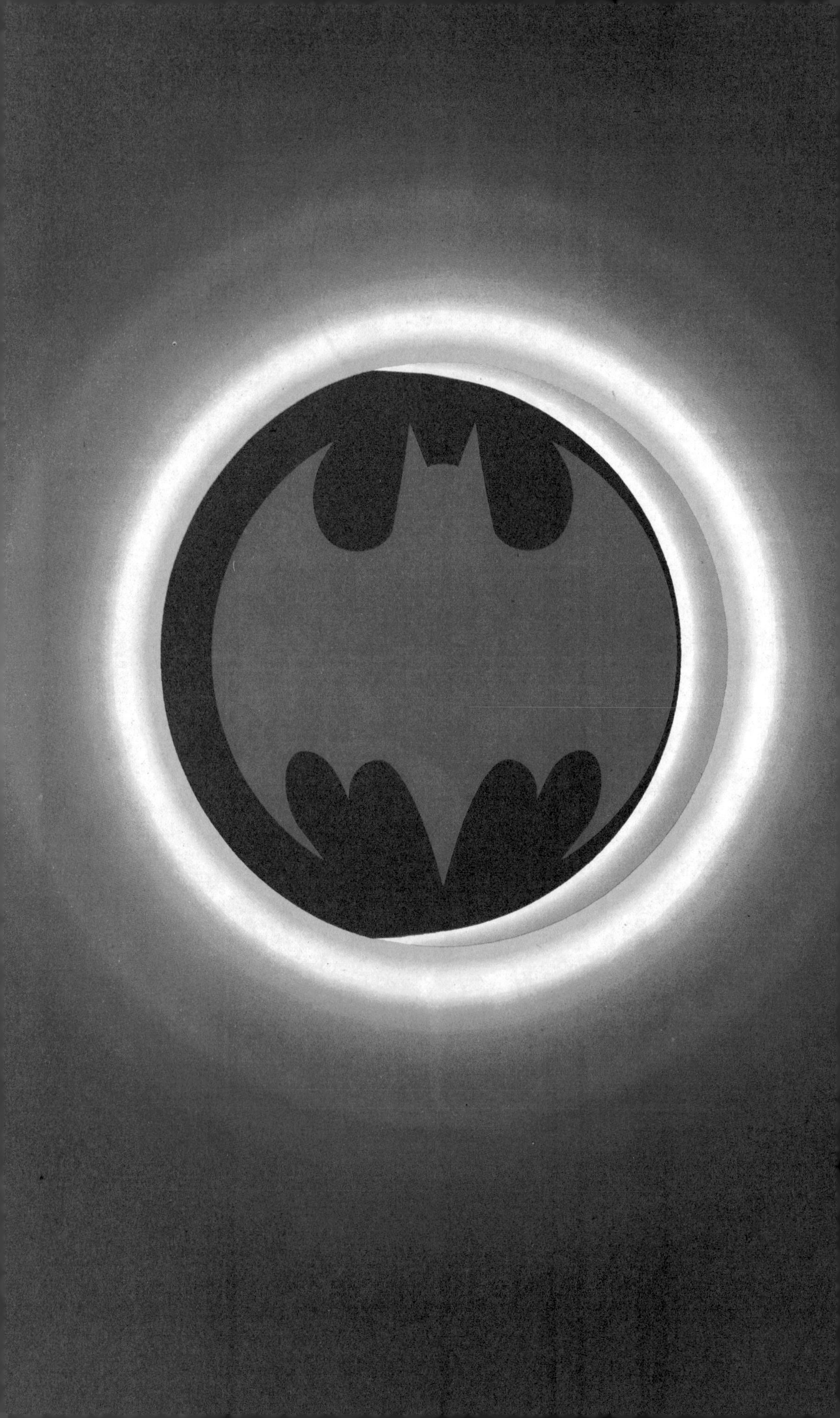

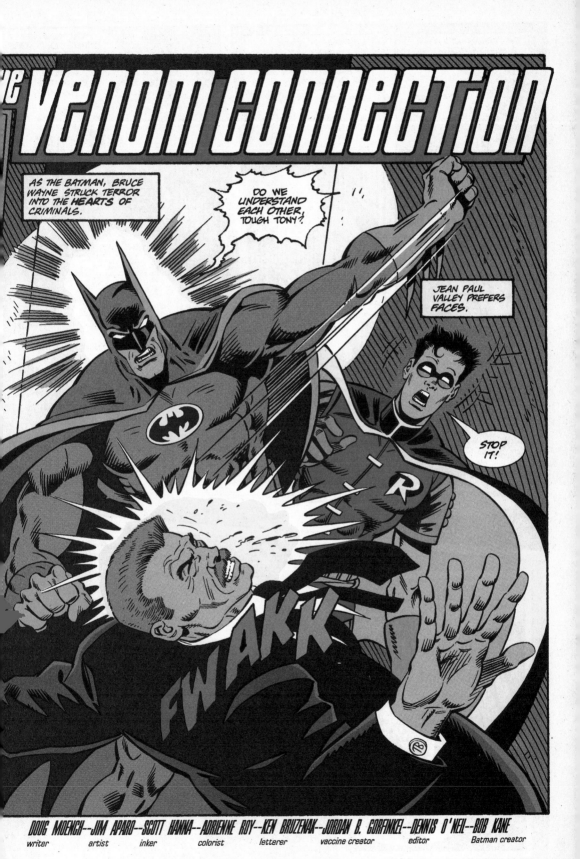

THE VENOM CONNECTION

AS THE BATMAN, BRUCE WAYNE STRUCK TERROR INTO THE *HEARTS* OF CRIMINALS.

DO WE UNDERSTAND EACH OTHER, TOUGH TONY?

JEAN PAUL VALLEY PREFERS *FACES.*

STOP IT!

FWAKK

DOUG MOENCH--JIM APARO--SCOTT HANNA--ADRIENNE ROY--KEN BRUZENAK--JORDAN B. GORFINKEL--DENNIS O'NEIL--BOB KANE

writer   artist   inker   colorist   letterer   vaccine creator   editor   Batman creator

IT'S TURNING INTO A NIGHTMARE...

THERE'S NO NEED TO BEAT HIM LIKE--

HE'S OUT OF CONTROL-- AND THERE'S NOT MUCH MORE I CAN SAY IN FRONT OF BRESSI WITHOUT BLOW-ING OUR COVER.

NOW--DO WE HAVE AN UNDERSTANDING, TOUGH TONY?

YOU KEEP THE OTHER DONS HERE LONG ENOUGH FOR ME TO CONVINCE BANE WE'RE HANDING OVER THE UNIONS...

YOU SHUT UP!

...THE WHOLE IDEA OF THE BATMAN-ROBIN TEAM IS NOTHING BUT A BAD JOKE.

Y-YEAH... SURE...

...SO HE HANDS OVER MY KIDS.

...AND WHEN THE RELEASE IS SET, YOU LEAVE WORD FOR ME RIGHT HERE.

G-GOT IT.

THEN GET OUT OF HERE--AND START CONTACTING BANE'S PEOPLE!

FORGET YOUR KIDS! YOU CROSS ME ON THIS, TOUGH TONY, AND I'LL MAKE YOU EAT YOUR EYES.

I...I'LL DO IT--YOU KNOW I'LL DO IT--ANYTHING TO GET MY KIDS BACK.

BRUCE WAS TOUGH, BUT NEVER LIKE THIS, WHATEVER THE SCORE, HE PLAYED IT STRAIGHT AND HE WON...

...AT LEAST UNTIL BANE.

SIR, ARE YOU CERTAIN YOU'RE UP TO--?

SHONDRA AND TIM'S FATHER HAVE BEEN KIDNAPPED, ALFRED.

AFTER WHAT I'VE ALREADY BEEN THROUGH, IT'LL TAKE MORE THAN ANOTHER BUMP ON THE HEAD TO STOP ME FROM FINDING THEM.

BUT HOW, SIR? YOU SAID YOU LOST CONSCIOUSNESS BEFORE YOU COULD MEMORIZE THE ABDUCTORS' LICENSE PLATE...

WHICH WAS PROBABLY STOLEN ANYWAY.

IF THERE'S A CLUE TO BE HAD, IT'S IN THIS MASK THEY LEFT BEHIND...

IT WON'T BE EASY... BUT MAYBE BY EXAMINING THE WEAVE OF THE MASK...

...OR EVEN ANALYZING THE BLOOD SOAKED INTO IT...

3

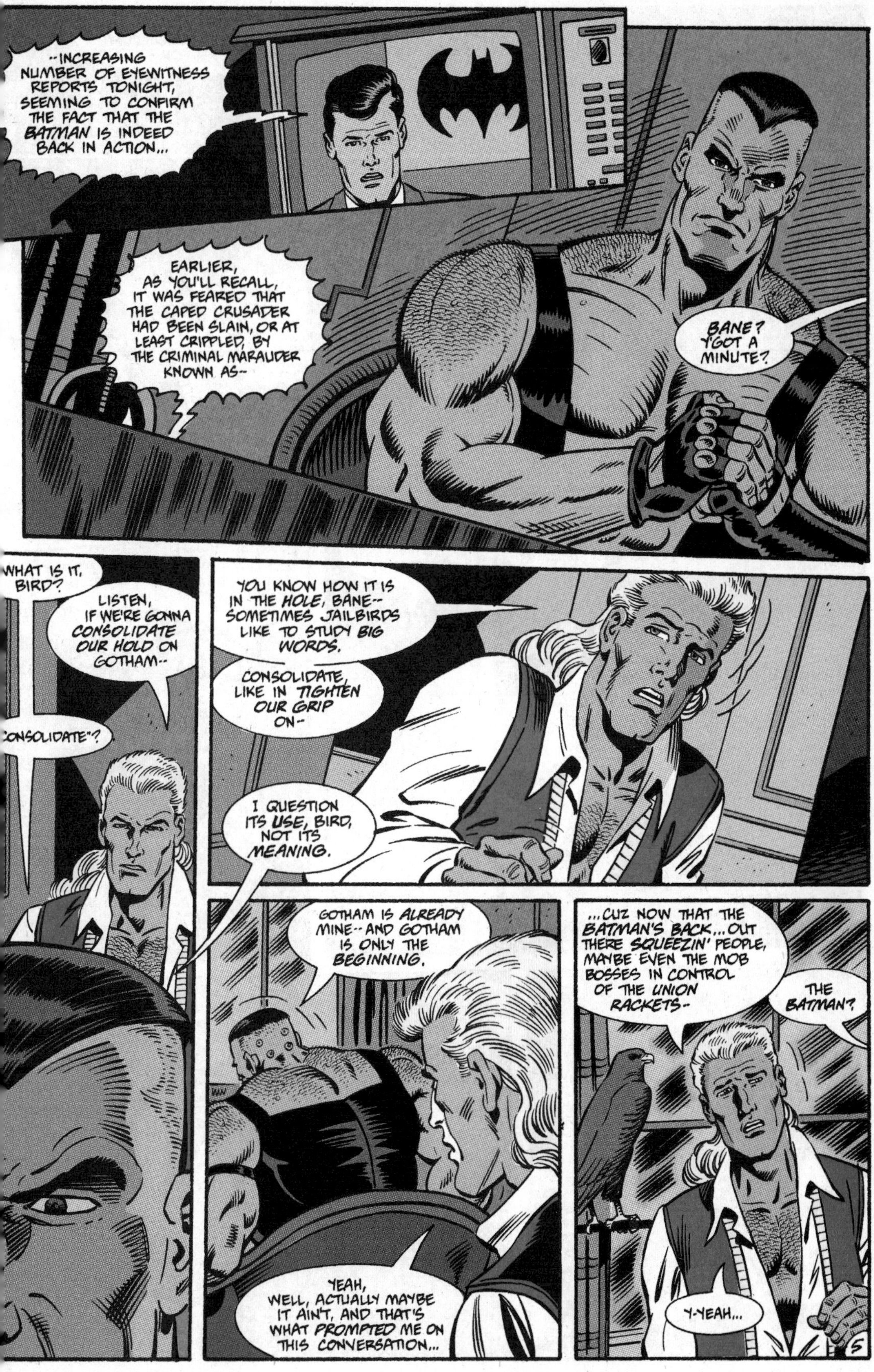
--INCREASING NUMBER OF EYEWITNESS REPORTS TONIGHT, SEEMING TO CONFIRM THE FACT THAT THE BATMAN IS INDEED BACK IN ACTION...
EARLIER, AS YOU'LL RECALL, IT WAS FEARED THAT THE CAPED CRUSADER HAD BEEN SLAIN, OR AT LEAST CRIPPLED, BY THE CRIMINAL MARAUDER KNOWN AS--
BANE? Y'GOT A MINUTE?
WHAT IS IT, BIRD?
LISTEN, IF WE'RE GONNA CONSOLIDATE OUR HOLD ON GOTHAM--
"CONSOLIDATE"?
YOU KNOW HOW IT IS IN THE HOLE, BANE-- SOMETIMES JAILBIRDS LIKE TO STUDY BIG WORDS.
CONSOLIDATE, LIKE IN TIGHTEN OUR GRIP ON--
I QUESTION ITS USE, BIRD, NOT ITS MEANING.
GOTHAM IS ALREADY MINE-- AND GOTHAM IS ONLY THE BEGINNING.
YEAH, WELL, ACTUALLY MAYBE IT AIN'T, AND THAT'S WHAT PROMPTED ME ON THIS CONVERSATION...
...CUZ NOW THAT THE BATMAN'S BACK... OUT THERE SQUEEZIN' PEOPLE, MAYBE EVEN THE MOB BOSSES IN CONTROL OF THE UNION RACKETS--
THE BATMAN?
Y-YEAH...
5

I MEAN, NOBODY'S EVEN *SEEN* TOUGH TONY BRESSI FOR--

THE BATMAN... IS...*NOT*... BACK.

BUT BANE... HE *HADDA* BE THE ONE BUSTED UP THE *GOTHAMDOME* SKYBOX... AND HE MAN EVEN KNOW WE'VE GOT BRESSI'S *KIDS* STASHED AWAY IN--

IT'S *NOT* HIM.

IT'S NOTHING BUT A *COSTUME.*

OKAY, ALL RIGHT... BUT DOES THAT MEAN WE'RE JUST GONNA REST ON OUR--

I *BROKE* THE *REAL* BATMAN... AND I WILL *CRUS* THIS PRETENDER

BRIIINNG

RIGHT... YES... RIGHT.

I'LL TELL HIM.

BRESSI JUST MADE *CONTACT.*

SAYS THE UNIONS ARE *OURS.*

WANTS HIS *KIDS* BACK.

I DON'T KNOW ABOUT THIS, BANE.

IF THE BATMAN'S SQUEEZING BRESSI--

ALL RIGHT... WHOEVER'S IN THE BAT OUTFIT... WHAT IF HE'S USING BRESSI TO--

--AN APPARENTLY RARE STRAIN, CALLED MALARIA SECORUM.

I TOLD YOU, BIRD... THE BATMAN IS BROKEN.

THEN YOU'LL TAKE ZOMBI AND TROGG AND FIND OUT-- WHEN YOU SUPERVISE THE RETURN OF BRESSI'S CHILDREN.

THANK YOU.

SHE'LL TRACE IT FOR US, ALFRED.

IF ANYONE CAN DO IT, SHE CAN.

CAN'T LET HIM DO IT-- CAN'T LET HIM GET MORE AND MORE RUTHLESS WITH EACH PASSING NIGHT.

PART OF IT MUST BE "THE SYSTEM"...

...ALL THE HIDDEN TRAINING HYPNOTICALLY IMPLANTED WHEN THE ORDER OF SAINT DUMAS WAS PREPARING HIM TO BECOME AZRAEL.

SHSH SH

WE STILL DON'T KNOW HOW MUCH HIS BRAIN WAS WASHED...

BUT THAT'S NOT THE *ONLY* THING CHANGING JEAN PAUL.

IT'S ALSO BECAUSE HE'S SHUTTING ME OUT, TRYING TO GO IT *ALONE*...

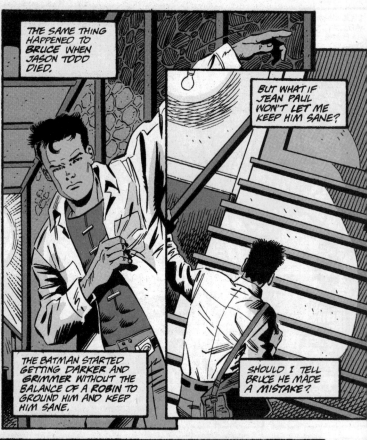

THE SAME THING HAPPENED TO *BRUCE* WHEN JASON TODD DIED.

THE BATMAN STARTED GETTING DARKER AND GRIMMER WITHOUT THE BALANCE OF A *ROBIN* TO GROUND HIM AND KEEP HIM *SANE.*

BUT WHAT IF JEAN PAUL WON'T LET ME KEEP HIM SANE?

SHOULD I TELL BRUCE HE MADE A *MISTAKE?*

NO, NOT YET... NOT WHILE BRUCE HAS ENOUGH ON HIS MIND JUST TRYING TO RECOVER FROM A BROKEN BACK.

BESIDES, HE *DIDN'T* MAKE A MISTAKE, NOT IN THE AREAS OF SKILL AND CONFIDENCE. OTHER THAN *NIGHTWING,* JEAN PAUL'S THE ONLY ONE WHO COULD WEAR THAT CAPE.

DAD MUST BE SOUND ASLEEP FOR A CHANGE-- AND THAT'S JUST WHAT *I* NEED.

KEEPING UP WITH JEAN PAUL *TONIGHT* WAS BAD ENOUGH...

TOMORROW NIGHT COULD BE *WICKED.*

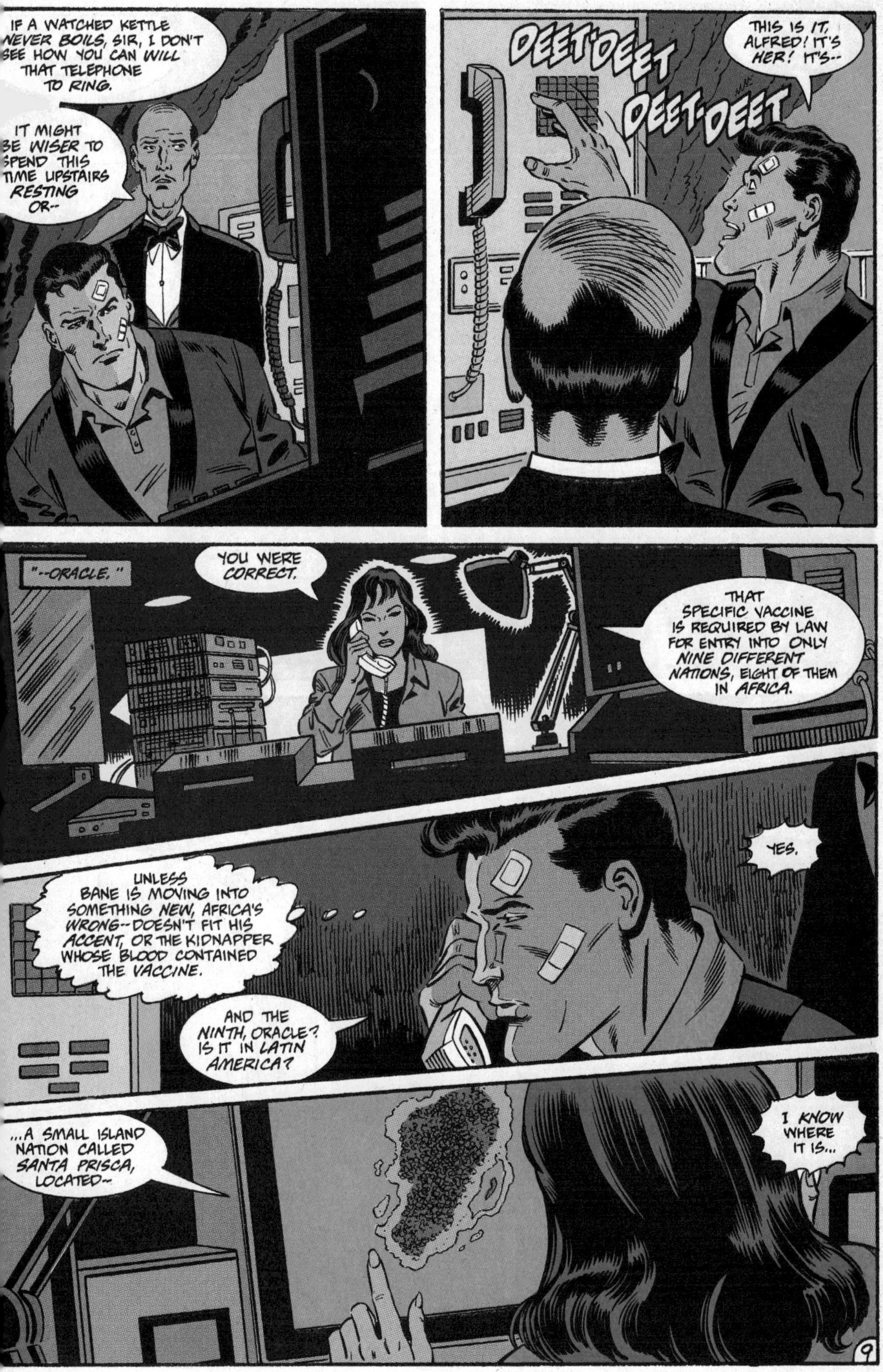
IF A WATCHED KETTLE NEVER BOILS, SIR, I DON'T SEE HOW YOU CAN WILL THAT TELEPHONE TO RING.
IT MIGHT BE WISER TO SPEND THIS TIME UPSTAIRS RESTING OR--
DEET DEET DEET DEET
THIS IS IT, ALFRED! IT'S HER! IT'S--
"--ORACLE."
YOU WERE CORRECT.
THAT SPECIFIC VACCINE IS REQUIRED BY LAW FOR ENTRY INTO ONLY NINE DIFFERENT NATIONS, EIGHT OF THEM IN AFRICA.
YES.
UNLESS BANE IS MOVING INTO SOMETHING NEW, AFRICA'S WRONG--DOESN'T FIT HIS ACCENT, OR THE KIDNAPPER WHOSE BLOOD CONTAINED THE VACCINE.
AND THE NINTH, ORACLE? IS IT IN LATIN AMERICA?
...A SMALL ISLAND NATION CALLED SANTA PRISCA, LOCATED--
I KNOW WHERE IT IS...
9

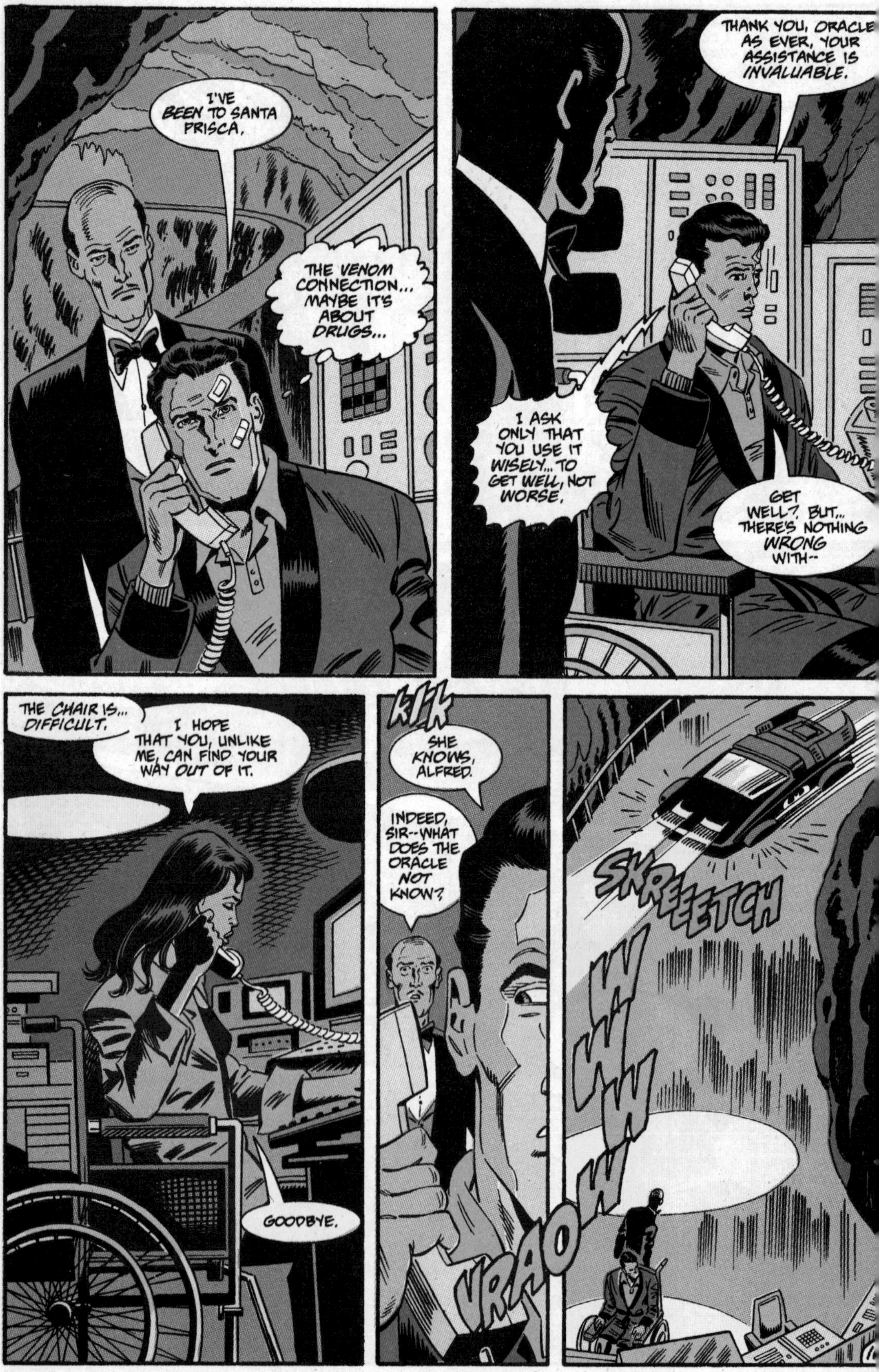
I'VE BEEN TO SANTA PRISCA.
THE VENOM CONNECTION... MAYBE IT'S ABOUT DRUGS...
THANK YOU, ORACLE AS EVER, YOUR ASSISTANCE IS INVALUABLE.
I ASK ONLY THAT YOU USE IT WISELY... TO GET WELL, NOT WORSE.
GET WELL? BUT... THERE'S NOTHING WRONG WITH--
THE CHAIR IS... DIFFICULT.
I HOPE THAT YOU, UNLIKE ME, CAN FIND YOUR WAY OUT OF IT.
GOODBYE.
KLIK
SHE KNOWS, ALFRED.
INDEED, SIR--WHAT DOES THE ORACLE NOT KNOW?
SKREEETCH
VRAOWWWWW

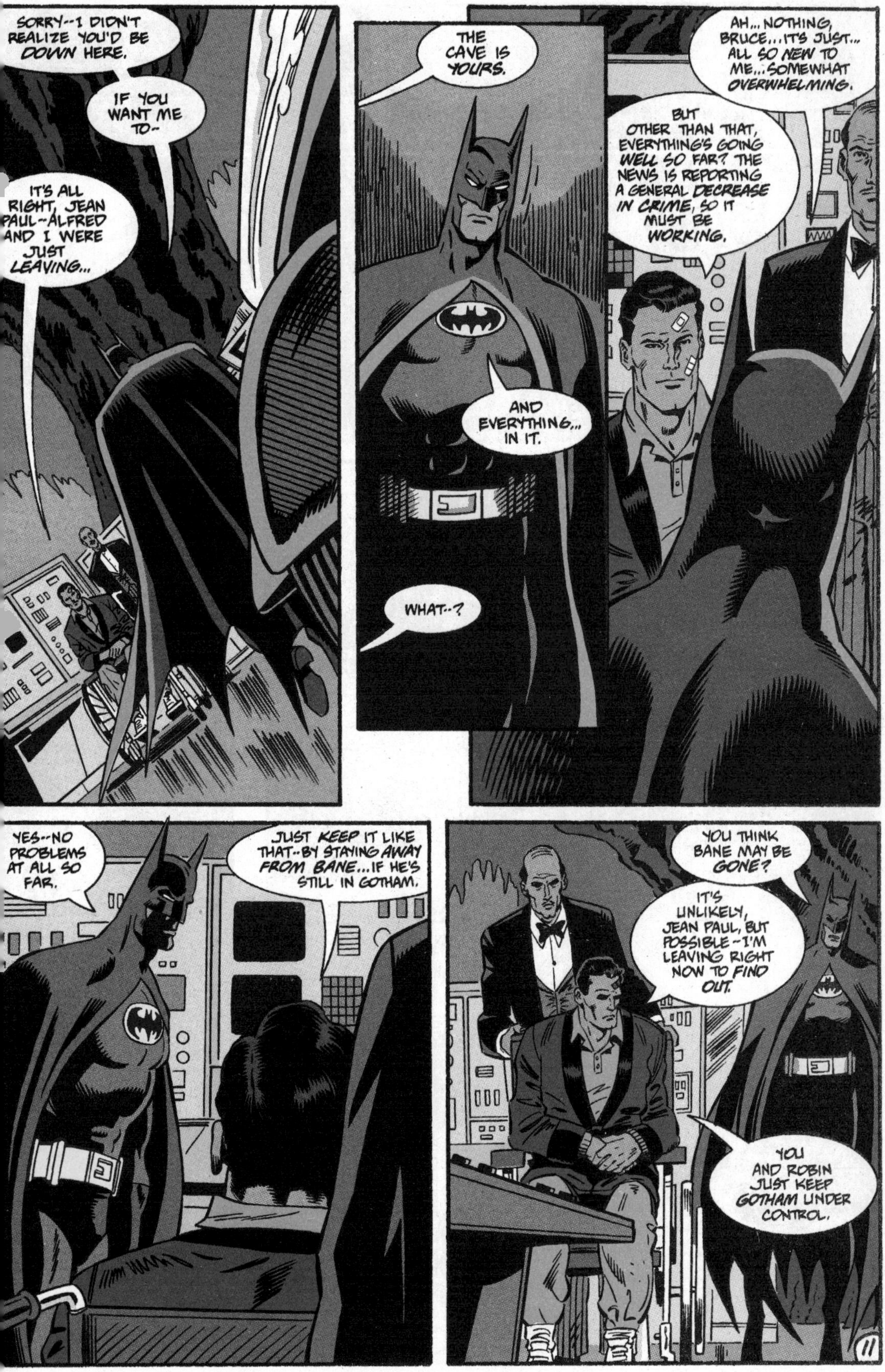
SORRY--I DIDN'T REALIZE YOU'D BE DOWN HERE.
IF YOU WANT ME TO-
IT'S ALL RIGHT, JEAN PAUL--ALFRED AND I WERE JUST LEAVING...
THE CAVE IS YOURS.
AND EVERYTHING... IN IT.
WHAT--?
AH... NOTHING, BRUCE... IT'S JUST... ALL SO NEW TO ME... SOMEWHAT OVERWHELMING.
BUT OTHER THAN THAT, EVERYTHING'S GOING WELL SO FAR? THE NEWS IS REPORTING A GENERAL DECREASE IN CRIME, SO IT MUST BE WORKING.
YES--NO PROBLEMS AT ALL SO FAR.
JUST KEEP IT LIKE THAT--BY STAYING AWAY FROM BANE... IF HE'S STILL IN GOTHAM.
YOU THINK BANE MAY BE GONE?
IT'S UNLIKELY, JEAN PAUL, BUT POSSIBLE--I'M LEAVING RIGHT NOW TO FIND OUT.
YOU AND ROBIN JUST KEEP GOTHAM UNDER CONTROL.
11

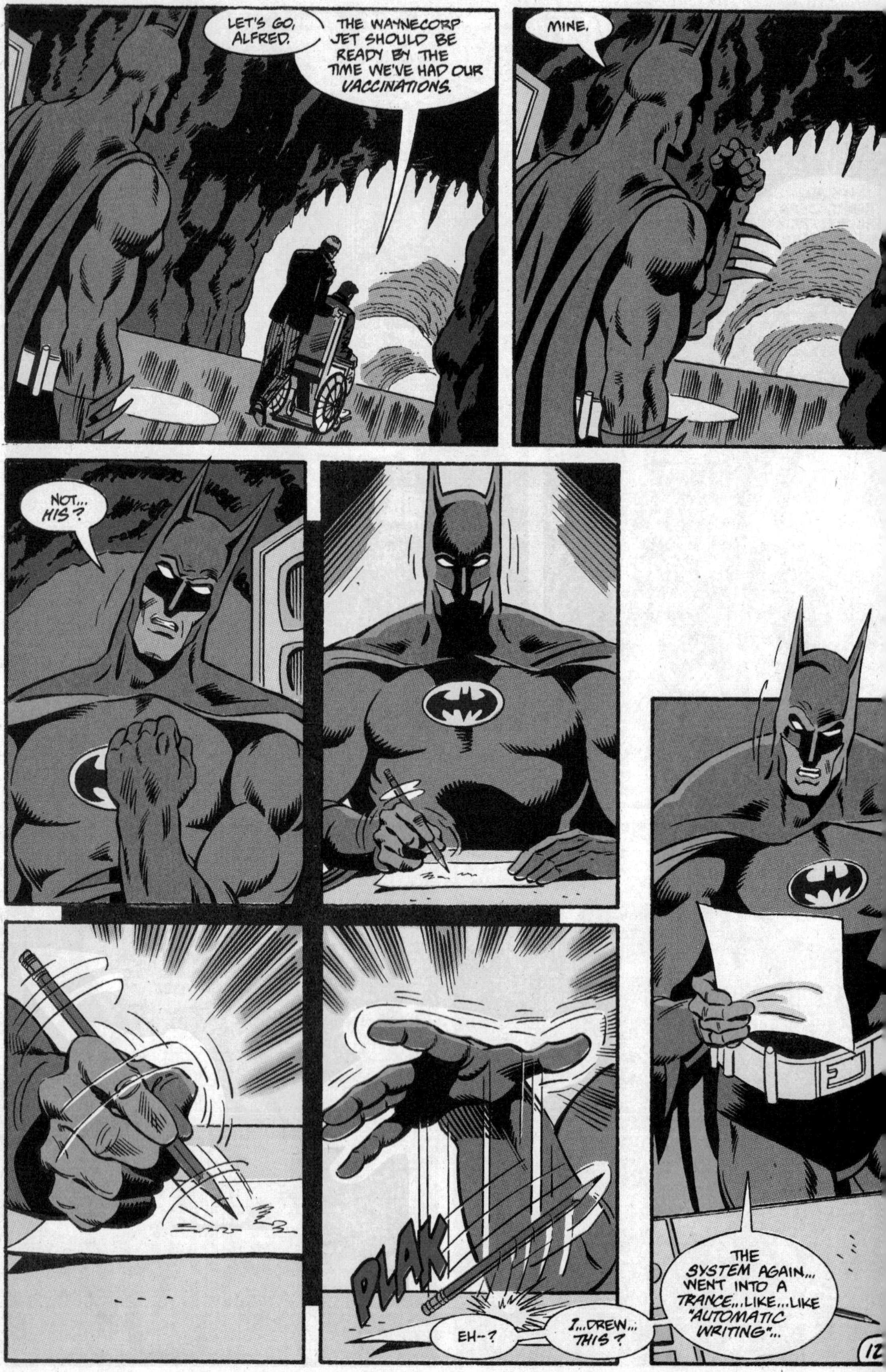
LET'S GO, ALFRED.
THE WAYNECORP JET SHOULD BE READY BY THE TIME WE'VE HAD OUR VACCINATIONS.
MINE.
NOT... HIS?
PLAK
EH--?
I...DREW... THIS?
THE SYSTEM AGAIN... WENT INTO A TRANCE...LIKE...LIKE "AUTOMATIC WRITING"...
12

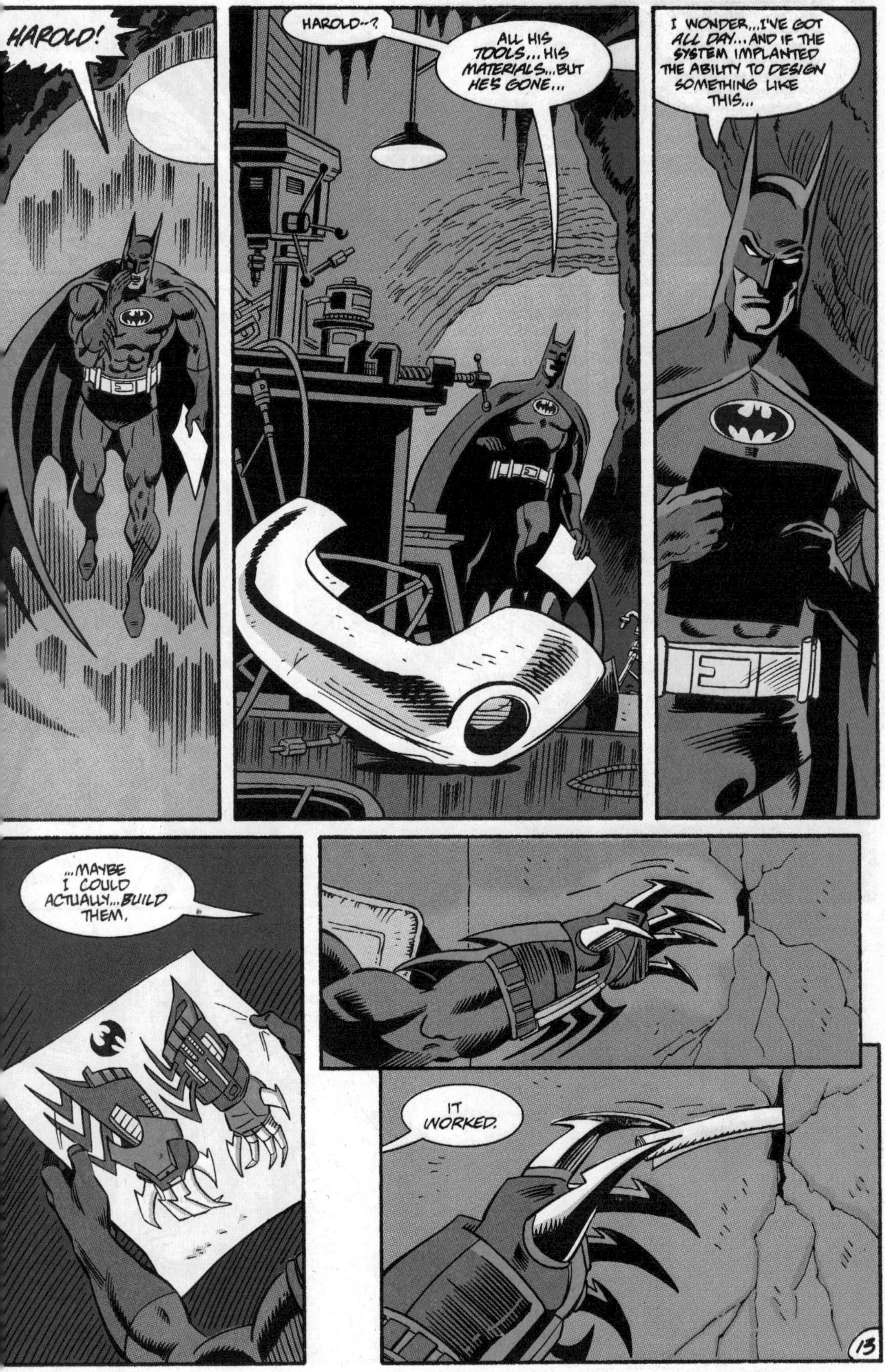
HAROLD!
HAROLD--?
ALL HIS TOOLS... HIS MATERIALS... BUT HE'S GONE...
I WONDER... I'VE GOT ALL DAY... AND IF THE SYSTEM IMPLANTED THE ABILITY TO DESIGN SOMETHING LIKE THIS...
...MAYBE I COULD ACTUALLY... BUILD THEM.
IT WORKED.
13

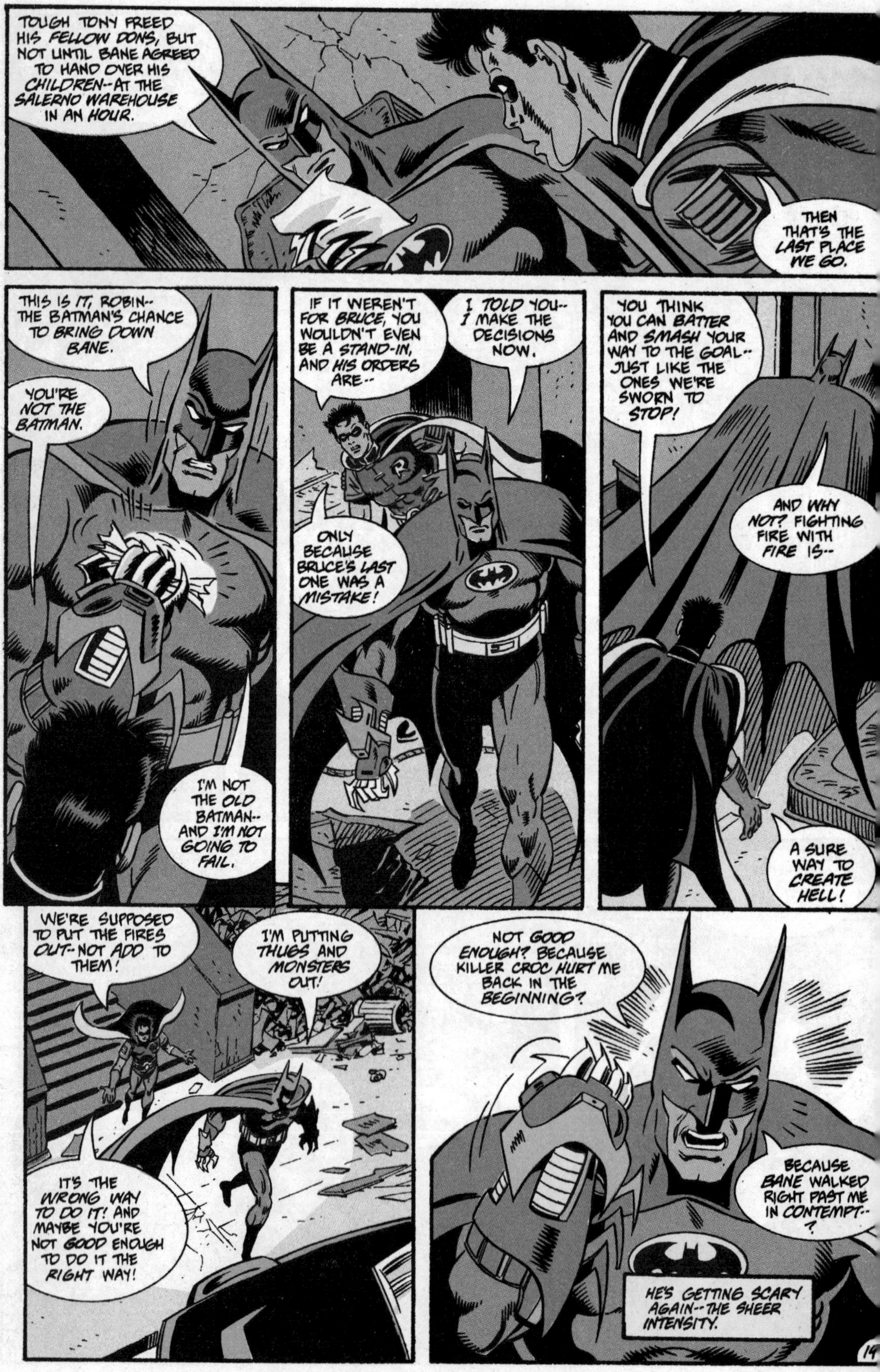
TOUGH TONY FREED HIS FELLOW DONS, BUT NOT UNTIL BANE AGREED TO HAND OVER HIS CHILDREN--AT THE SALERNO WAREHOUSE IN AN HOUR.
THEN THAT'S THE LAST PLACE WE GO.
THIS IS IT, ROBIN-- THE BATMAN'S CHANCE TO BRING DOWN BANE.
YOU'RE NOT THE BATMAN.
I'M NOT THE OLD BATMAN-- AND I'M NOT GOING TO FAIL.
IF IT WEREN'T FOR BRUCE, YOU WOULDN'T EVEN BE A STAND-IN, AND HIS ORDERS ARE--
I TOLD YOU-- I MAKE THE DECISIONS NOW.
ONLY BECAUSE BRUCE'S LAST ONE WAS A MISTAKE!
YOU THINK YOU CAN BATTER AND SMASH YOUR WAY TO THE GOAL-- JUST LIKE THE ONES WE'RE SWORN TO STOP!
AND WHY NOT? FIGHTING FIRE WITH FIRE IS--
A SURE WAY TO CREATE HELL!
WE'RE SUPPOSED TO PUT THE FIRES OUT--NOT ADD TO THEM!
I'M PUTTING THUGS AND MONSTERS OUT!
IT'S THE WRONG WAY TO DO IT! AND MAYBE YOU'RE NOT GOOD ENOUGH TO DO IT THE RIGHT WAY!
NOT GOOD ENOUGH? BECAUSE KILLER CROC HURT ME BACK IN THE BEGINNING?
BECAUSE BANE WALKED RIGHT PAST ME IN CONTEMPT--?
HE'S GETTING SCARY AGAIN--THE SHEER INTENSITY.
14

NEVER AGAIN, BOY WONDER...

NEVER AGAIN!

GREAT--NOW I HAVE TO RACE HIM TO THE WAREHOUSE ON FOOT...

VRRAOWN

...AND I HOPE I GET THERE BEFORE HE DESTROYS THE MANTLE OF THE BAT FOR GOOD.

I'M SORRY, MS. KYLE--BUT THERE ARE NO DEPARTURES FOR THAT DESTINATION--BY ANY AIRLINE--UNTIL WEDNESDAY.

BUT IT'S VITAL THAT I LEAVE FOR SANTA PRISCA IMMEDIATELY.

I'M SORRY, BUT--

GOTHAM INTERNATIONAL

SOUTHWAY AIRLINES

WHAT ABOUT A CHARTERED FLIGHT?

I'M AFRAID WITH ALL THE RECENT CUTBACKS AMONG THE INDEPEN--

THERE'S ABSOLUTELY NOTHING?

WELL, IT'S ODD...I MEAN, I'D BARELY HEARD OF SANTA PRISCA BEFORE TODAY, BUT...

BUT WHAT?

WELL, THERE IS A PRIVATE PLANE SCHEDULED TO USE ONE OF OUR RUNWAYS IN ABOUT AN HOUR...OWNED BY BRUCE WAYNE...BUT OF COURSE THERE'S NO WAY WE COULD BOOK YOU ON...

EH--?

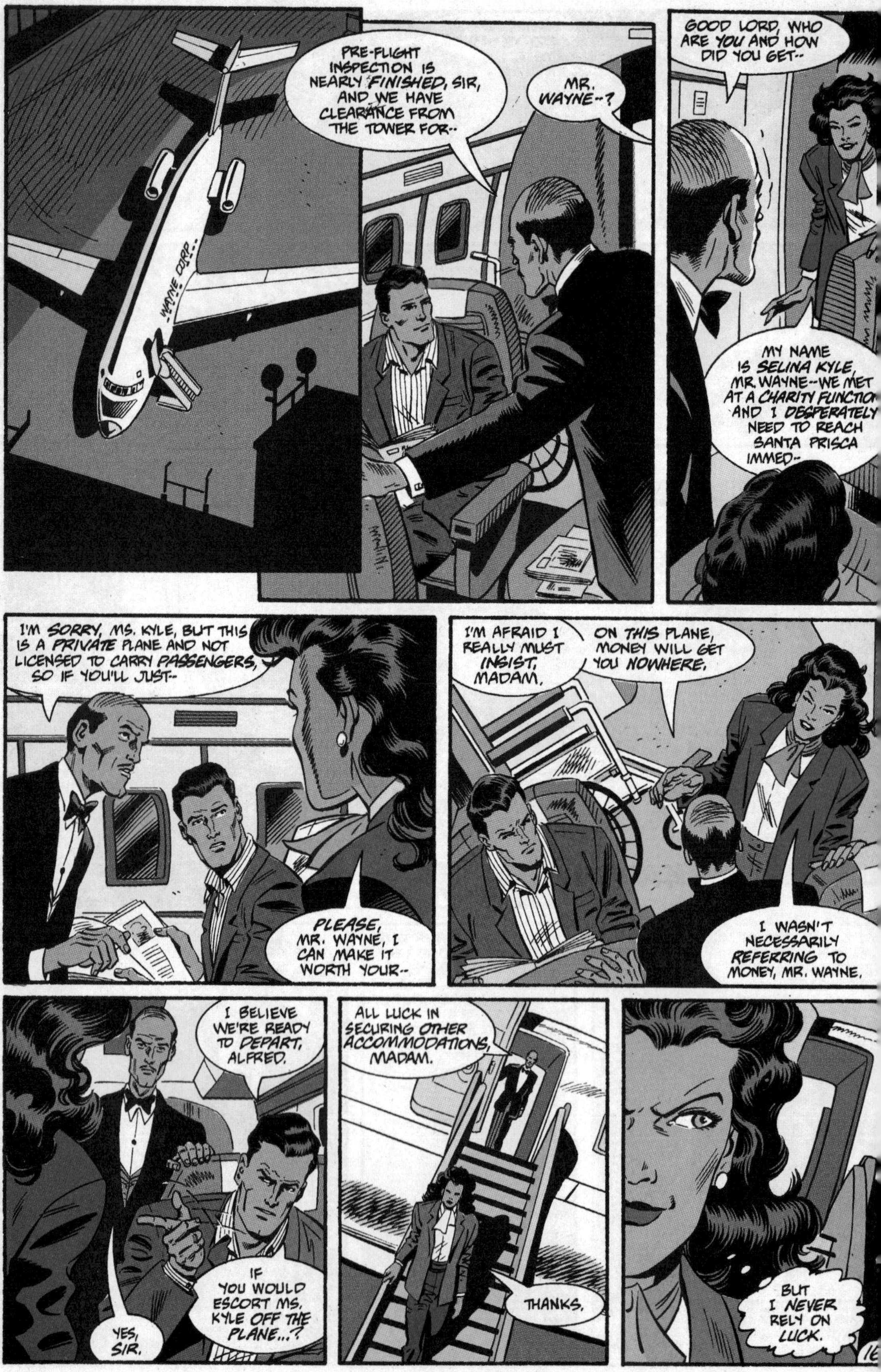
WAYNE CORP.
PRE-FLIGHT INSPECTION IS NEARLY FINISHED, SIR, AND WE HAVE CLEARANCE FROM THE TOWER FOR--
MR. WAYNE--?
GOOD LORD, WHO ARE YOU AND HOW DID YOU GET--
MY NAME IS SELINA KYLE, MR. WAYNE--WE MET AT A CHARITY FUNCTION AND I DESPERATELY NEED TO REACH SANTA PRISCA IMMED--
I'M SORRY, MS. KYLE, BUT THIS IS A PRIVATE PLANE AND NOT LICENSED TO CARRY PASSENGERS, SO IF YOU'LL JUST--
PLEASE, MR. WAYNE, I CAN MAKE IT WORTH YOUR--
I'M AFRAID I REALLY MUST INSIST, MADAM.
ON THIS PLANE, MONEY WILL GET YOU NOWHERE.
I WASN'T NECESSARILY REFERRING TO MONEY, MR. WAYNE.
I BELIEVE WE'RE READY TO DEPART, ALFRED.
IF YOU WOULD ESCORT MS. KYLE OFF THE PLANE...?
YES, SIR.
ALL LUCK IN SECURING OTHER ACCOMMODATIONS, MADAM.
THANKS.
BUT I NEVER RELY ON LUCK.
16

HERE ARE YOUR KIDS, BRESSI...

AND I HOPE FOR YOUR SAKE YOU CAME TO COLLECT THEM ALONE.

OF COURSE I CAME ALONE! YOU THINK I'M CRAZY ENOUGH TO--

WHERE'S BANE?

UP THERE! WASTE HIM!

NO! NOT YET! NOT TILL THE KIDS ARE IN THE CLEAR!!

HE DOESN'T EVEN HEAR ME.

HE'S A DEMON...HELLBENT ON SHOCK AND PAIN...

17

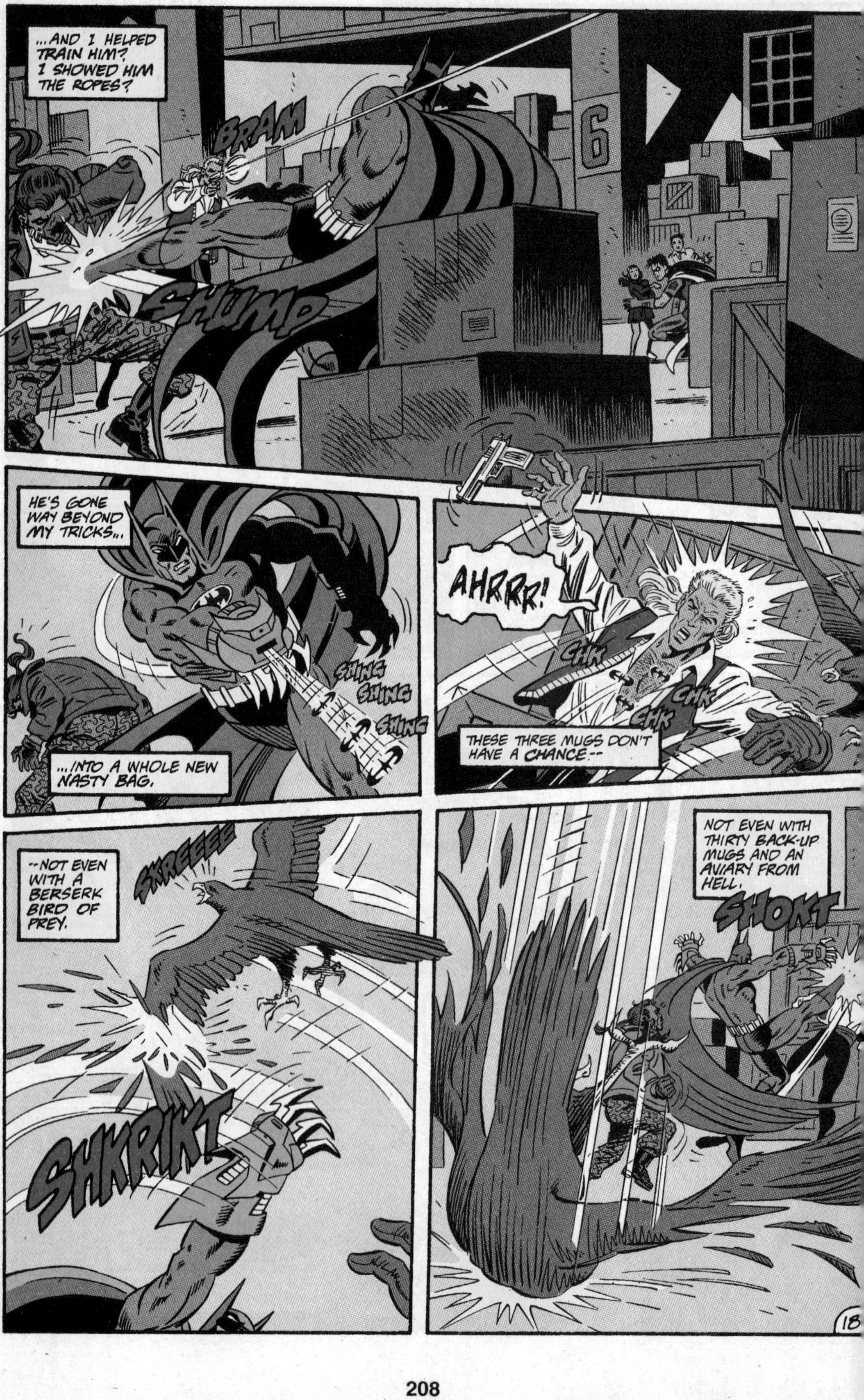

...AND I HELPED TRAIN HIM? I SHOWED HIM THE ROPES?
BRAM
SHUMP
HE'S GONE WAY BEYOND MY TRICKS...
SHING
SHING
SHING
...INTO A WHOLE NEW NASTY BAG.
AHRRR!
CHK
CHK
CHK
THESE THREE MUGS DON'T HAVE A CHANCE--
--NOT EVEN WITH A BERSERK BIRD OF PREY.
SKREEEE
SHKRIKT
NOT EVEN WITH THIRTY BACK-UP MUGS AND AN AVIARY FROM HELL.
SHOKT
18

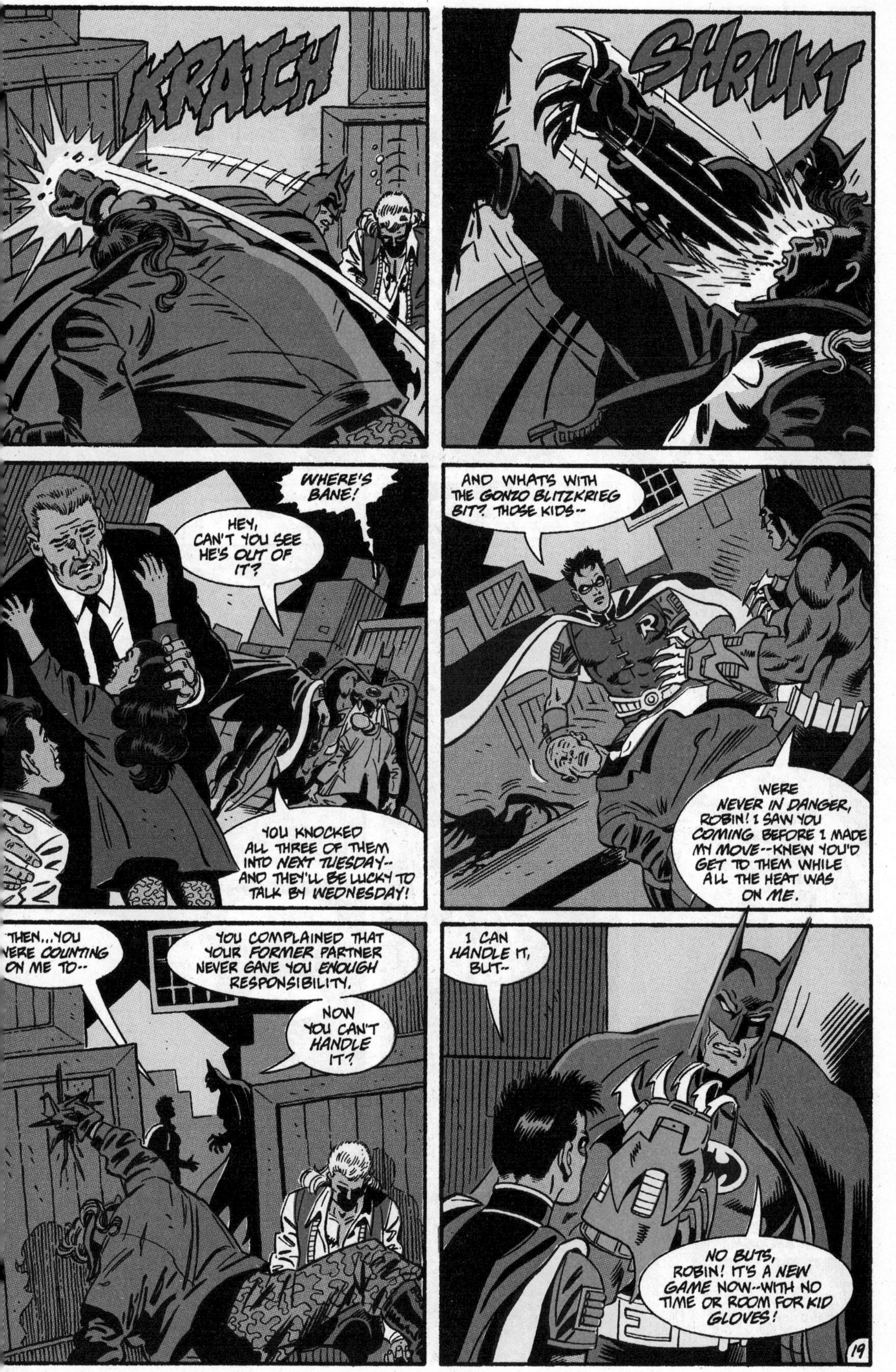
KRATCH
SHRUKT
WHERE'S BANE!
HEY, CAN'T YOU SEE HE'S OUT OF IT?
YOU KNOCKED ALL THREE OF THEM INTO NEXT TUESDAY-- AND THEY'LL BE LUCKY TO TALK BY WEDNESDAY!
AND WHAT'S WITH THE GONZO BLITZKRIEG BIT? THOSE KIDS--
WERE NEVER IN DANGER, ROBIN! I SAW YOU COMING BEFORE I MADE MY MOVE--KNEW YOU'D GET TO THEM WHILE ALL THE HEAT WAS ON ME.
THEN...YOU WERE COUNTING ON ME TO--
YOU COMPLAINED THAT YOUR FORMER PARTNER NEVER GAVE YOU ENOUGH RESPONSIBILITY.
NOW YOU CAN'T HANDLE IT?
I CAN HANDLE IT, BUT--
NO BUTS, ROBIN! IT'S A NEW GAME NOW--WITH NO TIME OR ROOM FOR KID GLOVES!
19

SPEAKING OF THOSE THINGS, AREN'T THEY A LOT MORE AZRAEL THAN THEY ARE BAT--

"THAT WAS STUPID, ROBIN--A MOCKERY OF EVERYTHING WE'RE SUPPOSED TO BE."

EEOOEEOOo

SKREETCH

SKREETCH

POLICE

GORFINKEL

YOU CALLED THE POLICE BEFORE YOU CAME HERE--?

AND HE'S GONE, GETTING THE WHOLE THING BACKWARDS.

EVEN IF HE WAS RIGHT--EVEN IF HE IS GOOD ENOUGH TO KNOW HE'D PULL IT OFF WITHOUT ENDANGERING THE KIDS--IT'S NOT GOOD ENOUGH...

...BECAUSE ONE WAY OR ANOTHER, SOONER OR LATER, HE'S GOING TO CRASH INTO BANE HIMSELF--THE MONSTER WHO BROKE THE REAL BATMAN.

I CAN'T LET THAT HAPPEN.

I'VE GOT TO TELL...

BRUCE--?

Nhn?

BRUCE, ARE YOU HERE?

OH--JEAN PAUL...

BRUCE IS GONE... WITH ALFRED...ON SOME SORT OF... TRIP.

A TRIP? WHERE'S HAROLD?

I DON'T KNOW.

YOU ALL RIGHT, JEAN PAUL?

I'M FINE... SORRY WE HAD TO ARGUE LIKE THAT.

HE TOLD ME TO...MOVE IN.

ACE?

NO IDEA.

YEAH... SO WHAT ARE YOU DOING?

JUST SOME... NEW DESIGNS. THE COSTUME NEEDS... IMPROVEMENT.

AND WHAT YOU NEED IS TO GET HOME, ROBIN... BEFORE YOUR FATHER MISSES YOU.

YEAH... YEAH, I'LL DO THAT.

A TRIP? FUNNY ALFRED DIDN'T MENTION IT...

LAVATORY

EH? LOCKED?

KKTCH

SORRY, BUT IT WAS AN EMERGENCY--I JUST HAD TO USE THE FACILITIES...

YOU--?

21

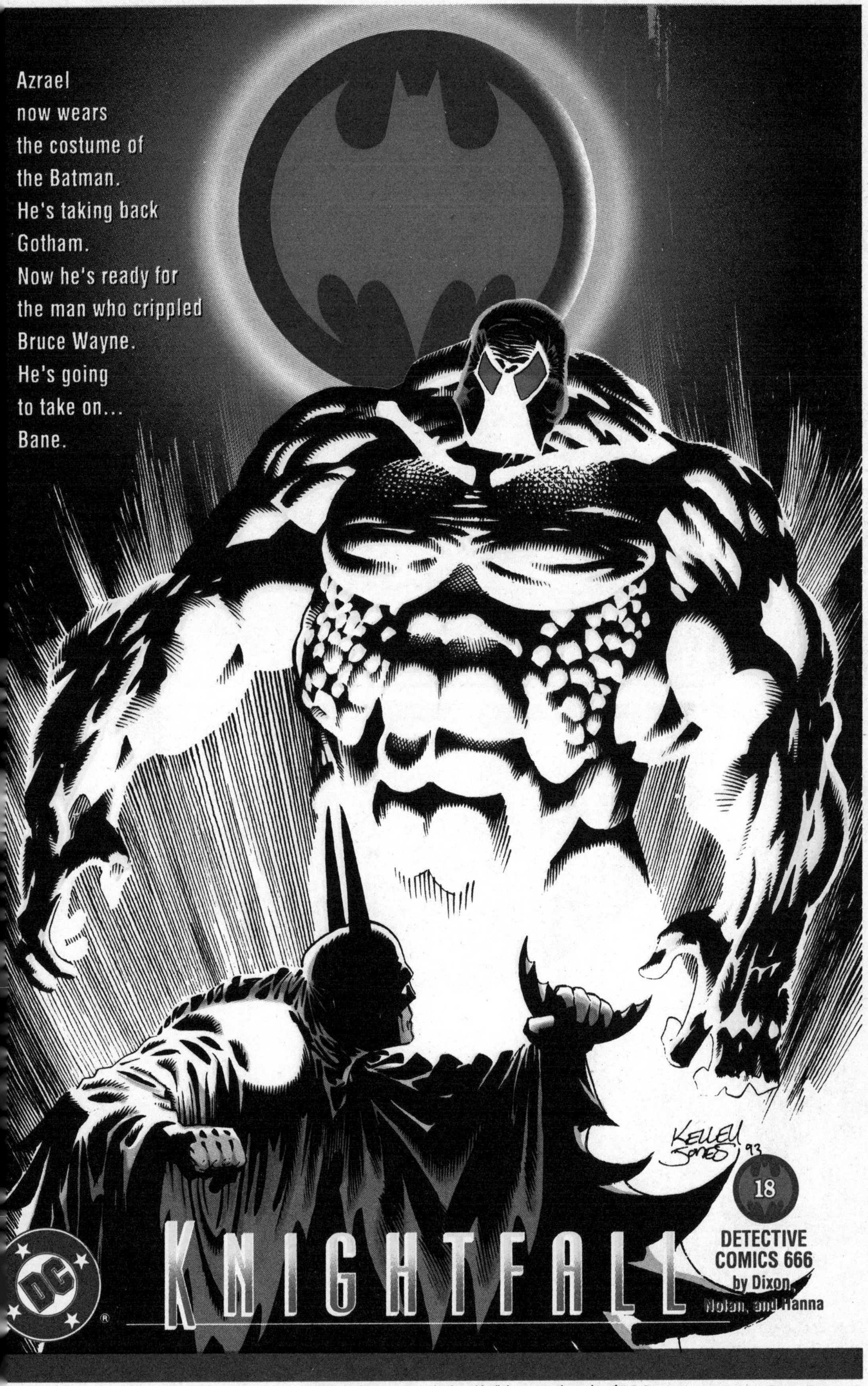
Azrael
now wears
the costume of
the Batman.
He's taking back
Gotham.
Now he's ready for
the man who crippled
Bruce Wayne.
He's going
to take on...
Bane.
KELLEY JONES '93
18
KNIGHTFALL
DETECTIVE COMICS 666
by Dixon, Nolan, and Hanna
DC

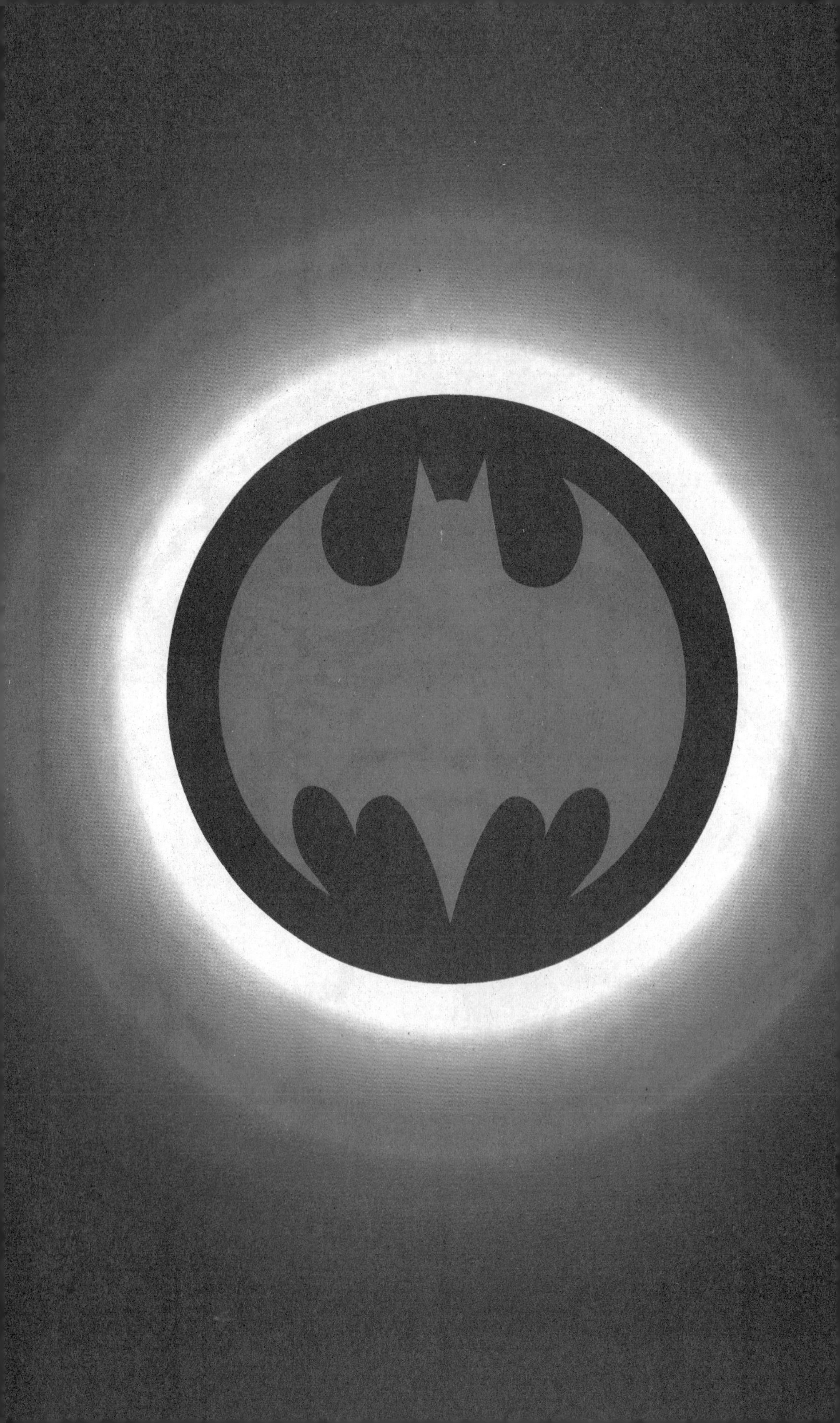

215

THE MANTLE OF THE BAT IS HIS.

BANE MUST FALL IF *GOTHAM* IS TO BE HIS.

BUT BANE STILL RULES THE NIGHT.

FOR NOW.

BUT FIRST HE MUST FIND BANE.

HE'LL FIND THE MONSTER AND IT WILL ALL BE HIS.

THE NIGHT, THE CITY AND EVERY-THING.

COMMISSIONER

THE DETECTIVE WORK BORES HIM.

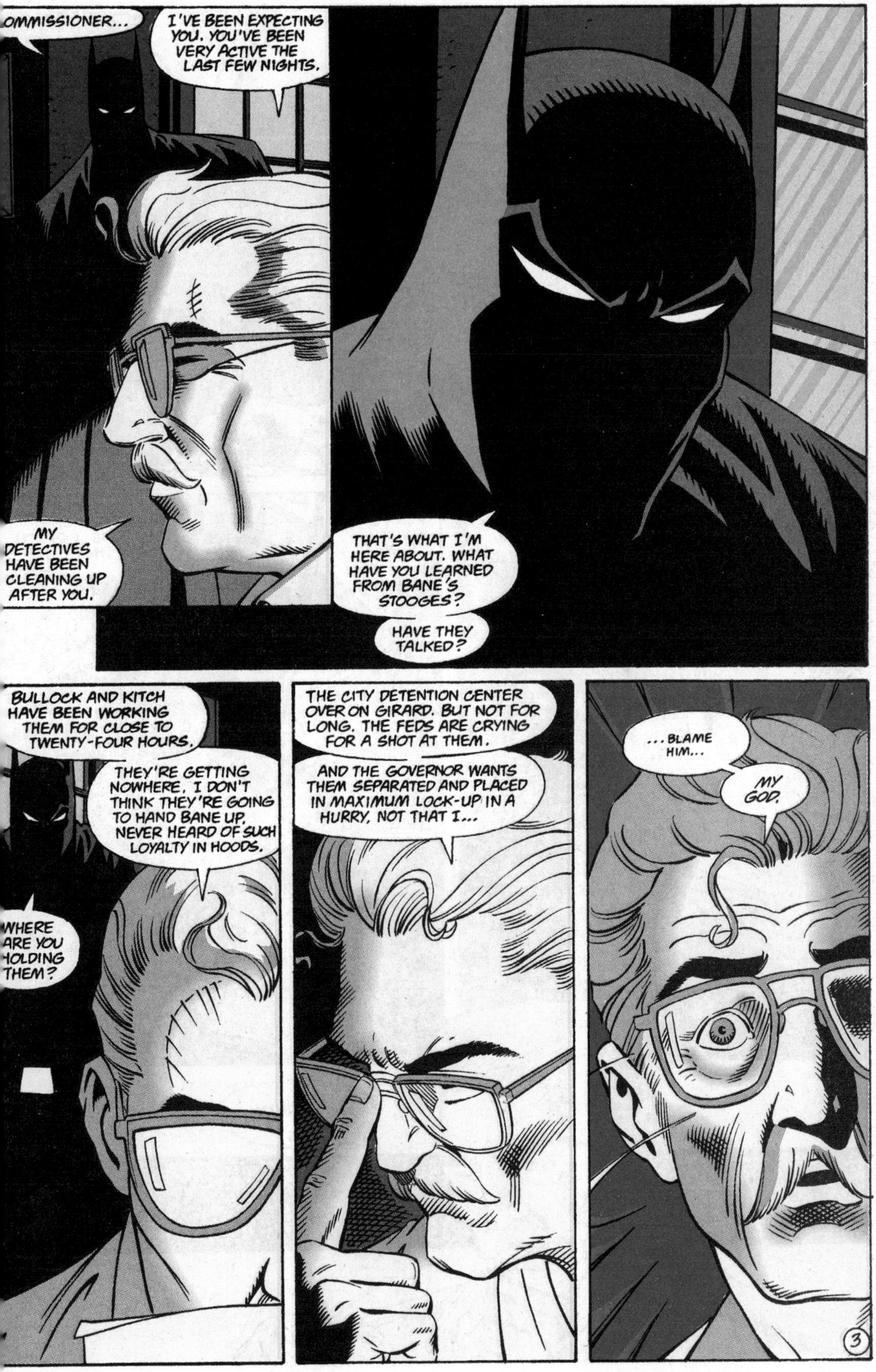
OMMISSIONER...
I'VE BEEN EXPECTING YOU. YOU'VE BEEN VERY ACTIVE THE LAST FEW NIGHTS.
MY DETECTIVES HAVE BEEN CLEANING UP AFTER YOU.
THAT'S WHAT I'M HERE ABOUT. WHAT HAVE YOU LEARNED FROM BANE'S STOOGES?
HAVE THEY TALKED?
BULLOCK AND KITCH HAVE BEEN WORKING THEM FOR CLOSE TO TWENTY-FOUR HOURS.
THEY'RE GETTING NOWHERE. I DON'T THINK THEY'RE GOING TO HAND BANE UP. NEVER HEARD OF SUCH LOYALTY IN HOODS.
WHERE ARE YOU HOLDING THEM?
THE CITY DETENTION CENTER OVER ON GIRARD. BUT NOT FOR LONG. THE FEDS ARE CRYING FOR A SHOT AT THEM.
AND THE GOVERNOR WANTS THEM SEPARATED AND PLACED IN MAXIMUM LOCK-UP IN A HURRY. NOT THAT I...
...BLAME HIM...
MY GOD.
3

YOU GUYS ARE NEVER GONNA SEE THE LIGHT OF DAY, YOU KNOW THAT?

ARE YOU TRYING TO FRIGHTEN ME, SERGEANT?

WITH *WHAT*, SERGEANT? IMPRISONMENT?

I HAVE SERVED HARD TIME IN *PENA DURO*, THE HELLHOLE OF THE UNIVERSE. YOUR PRISONS ARE SOFT, EASY.

SURE. THEY'RE *COUNTRY* CLUBS.

BUT YOU'LL SERVE *ALONE*, ZOMBIE. THE FEDS ARE COMING TOMORROW AND SPLITTING YOU AND YOUR TWO BUNKIES UP, YOU'LL BE COUNTIN' THE YEARS IN THREE SEPARATE PENS.

HARD TIME IS *HARDER* WITHOUT FRIENDS.

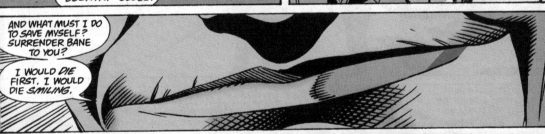

AND WHAT MUST I DO TO SAVE MYSELF? SURRENDER BANE TO YOU?

I WOULD *DIE* FIRST. I WOULD DIE *SMILING*.

GET THIS GOON OUTTA HERE BEFORE I PUT A SLUG IN HIM, LIEUTENANT.

LET'S GO, ZOMBIE. WE'RE FINISHED WITH YOU.

IMAGINE MY RELIEF.

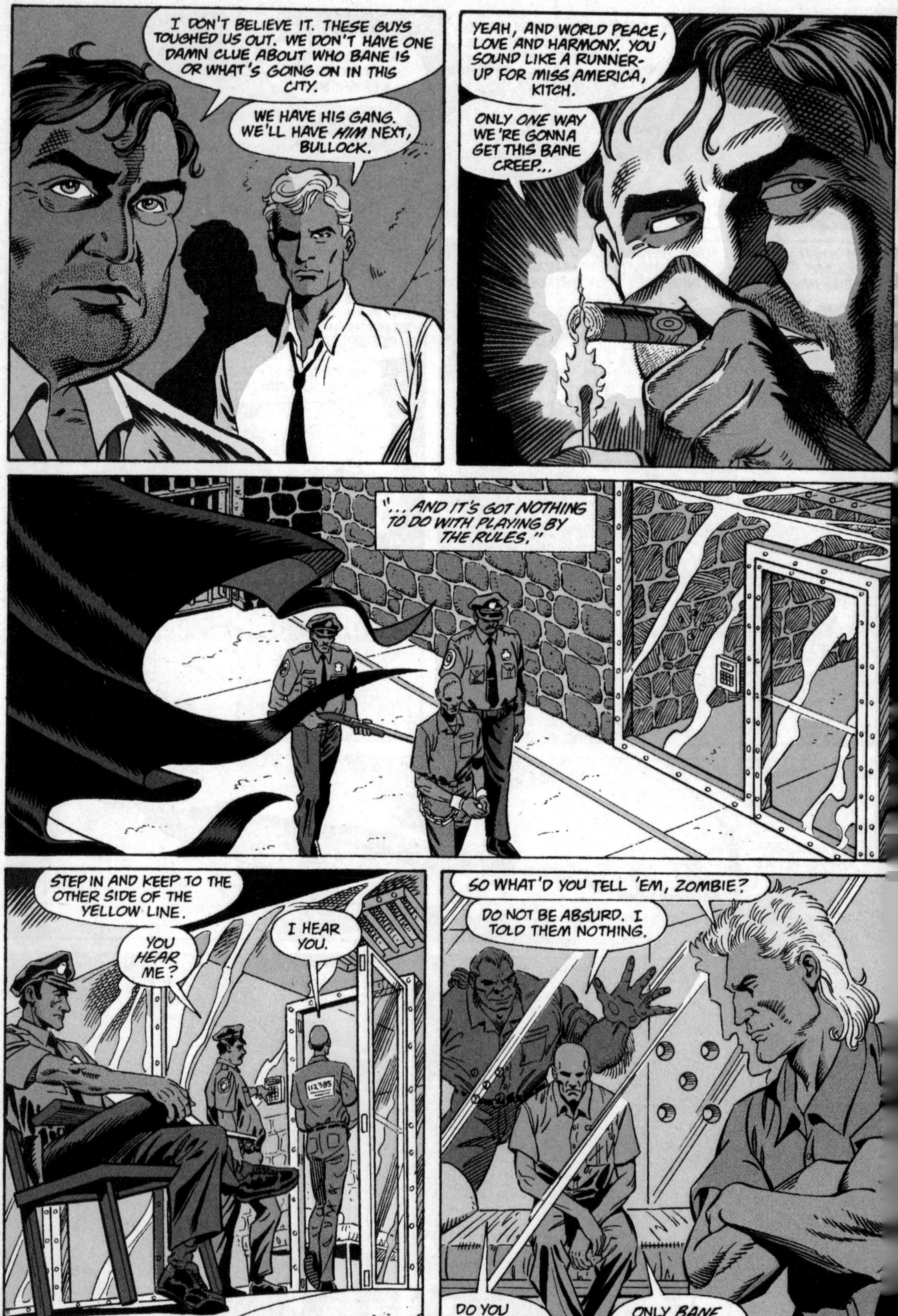

I DON'T BELIEVE IT. THESE GUYS TOUGHED US OUT. WE DON'T HAVE ONE DAMN CLUE ABOUT WHO BANE IS OR WHAT'S GOING ON IN THIS CITY.
WE HAVE HIS GANG. WE'LL HAVE *HIM* NEXT, BULLOCK.
YEAH, AND WORLD PEACE, LOVE AND HARMONY. YOU SOUND LIKE A RUNNER-UP FOR MISS AMERICA, KITCH.
ONLY *ONE* WAY WE'RE GONNA GET THIS BANE CREEP...
"...AND IT'S GOT NOTHING TO DO WITH PLAYING BY THE RULES."
STEP IN AND KEEP TO THE OTHER SIDE OF THE YELLOW LINE.
YOU *HEAR* ME?
I HEAR YOU.
SO WHAT'D YOU TELL 'EM, ZOMBIE?
DO NOT BE ABSURD. I TOLD THEM NOTHING.
DO YOU THINK BANE WILL *FREE* US?
ONLY *BANE* CAN KNOW WHAT HE WILL DO, TROGG.
6

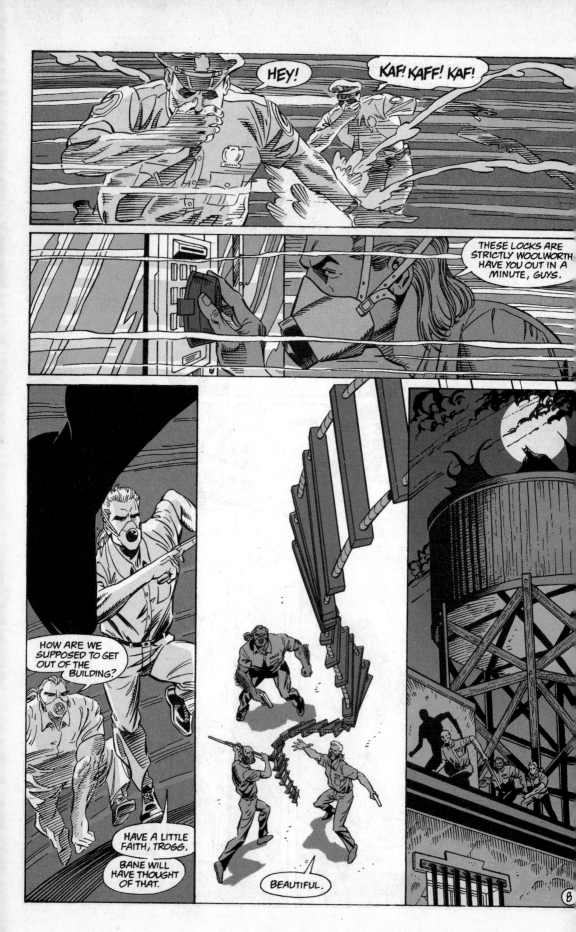

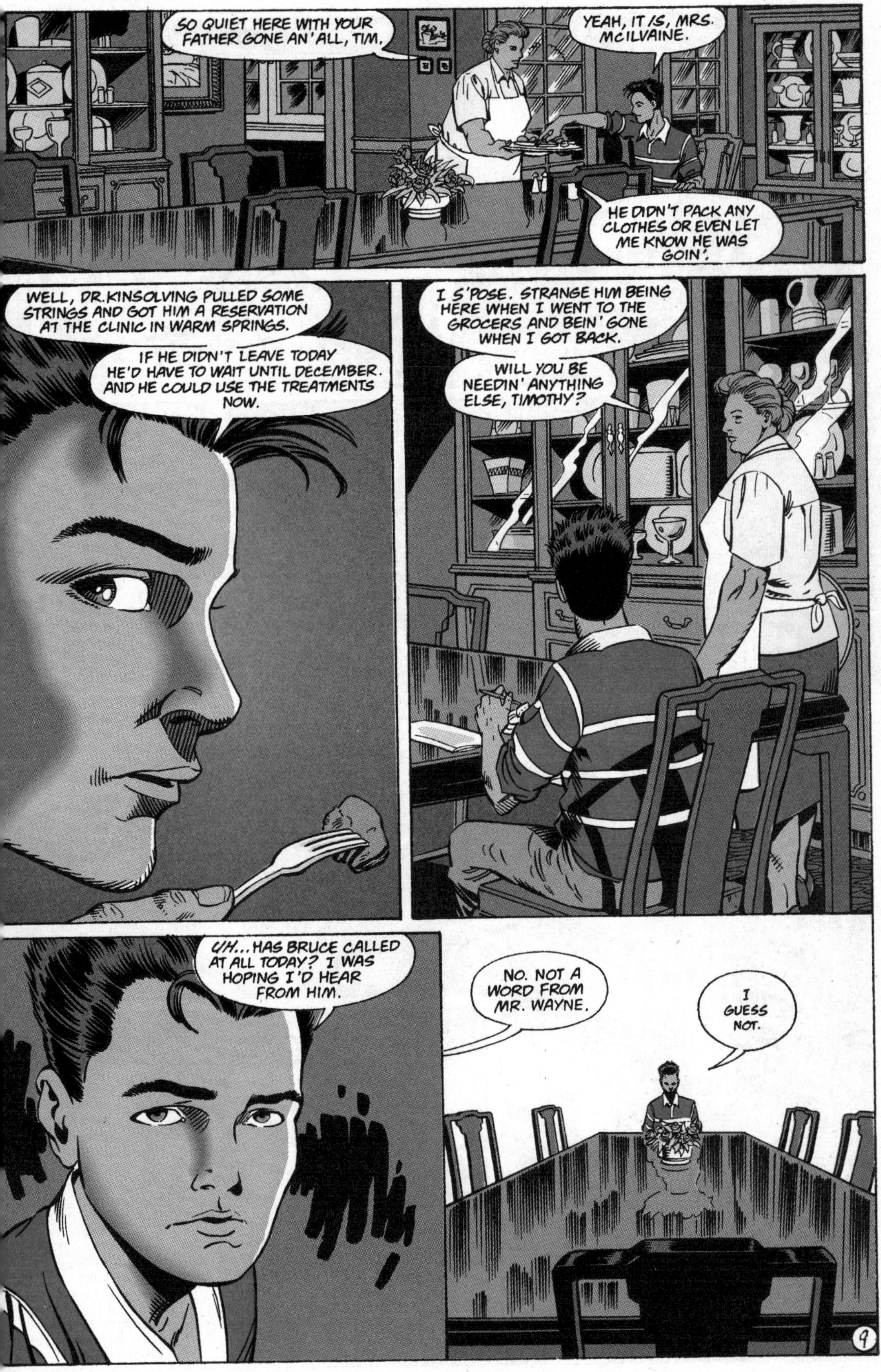
SO QUIET HERE WITH YOUR FATHER GONE AN' ALL, TIM.
YEAH, IT IS, MRS. McILVAINE.
HE DIDN'T PACK ANY CLOTHES OR EVEN LET ME KNOW HE WAS GOIN'.
WELL, DR. KINSOLVING PULLED SOME STRINGS AND GOT HIM A RESERVATION AT THE CLINIC IN WARM SPRINGS.
IF HE DIDN'T LEAVE TODAY HE'D HAVE TO WAIT UNTIL DECEMBER. AND HE COULD USE THE TREATMENTS NOW.
I S'POSE. STRANGE HIM BEING HERE WHEN I WENT TO THE GROCERS AND BEIN' GONE WHEN I GOT BACK.
WILL YOU BE NEEDIN' ANYTHING ELSE, TIMOTHY?
UH... HAS BRUCE CALLED AT ALL TODAY? I WAS HOPING I'D HEAR FROM HIM.
NO. NOT A WORD FROM MR. WAYNE.
I GUESS NOT.
9

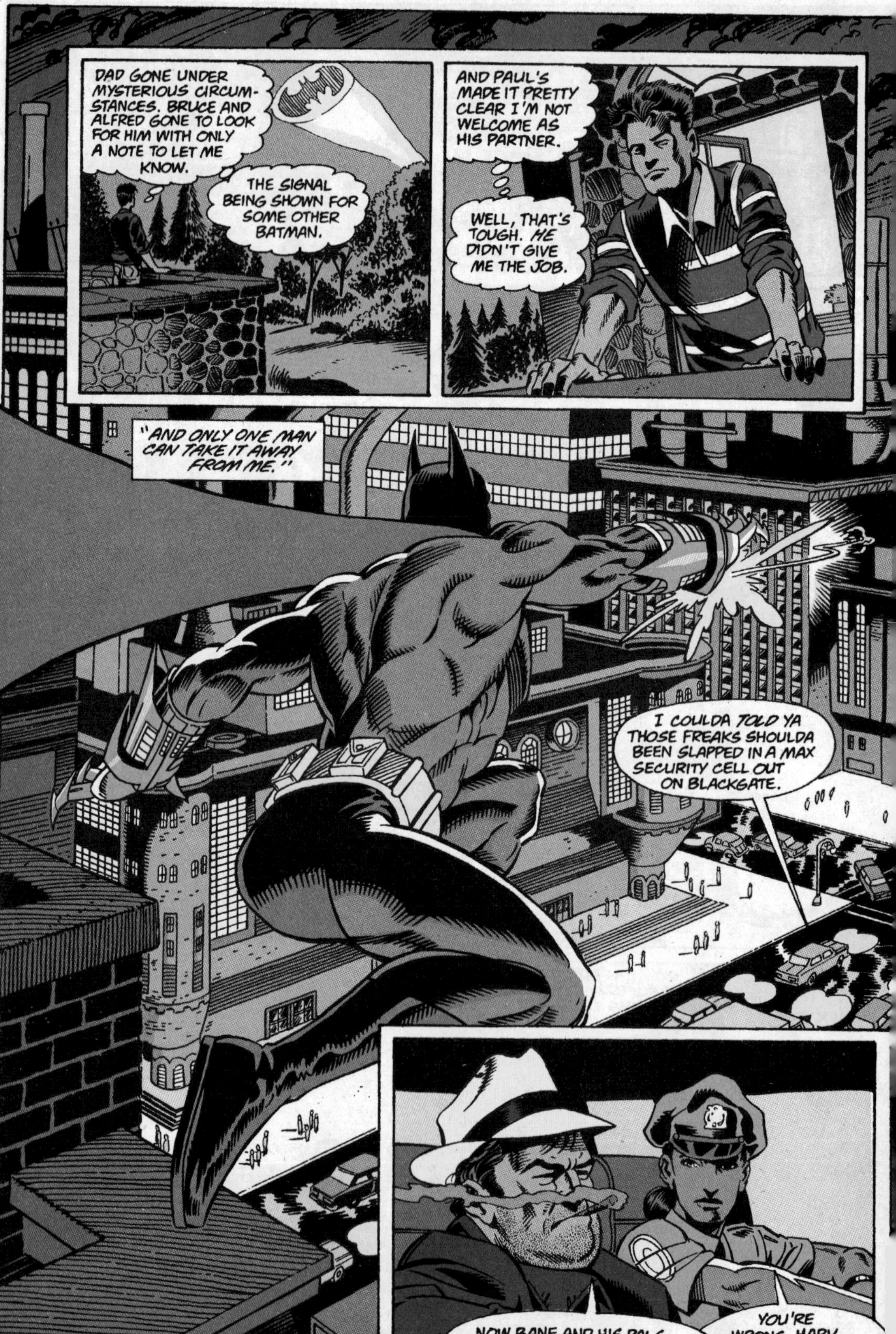
DAD GONE UNDER MYSTERIOUS CIRCUMSTANCES. BRUCE AND ALFRED GONE TO LOOK FOR HIM WITH ONLY A NOTE TO LET ME KNOW.
THE SIGNAL BEING SHOWN FOR SOME OTHER BATMAN.
AND PAUL'S MADE IT PRETTY CLEAR I'M NOT WELCOME AS HIS PARTNER.
WELL, THAT'S TOUGH. HE DIDN'T GIVE ME THE JOB.
"AND ONLY ONE MAN CAN TAKE IT AWAY FROM ME."
I COULDA TOLD YA THOSE FREAKS SHOULDA BEEN SLAPPED IN A MAX SECURITY CELL OUT ON BLACKGATE.
NOW BANE AND HIS PALS ARE PROBABLY HALFWAY TO RIO AND LAUGHING THEMSELVES STUPID AT GOTHAM'S "FINEST".
YOU'RE WRONG, HARV. BANE WORKED TOO HARD TO GET HIS GRIP ON THIS TOWN'S UNDERWORLD.

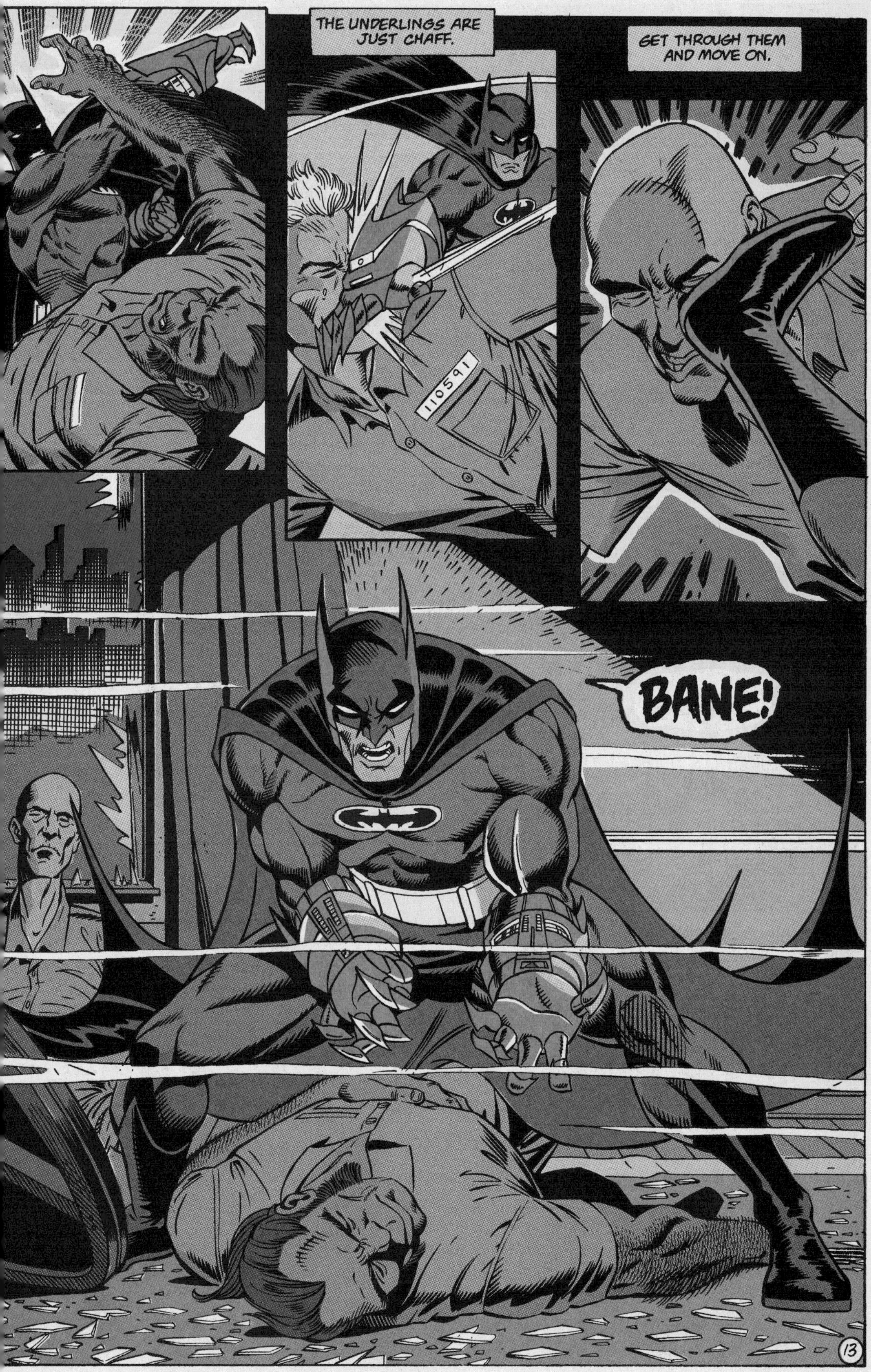
THE UNDERLINGS ARE JUST CHAFF.
GET THROUGH THEM AND MOVE ON.
110591
BANE!
13

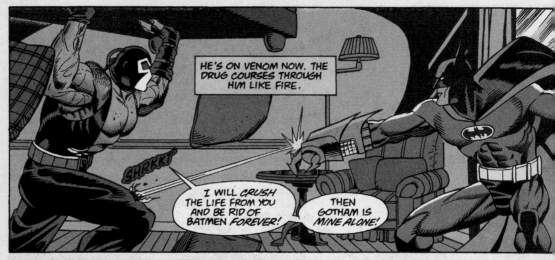

HE'S ON VENOM NOW. THE DRUG COURSES THROUGH HIM LIKE FIRE.

SHRKKT

I WILL *CRUSH* THE LIFE FROM YOU AND BE RID OF BATMEN *FOREVER!*

THEN GOTHAM IS *MINE ALONE!*

THE DANGER IS GREATER. THE RISKS ARE HIGHER.

AND THIS TIME I *KILL* YOU!

THE MONSTER IS AT THE HEIGHT OF HIS POWERS.

I WILL MAKE YOUR DEATH A *MONUMENT.*

HE SHOULD HAVE SKIPPED THE BRAVADO AND TAKEN BANE DOWN AT THE OUTSET.

THERE WILL BE *NO* MORE TO FOLLOW YOU! THE MANTLE OF THE BAT WILL BE A *FUNERAL SHROUD!*

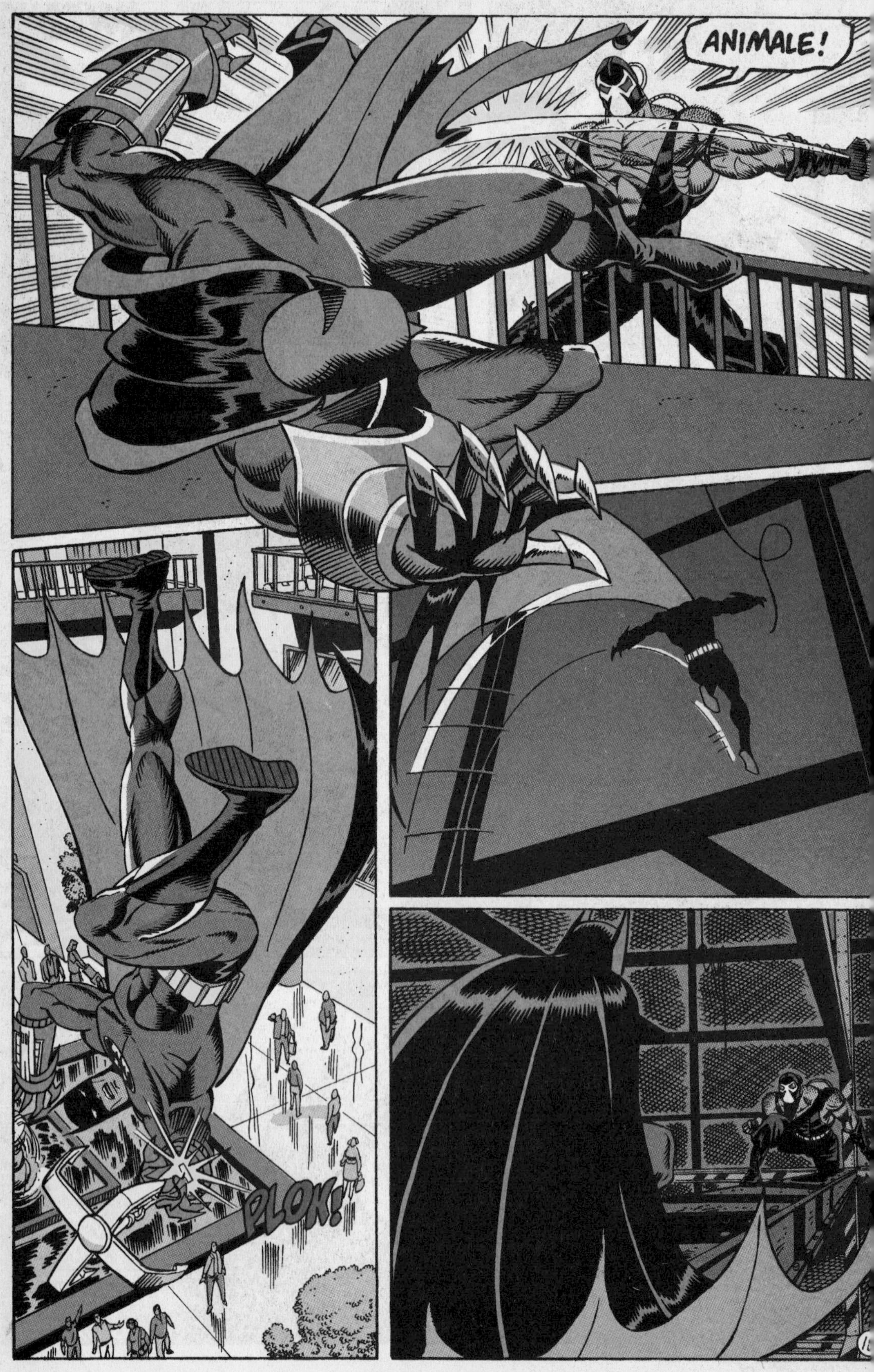
ANIMALE!
PLOK!

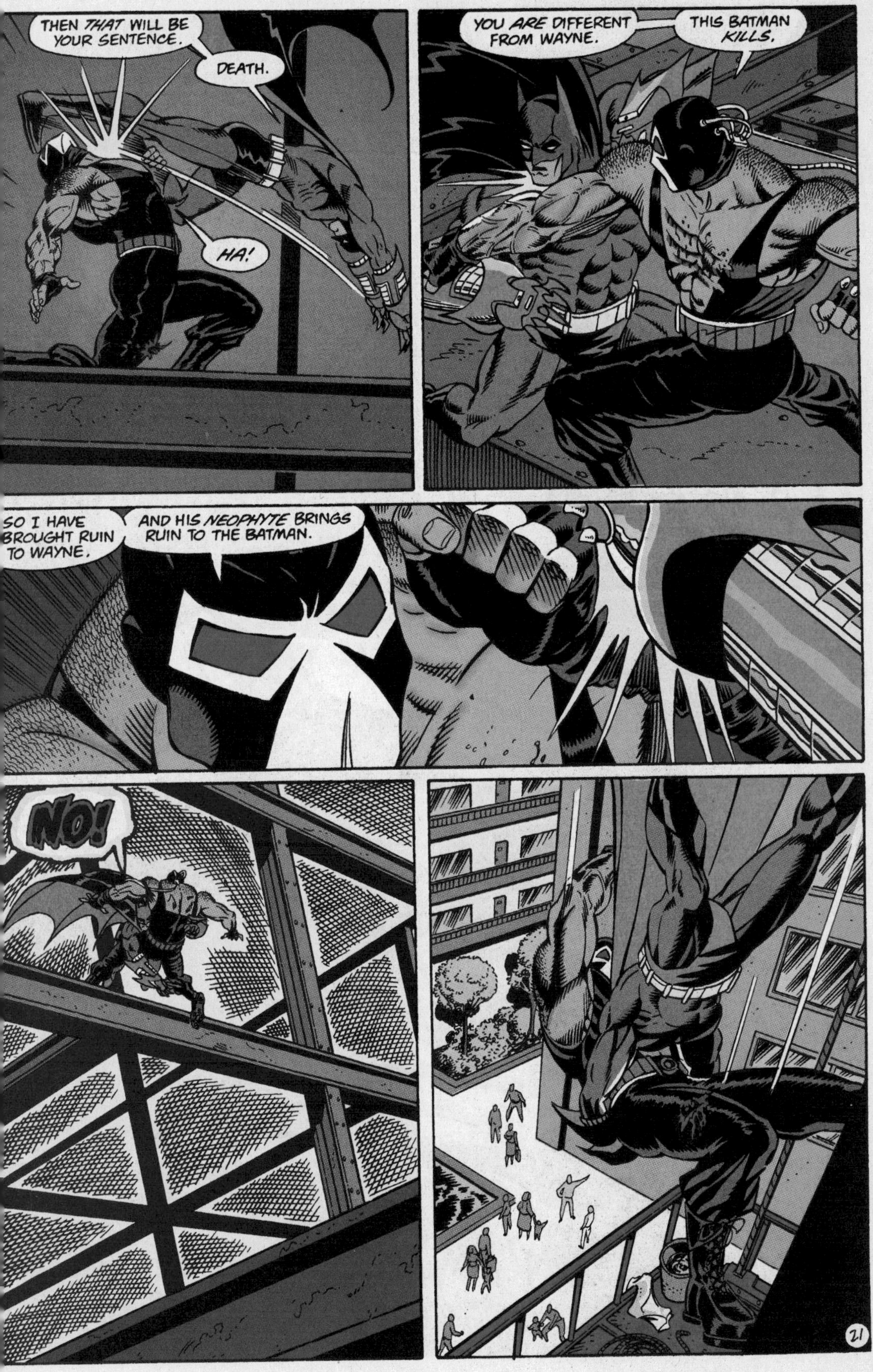
THEN THAT WILL BE YOUR SENTENCE.
DEATH.
HA!
YOU ARE DIFFERENT FROM WAYNE.
THIS BATMAN KILLS.
SO I HAVE BROUGHT RUIN TO WAYNE.
AND HIS NEOPHYTE BRINGS RUIN TO THE BATMAN.
NO!
21

BATMAN

500

ON SALE IN AUGUST

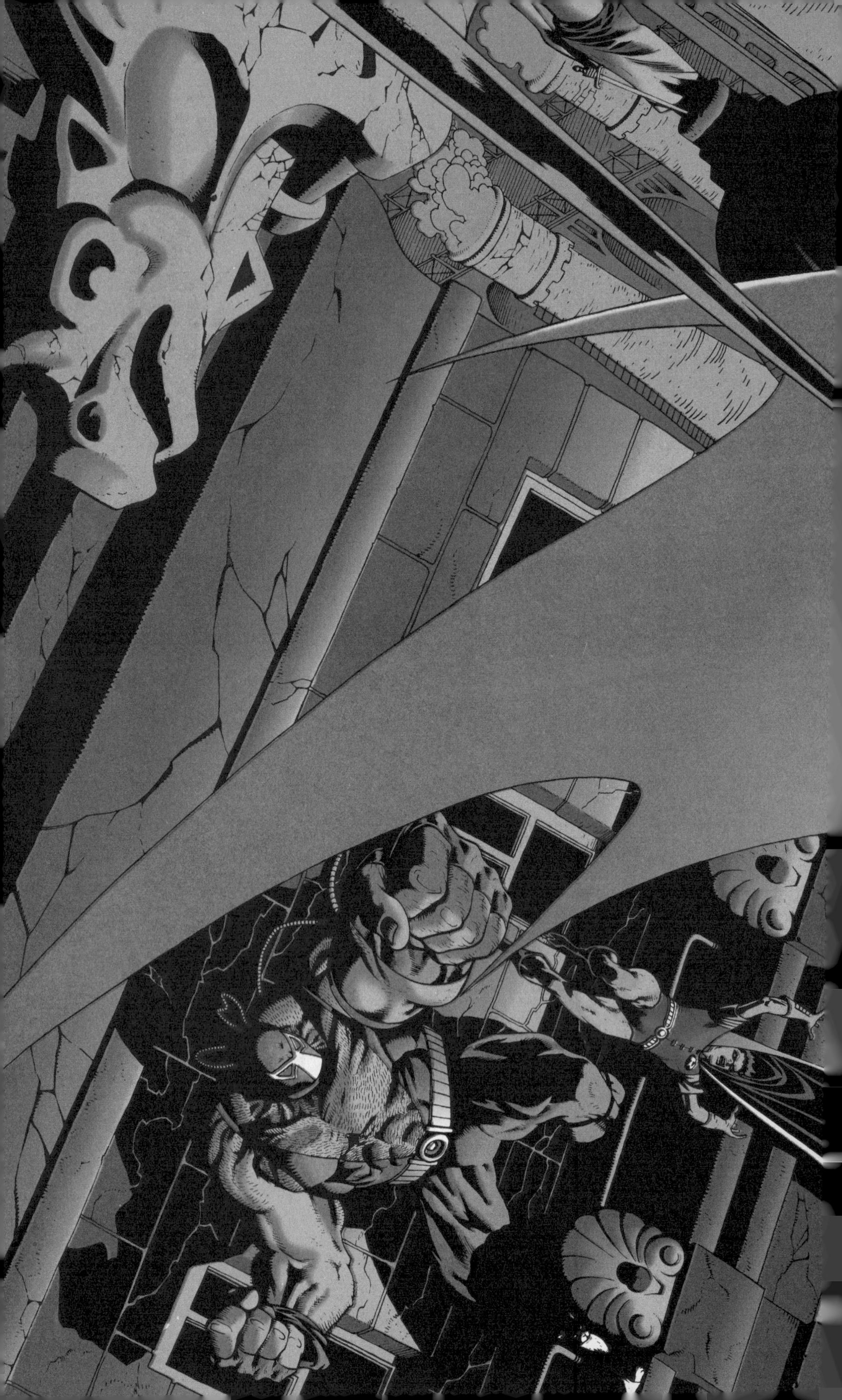

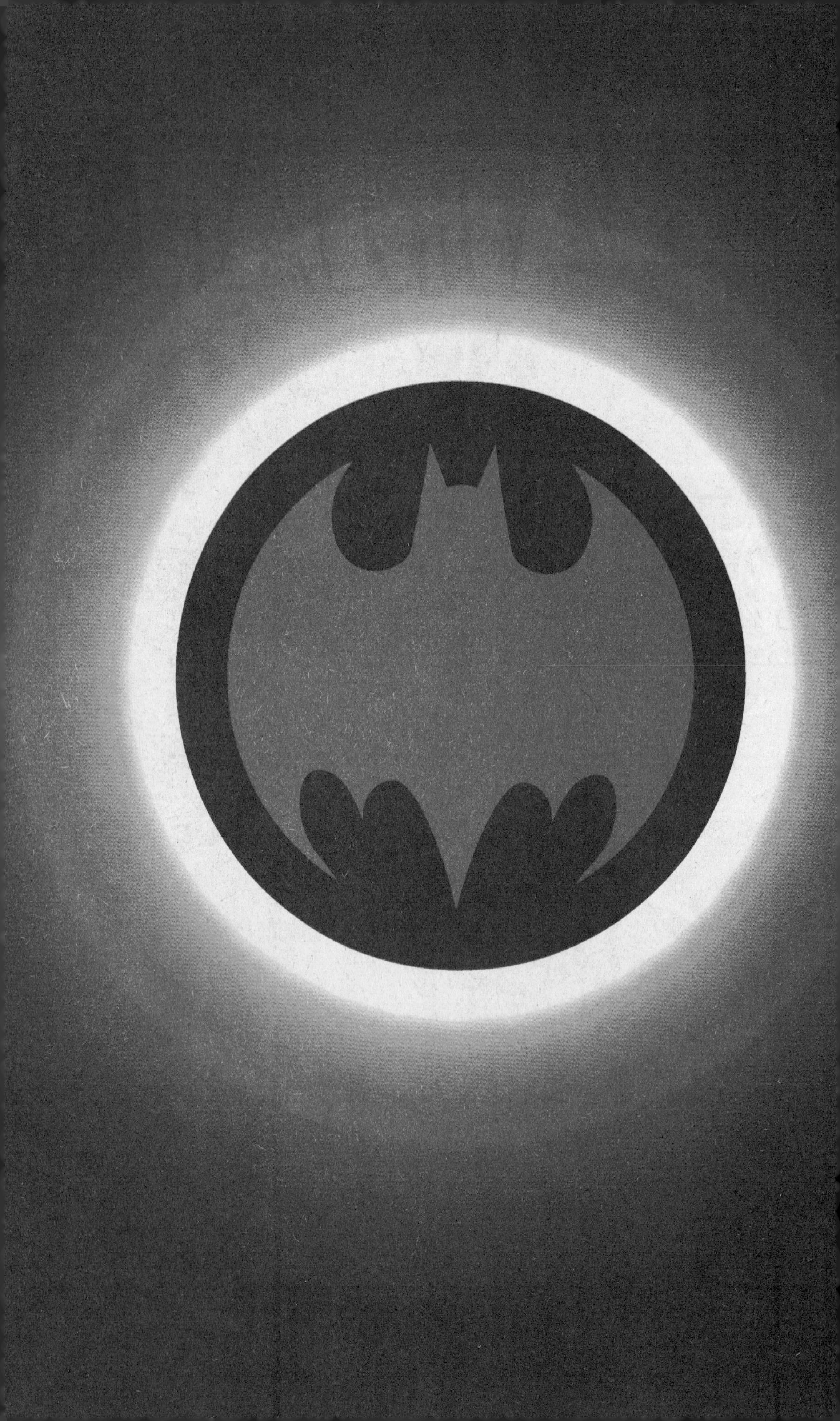

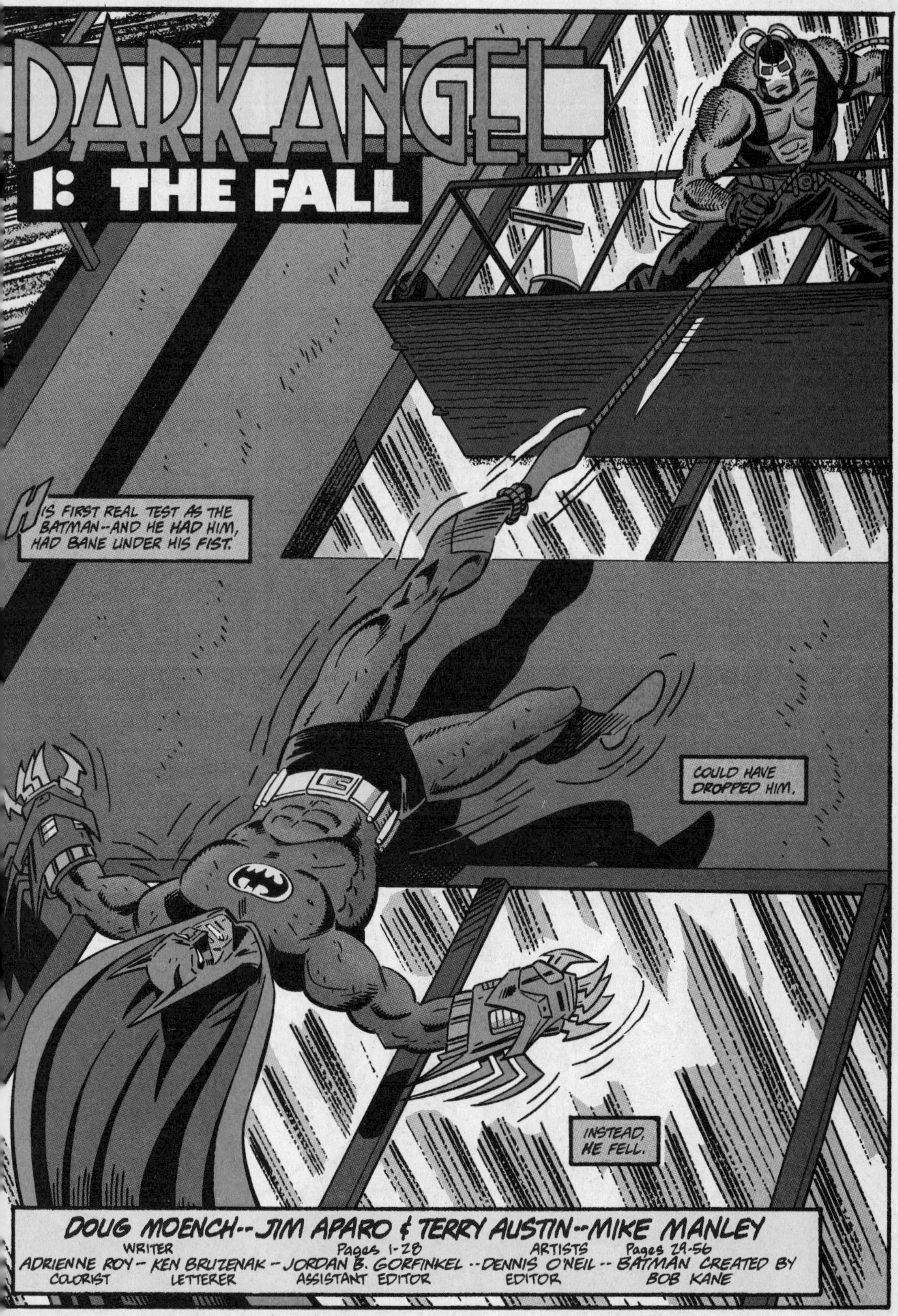
DARK ANGEL
1: THE FALL
HIS FIRST REAL TEST AS THE BATMAN--AND HE HAD HIM, HAD BANE UNDER HIS FIST.
COULD HAVE DROPPED HIM.
INSTEAD, HE FELL.
DOUG MOENCH--JIM APARO & TERRY AUSTIN--MIKE MANLEY
WRITER Pages 1-28 ARTISTS Pages 29-56
ADRIENNE ROY-- KEN BRUZENAK -- JORDAN B. GORFINKEL --DENNIS O'NEIL -- BATMAN CREATED BY
COLORIST LETTERER ASSISTANT EDITOR EDITOR BOB KANE

AND NOW BANE IS USING A SHURIKEN-- ONE OF HIS OWN NEW WEAPONS--TO MAKE THE FALL PERMANENT.

RNCH
RNCH

TO HELL WITH BUYING TIME.

HE TRIES TO SMASH AND GRAB IT, SHOOTING MORE OF THE BLADES.

SHING
SHING
SHING

DRIVING BANE BACK.

PRESERVING THE ROPE.

CHTCH
CHUT
SHING

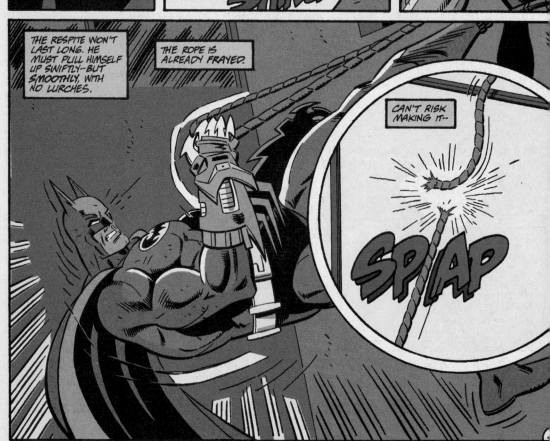

THE RESPITE WON'T LAST LONG. HE MUST PULL HIMSELF UP SWIFTLY--BUT SMOOTHLY, WITH NO LURCHES.

THE ROPE IS ALREADY FRAYED.

CAN'T RISK MAKING IT--

SPLAP

SEVERED, THE ROPE IS USELESS.

HE KICKS IT FREE.

ABOVE, BANE THINKS HE IS DEAD.

HRHHH!

AND WITH NO SECURE PURCHASE FOR HIS GRAPNEL, IT WOULD BE HARD TO ARGUE.

CHT

HE SHOOTS FOR LIFE ANYWAY,

THE GRAPNEL CATCHES POORLY, AS EXPECTED, AND EVEN AS THE BREATH IS SLAMMED FROM HIS BODY--

WUMPT

SKRIKKT

--HE FEELS THE LINE SLACKEN IN HIS GRASP.

HE WISHES HE COULD FLY.

3

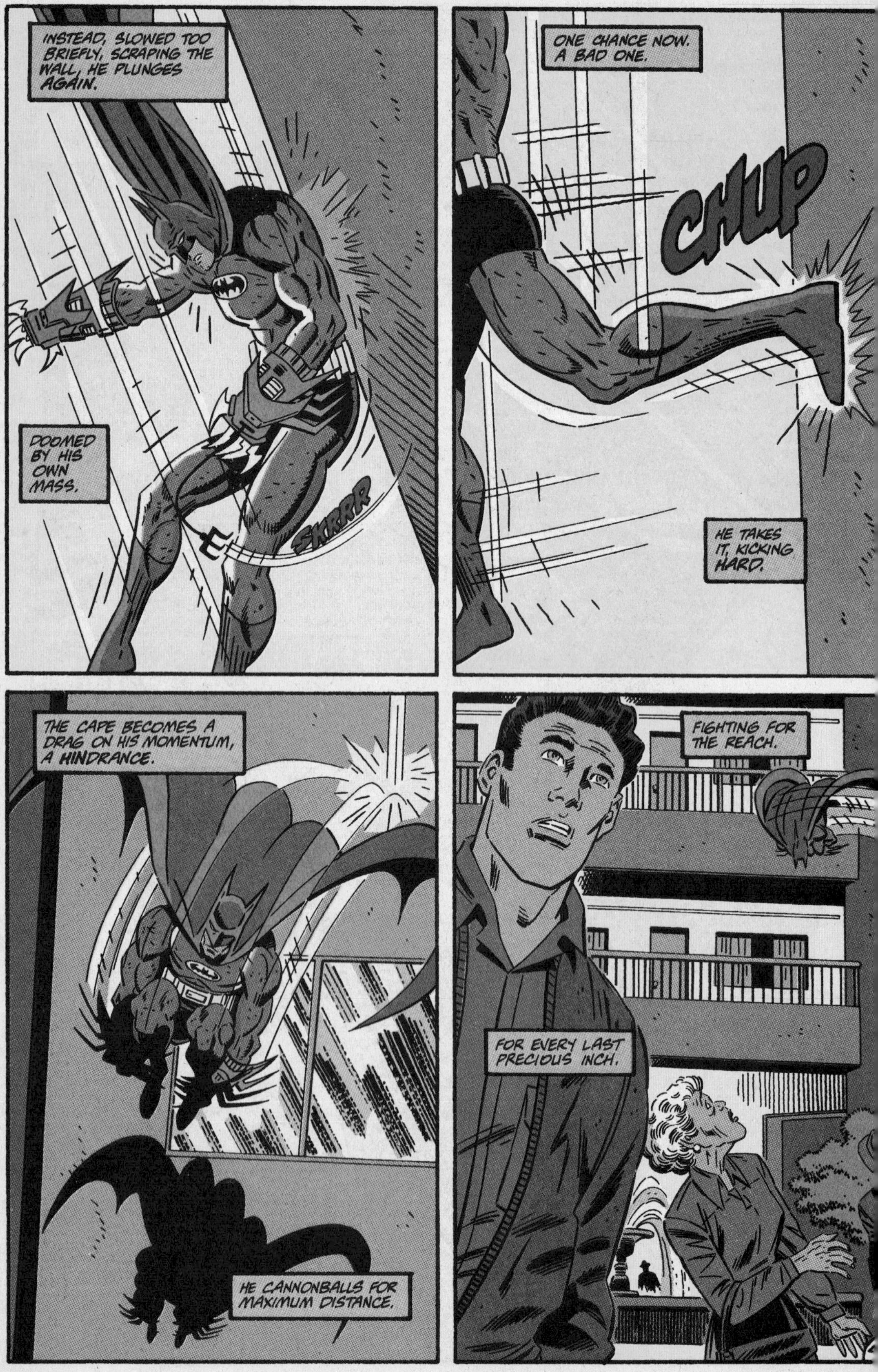
INSTEAD, SLOWED TOO BRIEFLY, SCRAPING THE WALL, HE PLUNGES AGAIN.
DOOMED BY HIS OWN MASS.
SKRRR
ONE CHANCE NOW. A BAD ONE.
CHUP
HE TAKES IT, KICKING HARD.
THE CAPE BECOMES A DRAG ON HIS MOMENTUM, A HINDRANCE.
HE CANNONBALLS FOR MAXIMUM DISTANCE.
FIGHTING FOR THE REACH.
FOR EVERY LAST PRECIOUS INCH.

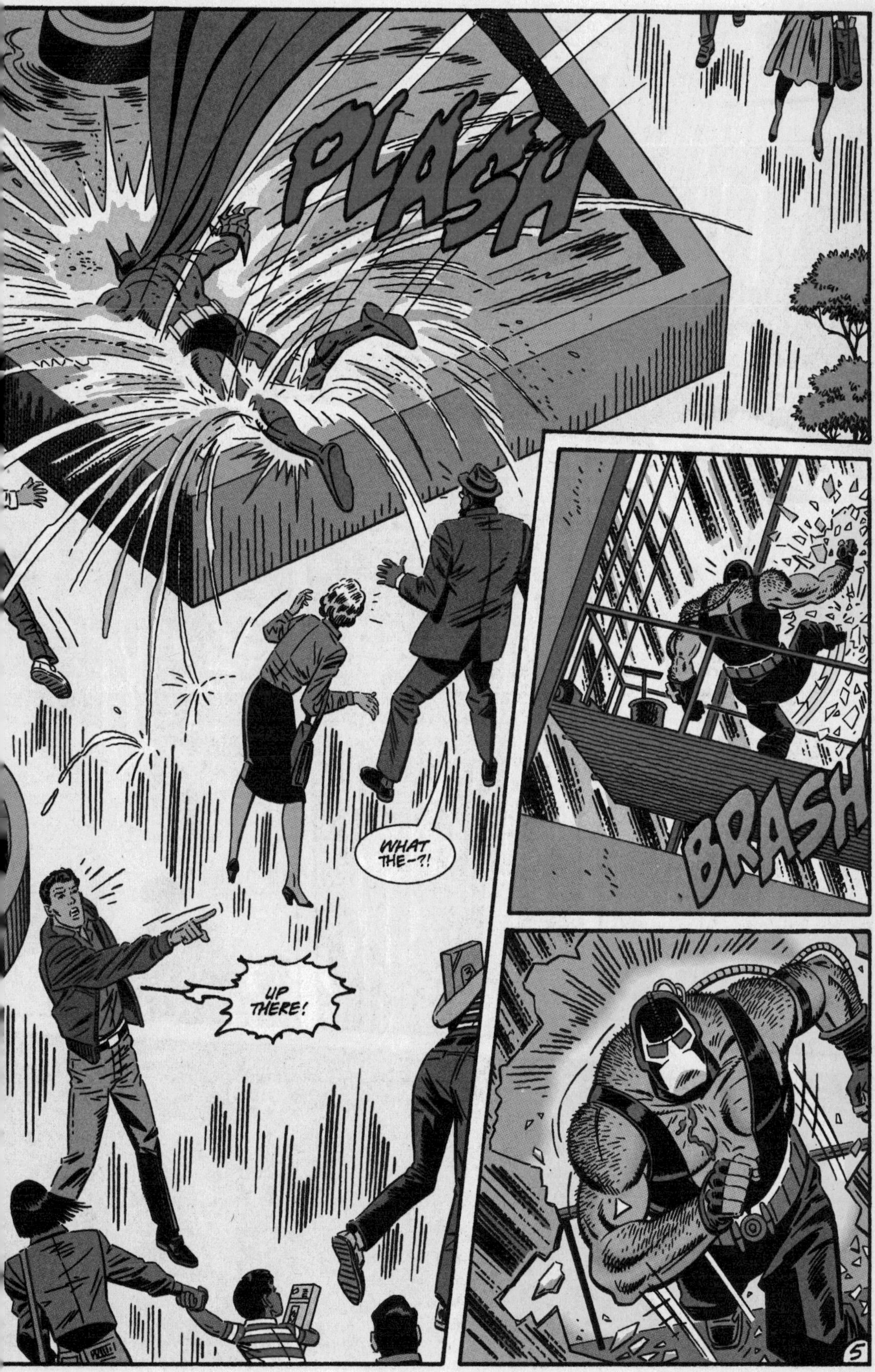
PLASH
BRASH
WHAT THE-?!
UP THERE!
5

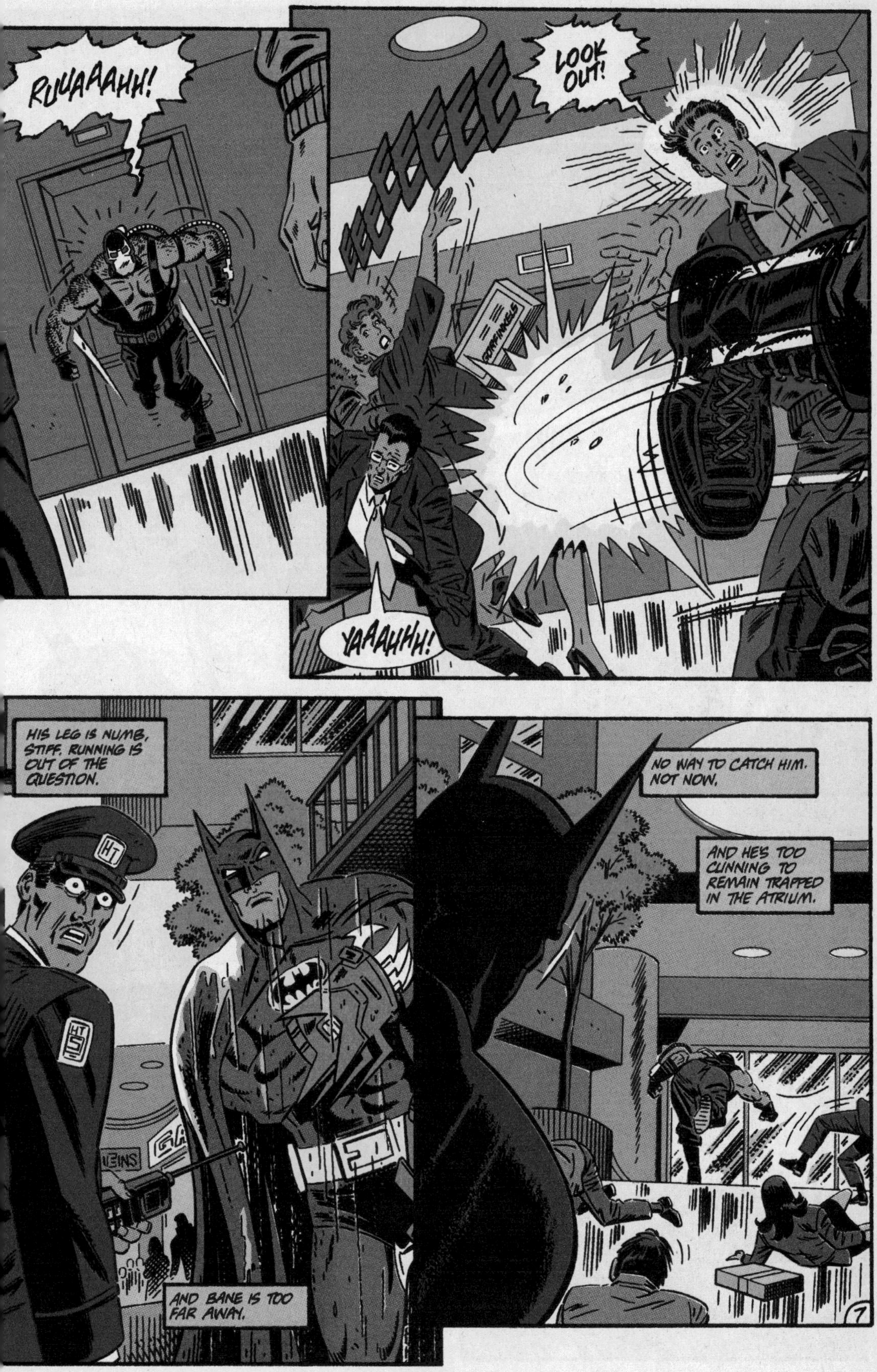
RUUAAAHH!
EEEEEEEEE
LOOK OUT!
YAAAHHH!
HIS LEG IS NUMB, STIFF. RUNNING IS OUT OF THE QUESTION.
AND BANE IS TOO FAR AWAY.
NO WAY TO CATCH HIM. NOT NOW.
AND HE'S TOO CUNNING TO REMAIN TRAPPED IN THE ATRIUM.
7

WHEN THEY NEXT MEET, IT WILL BE OUTSIDE, IN THE WILD.

HARBORGATE

TWO BEASTS HUNTING THE URBAN JUNGLE.

A LITTLE LATE FOR SEALING EXITS.

BUT DON'T WORRY.

HE WON'T RUN FAR.

YOUR GUEST JUST CHECKED OUT.

NEVER KNEW HE HAD...

AND I'LL FIND HIM.

...CLAWS.

249

WHAT'S THE SITUATION, SERGEANT BULLOCK?

BACK TO SQUARE ONE, LIEUTENANT--BATMAN DROPPED THE THREE STOOGES AGAIN, BUT BANE GOT AWAY.

AND THE BATMAN?

HE'S GONE, TOO WITNESSES JUDGE ROUND ONE A DRAW.

ROUND ONE?

OF THE REMATCH-- AN' YA ASK ME, IT'S AN EVEN BET.

WAY I SEE IT, THAT FIRST LOSS WOKE THE BATMAN UP. SEEMS LIKE HE'S TOUGHER NOW, ALL BUSINESS. MIGHT EVEN BE THE GLOVES ARE OFF.

LIEUTENANT KITCH? WE JUST GOT A CALL. THE MAYOR WANTS TO SEE YOU-- NOW.

KROL WANTS ME?

WORD IS, HE AND COMMISSIONER GORDON AREN'T ON SPEAKING TERMS RIGHT NOW.

I CAN VOUCH FOR THAT--AN' THE COMMISH AIN'T CRYIN' OVER IT NEITHER.

ALL RIGHT, GET THESE THREE BACK TO LOCKUP-- AND DOUBLE THE SECURITY.

TOLD ARIANA
IM "BUSY"--BUT
DOING *WHAT*?

JEAN PAUL
DOESN'T WANT
ME *AROUND*--
AND BRUCE TOLD
ME NOT TO GO
AFTER *BANE*.

PAUL--?

OVER
HERE...

...STRETCHING
OUT SOME
KINKS.

YOU'RE
HURT?

I'LL BE
FINE. WHAT
DO YOU
WANT?

WHAT YOU'RE DOING
ISN'T *RIGHT*, PAUL.
IT ISN'T THE BATMAN.
IT'S TOO *BRUTAL*, I
MEAN, WHAT
ABOUT BASIC
DECENCY?

I'LL *PRESERVE*
DECENCY, BUT I DON'T
NEED IT-- AND I
WON'T NECESSARILY
USE IT.

THEN YOU'RE
NOT PRESERVING
IT.

YES
I *AM*--ANY
WAY I *CAN*.
I'M SAVING THE
CITY, NOT
MYSELF.

BUT
THERE'S NO
HONOR--

AMONG *THIEVES*--
AND WE'RE DEALING
WITH A LOT *WORSE*
THAN THIEVES.

ON
THEIR
LEVEL.

11

251

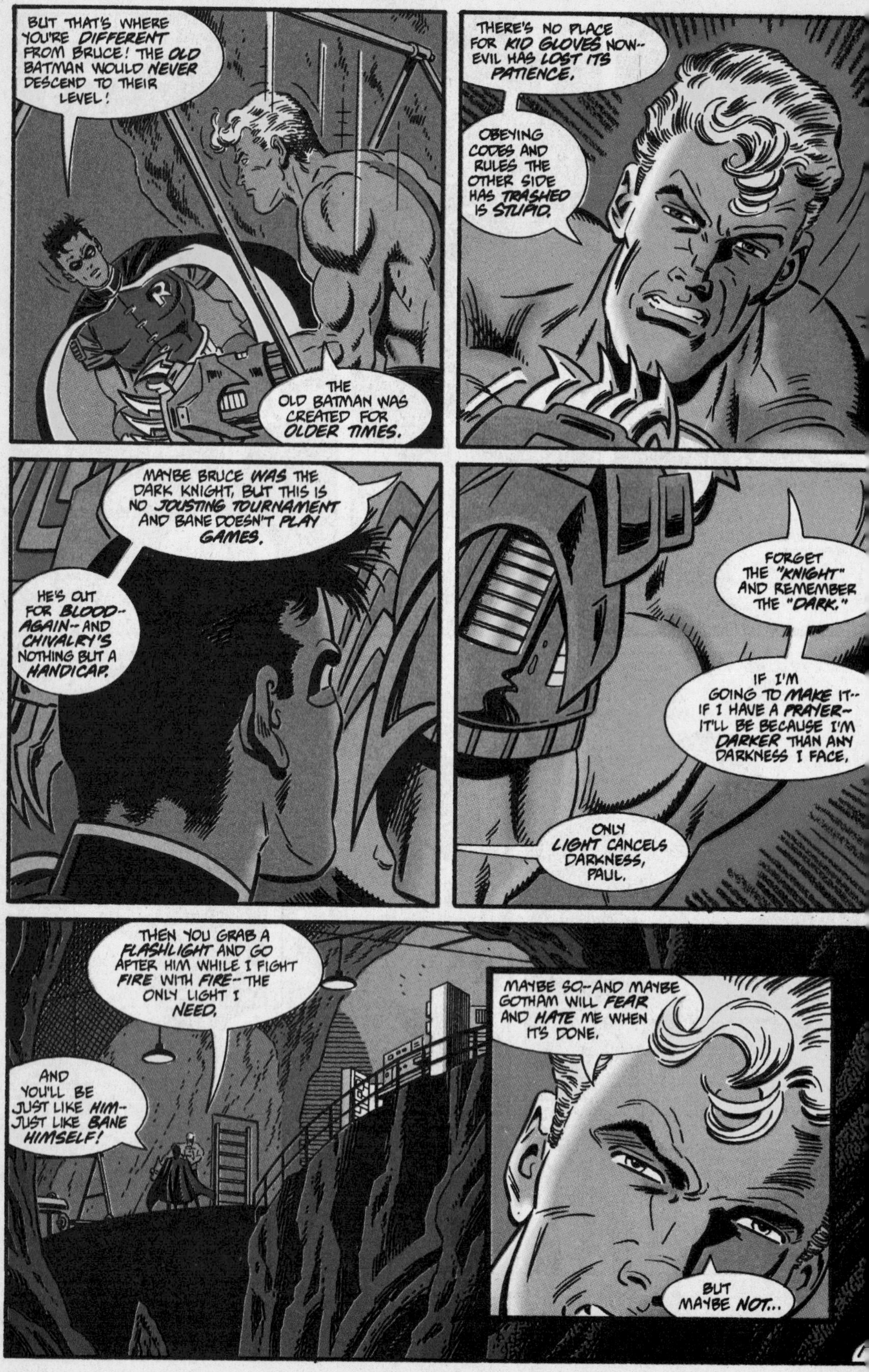
BUT THAT'S WHERE YOU'RE DIFFERENT FROM BRUCE! THE OLD BATMAN WOULD NEVER DESCEND TO THEIR LEVEL!
THE OLD BATMAN WAS CREATED FOR OLDER TIMES.
THERE'S NO PLACE FOR KID GLOVES NOW-- EVIL HAS LOST ITS PATIENCE.
OBEYING CODES AND RULES THE OTHER SIDE HAS TRASHED IS STUPID.
MAYBE BRUCE WAS THE DARK KNIGHT, BUT THIS IS NO JOUSTING TOURNAMENT AND BANE DOESN'T PLAY GAMES.
HE'S OUT FOR BLOOD-- AGAIN-- AND CHIVALRY'S NOTHING BUT A HANDICAP.
FORGET THE "KNIGHT" AND REMEMBER THE "DARK."
IF I'M GOING TO MAKE IT-- IF I HAVE A PRAYER-- IT'LL BE BECAUSE I'M DARKER THAN ANY DARKNESS I FACE.
ONLY LIGHT CANCELS DARKNESS, PAUL.
THEN YOU GRAB A FLASHLIGHT AND GO AFTER HIM WHILE I FIGHT FIRE WITH FIRE-- THE ONLY LIGHT I NEED.
AND YOU'LL BE JUST LIKE HIM-- JUST LIKE BANE HIMSELF!
MAYBE SO-- AND MAYBE GOTHAM WILL FEAR AND HATE ME WHEN IT'S DONE.
BUT MAYBE NOT...

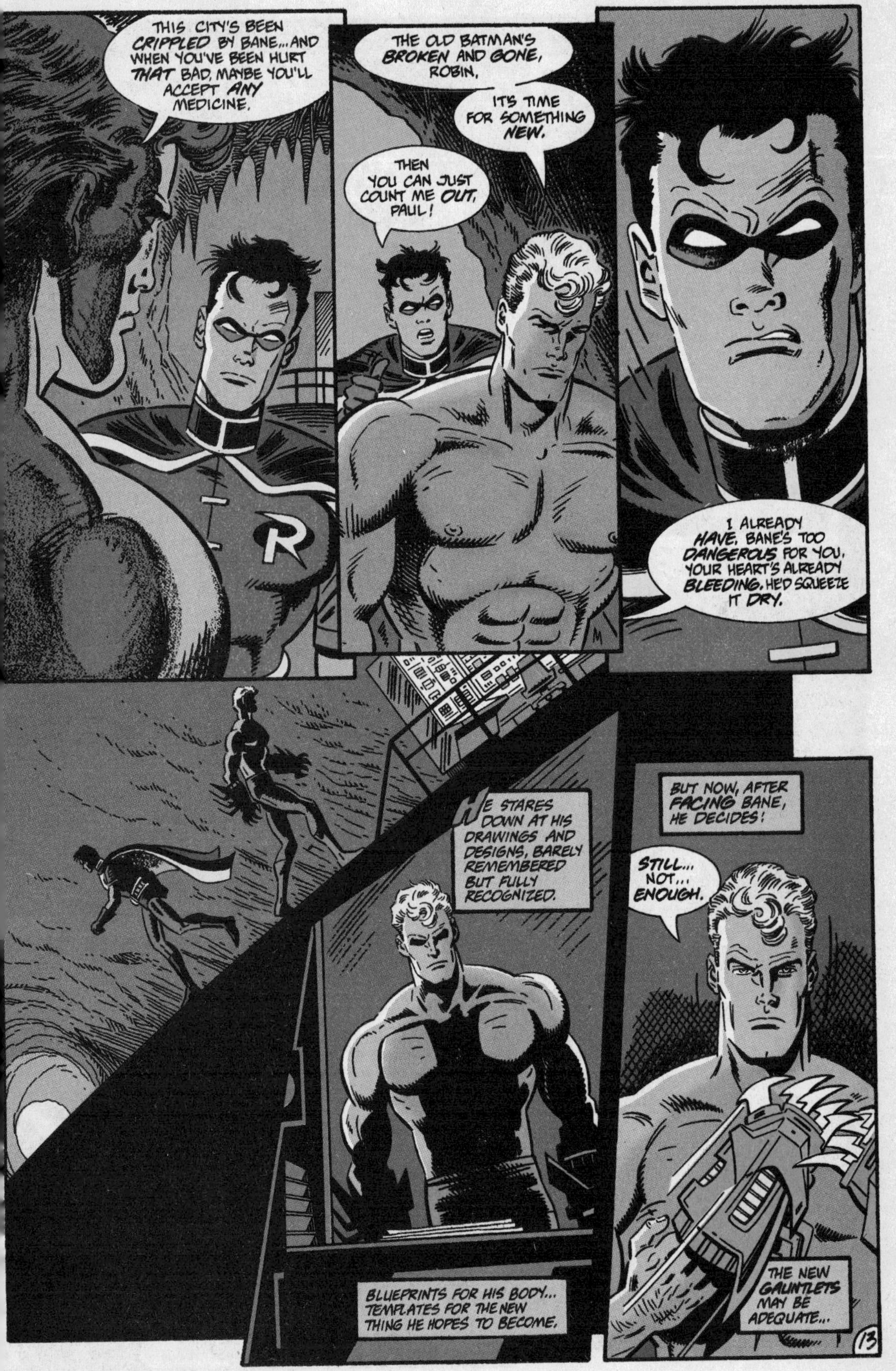
THIS CITY'S BEEN CRIPPLED BY BANE... AND WHEN YOU'VE BEEN HURT THAT BAD, MAYBE YOU'LL ACCEPT ANY MEDICINE.
THE OLD BATMAN'S BROKEN AND GONE, ROBIN.
IT'S TIME FOR SOMETHING NEW.
THEN YOU CAN JUST COUNT ME OUT, PAUL!
I ALREADY HAVE. BANE'S TOO DANGEROUS FOR YOU. YOUR HEART'S ALREADY BLEEDING. HE'D SQUEEZE IT DRY.
HE STARES DOWN AT HIS DRAWINGS AND DESIGNS, BARELY REMEMBERED BUT FULLY RECOGNIZED.
BLUEPRINTS FOR HIS BODY... TEMPLATES FOR THE NEW THING HE HOPES TO BECOME.
BUT NOW, AFTER FACING BANE, HE DECIDES!
STILL... NOT... ENOUGH.
THE NEW GAUNTLETS MAY BE ADEQUATE...
13

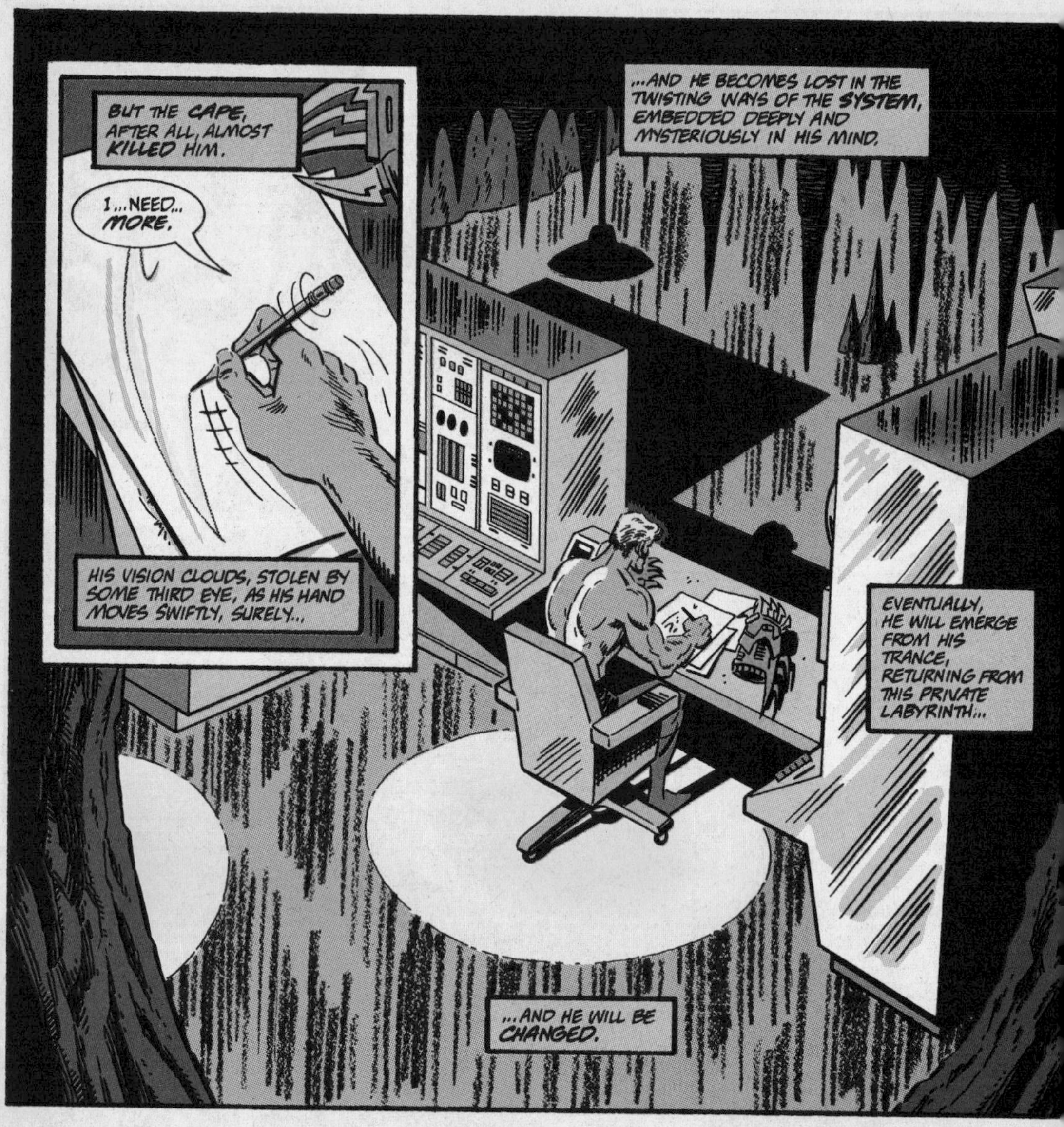

BUT THE CAPE, AFTER ALL, ALMOST KILLED HIM.
I...NEED... MORE.
HIS VISION CLOUDS, STOLEN BY SOME THIRD EYE, AS HIS HAND MOVES SWIFTLY, SURELY...
...AND HE BECOMES LOST IN THE TWISTING WAYS OF THE SYSTEM, EMBEDDED DEEPLY AND MYSTERIOUSLY IN HIS MIND.
EVENTUALLY, HE WILL EMERGE FROM HIS TRANCE, RETURNING FROM THIS PRIVATE LABYRINTH...
...AND HE WILL BE CHANGED.

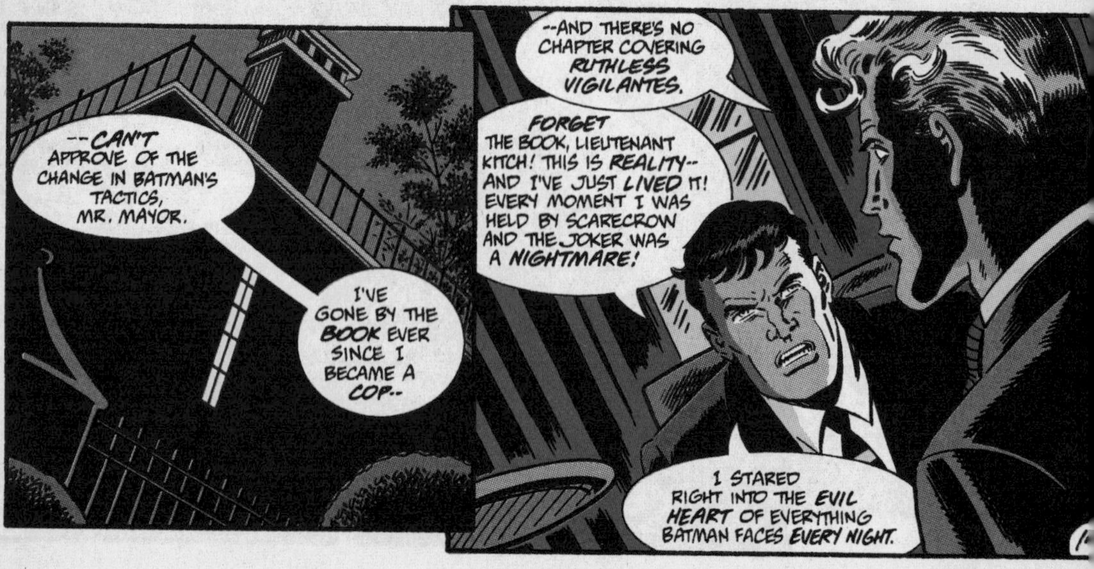

--CAN'T APPROVE OF THE CHANGE IN BATMAN'S TACTICS, MR. MAYOR.
I'VE GONE BY THE BOOK EVER SINCE I BECAME A COP--
--AND THERE'S NO CHAPTER COVERING RUTHLESS VIGILANTES.
FORGET THE BOOK, LIEUTENANT KITCH! THIS IS REALITY-- AND I'VE JUST LIVED IT! EVERY MOMENT I WAS HELD BY SCARECROW AND THE JOKER WAS A NIGHTMARE!
I STARED RIGHT INTO THE EVIL HEART OF EVERYTHING BATMAN FACES EVERY NIGHT.

E SAVED MY 'FE, KITCH--AND HE 'DN'T DO IT BY 'OLLOWING ANY BOOK!

YOU'RE NOT SUGGESTING THE *POLICE FORCE* SHOULD CHANGE ITS--

OF COURSE NOT! YOU *HAVE* TO FOLLOW THE BOOK, KITCH--*CHAPTER AND VERSE*--NO MATTER HOW MUCH IT *HAMPERS* YOU.

BUT *THEY DON'T*-- AND NEITHER DOES HE.

THAT'S WHY I'M GLAD HE'S *OUT* THERE-- AND THAT'S WHY YOUR PEOPLE WILL *NOT INTERFERE.*

...NOTHING BUT SIT HERE AND *WAIT.*

BUT IF YOU'RE NOT COMING *HOME*, JAMES, THEN WHAT ARE YOU--

NOTHING, SARAH...THERE'S NOTHING I *CAN* DO NOW...

FOR *HIM.* FOR THE *BATMAN.*

15

255

YES... FOR HIM TO MAKE A *MOVE*... AS EVER.

HE'S NEVER LET YOU DOWN *BEFORE*.

YOU'VE NEVER LET M DOWN *EITHER*, SARAI AND NOW... JUST AS YOU'RE PREPARED T *ACCEPT* THE *BATMAN*...

YOU'RE HAVING *DOUBTS*?

HE'S NOT THE *SAME*, SARAH. *SOMETHING'S* HAPPENED TO HIM.

HE'S *CHANGED*.

HE'S *DIFFERENT*.

HE FINDS HAROLD STILL *GONE*, NO MATTER. STILL *LOST* IN THE SYSTEM, HE IS CAPABLE OF *ANYTHING*.

HE WILL DO IT HIMSELF.

AND HERE IN THESE COOL CAVERN DEPTHS HE WILL FIND THE HEAT TO *FORGE* SOMETHING *NEW*.

SOON HE IS AWARE OF NOTHING BUT THE TASK AT HAND.

NOTHING ELSE MATTERS.

ALONE WITH HIS SECRET SKILLS, NOTHING ELSE IS IMPORTANT.

NOTHING BUT FINDING HIS WAY THROUGH NEW REGIONS OF THE SYSTEM'S LABYRINTH.

NOTHING BUT...

TSHH

...PRIVACY.

SHUT OUT OF THE *MANOR*, THE *CAVE*, EVEN THE *TEAM* ITSELF,

AND ALL BECAUSE--

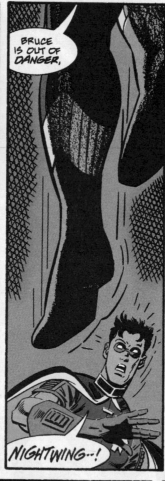

BRUCE IS OUT OF *DANGER*,

NIGHTWING--!

HOW DID YOU *KNOW* HE WAS--

I HAD TO LEARN IT FROM *ORACLE*.

UH, SORRY... BUT BRUCE FIGURED IT'D BE BEST TO KEEP IT *SECRET*.

EVEN FROM *ME*?

HEY, IT'S BEEN KINDA *FRANTIC* AROUND HERE.

NO DOUBT--BUT I'LL LET *BRUCE* TELL ME ABOUT IT.

HE'S NOT *HERE*-- AND NEITHER IS *ALFRED*.

AND YET THE *BATMAN* LOOMS *LARGE* IN TODAY'S *NEWS*.

IT'S NOT *HIM* NIGHTWIN--

HE'S OUT OF *DANGER*, BUT...HE'S STILL IN A *WHEELCHAIR*.

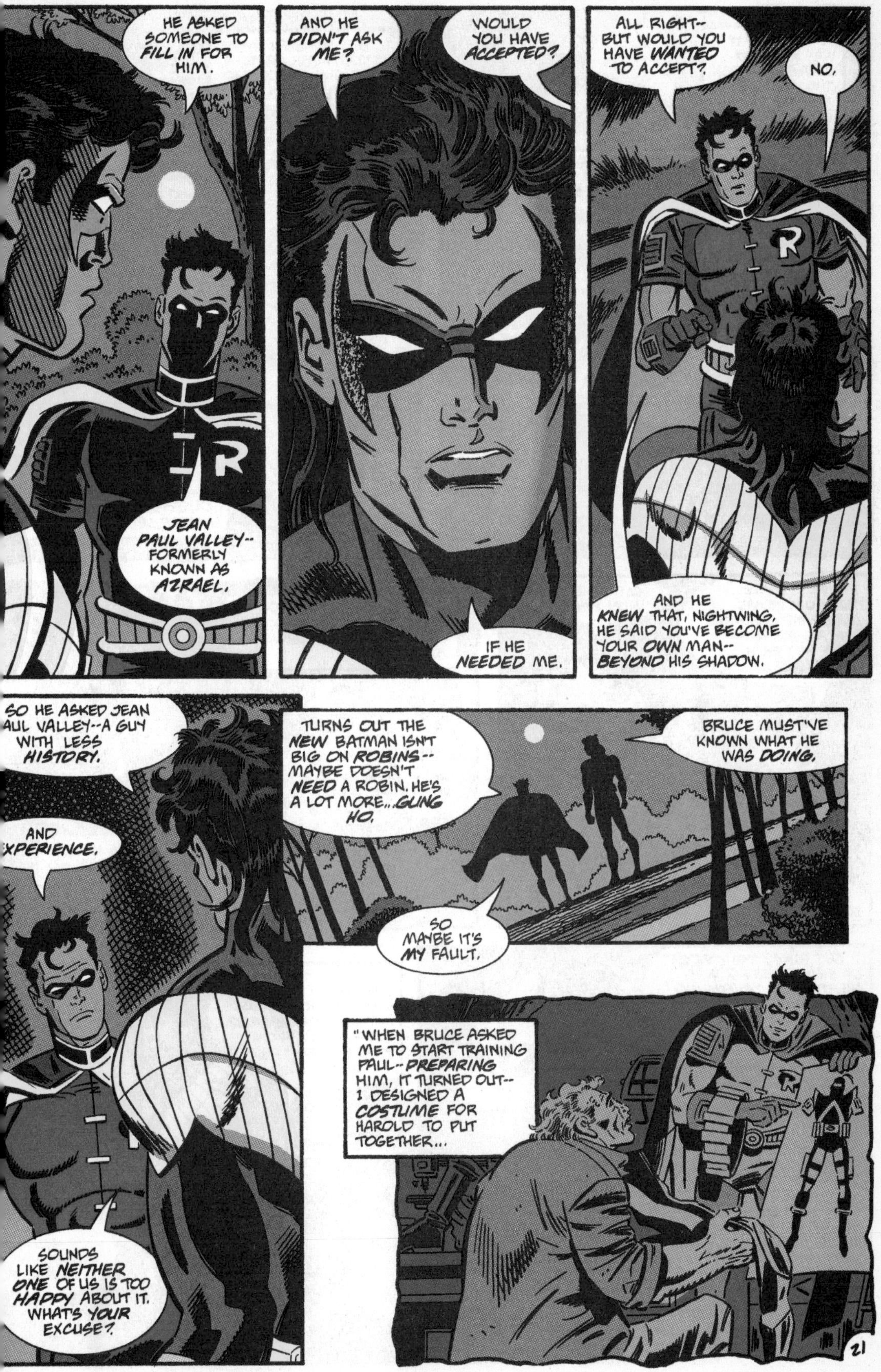

HE ASKED SOMEONE TO FILL IN FOR HIM.
JEAN PAUL VALLEY-- FORMERLY KNOWN AS AZRAEL.
AND HE DIDN'T ASK ME?
WOULD YOU HAVE ACCEPTED?
IF HE NEEDED ME.
ALL RIGHT-- BUT WOULD YOU HAVE WANTED TO ACCEPT?
NO.
AND HE KNEW THAT, NIGHTWING. HE SAID YOU'VE BECOME YOUR OWN MAN-- BEYOND HIS SHADOW.
SO HE ASKED JEAN PAUL VALLEY--A GUY WITH LESS HISTORY.
AND EXPERIENCE.
SOUNDS LIKE NEITHER ONE OF US IS TOO HAPPY ABOUT IT. WHAT'S YOUR EXCUSE?
TURNS OUT THE NEW BATMAN ISN'T BIG ON ROBINS-- MAYBE DOESN'T NEED A ROBIN. HE'S A LOT MORE... GUNG HO.
BRUCE MUST'VE KNOWN WHAT HE WAS DOING.
SO MAYBE IT'S MY FAULT.
"WHEN BRUCE ASKED ME TO START TRAINING PAUL--PREPARING HIM, IT TURNED OUT-- I DESIGNED A COSTUME FOR HAROLD TO PUT TOGETHER...
21

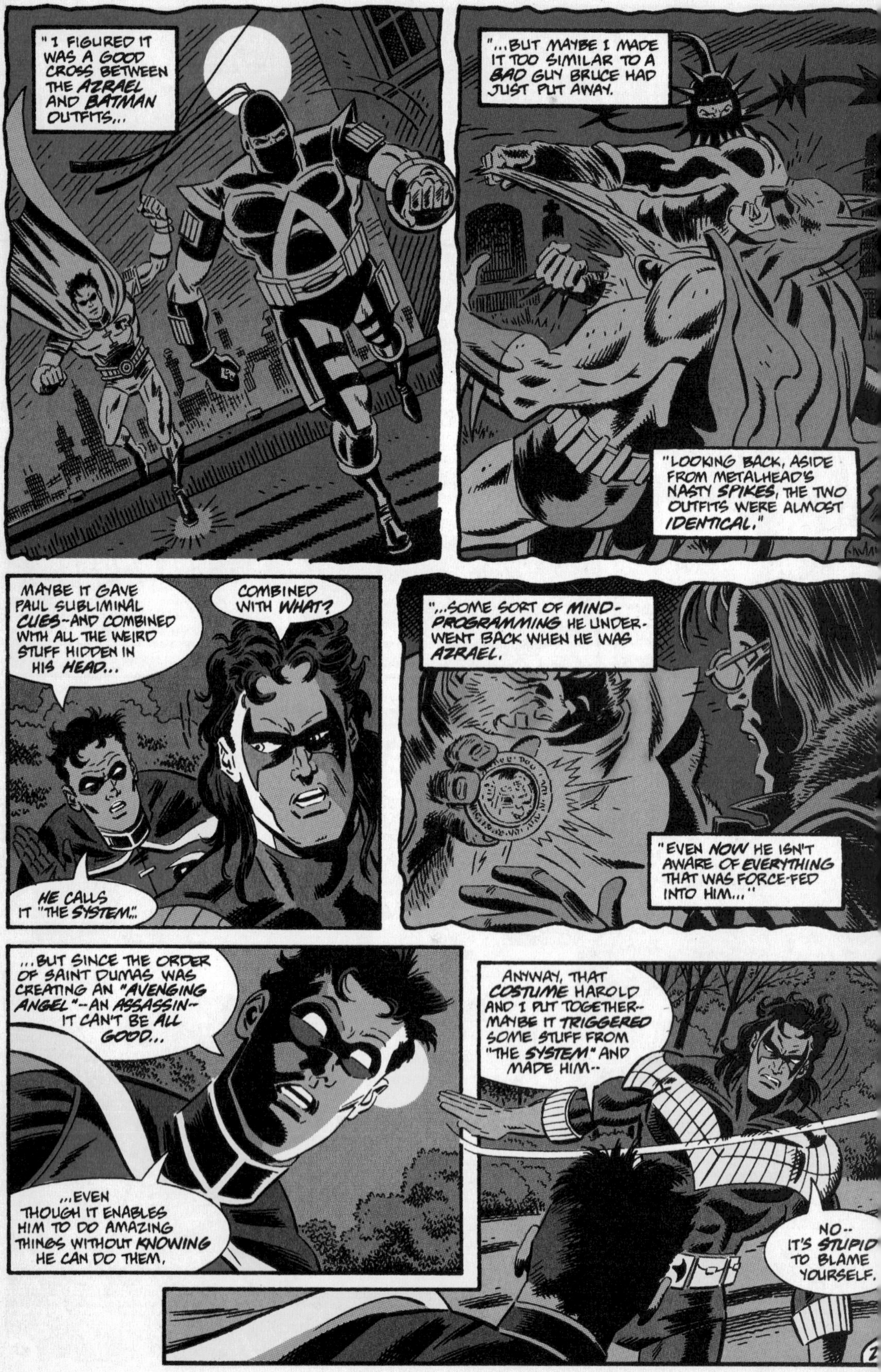
"I FIGURED IT WAS A GOOD CROSS BETWEEN THE AZRAEL AND BATMAN OUTFITS...
"...BUT MAYBE I MADE IT TOO SIMILAR TO A BAD GUY BRUCE HAD JUST PUT AWAY.
"LOOKING BACK, ASIDE FROM METALHEAD'S NASTY SPIKES, THE TWO OUTFITS WERE ALMOST IDENTICAL."
MAYBE IT GAVE PAUL SUBLIMINAL CUES--AND COMBINED WITH ALL THE WEIRD STUFF HIDDEN IN HIS HEAD...
COMBINED WITH WHAT?
HE CALLS IT "THE SYSTEM."
"...SOME SORT OF MIND-PROGRAMMING HE UNDERWENT BACK WHEN HE WAS AZRAEL.
"EVEN NOW HE ISN'T AWARE OF EVERYTHING THAT WAS FORCE-FED INTO HIM..."
...BUT SINCE THE ORDER OF SAINT DUMAS WAS CREATING AN "AVENGING ANGEL"--AN ASSASSIN--IT CAN'T BE ALL GOOD...
...EVEN THOUGH IT ENABLES HIM TO DO AMAZING THINGS WITHOUT KNOWING HE CAN DO THEM.
ANYWAY, THAT COSTUME HAROLD AND I PUT TOGETHER--MAYBE IT TRIGGERED SOME STUFF FROM "THE SYSTEM" AND MADE HIM--
NO-- IT'S STUPID TO BLAME YOURSELF.

EITHER THIS JEAN PAUL VALLEY IS GOOD ENOUGH OR HE ISN'T.

BRUCE THINKS HE IS,

THEN THAT'S IT--

--AND THERE'S NOTHING HERE FOR US TO DO.

MAYBE NOT...

...BUT I'M GAME FOR ONE LAST TRY,

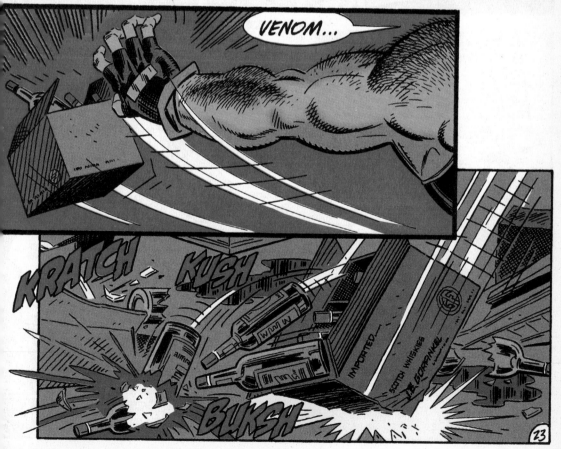

VENOM...

KRATCH KUSH

BUKSH

IMPORTED--

SCOTCH WHISKY

23

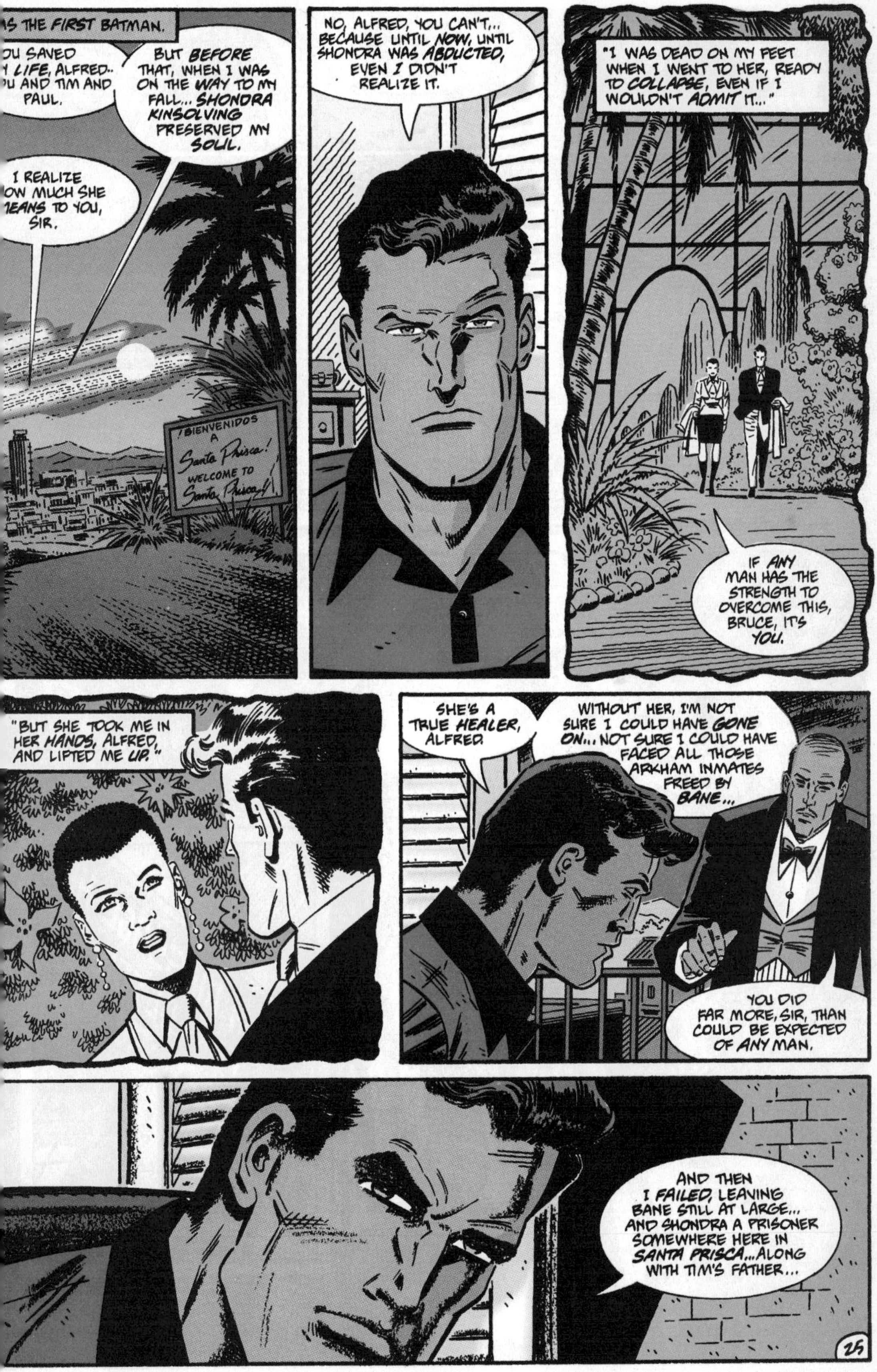
...AS THE FIRST BATMAN.
...OU SAVED ...Y LIFE, ALFRED.. ...OU AND TIM AND PAUL.
BUT BEFORE THAT, WHEN I WAS ON THE WAY TO MY FALL... SHONDRA KINSOLVING PRESERVED MY SOUL.
I REALIZE ...OW MUCH SHE ...EANS TO YOU, SIR.
!BIENVENIDOS A Santa Prisca! WELCOME TO Santa Prisca!
NO, ALFRED, YOU CAN'T... BECAUSE UNTIL NOW, UNTIL SHONDRA WAS ABDUCTED, EVEN I DIDN'T REALIZE IT.
"I WAS DEAD ON MY FEET WHEN I WENT TO HER, READY TO COLLAPSE, EVEN IF I WOULDN'T ADMIT IT..."
IF ANY MAN HAS THE STRENGTH TO OVERCOME THIS, BRUCE, IT'S YOU.
"BUT SHE TOOK ME IN HER HANDS, ALFRED, AND LIFTED ME UP."
SHE'S A TRUE HEALER, ALFRED.
WITHOUT HER, I'M NOT SURE I COULD HAVE GONE ON... NOT SURE I COULD HAVE FACED ALL THOSE ARKHAM INMATES FREED BY BANE...
YOU DID FAR MORE, SIR, THAN COULD BE EXPECTED OF ANY MAN.
AND THEN I FAILED, LEAVING BANE STILL AT LARGE... AND SHONDRA A PRISONER SOMEWHERE HERE IN SANTA PRISCA...ALONG WITH TIM'S FATHER...
25

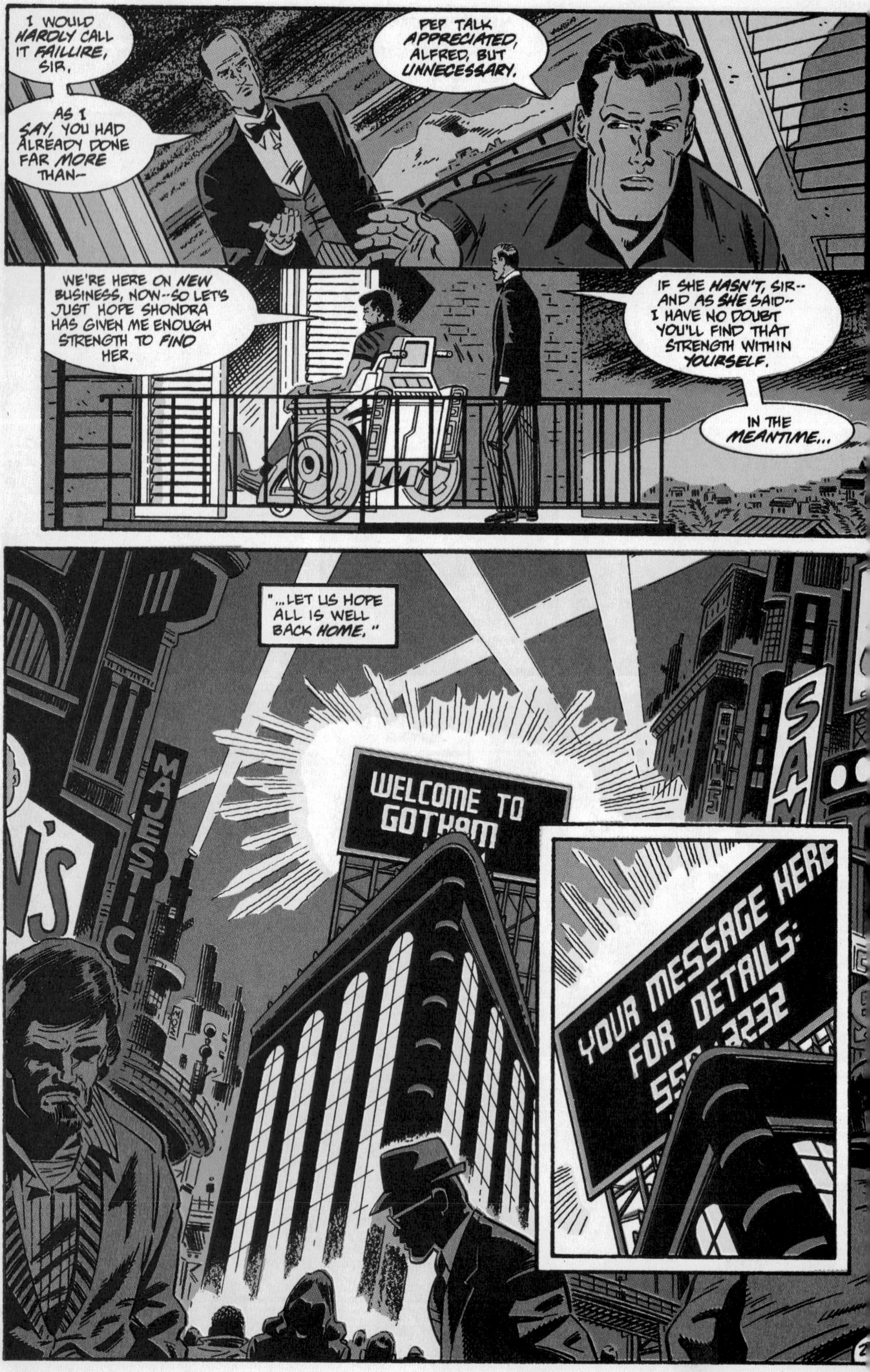
I WOULD HARDLY CALL IT FAILURE, SIR.
AS I SAY, YOU HAD ALREADY DONE FAR MORE THAN–
PEP TALK APPRECIATED, ALFRED, BUT UNNECESSARY.
WE'RE HERE ON NEW BUSINESS, NOW--SO LET'S JUST HOPE SHONDRA HAS GIVEN ME ENOUGH STRENGTH TO FIND HER.
IF SHE HASN'T, SIR-- AND AS SHE SAID-- I HAVE NO DOUBT YOU'LL FIND THAT STRENGTH WITHIN YOURSELF.
IN THE MEANTIME...
"...LET US HOPE ALL IS WELL BACK HOME."
WELCOME TO GOTHAM
MAJESTIC
YOUR MESSAGE HERE
FOR DETAILS:

WHAT'S NEXT?
NEWS AND WEATHER,
OR ANOTHER
AO?

AN AO,
OF COURSE, AND
FOR NOTHING LESS
THAN GOOD OLD--

AGHK!

KRAKT

DEATH.

NO MORE
RUNNING.

K-KLUMP

TIME TO
END IT.

27

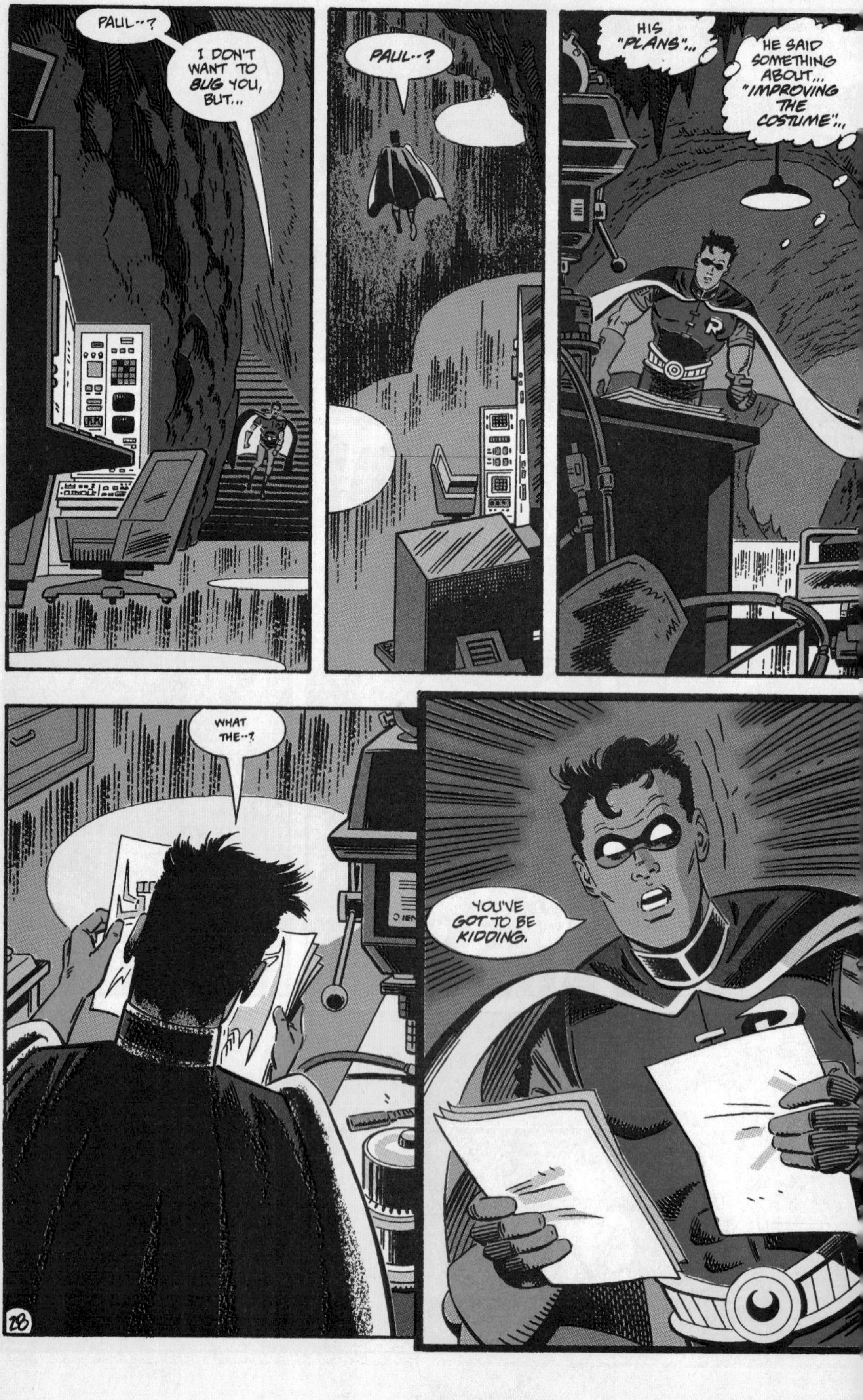
PAUL--?
I DON'T WANT TO BUG YOU, BUT...
PAUL--?
HIS "PLANS"...
HE SAID SOMETHING ABOUT... "IMPROVING THE COSTUME"...
WHAT THE--?
YOU'VE GOT TO BE KIDDING.
28

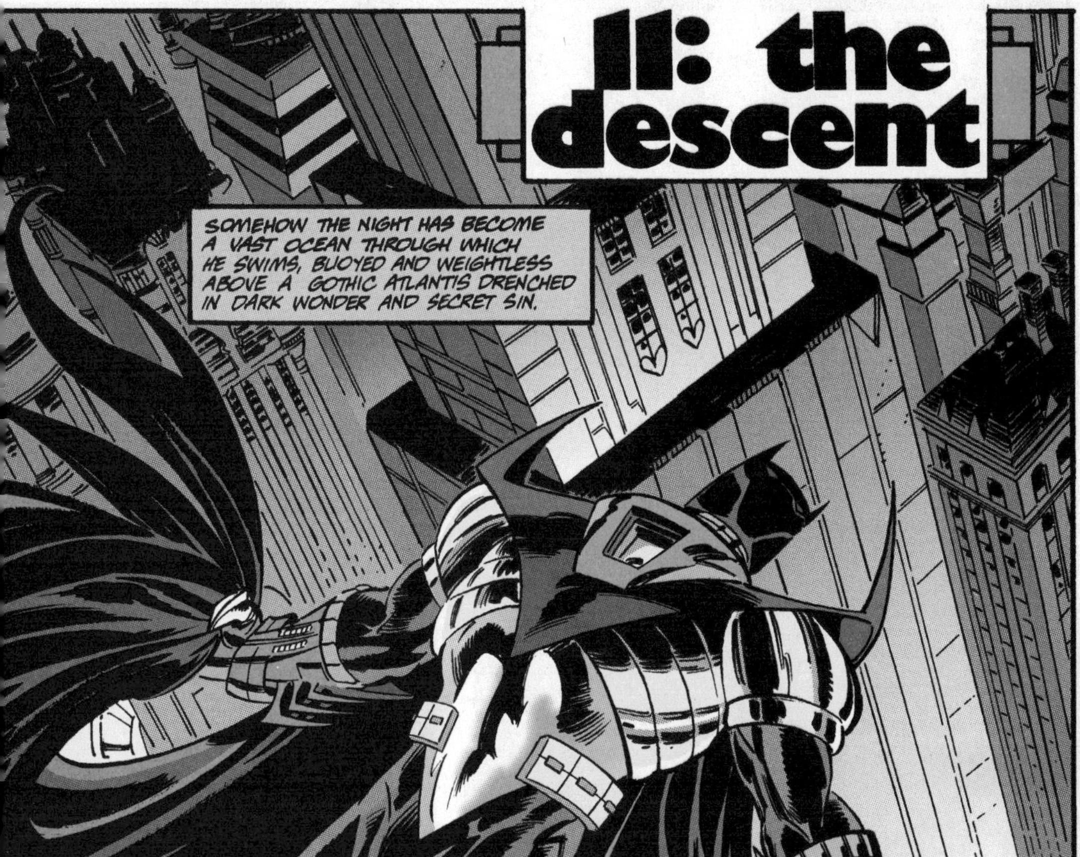
II: the descent
SOMEHOW THE NIGHT HAS BECOME A VAST OCEAN THROUGH WHICH HE SWIMS, BUOYED AND WEIGHTLESS ABOVE A GOTHIC ATLANTIS DRENCHED IN DARK WONDER AND SECRET SIN.
IT IS A PLACE LONG SINCE CURSED BY A FLOOD FROM HEAVEN, AND FORSAKEN BY TRUE LIGHT.

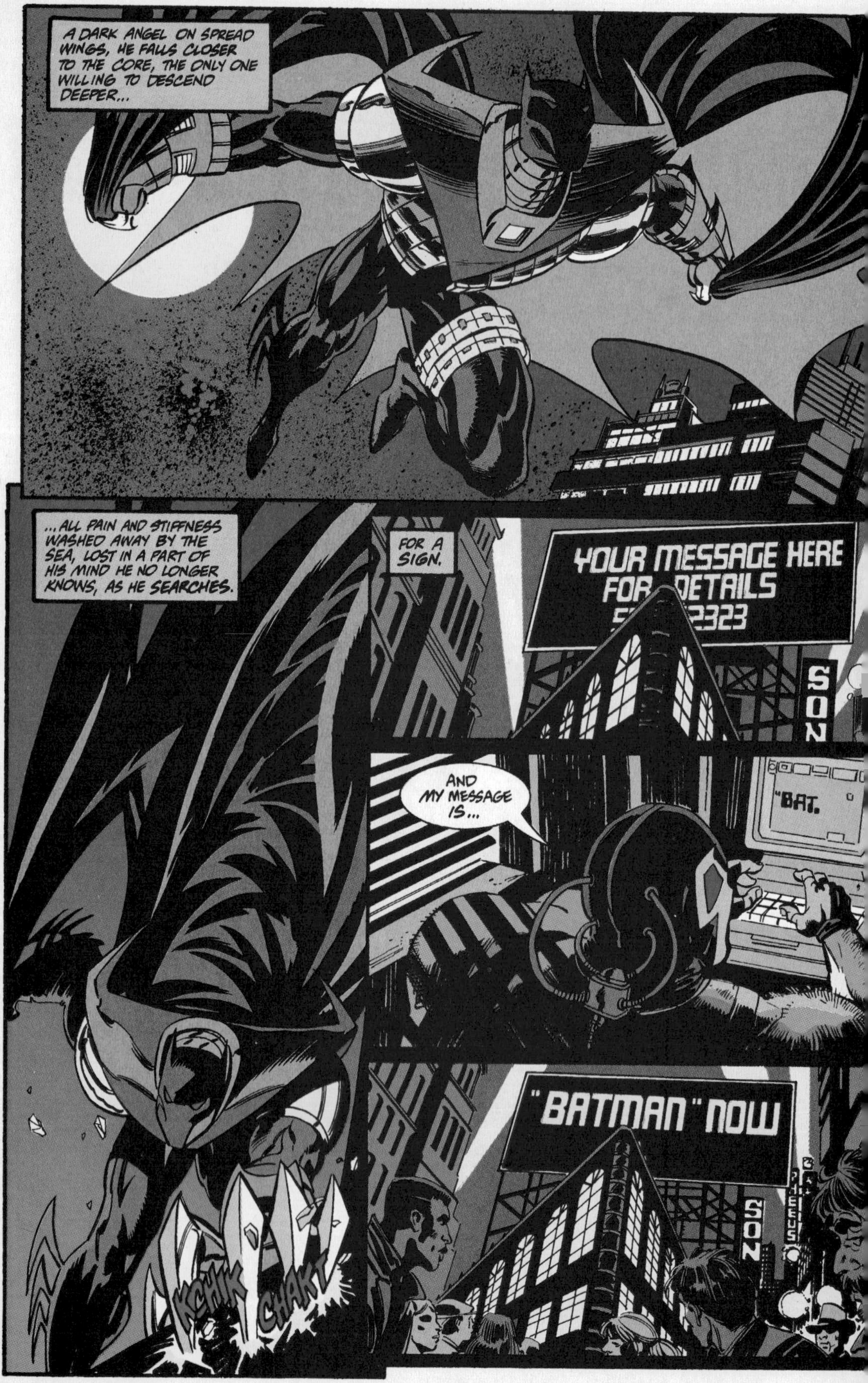
A DARK ANGEL ON SPREAD WINGS, HE FALLS CLOSER TO THE CORE, THE ONLY ONE WILLING TO DESCEND DEEPER...
...ALL PAIN AND STIFFNESS WASHED AWAY BY THE SEA, LOST IN A PART OF HIS MIND HE NO LONGER KNOWS, AS HE SEARCHES.
FOR A SIGN.
YOUR MESSAGE HERE
FOR DETAILS
SON
AND MY MESSAGE IS...
"BAT.
"BATMAN" NOW
SON
KCHIK
CHAKT

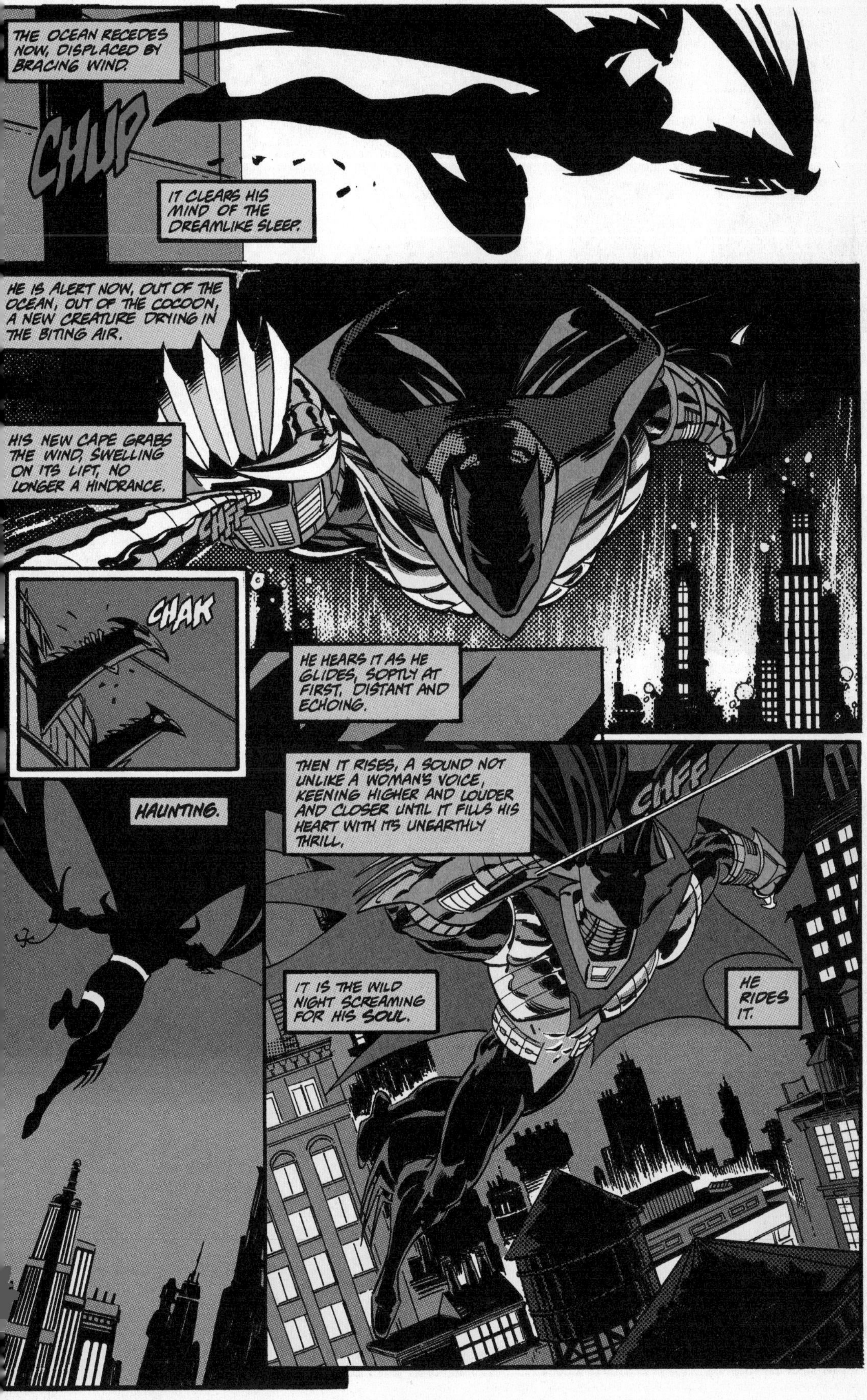

THE OCEAN RECEDES NOW, DISPLACED BY BRACING WIND.
CHUP
IT CLEARS HIS MIND OF THE DREAMLIKE SLEEP.
HE IS ALERT NOW, OUT OF THE OCEAN, OUT OF THE COCOON, A NEW CREATURE DRYING IN THE BITING AIR.
HIS NEW CAPE GRABS THE WIND, SWELLING ON ITS LIFT, NO LONGER A HINDRANCE.
CHAK
HE HEARS IT AS HE GLIDES, SOFTLY AT FIRST, DISTANT AND ECHOING.
HAUNTING.
THEN IT RISES, A SOUND NOT UNLIKE A WOMAN'S VOICE, KEENING HIGHER AND LOUDER AND CLOSER UNTIL IT FILLS HIS HEART WITH ITS UNEARTHLY THRILL,
CHFF
IT IS THE WILD NIGHT SCREAMING FOR HIS SOUL.
HE RIDES IT.

EVERYTHING IS BRIGHT AND GLITTERY NOW, A MILLION LIGHTS SHIMMERING THROUGH A WIND WHIPPING STRAIGHT TO HELL OR SALVATION.

HE DOESN'T CARE WHICH.

HE JUST WANTS AN END OR A BEGINNING--SOMETHING, ANYTHING, AS LONG AS IT IS HARD, FRESH AND FINAL.

HE IS STILL HIGH ON THE CREATION, STRETCHING OUT TO FILL THIS NEW THING HE HAS FASHIONED WITHOUT THINKING, SOMEHOW KNOWING IT IS RIGHT.

IT IS A THING BORN ONLY WHEN NOTHING ELSE MATTERS, FILLING HIM NOW, EVEN AS HE RIDES IT HARDER, A PERFECT CAST, FORGED IN A FIRE HE NEVER FELT.

HE ONLY FEELS LARGER, STRONGER.

HE TOUCHES ANOTHER CREATION, ONE WHICH HAS NOT FELT A HAND IN A HUNDRED YEARS.

FEELING LIKE A BLACK COMET SLASHING THE SKY, SCATTERING STARS IN HIS WAKE.

HE WISHES IT WOULD TAKE FLIGHT, FOR THE SHEER THRILL OF CHASING IT.

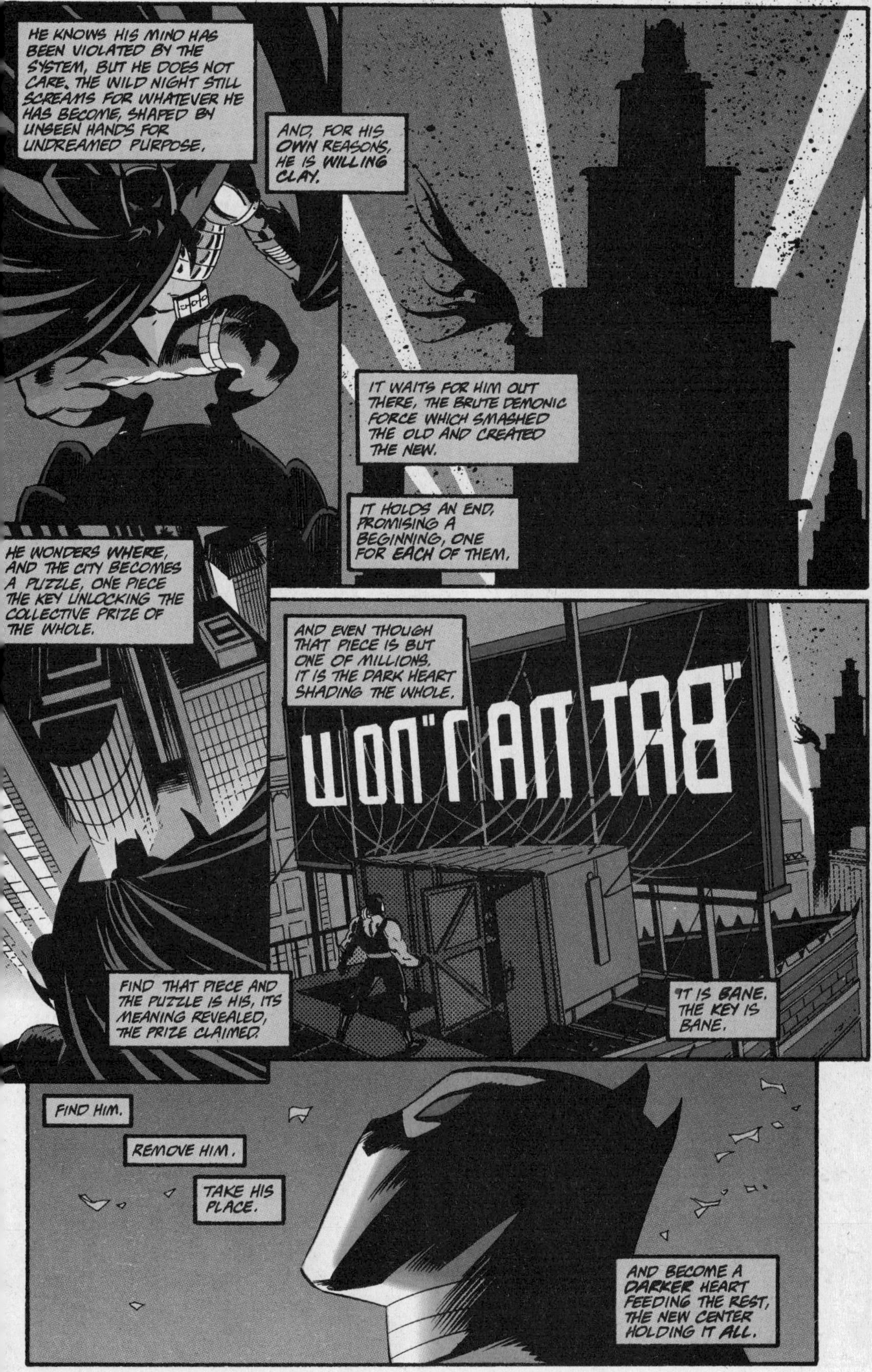
HE KNOWS HIS MIND HAS BEEN VIOLATED BY THE SYSTEM, BUT HE DOES NOT CARE. THE WILD NIGHT STILL SCREAMS FOR WHATEVER HE HAS BECOME, SHAPED BY UNSEEN HANDS FOR UNDREAMED PURPOSE.
AND, FOR HIS OWN REASONS, HE IS WILLING CLAY.
IT WAITS FOR HIM OUT THERE, THE BRUTE DEMONIC FORCE WHICH SMASHED THE OLD AND CREATED THE NEW.
IT HOLDS AN END, PROMISING A BEGINNING, ONE FOR EACH OF THEM.
HE WONDERS WHERE, AND THE CITY BECOMES A PUZZLE, ONE PIECE THE KEY UNLOCKING THE COLLECTIVE PRIZE OF THE WHOLE.
AND EVEN THOUGH THAT PIECE IS BUT ONE OF MILLIONS, IT IS THE DARK HEART SHADING THE WHOLE.
FIND THAT PIECE AND THE PUZZLE IS HIS, ITS MEANING REVEALED, THE PRIZE CLAIMED.
IT IS BANE. THE KEY IS BANE.
FIND HIM.
REMOVE HIM.
TAKE HIS PLACE.
AND BECOME A DARKER HEART FEEDING THE REST, THE NEW CENTER HOLDING IT ALL.

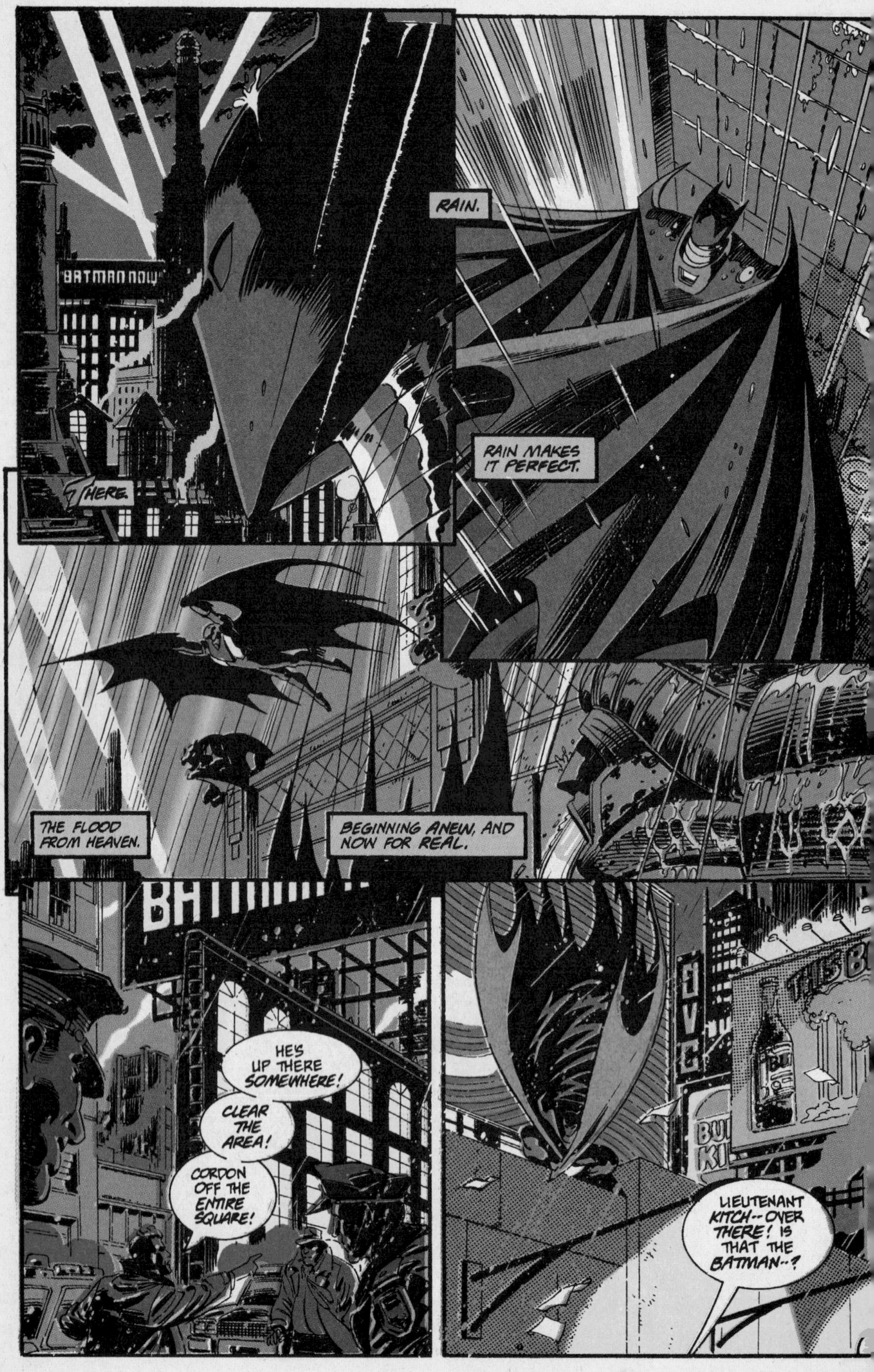
BATMAN NOW
THERE.
RAIN.
RAIN MAKES IT PERFECT.
THE FLOOD FROM HEAVEN.
BEGINNING ANEW, AND NOW FOR REAL.
HE'S UP THERE SOMEWHERE!
CLEAR THE AREA!
CORDON OFF THE ENTIRE SQUARE!
LIEUTENANT KITCH-- OVER THERE! IS THAT THE BATMAN--?

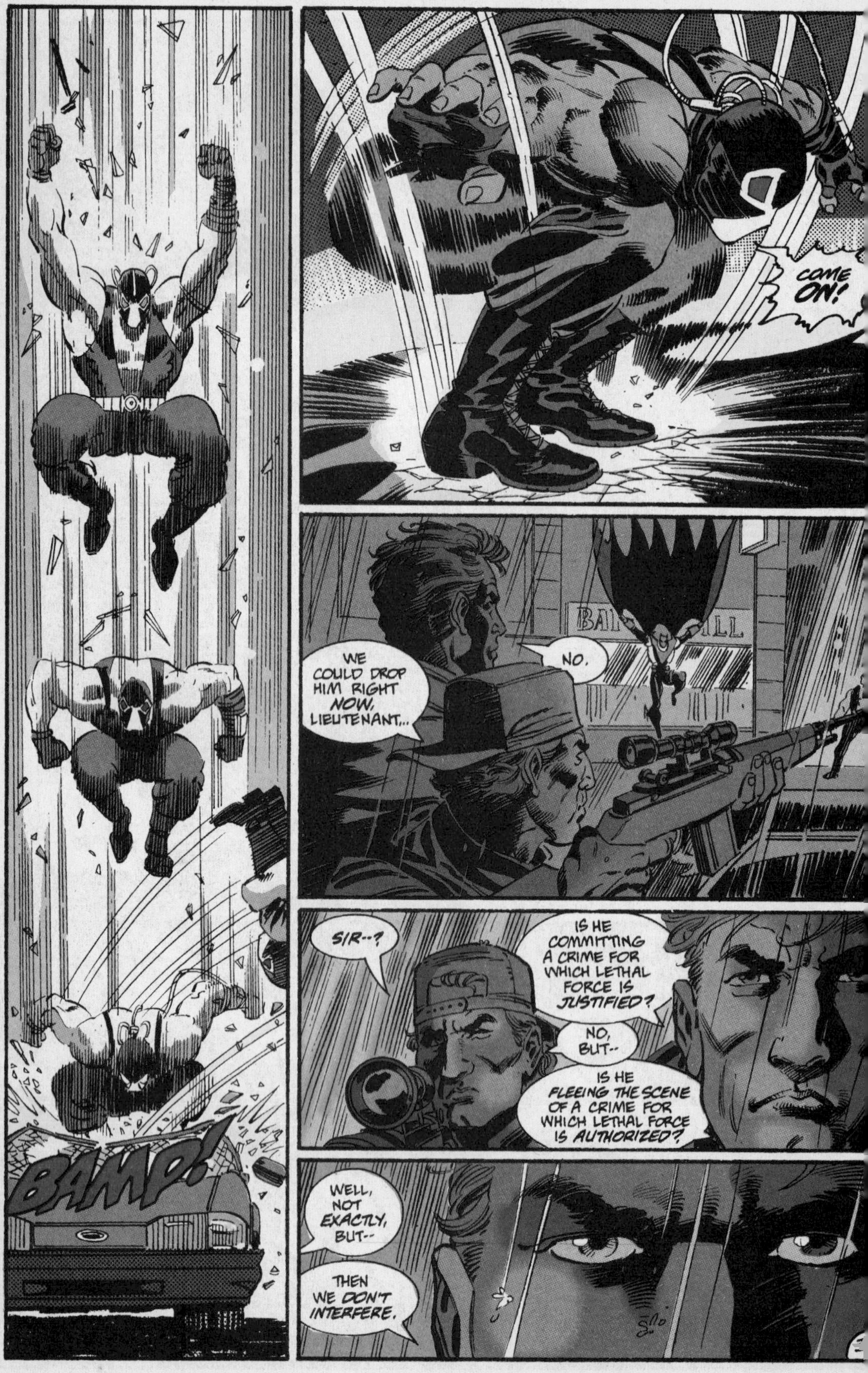

BAMP!
COME ON!
WE COULD DROP HIM RIGHT NOW, LIEUTENANT...
NO.
SIR--?
IS HE COMMITTING A CRIME FOR WHICH LETHAL FORCE IS JUSTIFIED?
NO, BUT--
IS HE FLEEING THE SCENE OF A CRIME FOR WHICH LETHAL FORCE IS AUTHORIZED?
WELL, NOT EXACTLY, BUT--
THEN WE DON'T INTERFERE.

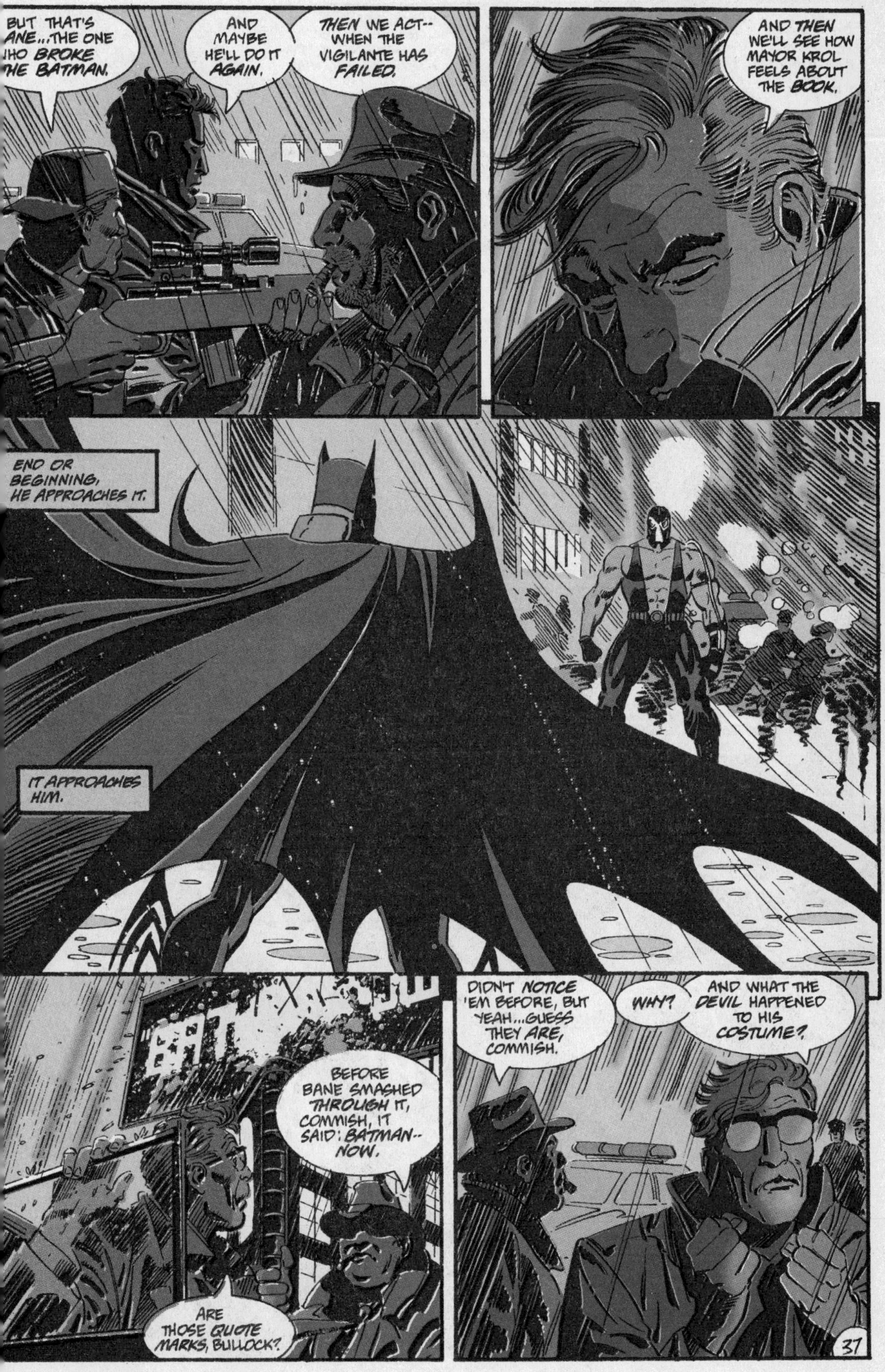
BUT THAT'S
ANE...THE ONE
WHO BROKE
THE BATMAN.
AND MAYBE HE'LL DO IT AGAIN.
THEN WE ACT-- WHEN THE VIGILANTE HAS FAILED.
AND THEN WE'LL SEE HOW MAYOR KROL FEELS ABOUT THE BOOK.
END OR BEGINNING, HE APPROACHES IT.
IT APPROACHES HIM.
BEFORE BANE SMASHED THROUGH IT, COMMISH, IT SAID: BATMAN-- NOW.
ARE THOSE QUOTE MARKS, BULLOCK?
DIDN'T NOTICE 'EM BEFORE, BUT YEAH...GUESS THEY ARE, COMMISH.
WHY?
AND WHAT THE DEVIL HAPPENED TO HIS COSTUME?
37

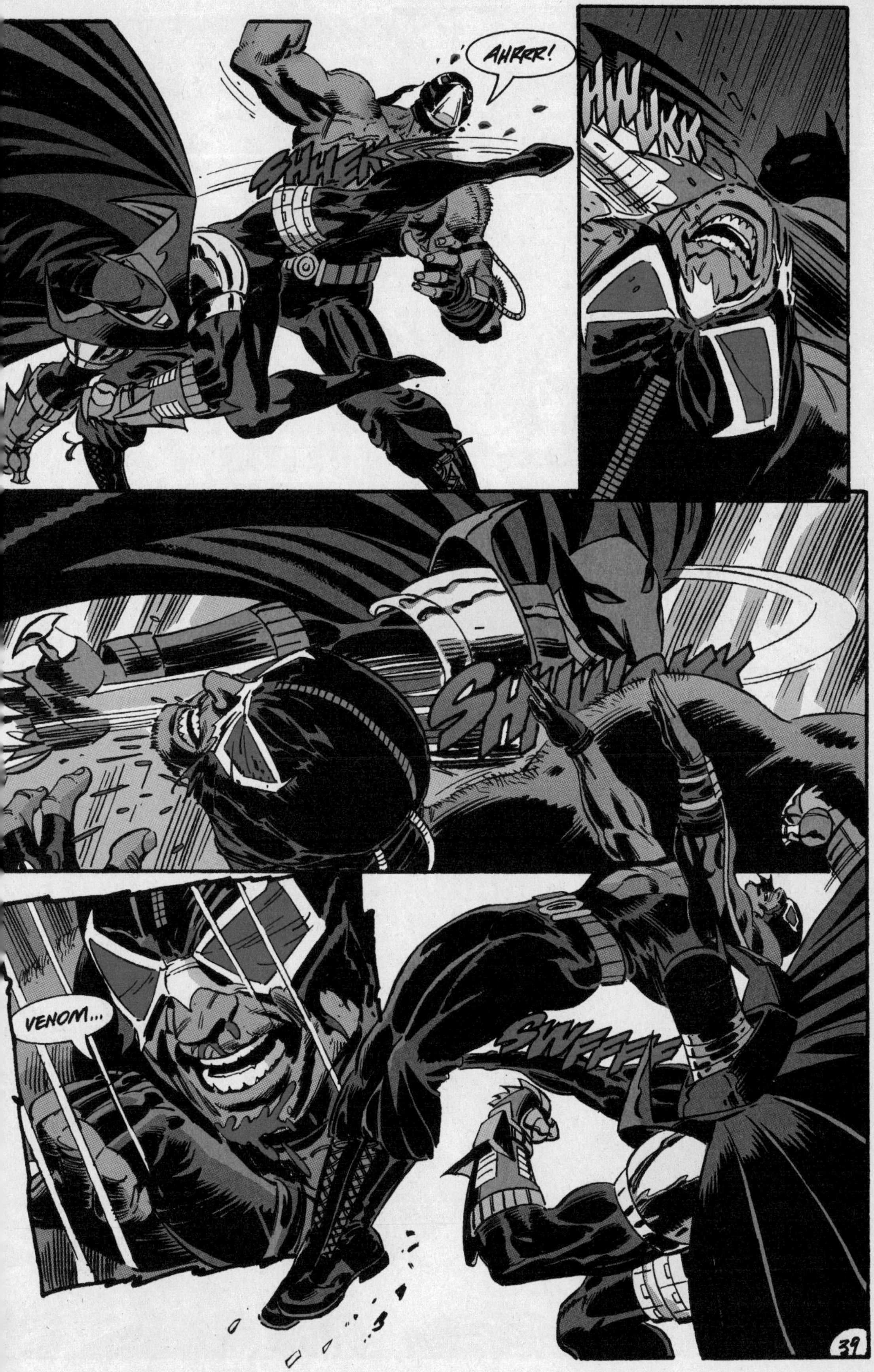
AHRRR!
SHHEN
HWUKK
SHWWW
VENOM...
SWFFFF
39

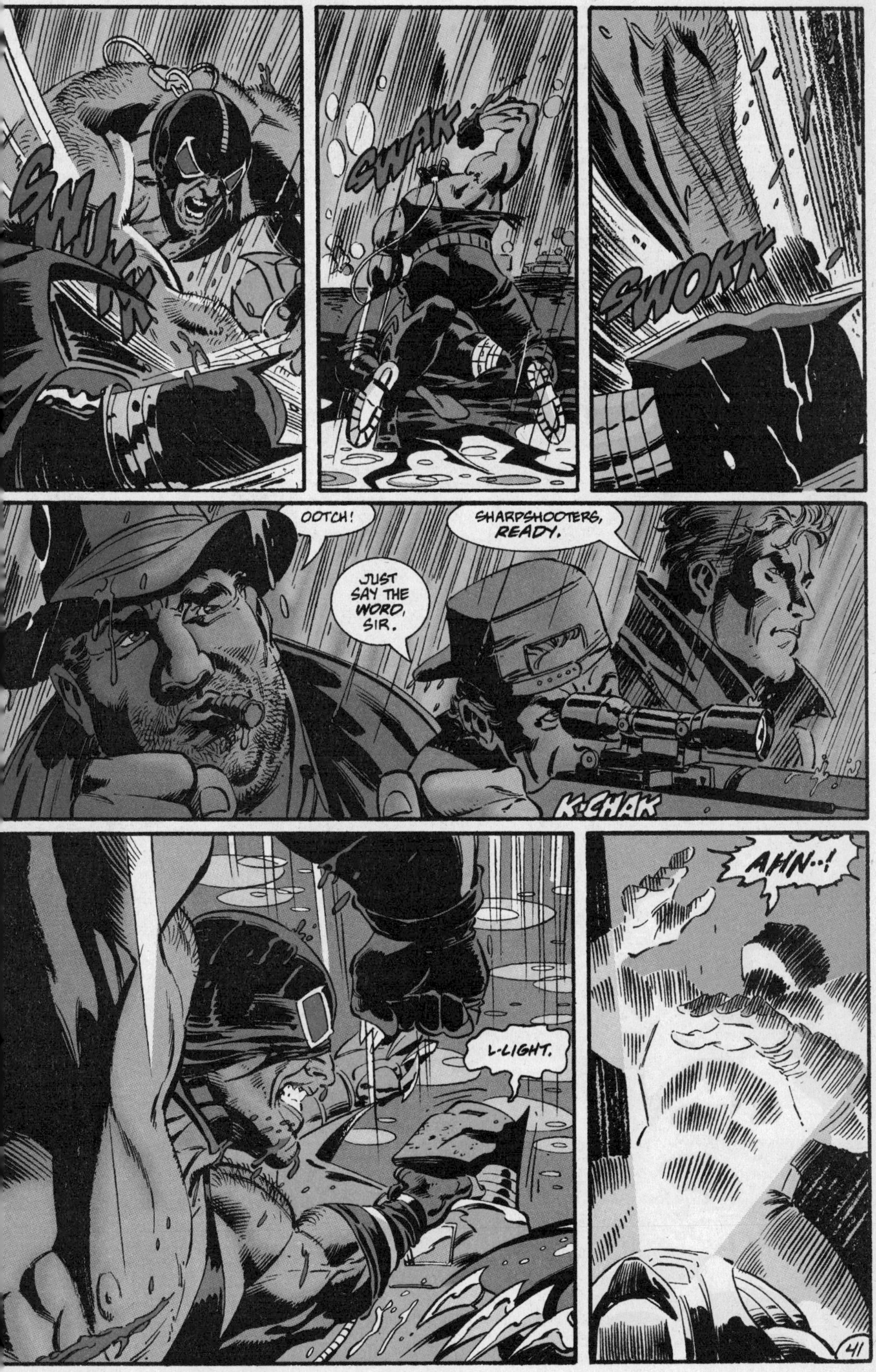
SWUNK
SWAK
SWOKK
OOTCH!
SHARPSHOOTERS, READY.
JUST SAY THE WORD, SIR.
K-CHAK
AHN..!
L-LIGHT.
41

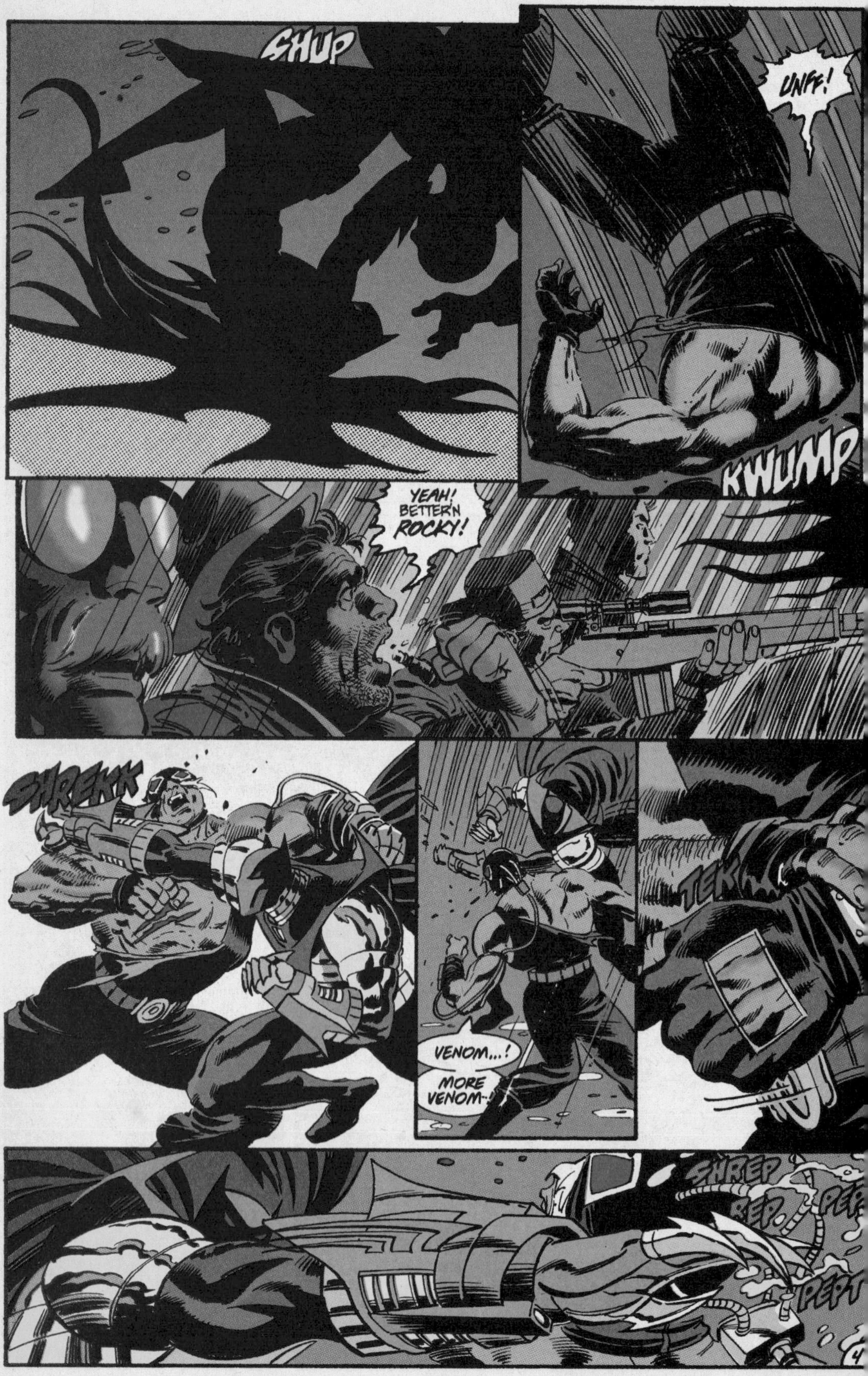
SHUP
UNFF!
KWUMP
YEAH! BETTER'N ROCKY!
SHREKK
TEK
VENOM...!
MORE VENOM...!
SHREP
BEP
PEP
PEPT
4

HE SIMPLY DIGS IN.

SPROKT

AND HAULS.

PROKT

EVERYONE OUT-- INTO THE NEXT CAR!

NOW!!

WHAT THE--? ONE OF THE HEADLIGHTS JUST WENT OU--

CHUS

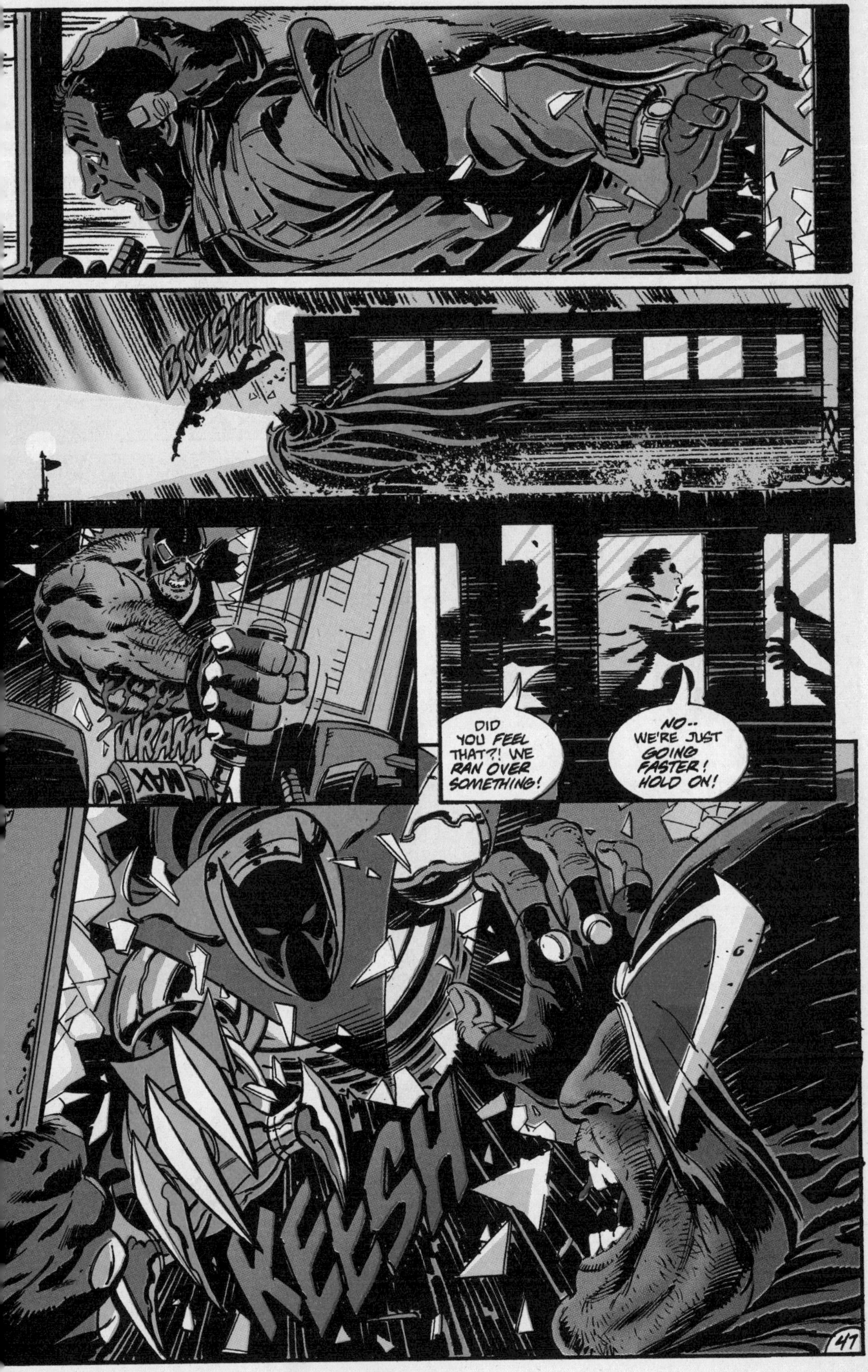

BRUSH
DID YOU FEEL THAT?! WE RAN OVER SOMETHING!
NO.. WE'RE JUST GOING FASTER! HOLD ON!
WRAKK
KEESH
47

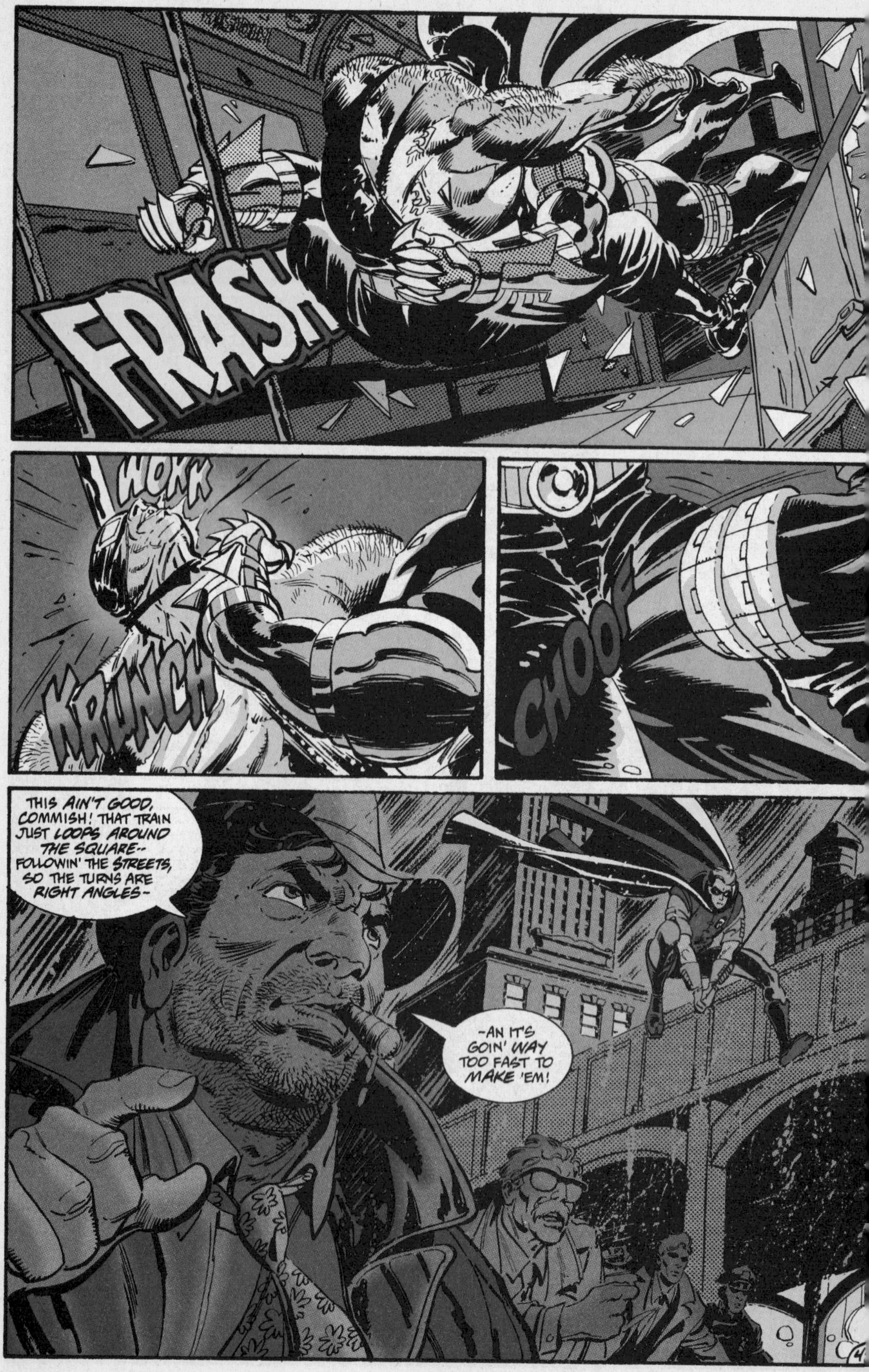
FRASH
WOKK
KRUNCH
CHOOF
THIS AIN'T GOOD, COMMISH! THAT TRAIN JUST LOOPS AROUND THE SQUARE-- FOLLOWIN' THE STREETS, SO THE TURNS ARE RIGHT ANGLES-
-AN IT'S GOIN' WAY TOO FAST TO MAKE 'EM!

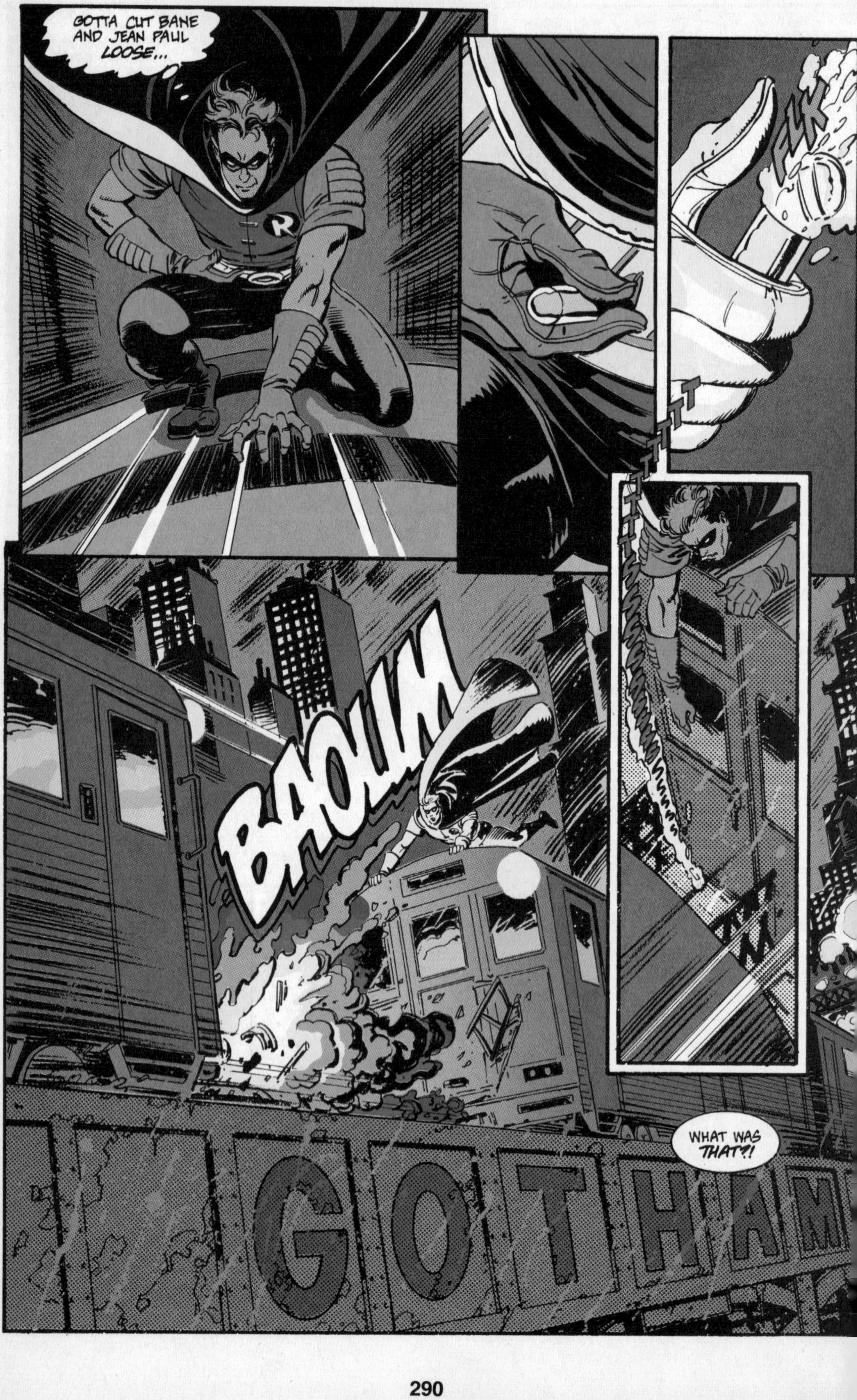
GOTTA CUT BANE AND JEAN PAUL LOOSE...
FLK
TTTTTTT
BAOUM
WHAT WAS THAT?!
GOTHAM

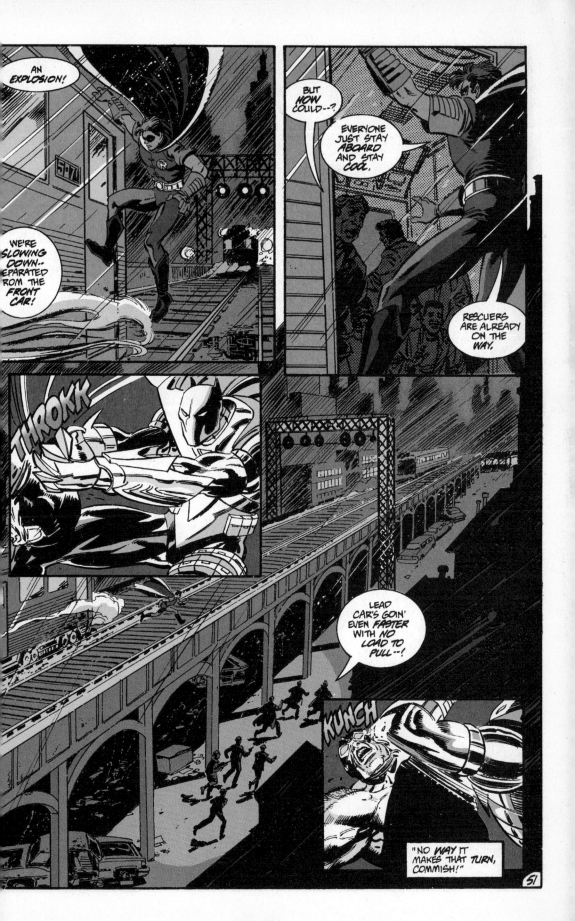

291

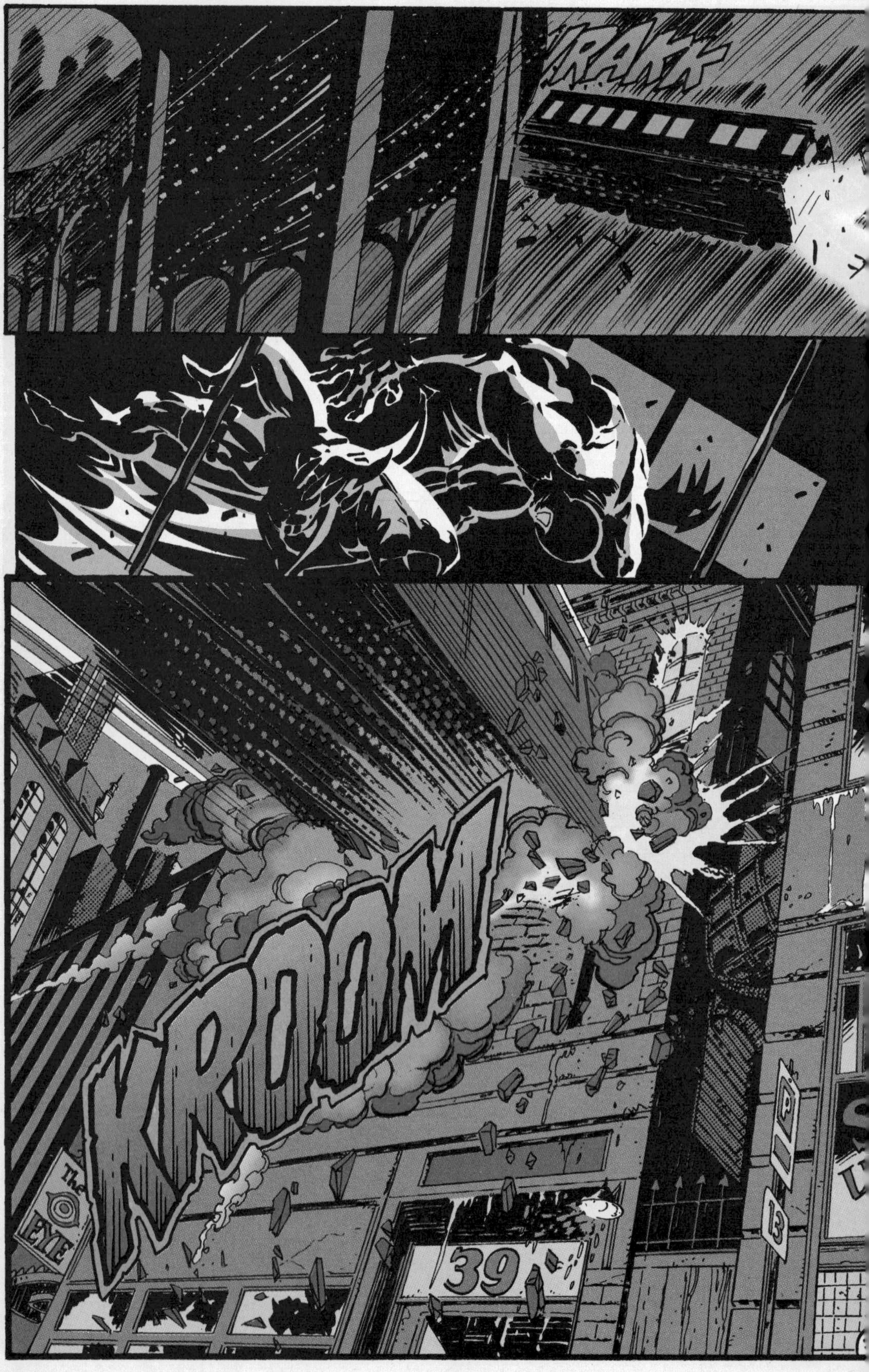
RAKK
KRROOM
The EYE
39
P
13

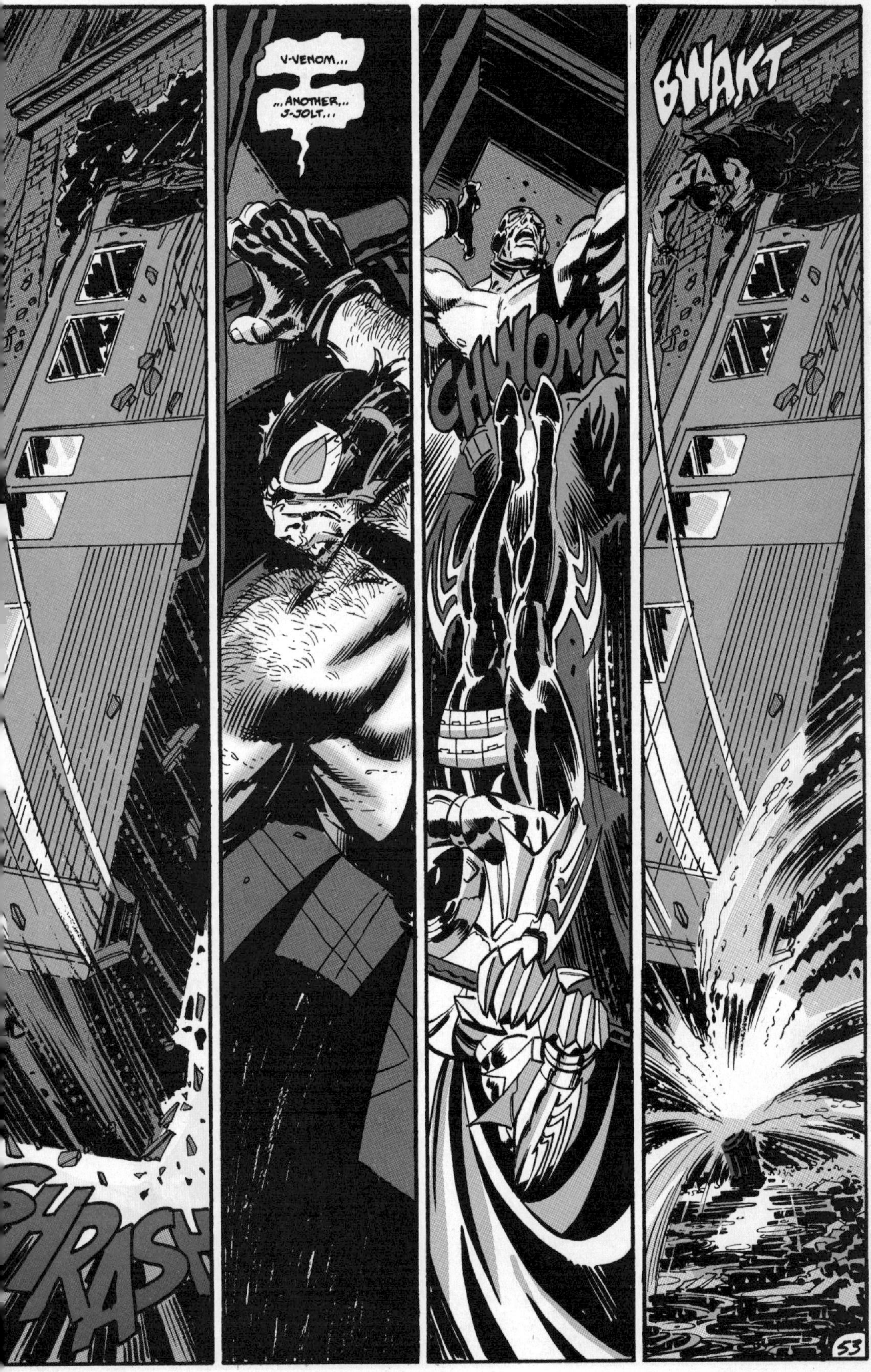
V-VENOM...
...ANOTHER... J-JOLT...
CHWOKK
BWAKT
SHRASH
53

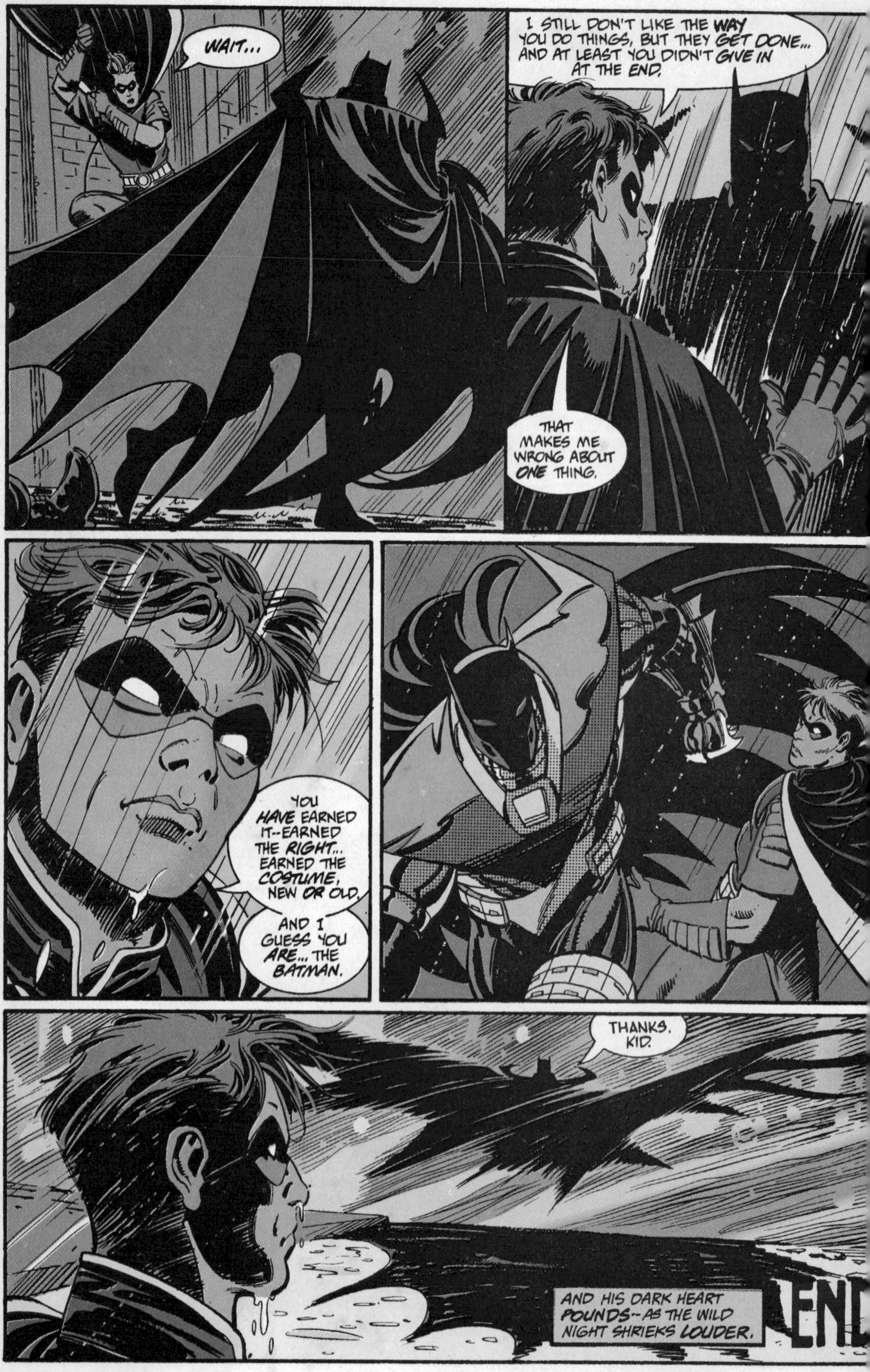
WAIT...
I STILL DON'T LIKE THE WAY YOU DO THINGS, BUT THEY GET DONE... AND AT LEAST YOU DIDN'T GIVE IN AT THE END.
THAT MAKES ME WRONG ABOUT ONE THING.
YOU HAVE EARNED IT--EARNED THE RIGHT... EARNED THE COSTUME, NEW OR OLD.
AND I GUESS YOU ARE... THE BATMAN.
THANKS, KID.
AND HIS DARK HEART POUNDS--AS THE WILD NIGHT SHRIEKS LOUDER.
END